THE Gansevoorts OF Albany

A NEW YORK STATE STUDY

THE Gansevoorts
OF Albany

Dutch Patricians in the
Upper Hudson Valley

ALICE P. KENNEY

SYRACUSE UNIVERSITY PRESS

ALICE P. KENNEY, assistant professor of history at Cedar Crest College, Allentown, Pennsylvania, is the author of *A History of the American Family* (1967) for young people, and articles in *New York History*, *New-York Historical Society Quarterly*, and *New England Galaxy*. She received her B.A. from Middlebury College and her M.A. and Ph.D. from Columbia University. Descended from several Hudson Valley Dutch families, including the remarkable Anneke Janse, she grew up in Albany and still considers it her home.

ACKNOWLEDGMENTS

This book could not have been written without the generosity of the owners of Gansevoort papers and of descendants of the Gansevoort family who have come forward with both interest and information. My greatest debt is of course to the New York Public Library for the use of the materials in the Gansevoort-Lansing Collection. I would like to express my particular appreciation to Robert W. Hill, curator of manuscripts, and to Paul Rugel and Jean McNiece of his staff for their unfailingly kind and courteous assistance, and also to the succession of pages who carried four hundred boxes of documents up the stairs and down again and refiled the quantities of material I sent to Photographic Service. Norman Rice of the Albany Institute of History and Art, Juliet Wolohan of the Manuscript Division, New York State Library, the New-York Historical Society, the Metropolitan Museum of Art, and the Fort Stanwix Museum, Rome, New York, were also most helpful in supplying material from their collections. Mrs. Frank Buturla permitted me to use a Leonard Gansevoort account book in her possession. Mr. Clifford Rugg, Saratoga County historian, and Mrs. Robert Leddick showed me the Gansevoort homes and passed on traditions about the family in the town of Gansevoort, New York.

Of Gansevoort descendants, the most helpful by far were Mr. and Mrs. Peter G. D. Ten Eyck, who permitted me to use their valuable collection of two hundred letters to Leonard Gansevoort. Mr. and Mrs. Robert Ten Eyck permitted me to use other Gansevoort documents in their possession. Robert Ten Eyck and Duncan L. Edwards took photographs for me of their Gansevoort heirlooms, and Mr. and Mrs. Stephen C. Clark contributed portraits of her Gansevoort ancestors. Jeannette Chapin, Duncan L. Edwards, Josephine Sofio, Robert C. Sofio, and Lorene Stirling sent me genealogical and other information. The late Huybertje Pruyn Hamlin, who knew Catherine Gansevoort Lansing well, and the late Dr. Charles K. Winne, were also most gracious and helpful.

This is also the place to thank Richard B. Morris and Robert

ACKNOWLEDGMENTS

D. Cross for their prompt and patient attention to that part of the manuscript which was once a dissertation. The research was partly supported by an American Association of University Women National Fellowship, and the administration, faculty, and students of Cedar Crest College have done everything in their power to be helpful. Benjamin Hunningher provided an authentic introduction to the Dutch tradition; Leslie Workman and David Armour permitted me to share imaginative insights and results of their unpublished research; and Don W. Gerlach offered perceptive comments on an early draft. Staff members of Syracuse University Press gave penetrating and thoughtful assistance in preparing the manuscript for publication, and Kenneth McFarlane and Edna Jacobsen rendered help beyond the call of duty at short notice. Various members of my own family have contributed books, transportation, research assistance, insight, and moral support.

CONTENTS

Map

Places in the Hudson Valley Important to the Gansevoorts   xxviii

Illustrations following page 132

1. Albany Dutch Reformed Church; 2. Market St., Albany; 3, 4. Leendert and Catarina Gansevoort; 5. Tankard; 6. Funeral spoon; 7. Gansevoort coat-of-arms; 8. Teapot; 9. Gen. Peter Gansevoort; 10. Catherine Van Schaick Gansevoort; 11. Ft. Stanwix; 12. Leonard Gansevoort; 13. Andirons; 14. Maria Gansevoort; 15. L. H. and Mary Ann Gansevoort; 16. Herman Gansevoort mansion; 17. "Old yellow house"; 18. Reformed Church of Gansevoort; 19. Parlor at 115 Washington Ave., Albany; 20. 115 Washington Ave., Albany; 21. State Capitol; 22. Albany Academy; 23. Family party; 24. Col. Henry Gansevoort and officers; 25. Abe Lansing; 26. Albany "North Dutch Church"; 27. Albany City Hall; 28. Stanwix Hall; 29. Gen. Peter Gansevoort; 30. Albany ca. 1850.

Picture Credits

Courtesy of Albany Institute of History and Art: 1, 2, 10.
Courtesy of Mr. and Mrs. Stephen C. Clark, Cooperstown, N.Y.: 3, 4.
Courtesy of Metropolitan Museum of Art, New York, N.Y.: 5, gift of Mrs. Abraham Lansing, 1901; 6, gift of Robert Olcott, executor to the estate of Mrs. Abraham Lansing, 1929.
From the Gansevoort-Lansing Collection, Manuscript Division, Courtesy of New York Public Library, Astor, Lenox, and Tilden Foundations, New York, N.Y.: 7, 11, 14, 15, 19, 20, 21, 22, 23, 24, 25, 27, 28, 29.
Courtesy of Duncan L. Edwards, Little Tongue Ranch, Dayton, Wyo.: 8.
Courtesy of Munson-Williams-Proctor Institute, Utica, N.Y.: 9.
Courtesy of Robert Ten Eyck, Loudonville, N.Y.: 12, 13.
Photographs by the author: 16, 17, 18.
Courtesy of First Church in Albany, Reformed: 26.
Courtesy of New-York Historical Society, New York, N.Y.: 30.

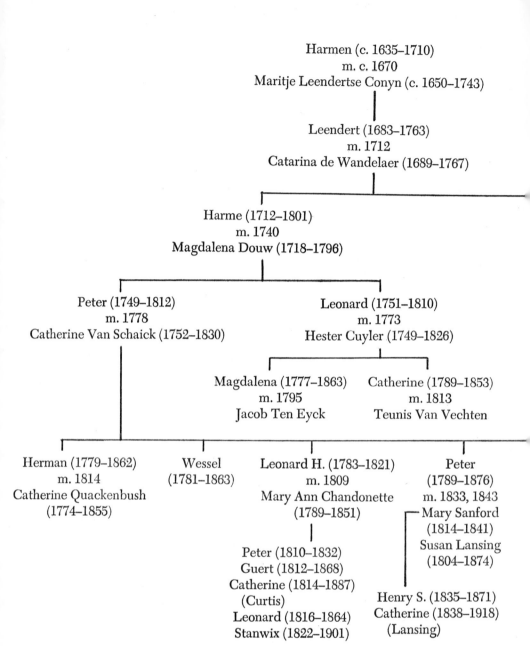

Harmen (c. 1635–1710)
m. c. 1670
Maritje Leendertse Conyn (c. 1650–1743)

Leendert (1683–1763)
m. 1712
Catarina de Wandelaer (1689–1767)

Harme (1712–1801)
m. 1740
Magdalena Douw (1718–1796)

Peter (1749–1812)
m. 1778
Catherine Van Schaick (1752–1830)

Leonard (1751–1810)
m. 1773
Hester Cuyler (1749–1826)

Magdalena (1777–1863)
m. 1795
Jacob Ten Eyck

Catherine (1789–1853)
m. 1813
Teunis Van Vechten

Herman (1779–1862)
m. 1814
Catherine Quackenbush
(1774–1855)

Wessel
(1781–1863)

Leonard H. (1783–1821)
m. 1809
Mary Ann Chandonette
(1789–1851)

Peter (1810–1832)
Guert (1812–1868)
Catherine (1814–1887)
(Curtis)
Leonard (1816–1864)
Stanwix (1822–1901)

Peter
(1789–1876)
m. 1833, 1843
Mary Sanford
(1814–1841)
Susan Lansing
(1804–1874)

Henry S. (1835–1871)
Catherine (1838–1918)
(Lansing)

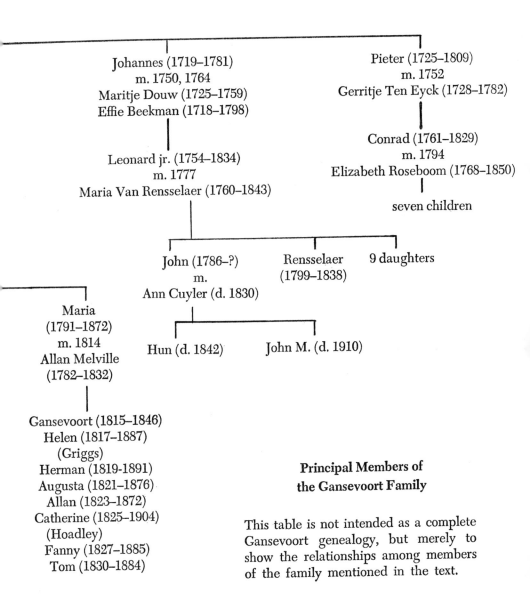

Johannes (1719–1781)
m. 1750, 1764
Maritje Douw (1725–1759)
Effie Beekman (1718–1798)

Pieter (1725–1809)
m. 1752
Gerritje Ten Eyck (1728–1782)

Leonard jr. (1754–1834)
m. 1777
Maria Van Rensselaer (1760–1843)

Conrad (1761–1829)
m. 1794
Elizabeth Roseboom (1768–1850)

seven children

John (1786–?)
m.
Ann Cuyler (d. 1830)

Rensselaer
(1799–1838)

9 daughters

Maria
(1791–1872)
m. 1814
Allan Melville
(1782–1832)

Hun (d. 1842)

John M. (d. 1910)

Gansevoort (1815–1846)
Helen (1817–1887)
(Griggs)
Herman (1819-1891)
Augusta (1821–1876)
Allan (1823–1872)
Catherine (1825–1904)
(Hoadley)
Fanny (1827–1885)
Tom (1830–1884)

**Principal Members of
the Gansevoort Family**

This table is not intended as a complete
Gansevoort genealogy, but merely to
show the relationships among members
of the family mentioned in the text.

INTRODUCTION

New Worlds From Old

Most people associate the Dutch with the Hudson Valley, but few know much about the Hudson Valley Dutch tradition. Schoolbooks show Peter Minuit shrewdly purchasing Manhattan Island from the Indians and Peter Stuyvesant unwillingly surrendering it to the English; General Philip Schuyler stubbornly fighting for independence from the British Empire and "Commodore" Cornelius Vanderbilt efficiently organizing an empire in steamboats and railroads; Martin Van Buren and two Roosevelts affably persuading the voters to elect them to the highest office in the nation. Research has uncovered much information about the people from whom these men sprang, who came to America very early in the period of settlement, maintained their ethnic identity throughout the colonial period, and retained many distinctive characteristics until the end of the nineteenth century. This book tries to show what the Hudson Valley Dutch tradition was in itself and to place it in the context of the other traditions with which it lived in close contact, sometimes in conflict.

One reason why the way of life of the Dutch in America has yet to be adequately described is inherent in the nature of the Dutch tradition. The basic assumptions of the American way of life are English, brought from seventeenth-century England by English speaking colonists, expounded in the eighteenth century by Founding Fathers largely of English descent and legal training, propagated in the nineteenth century by public schools designed to produce intelligent, responsible citizens, and expanded from within in the twentieth century by immigrants and their children Americanized in these schools. This fundamentally English tradition, which is the common denominator of American patriotism as of the schoolbooks which inculcate it, stresses the individual as the moving power of history, and liberty as his objective. American historical writing, on the other hand, has adapted its standards in language, methods, and concepts from nineteenth-century German scholars who emphasized the importance of mass movements in history and believed that the goal of such movements was the possession of power. In the Dutch tradition, neither the individual nor the mass, but the local community, was the significant entity, and its purpose in acting was neither to preserve liberty nor to seize power, but to protect and extend its particular privileges. For the description of such a tradition no American framework exists—yet this tradition is an integral part of the history of the Hudson Valley and of the United States.

The communal nature of the Dutch tradition reflected the fact that the significant unit of human organization in the Low Countries was the town. The earliest of these towns originated in the Dark Ages, when a group of traders gathered at a location possessing geographical advantages for commerce and defense and organized informal institutions—as opposed to the "sworn communes" of France—for keeping order among themselves and defending themselves against their enemies. Against other towns, who interfered with their trade, feudal lords, who attacked them with troops of knights, and churchmen, who controlled many forces of popular opinion, the townsmen employed the power of their wealth. They erected solid city walls, hired mercenaries when the town militia proved inadequate, endowed churches and monasteries, and, above all, they purchased from the lord of the land on which the town stood, or from his overlord, statements, restatements, and extensions of the privileges he was willing to grant to them. Thus, the territory on the lower Rhine, in ancient times the frontier between Roman civilization and Germanic barbarism, became in the Middle Ages the heartland of an indigenous civilized society.

It became usual, quite early in the Middle Ages, for Dutch

xiv

towns to be dominated by a closely intermarried group of the wealthiest commercial families, who have been called *patricians* by broad analogy with the ruling class of ancient Rome. These families made the largest contributions to sums raised for the purchase or re-purchase of the town's privileges, and all the townsmen accepted as right and proper the principle that these privileges should be exercised in behalf of the community by those who had been instrumental in acquiring them. One widely cherished privilege was the right of *co-optation,* a custom whereby Dutch town councils nominated their own successors with the consent of the town's overlord, but without reference to any wishes of the townsmen in general. This privilege enabled the merchant patricians to keep control of the city government and to use their power in the social and economic interests of their families. In primarily mercantile towns the best interest of the patricians often really was the best interest of the town; in towns with much manufacturing it often was not, and both craftsmen and laborers rebelled against patrician domination.

In the early Middle Ages most towns in the Low Countries purchased their privileges from local lords and regional overlords, resisting repeated attempts at domination by the King of France, most notably at the battle of Courtrai in 1302. Later in the fourteenth century, a younger branch of the French royal family, the house of Burgundy, acquired many lordships in the Netherlands by inheritance, marriage, and purchase, but they were no more anxious to be ruled by France than were the Netherlanders, and instead supported England until nearly the end of the Hundred Years War (1340–1453). After a century of virtual independence, the Duke of Burgundy tried to win acknowledgment as king, but this effort was frustrated when Duke Charles the Bold was killed in battle in 1477 leaving only a daughter, Mary, upon whose marriage to Holy Roman Emperor Maximilian of Hapsburg the Low Countries became part of the widely scattered Hapsburg family territories.

The Dukes of Burgundy seldom interfered with the established customs and local privileges of the towns and made little attempt to establish any central administration, but their courts did provide a center for a flowering of literature, art, and music. This development was contemporary with the Italian Renaissance and sprang from similar social, economic, and technological conditions, but it drew its inspiration from the medieval Gothic tradition rather than that of classical antiquity. When one remembers, however, that classical antiquity is local history in Italy and that all the local history possessed by the Low Countries was medieval, it becomes evident that both Flemish and Italian artists went back to their local traditions and developed them in new forms. A major difference between them was that while the classical tradition centered around a highly developed and formal literature so that the reconstruction of classical Latin was as important to the Italian Renaissance as the rediscovery of ancient works of art, the northern movement depended on an oral and nonverbal tradition perhaps equally highly developed but less easy to describe in familiar terms. It found written expression in histories of chivalry, most notably those of Froissart and Philippe de Comines, pictorial expression in the altar pieces and portraits of the great Flemish masters, and musical expression in a tradition traceable at least from the twelfth century to the great polyphonic compositions of fifteenth-century organists and choirmasters.

Another major concern of these medieval Dutch burghers was religion. Many Dutch cities had ecclesiastical overlords (bishops and abbots), and many others were the sees of dioceses or the homes of venerable monastic foundations. The burghers, therefore, looked upon such religious establishments as integral parts of the civic community, which for most of the Middle Ages conducted their affairs on a local basis, only distantly supervised by Rome and not at all by pious kings. At the same time the burghers responded to popular preachers in the tradition of St. Francis of Assisi, who exhorted laymen to practice their religion in their everyday lives. Typical Dutch religious orders were the Brethren of the Common Life and their sisterhood, the Beguines, who followed the example of Thomas à Kempis' *Imitation of Christ*, putting their communal mystical experience of the love of God to work in such everyday practical areas as education. The greatest

xvi

northern humanist, Erasmus, received his earliest teaching in their schools, and his ideas about religion always reflected their attitudes and emphasis.

In the sixteenth century the Dutch tradition was put under severe pressure. After the death of Charles the Bold dynastic accidents merged his nearly independent principality into the largest European empire since that of Charlemagne. Charles V, the grandson of Mary and Maximilian, inherited the Low Countries from his grandmother and the Hapsburg family lands in Austria from his grandfather. He also inherited from his mother's parents, Ferdinand and Isabella, their newly united kingdom of Spain, its newly conquered dependencies in Italy, and its newly discovered empire in America. Furthermore, in 1519 Charles was elected Holy Roman Emperor, which gave him supreme power in all Germany. Charles' tremendous empire, comprising half of Europe, was immediately threatened by the Turks, whose expansion through the Balkans after their conquest of Constantinople in 1453 overran Hungary in 1526, and the French, whom Charles expelled from Italy in 1527 in a decisive campaign which included the sack of Rome by his Lutheran German mercenaries. Charles also had to put down internal opposition in Spain and in Germany, where many princes used the Lutheran movement as an excuse to escape from his authority. He expected the cities of the Low Countries to contribute tremendous amounts of money for all these purposes. When they became restive in 1539, he besieged and captured Ghent with an imperial army, and although it was his birthplace he revoked all its cherished privileges.

In the meantime the doctrines of the Protestant Reformation were attracting many burghers in the Netherlands and western Germany. The most successful of numerous reformers who emerged from the religious tradition of medieval towns was John Calvin. His system of theology and church government, worked out in the city of Geneva in the 1540's and 1550's, became widely accepted in the Netherlands. In 1565 Calvinists of Antwerp who had been prevented by the authorities from assembling publicly to hear their preachers broke into open rebellion. King Philip II of Spain, the son of Charles V, sent Spanish troops to quell the disorders and Spanish Inquisitors to root out the heretics. This external interference with time-honored local privileges provoked many Protestant—and Roman Catholic—towns to full-scale revolt. Thus, with the very beginning of the Dutch struggle for national independence, theological doctrines came to serve many of the purposes of modern revolutionary and national ideology. The Calvinists were the most numerous Protestant sect and the most fervent for independence, and were particularly strong among the patrician class, but they never came anywhere near converting a majority of the whole population. Therefore, although patrician Dutch Calvinists who still viewed religious duties as a combination of doctrinal orthodoxy, mystical devotion, and practical piety were exceedingly strict with members of their own congregations, and in their capacity as magistrates were severe upon any burghers whose religious convictions appeared to threaten the security of the community, they were compelled by circumstances to adopt the general policy of religious toleration for which the United Netherlands became noted in the seventeenth century.

The Dutch struggle for independence, half religious, half political, went on for eighty years after its outbreak in 1565. Philip II poured Spanish troops into the ten southern (Belgian) provinces and soon reconquered them, but although his army repeatedly invaded the seven northern Dutch provinces and subjected them to such atrocities as the sack of Haarlem in 1572, it was unable to reduce them to submission. The Dutch people, protected to some extent by the great rivers which formed the mouth of the Rhine and defended by their dikes which could be cut to flood out besieging forces, rallied behind William the Silent of Orange and sustained such epic feats of endurance as the siege of Leyden in 1574. Indeed, the entire war was in a sense an extended siege, for the Dutch lacked resources to fight offensively and could hope at best to maintain themselves until Spain wearied of the conflict. This began to happen after the Netherlands' ally, England, defeated the Spanish Armada in 1589. Peace was unthinkable during the lifetime of Philip II, but in 1609, a decade after his death, the Twelve Years Truce was concluded. For all practical purposes the Netherlands were thereafter independent, although Spain refused to recognize them as such until the Peace of Westphalia in 1648.

The Dutch nation which thus won its independence by stubborn endurance was less than half—and by far the poorer and more obscure half—of the medieval Low Countries. The wealthy cities of Flanders entered a period of decline, having been battered into political submission by Spanish armies, deprived of their Protestant citizens by the Inquisition, and cut off from their trade by a combination of geographical changes, shifts in economic patterns, and the military success which placed the Dutch in a strategic position to ruin Antwerp by closing the mouth of the Scheldt. In the meantime, the cities of Holland and Zealand, led by Amsterdam, entered upon a period of tremendous commerical prosperity founded upon the sale of Dutch products such as salt herring, the carrying trade in grain from the Baltic to southern Europe, and the spice trade with the East Indies which the Dutch appropriated in 1602 from Portugal (from 1580 to 1640 under the rule of Spain and, therefore, technically part of the common enemy). These cities dominated the States-General, a medieval deliberative body which became the central government of the Dutch Republic more or less by default, as the Union of Utrecht of 1577, an offensive and defensive alliance among the seven provinces, served as its only approach to a federal constitution. Although divine right monarchy was the usual form of government in seventeenth-century Europe, the Dutch did not want a king. The Princes of Orange, whose title derived from a family territory in southern France utterly unconnected with the Netherlands, performed many functions of a royal executive and were regarded by the people with a respect and veneration that such kings as the Stuarts of England might well have envied, but their title was "Stadhouder" and they were clearly understood to be the servants, not the masters, of the States-General.

The work of the States-General was often impeded and sometimes interrupted altogether by the same sort of local particularism and factional rivalry that had characterized Dutch towns throughout the Middle Ages. A conspicuous example, which also shows how theological disputes turned into political issues, was the conflict between Remonstrants and Counter-Remonstrants which nearly paralyzed the Dutch Republic in the second decade of the seventeenth century. The Remonstrants were followers of a theologian named Arminius, who argued that man was saved by exercise of free will. The Counter-Remonstrants maintained the familiar Calvinist tradition that God predestined who should be saved and man could do nothing about it. The Arminian doctrine appealed to the Dutch sense of practical piety, but the Calvinist doctrine, which was consonant with familiar medieval beliefs, appealed to their sense of orthodox tradition. Both groups therefore acquired strong followings within Calvinist congregations, which groups then competed for control of the congregation. Since the leaders of the congregation were simultaneously civic leaders, and since Dutch factions traditionally used their total resources in their conflicts, these struggles soon became struggles for control of the city councils and of the cities' representatives in the States-General, who were appointed by the councils. In the face of mounting disorder the States-General and their executive official, Johan van Oldenbarnevelt, were powerless, and it was finally necessary for Maurice of Orange, William the Silent's son and the greatest soldier of his day, to use the army to seize power, to execute Oldenbarnevelt (the leader of the Remonstrants) for treason, and to compel the nation to accept the theological decisions of the Synod of Dort in 1619.

This nation, which could be rent to its foundations by religious controversy, was at the same time a haven for religious refugees from all over Europe, including the Pilgrim fathers. It was also a center of publishing of all sorts of books in many languages, although Dutch scholars much preferred Latin to their own language and the Dutch people were not great readers. Nor did they produce great writers of the stature of Shakespeare, Corneille, and Cervantes. Instead they supported Rembrandt, Hals, and Vermeer and many lesser artists whose paintings decorated civic buildings—though no longer churches as in the Middle Ages—and private homes. The Dutch appreciated particularly portraits of individuals and groups, "genre" paintings of objects and scenes from everyday life, and depictions of historical events or Bible stories. Allegorical and pagan classical subjects like those of the Flemish master, Rubens, and ecstasies of saints so popular with seventeenth-century Italian and Spanish painters were contrary to their Protestant religious convictions.

It was from this Netherlands in its Golden Age that Dutch colonists departed for the East Indies, South America, South Africa—and the Hudson Valley. They included traders, whose settlements followed the urban tradition which has been described —Albany adhered rather more closely to this pattern, telescoped into one hundred fifty years instead of several centuries, than did some Dutch cities—but also farmers who followed a rural tradition which Dutch historians themselves have not yet described. In the upper Hudson Valley many landholders were also traders, and the rural tradition resembled the urban—for example, the village of Kinderhook was governed by a "rural patriciate" similar to that of the city of Albany—but in the mid-Hudson region and in New Jersey the Dutch tradition was that of the rural Netherlands. Furthermore, the great Dutch landowners of the lower Hudson Valley, many of whom early intermarried with English landed and court families, developed an aristocratic way of life which differed in a number of important respects from the dominant urban Dutch tradition recapitulated in Albany. Albany was the first permanent Dutch settlement in the Hudson Valley; its Dutch name, Fort Orange, should be better known in American history as the contemporary of Jamestown and Plymouth. Most of its early settlers were of Dutch origin, in contrast to the cosmopolitan inhabitants of the seaport of New Amsterdam. Even after the English conquest few British settlers came to Albany. The Albanians continued to speak the Dutch language, retained Dutch forms of social and economic organization, and conducted their city government in a manner far more Dutch than English in spite of its reorganization by the conquerors. One of the most conspicuous developments in this Dutch town was the evolution of a merchant patriciate.

Until the middle of the eighteenth century the Albanians were sufficiently isolated to develop their Dutch society without external interference. Then the French and Indian War (1754–63) brought major British armies to Albany, and in 1763 the Peace of Paris opened nearby frontier lands to settlement. The Albany patricians dropped deep-seated rivalries among themselves to make common cause against the newcomers. The American Revolution gave them an opportunity to expel intrusive British merchants as Loyalists, but the Yankees who flooded into their places soon acquired, and were not backward in using, the advantage of numbers. After the War of 1812 they gained control of the city government and of most of its banks and businesses. They reinforced this control by allying themselves with the Dutch through intermarriage, while the Dutch families kept their considerable fortunes invested in local enterprises, contributed their talents inconspicuously to a wide variety of professions and civic undertakings, and maintained a tradition of generous hospitality. After the Civil War, however, the Dutch were an ever-decreasing proportion of an exploding population increasingly Irish, Italian, Polish, and Negro. City politics fell into the hands of a series of bosses. City banks and businesses broadened their sources of capital. Newly rich and politically prominent hostesses overshadowed the Dutch matrons. The Dutch patrician tradition ceased to be a recognizable ethnic entity.

The Gansevoort family represented the Albany Dutch patricians in many ways. For six generations they identified themselves with the city, living there, making their fortune there, participating in its civic affairs, and considering it their home even when their means of livelihood eventually took some of them away. As individuals they were not widely known, with the exception of Revolutionary General Peter Gansevoort and his grandson, Herman Melville. But this does not mean that they were merely part of the nameless, faceless mass of obscure men. Far from it, and least of all in their own estimation! Individual Gansevoorts contributed significantly to their community as they carried on their ordinary functions as members of a family which exercised community leadership. In remaining in Albany and performing these functions day in and day out for the entire period of their existence as a family, the Gansevoorts demonstrated the characteristic which distinguished Dutch patricians from landed aristocrats, whose power rested on large rural estates, and from the merchant oligarchs of English towns, whose ambition was to purchase and remove to country houses so their children could be accepted into the gentry.

Many of the Gansevoorts, especially the earlier ones, represented their Dutch tradition in another way which is most inconvenient for the historian. Busy making a fortune by brewing and improving their social position by marriage and civic participation, they kept few records of their transactions and preserved them carelessly. They had little need for personal correspondence, since most of them lived within walking distance of each other, and entrusted important business communications to agents who delivered them by word of mouth. Therefore the only information available about the first three generations of Gansevoorts is like that available about other Albany families in the public records: land holdings, court appearances, official acts in public positions, and formal church participation. Some of their portraits and a few of their personal possessions have been preserved by museums and interested descendants. All of this evidence tells far more about the Gansevoort family's position in its community than about the personalities of its individual members.

Several members of the fourth generation of Gansevoorts— the Revolutionary generation—thought differently about written records. Children when the British imperial army overwhelmed Albany on its way to conquer Canada, they grew up bilingual. Dutch was still their spoken domestic and social language—it was used in the services of the Albany Dutch Reformed Church until after the American Revolution—but even their family letters were written in fluent and accurate English. As soon as Revolutionary service scattered them from one end of the Hudson Valley to the other, they began corresponding frequently and at length about public events, local occurrences, and family affairs. Furthermore, they formed a habit of preserving their letters, their business records, and apparently almost every other piece of writing that came into their hands. This habit was imitated by General Peter Gansevoort's youngest son, also named Peter, and by Peter's daughter, Catherine Gansevoort Lansing. It was she who finally bequeathed the accumulation of three generations to the New York Public Library, where the Gansevoort-Lansing Collection is now cataloged at about 400 boxes and 295 volumes. These materials give as panoramic and minutely detailed a picture of the Gansevoorts' way of life as the paintings of the medieval Flemish masters give of the surroundings of their ancestors.

From the time that the Dutch located Fort Orange at a place geographically advantageous for trade, they found that their very location made them inescapably the focus of conflict among four different European cultures, to say nothing of two mutually hostile tribes of Indians. Always numerically inferior but possessing the advantages of being first comers and of holding the strategic center of communication, they allied with the Indians against all other Europeans, then with the French against the English, then with the English against the Yankees, and finally with the Yankees against the heterogeneous immigrants of the nineteenth century. For one generation these conflicts broke out into open warfare, but during most of their history the Albany Dutch patricians defended their community's identity and privileges with social, economic, and political weapons, wielded with the silent effectiveness which is possible when a group of people have lived together all their lives and know without being told how each other will react in given circumstances. Their stubborn, shrewd, efficient, tactful way of seeing the most necessary thing and getting it done is almost impossible to document exactly, yet it runs like an orange thread through American history wherever Hudson Valley Dutchmen have had anything to do with the making of it.

The fact that the Hudson Valley Dutch patricians were most concerned with acquiring and exercising the privileges of their own communities must not be construed to suggest that they cut themselves off from the developing American tradition. Instead, they contributed substantially to it. To make this clear, it must be pointed out that the proper legal term for Dutch civic "privileges" is "liberties." I have avoided it thus far only to prevent confusion with the habitual American (and English) usage. But by now it should be clear that in the Dutch tradition "liberty" was possessed by communities, whose members then shared its benefits among themselves, while in the English tradition "liberty" was possessed by individuals, who exercised it by joining in communities. In both cases "liberty" meant freedoms and rights, in many specific instances very similar freedoms and rights. The Albany Dutch patricians were just as much concerned about "liberty" as their English and Yankee neighbors, although they came to it by a different road. Therefore it was quite within their capacity to accept the ideology of the American Revolution, to bring their particular socio-economic system through it intact, and to make effective and important contributions to the emerging American tradition. Seldom popular, heroic, or brilliant, they provided experienced day-to-day leadership, overcoming small crises, marshalling limited resources, hanging on beyond hope or expectation until circumstances turned in their favor. Thus, Schuyler's army was at hand and ready to fight for liberty at Saratoga under Gates and Arnold; Van Buren's party was at hand and ready to sweep democracy into the White House under Andrew Jackson; Franklin Roosevelt's organization was at hand and ready to support the world struggle for freedom defined by Winston Churchill.

The Gansevoorts' story reflects this tenacious devotion to liberty, which their compatriots in the Netherlands had already demonstrated by their eighty-year struggle for independence from Spain. The first of the Gansevoorts arrived in the Hudson Valley about 1660 with no resources but his hands, but his descendants soon exerted themselves to become patricians and exercise the liberties of their community. When it became necessary to fight for these liberties they hurried into the war effort, and when it was time to form a new government they came forward to help with equal enthusiasm. These Revolutionary Gansevoorts and some of their children devoted their lives to courses of action designed to advance simultaneously their own fortunes and the liberties of their community and country, and when finally the mainstream of American liberty turned into a different channel, their grandchildren continued to associate the welfare of their family with the welfare of their community. The name of Gansevoort died out, but descendants of Gansevoort daughters are still aware of their Dutch tradition. Some of them, like the descendants of other Albany patricians, have carried that tradition to other locations, but some still live in Albany. These ninth- and tenth-generation Dutch patricians seldom go out of their way to attract attention, but they continue to participate in commercial, social, and civic affairs, and their actions rather than their words do much to benefit their community. It is to these heirs and maintainers of the Hudson Valley Dutch tradition, a number of whom have generously and thoughtfully given me every assistance in their power, that this book is dedicated.

THE Gansevoorts OF Albany

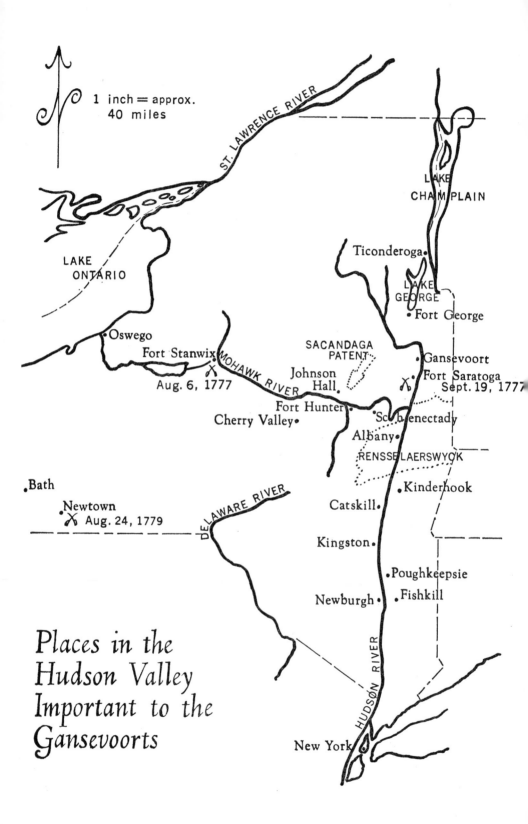

1 inch = approx.
40 miles

ST. LAWRENCE RIVER

LAKE
CHAMPLAIN

LAKE
ONTARIO

Ticonderoga.

LAKE
GEORGE

. Fort George

.Oswego

Fort Stanwix

MOHAWK RIVER

SACANDAGA
PATENT

.Gansevoort

Aug. 6, 1777

Johnson
Hall.

Fort Saratoga
Sept. 19, 1777

Fort Hunter

Cherry Valley.

.Schenectady

Albany.

RENSSELAERSWYCK

.Bath

.Kinderhook

Newtown
Aug. 24, 1779

DELAWARE RIVER

Catskill.

Kingston.

.Poughkeepsie

Newburgh.

.Fishkill

Places in the
Hudson Valley
Important to the
Gansevoorts

HUDSON RIVER

New York.

I

Plebeians to Patricians

The one thing that the Dutch traders, soldiers, and farmers who founded Fort Orange in 1624 had in common was plebeian origin; none of them, so far as is known, were related to the patrician families which ruled the cities of the Netherlands and, through them, the recently-independent Dutch Republic. Most of their names have been lost, and very little is known about them except that the eighteen families of farmers were Protestant Walloons, French-speaking religious refugees from the part of the Low Countries under Spanish rule. Like the vast majority of their successors in the forty years of Dutch rule over the Hudson Valley, the traders who came to barter for furs with the Indians and the soldiers sent by the Dutch West India Company to protect their goods probably emigrated from different cities, towns, and villages in the Netherlands or from nearby northern Germany. Certainly the community they developed on the American frontier bore many resemblances to the communities their ancestors had established on the ancient frontier between Roman civilization and the forests of Germany.

These settlers came to a part of the world geographically far different from the Netherlands. Many parts of the Low Countries were actually below sea level, made habitable and fruitful only by elaborate systems of dikes and drainage ditches which required constant vigilance and frequent repair. Even away from the sea and the great rivers, the Rhine and the Scheldt, the total elevation of the land was never great. From this level homeland the ship *Nieu Nederlandt* brought the settlers to the not-so-different low shores of Long Island and Staten Island. Then suddenly the little vessel entered the mighty tidal stream which poured between the heights of upper Manhattan and the Palisades. When the towering wall of volcanic columns at last came to an end, the *Nieu Nederlandt* sailed across the broad Tappan Zee and on into the rugged Highlands, their ancient rocks twisted and split into indescribably complex masses. It is little wonder that the settlers and their descendants peopled these mysterious crags and crannies with ghosts and supernatural beings. Tacking farther up the beautiful "reaches" of the river—fourteen in all—the *Nieu Nederlandt* passed beneath the bold Catskills, with their characteristic thick layers of red sandstone formed in the delta of an ancient river incomparably greater than the Hudson. On the east bank the hills rose gradually over hard rocks, like the Highlands even more ancient than the Catskills, to the main Taconic range twenty miles away.

The Hudson River estuary is about one hundred fifty miles long. Salt water followed the *Nieu Nederlandt* halfway, to the site of Newburgh; the pressure of the tide could be discerned all the way to Fort Orange. Solid mountain walls still confined the river, broken only by occasional creeks whose level bottoms were fertile and suitable for farming. As the river grew shallower, the ship passed low islands wooded with willow and alder. The Catskills fell away behind, and atop the steep banks level country rolled westward. Past the mouth of the Normanskill the river became too shallow for safe navigation, although the tide was still noticeable ten miles farther upstream, where the Hudson's greatest tributary, the Mohawk River, thundered in from the west over majestic Cohoes Falls.

The *Nieu Nederlandt* anchored near the Normanskill while the settlers built their fort. On a nearby island they found remains of buildings erected by various independent traders who had been visiting the area since 1614, but they quickly abandoned this site because it had been repeatedly flooded out. Instead, they threw up a palisade on the narrow shelf between the water's edge and the steep western bank. This bank, which rose slightly over

2

two hundred feet before it leveled off into miles of flat, sandy pine plains, was cut by five streams, of which the Normanskill—actually a small river about thirty miles long—was the southernmost and most considerable. Beaver Kill, Foxen Kill, and Rutten Kill have long since been canalized into ponds, park lakes, and sewers, but the streets of Albany still climb up and down the steep slopes between which these creeks once flowed. Patroon Creek, the northernmost, retains its identity and even traces of its wilderness character, for beside it is the city's wildlife sanctuary.

When they followed the creeks to the top of the hill, the settlers undoubtedly recognized the three highest Catskills as three blue bumps on the southern horizon. They certainly also saw the sheer Helderberg escarpment a few miles to the southwest, too far away for them to visit immediately. Eventually, however, they climbed this two-thousand-foot cliff, the northernmost edge of the great Appalachian Plateau. First they must have marveled at the rocks under their feet, for the cliffs are composed of an ancient limestone formed at the same time as the red Catskill sandstone, and consisting almost entirely of strange fossil shells. When they looked off from the edge of the cliff they saw that Fort Orange lay in an oval basin fifteen miles by twenty, rimmed by the Helderbergs, the Catskills, the Berkshires, and, to the north, the Mayfield Hills, southern outliers of the unexplored Adirondacks. The basin, formed by a postglacial lake a long time ago by human standards but only yesterday if compared with the antiquity of the Helderbergs and Catskills, was flat and level, floored with sandy soil, and forested primarily with towering white pines. The courses of the Hudson, the Mohawk, and the Normanskill near the foot of the cliff barely creased its surface; the tiny palisade that was Fort Orange was screened from view by the riverbank.

The settlers of Fort Orange came to their little post in a vast wilderness from a world shaken by widespread war. In 1618 a dispute between Austria and Bohemia had touched off the Thirty Years War, in which most of the states of Europe finally became involved. Hapsburg Spain supported Hapsburg Austria, and in 1621, when the Twelve Years Truce expired, the war between the

Dutch and the Spanish was resumed as part of the general conflict.

It had been clearly demonstrated by 1609 that the Dutch were masters on the sea, while the Spaniards were masters on the land. There was no real hope of liberating the ten southern provinces, now thoroughly conquered and solidly Catholic after the forced conversion or expulsion of the Protestant Walloons. There was nothing for the Dutch to gain by invading Spain itself, had such a campaign been within the range of practical possibilities. But the rich commerce between the New World and Spain, carried in lumbering galleons which had to sail out of their way considerably to the northward of the West Indies to be sure of favorable winds, offered prizes worth the taking as an additional reward for the patriotic duty of removing this wealth from the hands of the enemy. So the sons and grandsons of the "Sea Beggars" who had supplied William the Silent and intercepted Spanish transports sailed for the Spanish Main where they engaged in privateering, piracy, or legitimate trade as opportunities offered. This enterprise was too big, too serious, and too much in the national interest to be allowed to go on in the state of anarchic competition which characterized unorganized Dutch enterprises. A group of powerful financiers therefore petitioned the States-General to form a West India Company similar to the East India Company chartered in 1602, which had seized the East Indies from Portugal and made fortunes for its investors by trading in pepper and other spices.

When the West India Company received its charter in 1621, it was granted a monopoly of Dutch trade in the New World and empowered to conduct military operations against the Spanish colonies. It was also granted permission to found forts, trading posts, and colonies in territory discovered or conquered by the Dutch. The Hudson Valley, claimed in 1609 by a Dutch expedition under Henry Hudson and frequented thereafter by anarchic, competitive, private fur traders, was only one of its many interests and, as it turned out, comparatively a minor one. In 1628, four years after the Company's settlers arrived at Fort Orange, Admiral Piet Heyn captured the entire Spanish treasure fleet.

4

Thereafter the investors, who included many ordinary Dutch citizens as well as wealthy merchants, demanded more military operations likely to yield similar spectacular returns. In 1644 the Company's soldiers, led by the intrepid Pieter Stuyvesant, conquered Curaçao, giving the Dutch a foothold in the West Indies. The Company also founded a tropical colony in Surinam and took Brazil away from Portugal as the East India Company had taken the East Indies, but unlike the East India Company proved unable to retain what it had seized after the Portuguese regained their independence from Spain in 1640.

The West India Company therefore expected the colonists it sent to Fort Orange and simultaneously to Manhattan Island, the Delaware River, and the Connecticut River, to take care of themselves and send over many shiploads of fur to make the expenses of establishing them worthwhile. Livestock, agricultural implements, and trading goods did follow on later ships, three of them appropriately named the *Cow,* the *Sheep,* and the *Horse.* These animals were supposed to be loaned to the settlers and their increase divided between the settlers and the Company, but many of them found their way into the possession of powerful individuals, such as Governor Wouter Van Twiller. The settlers were further expected to confine themselves to farming, being forbidden to manufacture any goods even for local sale or to take any part in the fur trade. All of these regulations were consistently evaded.

The Fort Orange settlers had been there for only two years when their Indian neighbors went to war. At this time, the Dutch were acquainted only with the Hudson River Indians who had welcomed Henry Hudson, an Algonkian tribe called the Mahicans. They knew the Maquase or Mohawks of the Mohawk Valley, the easternmost and most ferocious of the redoubtable Five Nations or Iroquois Confederacy, as the Mahicans' deadly enemies. After the usual practice in the East Indies then and later, the commandant of Fort Orange, Daniel van Krieckebeeck, agreed to send a small party of Dutchmen with firearms to accompany the Mahicans on one of their raids. But the Mohawks ambushed the party at the steep falls of the Beaver Kill, a mile or

5

so from the fort. The site of this falls, a popular nineteenth-century picnic spot, is now included in Lincoln Park; the kill forms Lincoln Park Lake. Four Dutchmen, including van Krieckebeeck, were killed. The others escaped, but the word that filtered back later, that the victorious Mohawks had celebrated their triumph by eating an arm and a leg of a victim named Tymen Bouwensen, increased the settlers' panic. The eighteen refugee families fled once more, this time to Manhattan where most of them probably stayed. Fort Orange remained in a state of suspended animation until the Mohawks decisively defeated the Mahicans and drove them eastward into the Berkshires, where they were later known as the Stockbridge Indians. The Dutch, having learned their lesson, established trading relations with the Mohawks but never again interfered in any of their wars with other Indians.

The next group of settlers came to Fort Orange for slightly different reasons. In 1629, the year after Heyn's golden victory, the West India Company decided to turn over the troubles and expense of colonization to individual entrepreneurs. By the "Charter of Privileges and Exemptions" it offered to give a very large tract of land and the title "Patroon" to anyone who would undertake to send fifty settlers within four years. "Patroon" was not a title of nobility or rank in the Netherlands; it was a new title for a new world much like King James I of England's "baronets" of Nova Scotia, and meant as much or as little as its purchaser could make of it. Of a number of men who applied for patroonships, only Kiliaen Van Rensselaer, a wealthy Amsterdam diamond merchant and a director of the West India Company, succeeded in his venture, but he was so successful that his descendants were called patroons for the next two centuries, and were wholly responsible for the continued use of the title. Van Rensselaer chose for his colony the land around Fort Orange, twelve miles along the Hudson and twenty-four miles back into the wilderness on both sides of the river; his boundaries are today the boundaries of Albany and Rensselaer Counties. His fifty settlers began to arrive in 1630, and laid out their farms on the fertile islands and the low-lying east bank of the river. Though patroons'

6

rights were a curious compound of feudal terminology and early modern Dutch practice, Van Rensselaer's settlement functioned in many ways like a medieval feudal lordship. He even had a little fort called Rensselaersteyn built on an island at the entrance to his domain, and for a time expected all ships, including those of the Company, to dip their flags as they passed.

So long as Kiliaen Van Rensselaer lived his power and pretensions went unchallenged, but within two years after his death in 1646, opposition appeared from both above and below. Governor Pieter Stuyvesant, who was by no means deficient in a sense of his own importance, immediately curbed such extensions of the patroon's privileges as the salute from Company ships at Rensselaersteyn. Brant Van Slichtenhorst, the agent sent by the guardians of the Van Rensselaer heirs, was tactless and overbearing. Then in 1648, after Indians provoked by the policies of former Governor Kieft had massacred Dutch settlers near New Amsterdam, Van Slichtenhorst ordered all the patroon's colonists to cross the river and settle around Fort Orange. He insisted that the purpose of this removal was defense, but Stuyvesant suspected that it was really an attempt to engross the Indian trade for the Van Rensselaers. He directed Van Slichtenhorst to clear away all the buildings immediately surrounding the fort. When Van Slichtenhorst did nothing, Stuyvesant came to Fort Orange in April, 1652, arrested him, and eventually shipped him back to the Netherlands.

Conflict between Stuyvesant and Van Slichtenhorst, representing a powerful commercial organization and a powerful family from the homeland, was only part of this upheaval. The settlers of Fort Orange had a share in it too. By this time most of those whose names are known had come over as employees of the Van Rensselaers, though some may have been soldiers or traders. But a number of the Van Rensselaer employees had served out the six years that paid for their passage, and others were dissatisfied over their—theoretical—exclusion from the fur trade. When they all settled around Fort Orange they formed a community as their ancestors had done in the Dark Ages, a little group of traders clustered for mutual protection at a site possessing geographical

7

advantages for commerce and means of defense. Like their ancestors, they sought relief from restraints imposed by a neighboring territorial lord by appealing to his overlord for a grant of civic privileges. On April 14, 1652, Stuyvesant accordingly established the independent town of Beverwyck. *Wyck* or *wik* is a common North European word-element meaning "trading district"; *bever* is, of course, the commodity in which this particular *wyck* traded almost exclusively. The town included all the land within cannon-shot of Fort Orange, which he granted in generous lots to the various settlers, who thus became householders or burghers. (Some of them, who were later fined for not having built on their lots, evidently became burghers first and householders afterwards.) For the government of the town Stuyvesant set up a council of six magistrates whom he appointed from the burghers but who were thereafter replaced by co-optation, whose function was to try disputes and promulgate local ordinances. The population of this little civic entity was perhaps four hundred people, of whom at least half were probably children, as was true nearly everywhere in America throughout the colonial period.

The men elevated to membership on the town council of Beverwyck were, judging by assessment lists and the amounts for which they brought suit and were sued, the wealthiest traders in the upper Hudson Valley, but their office did not automatically make them patricians. It is unlikely that any of them had ever participated in city government in the Netherlands. Therefore, like community leaders elsewhere on the American frontier, they conducted the affairs of Beverwyck on the basis of common sense, the governor's ordinances, and that general awareness of what is legitimate and what is not which is shared by all the adult members of any society, rather than by the venerable procedures of Dutch city councils. An occasional litigant cited legal authorities in their court, but they never referred for precedent to any juridical works, to the specific customs of any Dutch city, or to the technical rules of Roman-Dutch law. Nevertheless, the government they formed follows the general pattern common to Dutch towns far more closely than that developed in English settlements on the American frontier. From this it appears evident that the whole Dutch tradition in the Old World and the New may be seen in an additional dimension by stripping away the complexities of accumulated custom and observing what features of their community life were important enough to these ordinary people who participated in it from the bottom up to reproduce in their new homes in the wilderness.

Some specific examples will illustrate how the town council of Beverwyck applied the common customs of their people in typical cases of misdemeanor, personal injury, and indebtedness. All three involved a plebeian brewer named Harmen Harmense van Gansevoort. There is no indication of his date of birth, his place of origin, or his time of arrival in Beverwyck. In 1660 he was probably at least twenty-five, which was legal age among the Dutch, for in that year he executed several documents before a notary. "Van Gansevoort" might be expected to identify his birthplace, but there was no town of that name in the seventeenth-century Netherlands. His nineteenth-century descendants discovered records of a score of Gansevoorts, including a Hermanus and other names repeated among Harmen Harmense's descendants, in church registers of seventeenth-century Gröningen, and traced them to a manor called Harena or Harn a few miles outside of Lippe in Westphalia. No other possibility has been suggested. Harmen Harmense may have been a "Harmen, the brewer" cited in default in an unidentified court action in 1655, but since this identification is uncertain he can only be assumed to have come to Beverwyck sometime before the spring of 1657.

Harmen's first appearance in the Beverwyck court was as an unsuccessful peacemaker. On April 19, 1657, Pieter Bronck quarreled with Poulus Martensen in Hendrick Bierman's tavern. Harmen tried to intervene, but Bronck drew a knife. Three other bystanders became involved in the fray before it could be stopped, probably by the *schout*, Beverwyck's equivalent of a constable. The nature of the offense seemed obvious; the magistrates undoubtedly expected that the men would plead guilty, as usually happened in such cases, but any such expectations were dashed by the first day's testimony. It was well established that the fight had occurred and that Pieter Bronck had started it, but on the

9

crucial matter of the knife the defendants were obstinately non-committal. It was possible that a knife had been drawn, but none of them were willing to testify that they had actually seen it. They were trying to shield Bronck, who did not seem able to re-member what had happened, for Harmen gave as his reason for refusing to be definite "that he is not an informer and will not say it." [1] This did not satisfy the magistrates, who recalled him and Hendrick Bierman two days later. At that point both admitted that they had seen Bronck with a knife in his hand. Three days after this, the case was concluded by Bronck's trial and convic-tion. In spite of, or perhaps because of, his plea of intoxication, he was condemned to pay a fine of one hundred guilders, "according to the ordinance." The other four were not prosecuted.

In this incident Harmen showed himself quick to interrupt violence and loyal to his friends. Three years later, another quar-rel which involved him in legal proceedings showed that he also possessed a hair-trigger temper which he did not always keep un-der control. The incident occurred at the end of the harvest sea-son in 1660. Eight or nine of Harmen's neighbors had apparently dropped in at his brewery in the settlement of Bethlehem, south of the Normanskill, to sample the new beer. After a time one Claes Bever so far forgot himself that he taunted his host with having been a hog-driver in the old country. Harmen Harmense was quick to answer. "Swarten Marten says, and I will prove it by him, that you, Claes Bever, have been a shepherd." [2]

Swarten Marten—"Black Marten," Marten Cornelisz van Ysselsteyn—who was present, probably only half-heard this ex-change. When it was called to his attention he must have made some remark which Harmen interpreted as confirmation of his statement and Claes Bever did not. At any rate, Harmen offered to support his veracity by staking a half-cask of beer on it. Bever accepted the wager and demanded that it be paid at once. Har-men was not ready to give in, but under pressure from the com-pany he tapped the cask. If he hoped that the disagreement would be forgotten in renewed conviviality, he was doomed to disappointment. When the beer had been drunk the issue arose again and the wager was renewed for higher stakes—Harmen's

10

brewing kettle against Bever's canoe full of firewood which was moored to the nearby bank of the Hudson. Then a difficulty appeared, for the brewing kettle was built into the fireplace where it was used and could not easily be moved. Bever apparently accepted this disappointment, but the brewer cried, "I will nevertheless have the canoe and the firewood too, at my risk and fine, for I have a valid enough claim thereto."

The men rushed down to the river bank, and one of them pulled the canoe up on the shore. "You wrong me and do me an injustice!" cried Bever, but three of the men pushed by him and each took out a load of wood. Outraged, Bever warned them once more, "If you take out more you shall rue it!" and somehow, perhaps by the tone of his voice, perhaps with his fists—the records do not tell—he apparently made this one respected.

But neither this nor the sobering up of the participants ended the matter. Nursing his wrath, Bever marshaled witnesses in his favor before the notary, whose functions in Roman-Dutch law included the taking of sworn statements and the preservation of many documents we consider public records. The witnesses included the unfortunate Marten Cornelisz whose careless remark had given Harmen's statement a semblance of support but who now asserted for the record that "It may well be that Claes Bever has been a shepherd or a swineherd, but not as far as I know." Harmen heard of what was going on and produced witnesses of his own. The notary took down their testimony and preserved it carefully. When Bever's suit came before the court, all that would be necessary would be for the parties to appear and swear that the papers contained their testimony and that it was correct. But for some reason Harmen capitulated and the case was never tried. It is possible, though not particularly consistent with the other available evidence of his character, that he apologized voluntarily. Perhaps some of their friends managed to convince them that it was more sensible to forget the quarrel, or arbitrators settled it out of court. In any event, Harmen surrendered the kettle, which Bever eventually sold. Of course, the kettle which Bever sold may not have been the one that Harmen wagered, but the incident in October, the affidavits for a suit that was never brought, and the

11

sale of a kettle in December seem to fit together too well to be coincidental.

Like most of his neighbors, Harmen frequently went to court to press or protest the collection of debts, some of them large, others quite small. His most spectacular lawsuit was an attempt to break the hasty sale of a farm to an improvident neighbor. Although the case was tried in 1678, nearly a decade and a half after the English conquest, its only English feature was that it was the first civil cause in Albany to be heard by a jury, probably because of the value of the farm. As the story came out in court, Harmen sold the farm to John Conell, an immigrant, possibly Irish, with a long record of convictions for debt and misdemeanors, and rued the bargain afterward. Conell refused to undo it. Harmen's wife, Maritje, who brought the suit and conducted the entire cause herself, objected to the sale because she was sure Conell would never pay the two hundred beaver skins he had agreed to give. She asserted that her husband had sold the land while intoxicated, that his act would be the ruin of her children, and that if the court would not annul the contract the least it could do was to require the purchaser to give proper security that he would make his payments when they fell due. Harmen did not testify, presumably to support the plea of irresponsibility due to intoxication. But Maritje's eloquence was countered by the statements of several witnesses, most of whom agreed that whether or not Harmen had been intoxicated when the sale took place, they had heard him say subsequently that he was well satisfied with the transaction and that his wife would also be pleased. The jury agreed that the sale was valid and that the Gansevoorts must surrender the farm, but the court in its judgment required John Conell to give security as Maritje had requested. Her caution was justified, for the following spring and the spring thereafter Harmen had to sue Conell for the payment before he could collect it. Then Conell sold the farm to someone else who completed the rest of the payments promptly.[3]

Harmen's experiences in court were quite typical of the burghers of Beverwyck. Indeed, small disagreements so frequently produced lawsuits that it is impossible to avoid suspecting that at least some of the inhabitants thoroughly enjoyed the momentary importance such an action gave them. Men sued each other for hasty words, usually spoken in their cups. Women, who seldom advanced that particular extenuating circumstance, showed their dislike of their neighbors in such unladylike ways as shouting obscenities at them in the street or engaging them in physical conflict, also usually in the street. Complete equality of the sexes was practiced in this respect; more than once a doughty housewife was fined for having beaten some unfortunate male with a stick or even with her fists, and men and boys did not hesitate to reply in kind. The court heard all these cases patiently and fined whichever party appeared to be the aggressor, and in some cases both. In this casually violent frontier community, it is noteworthy that only once in twenty years was Harmen Gansevoort ever summoned concerning a disturbance in his taproom.

In 1664 the English conquered New Netherland. Little can be known of the immediate effect of the conquest on Beverwyck because the town records for much of the 1660's have disappeared. Governor Richard Nicolls tried to make the change of government as easy as possible for the common people by confirming local magistrates in office, permitting previous judicial decisions to stand, and retaining Dutch customs in such important matters as inheritance. Beverwyck was renamed Albany, one of the titles of the Duke of York, later King James II, but the magistrates made no attempt to use the English language even for official proceedings. Then a new threat came from an old quarter, for the Van Rensselaer family, one of whose relatives in the Netherlands had befriended King Charles II during his exile, tried to use this personal relationship with the Crown to get possession of Albany. They continued their pressure for twenty years, interrupted by the Dutch reconquest of the province in 1673–74. After the English returned in 1674, the Van Rensselaers obtained a decision from the King granting them the town, but the Albanians protested so effectively that Governor Edmund Andros evaded carrying the decision into effect for his entire term of office. His successor Governor Thomas Dongan finally flatly stated, after Charles II had been succeeded by James II, "that it was not to his majes-

13

ty's interest that the second town in the province should be in the hands of any particular men." [4]

The Albanians' response to this threat resembled that of their medieval ancestors in similar situations; they appealed to the encroaching lord's overlord and eventually purchased from him a restatement of their civic liberties. This was the Dongan Charter, issued in 1686, for which the Governor later admitted receiving £300 and was suspected of receiving considerably more. It was English in form, providing the city with extensive tracts of land and with government by a mayor appointed by the governor and a common council elected by the inhabitants. The mayor and common council were given power to regulate the city's economic life, as were the governing bodies of most cities both Dutch and English. The most conspicuously Dutch feature of the charter was the common council's explicit monopoly over the fur trade and control of Indian relations on the entire northern frontier. For the next ninety years the Albanians implemented this hybrid instrument of government in a manner far more Dutch than English.

In the forefront of the movement for the charter were a group of fur traders who had amassed the largest fortunes in Albany and who undoubtedly contributed most substantially to the expenses of securing it. Foremost among them was Pieter Schuyler, indispensably influential because the suspicious Mohawk Indians trusted him alone. His sister's husband, Robert Livingston, a self-made Scot who had accumulated a fortune by an advantageous marriage and remarkably shrewd dealings, was also invaluable because he knew both the Dutch and the English languages. Levinus Van Schaick, Schuyler's wife's brother, was a son of by far the wealthiest trader in Beverwyck. Dirck Wesselse Ten Broeck was another successful trader who worked with the others although he was not related to them. All four of these men were appointed by the charter to city offices, Schuyler as mayor, Livingston as clerk, Van Schaick as an alderman, and Ten Broeck as recorder. When elections began, they and their relatives and associates were elected. After all, they were probably the only men in Albany who really understood how the new system worked.

14

But trouble soon arose when other Albany fur traders, such as Johannes Cuyler, Johannes Wendell, and Hans Hendrickse [Hansen], competitors of the Schuyler group, found out that they were placed in its power by the monopoly provisions of the charter.

Another source of discontent in Albany at this time was religion. It is unlikely that the settlers of Fort Orange brought with them any more subtle knowledge of theology than they did of law, but the West India Company required them to be orthodox Reformed Calvinists and sent lay readers and pastors to care for their spiritual welfare. By the time of the English conquest the Dutch Reformed Church founded by Domine Johannes Megapolensis in 1646 had become a central element of the community's identity. From all that is known of this congregation in the seventeenth century, it emphasized the medieval Dutch traditions of doctrinal orthodoxy and practical piety, but did not practice the Dutch custom of toleration for other sects. In this respect it followed the policies of Governor Stuyvesant, whose refusal to permit any worship but the Reformed brought him a rebuke from the West India Company—which had learned that intolerance discouraged prospective settlers—to which he paid little attention. Domine Gideon Schaets, who entered upon the Albany charge in 1656, not only agreed with Stuyvesant that no other churches should exist, but preached to his parishioners that it was their religious duty to convert, or failing that, to exclude from the community all individuals who were not Calvinists.

Under these circumstances Harmen Harmense and other Albanians who, like him, happened to be Lutherans were in a difficult position. In 1656, about the time of Harmen's arrival, Lutherans in New Netherland generally called a pastor from the Netherlands, but Stuyvesant arrested him on his arrival and shipped him back to the homeland. The English conquest relieved this pressure, for though the Dutch Reformed Church remained that of most of the community, the local civil authorities were no longer encouraged or indeed permitted to interfere with other forms of worship. The Albany Lutherans— who included beside Harmen Harmense such leaders as Hans Hendrickse and magistrate Volkert Janse [Douw]—thereupon called a pastor whom they shared with the Lutherans of New York City, and built a church for which an unsubstantiated and probably erroneous family tradition states that Harmen Harmense gave the land. Their relations with Domine Schaets's congregation nevertheless continued to be stormy, and throughout the 1670's and the 1680's cases continued to come before the magistrates in which members of one sect sued members of the other for alleged defamation of their beliefs. The magistrates tried to be fair, but bad feelings between the two churches continued through the 1670's and 1680's.

In 1689, King James II, unpopular, Catholic, and pro-French, was forced by Parliament to abdicate his throne in favor of his Protestant daughter Mary and her husband William III of Orange, Stadhouder of the Netherlands. Since William had been leading European resistance to Louis XIV of France for nearly twenty years, war immediately broke out between England and France. When news of this "Glorious Revolution" reached the New World, New York, Massachusetts, and the other New England colonies, which had been joined briefly as the "Dominion of New England," went their separate ways. The Bostonians imprisoned King James's unpopular governor, Edmund Andros, and the New Yorkers deposed his deputy, Francis Nicholson. The New York insurgents chose Jacob Leisler as their leader and turned upon the clique of merchant and landed families who had dominated the city and colony of New York. Then they reached out to extend their control over the Hudson Valley. A number of Leisler's principal supporters in New York were related to Albanians like Johannes Cuyler, Johannes Wendell, and Jochim Staets, who became leaders of a local faction which favored Leisler and opposed the Schuyler group and its instrument, the city charter. In this Leislerian group, Harmen Gansevoort became a leader. Subsequent events showed that he had acquired a large measure of the popularity and influence commonly afforded to frontier tavernkeepers.

As soon as Leisler seized control of the province, Mayor Schuyler, his friends on the common council, and a few other leaders abandoned the charter form of government and formed themselves into an extralegal body called the Convention, proclaimed William and Mary independently, and organized for defense against the French in Canada, with whom William's accession automatically involved them in war. Leisler also took steps for the defense of the frontier, sending his son-in-law Jacob Milborne to Albany in November, 1689, with fifty-one men. Distrusting Milborne, the Convention refused to quarter the men in the town or to admit them to the fort. But these magistrates did not have the support of all the people. Only forty "Inhabitants, Principall men of the Towne" had signed an affirmation of their loyalty which the Convention had requested before Milborne came. Two days after his arrival, "near a hundred Persons, most youthes, and them that were no freeholders," signed an agreement to appoint Jochim Staets, a Leislerian alderman, as captain of the men Milborne had brought. The Convention was sure they had been whipped up to this by Milborne's demagogic oratory, in which he had denounced "Popish government and arbitrary Power Condemning all things which had been done and Passed in the late King James Stuarts time Particularly the Charter of this Citty." [5]

These demonstrations only confirmed the impasse. Mayor Schuyler shut himself up in the fort to insure the loyalty of the thirty-one English soldiers who defended it, while the Convention, supported by its forty "Principall men" but weakened by the presence within its ranks of such open Leislerians as Staets and Jan Nack and such men as Johannes Wendell and Johannes Cuyler, both still trying to be moderates, maintained in the town an uneasy balance with Milborne and a considerable number of the general population. Milborne's fifty-one men shivered in the November air on Marte Gerritse's Island below the city; on November 13, Milborne marched them into the city, where "the Burgers of that faction Received them in there houses without billeting or lawfull authority." [6]

The following day the Mayor came down to the city from the fort to try to convince the people that he had merely taken measures to prevent Milborne from trying "to make an absolute change of government, to carry some Persones Prisoners to New

17

York, and so to make a generall disturbance among the People." [7]
He also described Milborne's refusal to come to an agreement with
the Convention regarding the billeting of the troops, and read the
articles to which Milborne had agreed in substance, "which
Pleased the Burgers very well and wished they might be Syned." [8]
Milborne was thereupon sent for, and when he arrived was presented once again with the articles, which for the fourth time he
found an excuse to delay signing. A committee of twelve men
chosen by the burghers, which included Harmen Gansevoort, observed these proceedings and agreed that Milborne was being deliberately obstructive. The Convention then asked them to suggest a better way of breaking the impasse, for which purpose they
withdrew and held a meeting with Harmen Gansevoort in the
chair. When they returned to the Convention they agreed that
nothing more could have been done to accommodate Milborne,
and declined to "trouble themselves farther in this matter." [9]

The day after that Milborne, firmly in possession of the town,
prepared to storm the fort. But "A Company of Maquase [Mo-
hawks] who were come here for the assistance of their Majesties
Subjects" [10] appeared on the hill behind the fort and threatened
to intervene in behalf of the defenders. This warning, communicated by Domine Dellius of the Dutch Reformed Church to "the
said Milborne at the head of his Companie in the Presence of a
great many Burgers," [11] gave the Leislerians pause. It is quite
possible that the burghers, who would have been anxious to keep
the Mohawks' friendship and trade, gave Milborne to understand that he had gone far enough. At any rate, he dismissed his
company and departed the next day for New York. The fifty-one
men stayed behind under the command of Jochim Staets, quartered, to the chagrin of the Convention, under a contract between
Milborne and five Albanians including Harmen Gansevoort, "Private but Extream active men in these Revolutions." [12]

A week later, the Convention welcomed Captain Jonathan
Bull and eighty-seven men from Connecticut, sent in response to
a plea for help of September 23. By this time the French war was
a reality, and anguished cries for defenders were being heard
from the outlying settlements on the Mohawk River, Half Moon,
Canestigione, and Schenectady. Captain Bull detailed a few men

to each place, but in Schenectady they were resented as minions of Albany almost as much as they were welcomed as help against the French. The details of the dissensions in Schenectady in January, 1690, were never recorded. Echoes of them have come down to us in the accusations of neglect hurled from both sides after the town had been destroyed by raiding French and Indians. The immediate panic caused by that atrocity gradually subsided, but long-term horror remained. If Schenectady could be obliterated without a struggle, when might Albany's turn come? The Convention sent out appeals to Connecticut for more help; Connecticut observed in reply that Albany should seek support closer to home this time. Even Leisler was better than the Praying Indian Kryn and his savage warriors, so the Convention swallowed its pride and wrote to Leisler. Robert Livingston and Domine Dellius promptly found pressing business which called them elsewhere.

But in spite of the fears the Convention had expressed in November, events in Albany went on pretty much as usual once the transfer of power was accomplished. Leisler appointed a committee of three including Jacob Milborne to assist in the local government. He placed Jochim Staets, an Albany man, in command of the fort. The mayor and common council he left as they were, although in December he had suggested to Captain Staets a list of nine men, including Harmen Gansevoort, whom he wished to see on the common council. The next fall Leisler bypassed the charter by appointing not only a mayor and recorder, but also twelve justices of the peace, including Harmen Gansevoort. The common council records would indicate that aldermen were also elected, though Leisler made no mention of them.

But Leisler's appointees had very brief tenure of office. In the spring of 1691 William and Mary sent a military expedition to regularize the government of New York. The new governor, Henry Sloughter, hanged Leisler and Milborne and permitted the provincial faction which the Leislerians had driven from power to engage in all sorts of reprisals. For example, in 1694 Robert Livingston haled Harmen Gansevoort into court on a charge that he had not paid his beer excise in 1689–90. Without reminding the authorities of his own support of Leisler, Harmen could hardly

19

plead that Livingston had fled and therefore was not present to collect the tax. He contented himself with the lame defense that he had not tapped that year. Livingston produced a dozen witnesses to the contrary, including two prominent Leislerians, and Harmen was fined £6 and costs. The kind of pressure exerted on Harmen's little Lutheran congregation is not recorded, but member after member of its younger generation, including several of Harmen's daughters, joined Domine Dellius' Dutch Reformed Church in the 1690's. The obstinate brewer and his equally stubborn wife remained outside the fold, although the rest of Maritje's family had always been Dutch Reformed, but sometime after Harmen was buried in his church in 1710 the congregation ceased to exist.

The most lasting result of Leisler's Rebellion in Albany was the acknowledgement by the entire community that the Dongan Charter would continue to be the foundation of the city government. The Leislerian leaders gave up trying to overthrow it and turned their energies toward attaining their aims within its framework. At the same time, the Schuyler group recognized that it could not run the community without reference to the interests of the rest of its inhabitants, particularly the other fur traders. In 1695 Pieter Schuyler's youngest brother Johannes married Elizabeth Staets Wendell, sister of three prominent Leislerians and widow of a fourth. This was only the first of numerous marriages between younger members of families which had been bitterly opposed in 1689. By 1710 the two groups of fur traders, though still commercial competitors, had intermarried into a single complex of families which dominated the city so completely that in 1717 and 1718 it held eleven out of the twelve seats on the common council. At this point it is proper to begin to speak of these families as the Albany Dutch patricians. Like their counterparts in the cities of the medieval Netherlands, they were first recognized as such by their fellow citizens after they made substantial contributions to preserving order in the face of violence and the liberties of the community in the face of internal subversion and external attack.

II

Fortune-Seekers and Social Climbers

The aspect of the emergence of the Albany patriciate which appears most significant to modern readers is its rise to a dominant position in local government. But to the Dutch patricians themselves politics was only one of several community activities in which they participated primarily for the benefit of their families. The benefits they particularly desired were material profit and social prestige, each valued for its convertibility into the other as well as for itself. The size of a family's fortune determined the degree of respect that that family might claim from the community and the marriage alliances that its children might expect to contract; community offices of trust, profit, and prestige went to those relatives, by birth or marriage, of respected families who could command the resources necessary either to purchase them or to pay election expenses. Conflicts within the community arose as a rule between families, or sometimes between branches of the same family, over rivalries for the possession of these advantages rather than between factions or parties formed primarily over political issues, although families already at odds often added disputes over provincial or even imperial politics to their other differences.

Family relationship as the basis of economic and political organization was of course by no means peculiar to the Dutch, being very important in all the north European traditions. Dutch families were particularly noted for singleminded dedication to the family business by all their members including women, and for their custom of keeping the family fortune invested in the same business for generations, as a result of which the capital resources available to Dutch patrician merchants were greater than those of individual English and French merchants. This long-term cumulative concentration of capital reflected the fact that merchant patricians held an honorable place in Dutch society by reason of their wealth, while among the English, whose primary symbol of status was land, and among the French, to whom noble birth was preeminent, commerce was looked down upon. English merchants withdrew their fortunes from trade as soon as they had made enough to purchase an estate and introduce their children into the country gentry and French merchants similarly purchased public offices and patents of nobility, while Dutch merchants handed over their valuable but intangible network of credit and commercial contacts intact to their sons. The roster of patrician families in Dutch cities and in Albany, therefore, remained stable for generations while in English cities and English colonial towns the turnover of families in the merchant oligarchy was rapid.

To describe how the Gansevoort family acquired its fortune and its place among the patricians is a convenient way to demonstrate how the society of colonial Albany recapitulated that of the medieval and early modern Netherlands. Harmen Gansevoort remained a plebeian all his life, but the scanty information about him indicates that he possessed the shrewdness, acquisitiveness, and ambition necessary to found a patrician family. When he came to Beverwyck he was alone and without resources beyond the skills of his trade. In 1657, at the time of his appearance in Pieter Bronck's trial, he was employed by Jan Thomasz [Witbeck], who operated a brewery in partnership with Volkert Janse [Douw] and Pieter Hartgers. All three had emigrated as Van Rensselaer employees, but in the 1640's Witbeck and Douw had left the patroon's service and Hartgers had been fired. All three were men of standing in Beverwyck, serving terms as magistrates before the English conquest. By 1660, however, Harmen had left their employ to operate a brewery of his own in Bethlehem, a settlement of farmers on the south side of the Normanskill. Perhaps this venture was not very profitable, for soon after the incident of Claes Bever and the kettle, Harmen left both Bethlehem and brewing to try his hand at farming. His farm was twenty-two *morgens* (forty-four acres) in an isolated settlement on Catskill Creek, which entered the Hudson from the west about thirty miles south of Albany. He owned it in partnership with Elbert Gerbertse Cruyff, who had emigrated as a Van Rensselaer employee but who, like many of the patroon's settlers, minded his own profit at least as much as he minded the patroon's. "If you make a contract with him, it must be very carefully and definitely worded, otherwise you will perhaps not receive a cent," wrote Jan Baptist Van Rensselaer to Jeremias Van Rensselaer in 1659.[1] In spite of Cruyff's reputation for sharp dealings, Harmen remained his partner in this and other ventures for the rest of Cruyff's life; he finally settled Cruyff's debts to him by taking sole possession of the farm from Cruyff's heirs.

The settlement at Catskill, like its counterpart at Kinderhook on the east side of the river, was supposed to be south of the southern boundary of Rensselaerswyck, but after the conquest, when the Van Rensselaers petitioned for an English patent for their lands, they insisted that all these settlements, as well as Albany itself, were part of their domain. Therefore, when Governor Richard Nicolls visited Albany in 1667 to examine into land titles, Harmen and Cruyff, along with the other landholders of the upper Hudson Valley, appeared before him, showed their title, paid the fees, and received new patents confirming their ownership. In 1674, after the reconquest, Harmen had to go through the same process all over again. In the same year, King Charles II granted the Van Rensselaers their patent for the Manor of Rensselaerswyck, which extinguished their former quasi-feudal political privileges but gave them property rights in all the land they claimed, including Albany and Catskill. The Albanians, as has been seen, were able to delay enforcement of the Van Rensselaers' claims until the death of King Charles II ended their personal connection with the Crown, but the farmers on Catskill Creek were too few and too scattered to protest effectively. Those who, like Harmen Gansevoort, had obtained new patents were safe in possession; the unpatented land went to the Van Rensselaers. Early in 1677 Harmen agreed to buy another farm from them, but in November he cancelled this agreement and the following spring sold the farm he already had to John Conell and moved permanently back to Albany. The very gravity of Maritje's suit to break the sale indicates that the Gansevoorts had developed the farm into a valuable and important asset.

In the meantime, Harmen had by no means left Albany behind altogether. Some time before 1667 he worked for a time for Arendt Van Corlaer, the founder of Schenectady. In the spring of 1670 and again in 1671 Harmen bid unsuccessfully for the position of town herdsman. The herdsman's task was to take all the cattle of the village to the common pasture every morning from April 16 to November 16 and to bring them back at night. He would hire a boy to help him, but since he was responsible for the loss of any animals which strayed it is unlikely that he would leave the boy alone very regularly. This position is entirely compatible with brewing, which must wait for the harvest of grain and hops, but it calls up echoes of Claes Bever's drunken assertion—is it possible that Harmen actually was a hog-driver in the old country?

In 1671, Elbert Cruyff considered it a good investment to become Harmen's partner in a brewery in Albany, along with a third man, Jan Cornelisz Root. Cruyff, who was to receive half the profits, probably put up the capital. Harmen's contribution was to be "the work of brewing," for which he was to receive a quarter of the profits. Root received the last quarter "on condition that Gansevoort again was to receive one-half of the gains which Jan Cornelisz should earn by his work [in the brewery] during the term of the partnership." [2] The location of this brewery is not known. Not until 1677 did Harmen receive the final deed to the house and lot on the southeast corner of Brewer's Street and Maiden Lane which he thenceforward occupied, and in 1680 he was still renting a brewery from Geertruy Barentsz and Reyndert Pietersz. In that year, however, he bought the lot between his

24

home and the river where the Gansevoort brewery eventually stood.

Harmen's house, which stood until 1832 and was depicted by a local artist not long before it was destroyed by fire, looked like the other Dutch houses in Albany, and resembled the house built in West Coxsackie in 1663 by Harmen's brother-in-law Jan Bronck, which is still standing. The Bronck house is noteworthy because, like other upper Hudson Valley Dutch farmhouses, it follows traditions of urban Dutch architecture, which is much less true in New Jersey. These houses were built of wood and brick faced with tile, with steep-pitched roofs and gable ends to the street. In the gable end was a door, approached over a wide "stoep" and flanked by a pair of high-backed wooden benches. The door led into a shop, behind which was a large kitchen. The family slept in the loft, but the roof sloped so sharply that there was plenty of room for a second storage loft or a half-loft over their heads, and in some Dutch houses even for a third.

The extraordinarily wide street (now Broadway) outside of Harmen's door had been planned as a route of refuge to the blockhouse church at the main crossing a block to the south; ordinarily this broad space was used for a marketplace. The town was also defended by a palisade, built in 1670 by the governor's orders and maintained thereafter by the burghers. Whenever war threatened, the magistrates drew up a list assigning each citizen a certain number of rods of palisade to put in repair. In 1679 Harmen, like most other householders, was assessed two rods; Annetje Goosens, heiress of Goosen Van Schaick, was held responsible for five and half rods, and other substantial citizens for varying intermediate amounts. Since every rod contained twelve "straight oaken posts, eleven feet long, the least of them to measure eight inches across at the thin end" [3]—in 1680 increased to one foot by one foot by twelve feet—it is evident that cutting, shaping, and drawing the necessary logs constituted a considerable tax even if the whole dozen did not have to be replaced at once.

About the same time, Harmen established himself more firmly by marrying Maritje Leendertse Conyn, daughter of brewer Leendert Philipsz Conyn and his wife Agnietje. The date of

25

Maritje's birth, like that of her wedding, is unknown, but since her eldest daughter was married in 1689 and she herself lived until 1743, it seems unlikely that she was born much before 1650. In that case she would have been a little girl when Harmen came to Beverwyck, and probably married him about 1670, when he bought his house and established his brewery. The evident disparity in their ages—at least ten or fifteen years—suggests the possibility that the marriage was arranged sometime beforehand between the bridegroom and the father of the bride, although marriages directly arranged by parents are not mentioned by any writer as typical of the Hudson Valley Dutch. Nevertheless, matchmaking by the elders of the family in the interests of the family group was the usual practice of the medieval Netherlands, and in New Netherland the scarcity of women was so great that some such control over suitors of young girls must at times have been imperatively necessary. The number of young women who came to New Netherland was never very great; the West India Company made no attempt to send out prospective wives by the shipload, as was done at Jamestown, nor did the migration of large numbers of refugee families bring many grown and growing daughters as happened in New England. Many of the traders of Beverwyck were unmarried, hoping to make quick fortunes and then to advance them further by marriage in the homeland; most of the patroon's young farmers had married not long before leaving the Netherlands. Therefore, settlers like Harmen Gansevoort who wanted to establish families in America had to wait until a single young woman came over to join relatives or to enter domestic service—it was nearly impossible to hold maids to their contracted terms of employment—or until a local girl, like Maritje, reached marriageable age.

Harmen's marriage allied him with a whole complex of brewers' families. Maritje had two sisters and three brothers; one sister, Commertje, married Jan Bronck, a son of that Pieter whom Harmen had defended in 1657, and the other, Lysbeth, married a son of Jan Thomasz Witbeck. The children and grandchildren of these marriages—Gansevoorts, Conyns, Broncks, and Witbecks—intermarried frequently with each other and with each others' brothers-in-law, sisters-in-law, and cousins-in-law, until the descendants of Leendert Philipsz Conyn formed a compact core uniting several brewing and farming families. The full development of this family complex took place over a century and can only be properly appreciated by working out in detail the interrelationships among the spouses of Harmen's twelve children—ten daughters and two sons, of whom seven daughters and one son married and had families—Maritje's nieces and nephews, and all of their children. It is further worthwhile to trace the relationships of baptismal sponsors to their godchildren, for the pattern of reciprocation of such honors over a number of baptisms indicates which branches of this far-reaching cousinship kept up close contact with each other. From such analysis, it becomes obvious that kinship through females was quite as important to the Albanians as kinship through males. When groupings representing every possible form of human association are studied in this extended genealogical framework, it becomes strikingly obvious that the Gansevoorts represented a pattern usual in Albany when they organized all of their activities around this compact family core. Of course they had far too many relatives to associate with all of them at the same time, and with some of them they never associated, but in any venture they joined with relatives—usually quite close relatives—in preference to persons with whom they had no family connection.

Nevertheless, outsiders could enter this system; it was only necessary for one to convince some Dutch family of his fitness to marry one of their daughters. After the confused years of Leisler's Rebellion and the subsequent French war, when troops from New York City and from other colonies came to Albany, and when some Albany women were sent down the river out of the way of massacre, a number of Dutch families were willing to be so convinced. Among them were Harmen and Maritje Gansevoort, two of whose daughters found English mates during the Leislerian turmoil. Anna married a New York militia captain named Jacobus De Warren who soon left her a widow with two small daughters; returning to the family home, she eventually married an Albany tavernkeeper named Kitchener. Agnietje married Thomas Wil-

27

liams, identified in the marriage records as "yong man van New York." "Yong man" in this usage means bachelor rather than widower, but Williams had such a long career in Albany that it is probable he was literally a young man. He was probably not the same Thomas Williams who served on Leisler's council, since that Williams was in prison under sentence of death until a year after Agnietje's wedding, but he must have had some influence in New York to be appointed High Sheriff of Albany County by Governor Bellomont in 1699. Either in this position or in some other manner, he acquired sufficient knowledge of English law to guide his fellow citizens through the bewildering English procedures introduced into the Mayor's Court (the equivalent of the pre-charter magistrates' court) by another outsider, John Collins, an officer of the garrison in the fort, who practiced law in his spare time. Collins affiliated with the anti-Leislerian fur-trading patricians by marrying a niece of Pieter Schuyler; clients from plebeian families turned to Williams, while the Leislerian fur-traders, by no means entirely amalgamated with the Schuyler group, produced a lawyer of their own in Evert Wendel. These three men who, followed by their sons, divided Albany's local law business for the first half of the eighteenth century, had all begun to appear as attorneys in the Mayor's Court by 1705. The following year, Thomas Williams was elected to the common council simultaneously with two of Harmen Gansevoort's other sons-in-law. Agnietje died soon thereafter, but Williams evidently wished to maintain his relationship with her family; in 1712 he chose for his second wife her cousin Hillitje Bronck, with whom he later stood sponsor to several of Harmen Gansevoort's grandchildren.

By the time of Harmen's death in 1710, his family had thus attained a responsible, though not yet a patrician, position in the community. His only surviving son Leendert, his eighth child, was only twenty-seven, old enough to have cast a vote in the election of 1707 (although Harmen himself did not) and old enough in 1712 to be elected constable, an office usually allotted at this time to young men likely to serve on the common council later, but as yet unmarried and unready to exercise community leadership. But the positions of the husbands of Leendert's sisters, taken

28

together, are a good index of the Gansevoorts' status. Three of
them had sufficient influence to be elected and reelected to the
common council; Agnietje's husband Thomas Williams, who certainly had connections in New York, Elsje's husband Frans
Winne, whose family were prominent in the settlement of Bethlehem, and Lysbeth's husband Johannes de Wandelaer, the son of
a trader who had served on the common council in the 1690's and
then had removed to New York. Three of them removed to outlying settlements where they became progenitors of leading
families—Hillitje and Albert Van der Zee in Catskill, Catarina
and Arent Pruyn in Kinderhook, and Rachel and Teunis Lievense
in Half-Moon—but they and their children continued to ask the
Gansevoorts to stand sponsors to their offspring at baptism. Only
one sister, Maria, remained unmarried in the family home, surviving her mother, her sisters, and even her octogenarian younger
brother. There is no indication of the reason, but in a town where
nearly every woman married, one cannot help suspecting some
handicap which prevented her from undertaking responsibility
for a household.

Leendert's first recorded act after his father's death was to
marry his sister-in-law and neighbor across the street, Catarina de
Wandelaer. This alliance reinforced a connection already initiated by Lysbeth and Johannes, and further cemented by the
marriage of Anna de Wandelaer to the Gansevoorts' first cousin
Leendert Bronck of Coxsackie. Thus to become connected with
the family of a trader who had served on the common council,
though by no means a patrician family, was an indication of an
improvement in the Gansevoorts' status; on the other hand the
young de Wandelaers, who had to divide their father's fortune
ten ways, evidently considered Leendert's thriving brewery a
sound basis for close relationship. But then Leendert and Catarina encountered a common frontier problem, for Domine Johannes Lydius had died and no one knew when his successor
might be expected from the Netherlands. Some time in 1710 or
1711, therefore, Leendert and Catarina set up housekeeping without benefit of clergy. When Domine Petrus Van Driesen finally
reached Albany early in 1712, on Easter Sunday he baptized their

29

son Harme. A month later, having duly proclaimed their banns three Sundays in succession, he married the baby's parents.

Leendert then turned his attention to increasing his fortune. Most of it was invested in the brewery, which in 1714, when Leendert bought out the shares of his seven surviving sisters, was valued at £120. His father had made a few speculations in land in the 1680's, notably one in Dutchess County with Pieter Schuyler which Governor Bellomont considered vacating as an "extravagant grant." In the end he did not, but it was perhaps in apprehension of another such attack that Harmen sold his share in 1704. All of the exceedingly sparse evidence about Leendert's business affairs indicates that he increased his inheritance by operating the brewery and by investing the proceeds in mortgages on city property and developed farms. Only late in his career is there any suggestion that he possessed any wild lands.

Although very little is known about Leendert's brewery in particular, it is possible to reconstruct its mode of operation from what is known of brewing in the American colonies in general. Beer, like bread, was a basic commodity, in seventeenth-century Albany almost the universal beverage. Coffee and tea, which were only just coming into use, were imported luxuries. So were wines and gin and brandy, the spirituous liquors most familiar to the Dutch. Rum was primarily a product of New England; whiskey had not yet been made popular by the Scots and Irish. Milk the Dutch preferred to make into butter and cheese. Water the Albanians avoided drinking, like their ancestors in the Netherlands. Inhabitants of medieval cities had good reason for so doing, for their water supplies were often polluted. Albany well water had an unpleasant taste and sometimes made people who were unaccustomed to it ill; a foreign visitor once noted that the Albanians drew water from the river for both tea and brewing, and even then they had to let it stand until the silt settled.

The Gansevoort brewery stood right on the riverbank, behind the Gansevoort home, on a lot just about big enough to hold buildings the size of "a typical brewery advertised for sale at New Brunswick [which] was 70 by 48 feet, with a malt cellar 70 by 14 feet and a copper [kettle] holding 23 barrels. There was a malt mill operated by horsepower." [4] The beer was made of that Albany wheat which when ground into flour had the reputation of being the finest in the world. Since it was Dutch beer rather than English ale, it also contained hops, which added body to its flavor and acted as a preservative. The process of making it required great skill, judgment, and experience. First the grain had to be malted—dampened, permitted to germinate, then heated to arrest germination. This malt then had to be ground in a mill very like a flour-mill and boiled with hops and a quantity of water in the brewer's huge copper kettle—such a kettle as Harmen had wagered with Claes Bever. When it had boiled enough—and before the introduction of regulated heat and thermometers "enough" was a crucial test of the brewer's judgment—it was strained out into vats and left to cool. Yeast was then added, and the beer put aside to "work." After two or three weeks, when it had fermented enough—another test of the brewer's judgment—the yeast was skimmed off and the beer put into barrels. Leendert is known to have sold some of his beer to the commandant of the fort for the use of workmen repairing the defenses and to the common council for its annual corporation banquets, but his most regular customers were undoubtedly his neighbors in the city and on the thriving farms of Rensselaerswyck. Certainly he shared in the runaway prosperity among brewers that prompted the assembly to raise the excise tax on strong beer.

The reason for the spectacular expansion of the market for Leendert's beer was a population explosion in Albany County. After recovering slowly from the losses by flight which followed the Schenectady massacre, the county doubled its number of people between 1715 and 1723 and doubled it again by 1737, when there were slightly over 10,000 inhabitants. Some of this increase came from immigration, notably the 2,000 Palatine Germans brought to the southern part of the county by Robert Livingston in 1712, but most of it occurred in the course of nature. It was common everywhere at that time for women to bear numerous children, but in the crowded, unsanitary cities of the Old World most of them died in infancy or childhood. This was much less true in America, where towns and cities spread out on virgin sites rather than pil-

31

ing up on top of the accumulated filth of centuries. Instead of bringing up one or two of a dozen children, or leaving their fortunes to cousins or charitable foundations because no descendants survived them, many colonists raised families like Harmen Gansevoort's, in which eight out of twelve children lived to have comparable families of their own. Leendert and Catarina were less fortunate, for of their ten children, born between 1712 and 1731, only three sons survived to raise families in turn. One daughter died in 1723, two in the same week in a widely fatal but unidentified epidemic in 1731, a fourth in 1738, and the last, a young lady engaged to be married, in 1753. One son died in infancy and another at the age of thirty in a major yellow fever epidemic in 1746. But in spite of this severe infant and childhood mortality the Gansevoorts, like the rest of the Albany Dutch, continued to increase in numbers, maintaining both a prolific birth rate and a remarkable level of longevity. For six generations Gansevoorts who survived infancy as often as not lived well into their eighties, and many of their friends and relatives held onto life with equal tenacity.

This expansion of population created a number of problems for the Albany patricians which eventually gave the Gansevoorts the opportunity to break into their ranks. In the 1720's the patricians were the fur-trading families, led by the Schuylers on the one hand and the Cuylers on the other. Although Pieter Schuyler's unique personal influence over the Iroquois ended with his death in 1724, members of his family still felt themselves entitled to dominate the fur trade, particularly with the Indians to the west, as he had done. The Cuylers, ambitious to outdo the Schuylers, concentrated their efforts on selling trading goods to the French at Montreal, had discovered that the Indians preferred English manufactures to those of France. Of course, neither family had any formal monopoly, and each invaded the sphere of influence of the other on any advantageous occasion. This competition was occasionally punctuated by an intermarriage and interrupted by cooperation against some common threat, but in general the Schuylers and the Cuylers managed to be on opposite sides of major issues which arose between Leisler's

Rebellion and the American Revolution. Their rivalry developed wider ramifications through Pieter Schuyler's marriage connections with the Van Rensselaer and Livingston families, reinforced by the alliances of his descendants who became the only colonial Albany patrician family to intermarry closely with the river gentry and to acquire eventually a landed estate of their own.

In the 1720's these fur-trading patricians discovered that while they were competing with each other, the increasing population of Albany County outside the city was creating a number of threats to their domination. More people meant more farms, and settlers like the disappointed Palatines who moved from Livingston Manor to Schoharie were probing deep into the lands of the Mohawk Indians. The Mohawks therefore retreated westward, farther from the trading posts at Albany. In any case their hunting grounds were depleted, and the most profitable fur trade was now with the "Far Indians" of the Great Lakes basin. In this trade the Dutch patricians, whose monopoly required the Indians to come to Albany, were put at a disadvantage by French *coureurs de bois* who carried trade goods to the Indians. Governor William Burnet recognized this shift in the currents of trade by authorizing the establishment of a post at Oswego on Lake Ontario in 1724. Albany traders, led by the Schuylers, hastened to Oswego to trade directly with the "Far Indians," but there they had no monopoly and they could not prevent other traders from coming to compete with them. In the same decade Johannes Myndertse, representing the irate traders of the nearby town of Schenectady, upon whom the Albanians repeatedly tried to enforce their monopoly, challenged this provision of the charter in the courts and had it declared invalid in 1726. Meanwhile Governor Burnet tried to cut off the trade with Montreal, which contravened British mercantile regulations. In 1721 the assembly passed a law designed to tax this trade out of existence, but the Albanians simply ignored it until in 1729 the act was disallowed in London.

Besides undermining the patricians' control of the fur trade, the increasing population of the upper Hudson Valley threatened them with competition for power, profit, and prestige in Albany.

Leendert Gansevoort was by no means the only plebeian who made a fortune satisfying the needs of the farm families. Even more successful were the general merchants, who imported from England nearly all the manufactured goods the farmers used, for there was no manufacturing to speak of in pre-Revolutionary New York. Tools and implements beyond the skill of local smiths, textiles beyond the time and patience of farmers' wives too busy to spin and weave, tea, spices, and other luxuries from other parts of the world began to come to Albany merchants directly from England as well as through the great importers of New York City. Some of these merchants, like Sybrant Van Schaick, were scions of fur-trading families, and therefore already patricians, but others, like Jacob C. Ten Eyck, the son of a silversmith and a silversmith himself as well as a merchant, were plebeians by birth. Together with prominent artisans like Leendert Gansevoort, they formed a group whose interests were very different from those of the fur-trading patricians.

In 1730 there began the series of events which gave this group their opportunity to contest the fur-trading patricians' control of the Albany Common Council. Among the privileges granted to Albany by the charter were options to purchase two specific, widely separated tracts of land from the Indians whenever they should choose to sell. It seems probable that these tracts, both of them the sites of Indian villages, were locations particularly suitable for the establishment of rival trading posts. The tract at Schagticoke, a few miles north of Albany on the east side of the Hudson, had been duly purchased and leased to substantial tenant farmers, among whom were Johannes and Lysbeth Gansevoort de Wandelaer, who removed there from Albany about 1719. The other tract, at Tionderoga (Fort Hunter) on the Mohawk River, was still an important Indian settlement. Then Governor William Cosby began granting Mohawk Valley lands to his friends and political supporters. The Albany Common Council took the precaution of securing a deed to Tionderoga from the Indians, reserving to them their right to live there as long as they chose, but Cosby declared this deed to be fraudulent, prompted the Indians to revoke it, and granted the land to some of his henchmen.

Aghast at Cosby's high-handed action, the Albany patricians dropped their rivalries and closed ranks. The common council sent posthaste to New York with a protest to Cosby and a request to a lawyer for advice about resistance in the courts, and took steps to gain support for a protest by the assembly. Cosby retaliated by using his powers of appointment and patronage to drive the Albany patricians out of office. In 1732 he made one of his henchmen, a Scot named John Lindesay, high sheriff of the county, thus extending his influence over assembly elections. In 1733 he appointed as mayor of Albany Edward Holland, son of a former English commandant and sheriff, husband of a Dutch wife not fully identified but probably not a patrician, and former alderman from the first ward, in which the British garrison formed a substantial minority of the voters. The following year, 1734, Leendert Gansevoort was elected alderman for the third ward, which seat he continued to hold as long as Edward Holland was mayor. Enough other plebeians were elected in the same years to prevent the patricians from interfering further with Cosby's policies.

His seat on the common council and the honor of the freedom of the city, voted by the common council to him, Edward Holland, and seven others as they left office in 1740, the only such instance in the colonial period, were not the only distinctions bestowed upon Leendert at this time. Along with some of his common council colleagues and some of his relatives, he was permitted to share in two of the governor's Mohawk Valley land patents. In 1736 a group of aldermen, including Leendert Gansevoort, complained to Cosby about the excessive size of his Mohawk Valley grants. Evidently hoping that the newcomers to the common council would prove less implacably opposed to him than the patricians, Cosby then permitted three new aldermen, Leendert Gansevoort, Sybrant Van Schaick, and Jacob Ten Eyck, to share in the Cherry Valley patent. Most of the land went to Cosby, his secretary George Clarke, the Hollands, and John

Lindesay, who settled there after his term as sheriff expired, but Leendert and his co-patentees, the "trustees" who permitted their names to be used to evade the laws limiting land grants to 2,000 acres per person, received 1,700 choice acres among them for their services.

This speculation was soon followed by another. In February, 1739, after Cosby had died and been succeeded by Clarke, Leendert Gansevoort and others petitioned the governor's council for permission to purchase 24,000 acres on the north side of the Mohawk River from the Indians, which petition was granted. Two and a half years later the group applied for a patent for 28,000 acres in the same area, now more specifically located as being "over against Fort Hunter, beginning at the northwest corner of Hendrick Mancines." [5] From that point a complicated series of bounds ran through the woods north of the Mohawk River, tracing out a tract shaped on the map like an elongated keystone, which bore the name of the Sacandaga Patent. Among the fourteen grantees were four recent members of the common council, including Leendert; a brother of Holland's recorder; three sons of Holland's former common council colleague from the first ward, Harmanus Wendell; three nephews of Leendert's, all sons or sons-in-law of Frans and Elsje Winne; Edward Holland himself; his brother Henry; and John Lindesay. Leendert's further connection with the patent was brief. In 1742, Leendert executed a deed in partition with George Clarke and Henry Holland, by which Clarke and Holland in common received 2,000 acres and Holland alone received 3,750 acres. The odd 250 acres which seem to have been left out may have been Leendert's own share.

Probably the obvious eagerness of these newcomers to the common council to cooperate with powerful outsiders who would help them make their fortunes irritated the patricians as much as their own exclusion from office. In 1741, four years after Cosby's death, they prevailed upon Governor Clarke to appoint John Schuyler as mayor, and in the following year his brother-in-law Cornelis Cuyler, who held the mayoralty for four years. Simultaneously the patrician families took steps to secure their own election to the common council, so in 1741 Leendert Gansevoort was succeeded as alderman for the third ward by Gerrit C. Van den Bergh, a relative by marriage of the Schuylers. Then the contest extended to the county and took on province-wide ramifications, for when Edward Holland ran for the assembly in 1745 with the support of a new governor, George Clinton, the Schuylers joined with their relatives the Van Rensselaers and Livingstons to defeat him in a poll marked by unusually fierce mutual accusations of fraud. Holland claimed a majority, but the sheriff, controlled by the Schuyler group, refused to certify his election. Holland thereupon removed to New York, of which city Governor Clinton appointed him mayor in 1747 for the same sort of purpose that Cosby had appointed him mayor of Albany. After the outbreak of war between England and France in 1744, Clinton determined to break off Albany's trade with Canada, but his attempt broke down when he quarreled with his own supporters elsewhere in the province. In the course of it, however, he gave the mayoralty to Jacob C. Ten Eyck, and the Dutch general merchants retained control of the city government until 1770. Ten Eyck's mayoralty, which began in 1748, is a convenient point at which to recognize that group of families as a new patrician class. Leendert Gansevoort's eldest son Harme was a leader among them, being almost immediately elected to the common council, and holding one civic office or another—sometimes two at a time —for the next fifteen years.

Harme Gansevoort completed the family's rise to the patriciate in another sense, for he became a merchant while his younger brother Johannes learned the trade of brewing from their father. Their youngest brother Pieter studied medicine with a Dr. Cutler of Boston and became a physician. Their careers ranked in about that order of prestige in Dutch Albany, but the marked success of all of them indicates that the pressure of family ambition did not force them into vocations for which they had little aptitude. Perhaps Harme inherited his capacity for sustained desk work, his head for figures, and his shrewdness from his mother, the trader's daughter, who is reputed to have kept her husband's books, collected his debts, and managed his investments. Johannes certainly inherited from his father the ability to learn the skills of a complex craft requiring technical knowledge and careful judgment, but like his father he let the quality of his beer speak for him and left no documents which reveal anything of his character. Of Pieter's characteristics as a doctor nothing is known beyond the general fact that in the American colonies his training cannot have been other than practical, but perhaps he shared with several later members of the Gansevoort family their dexterous touch, their sensitivity to pain, and their reassuring bedside manner.

Harme began his mercantile career in April, 1735, when he and John R. Bleecker bought of Bleecker's father "100 gal. Rum, 2 stuck [pieces] Strood, 2 stuck Linnen, ½ lb. vermilion, 48 Kettles." [6] This was almost exactly the inventory which Mrs. Anne Grant later described young Albanians as loading into their canoes for their expeditions to the "Far Indians"—presumably at Oswego. She went on to describe how such young traders proudly learned to smoke, not only as a symbol of manhood but also for protection against insect pests and also probably to prepare them to participate in ceremonial exchanges of pipes with Indians. Then she told how they set off, each with his slave, or, as in Harme's case, with his partner, to spend the summer acquiring furs, experience, and wilderness lore.

With the profits of this excursion and probably with his father's backing, Harme opened a store in 1739. From its account books we learn that he sold general merchandise, including such fabrics as linen, "schalloen" (shalloon, a light woolen fabric used for linings), osnaburgh, mohair and calico, teas and wines, and a punch bowl and the rum to go in it. He took in payment mostly grain but also sugar, butter, a few beaver skins, and some money. This contrasts in a striking manner with the payments his grandfather collected from debtors, among which beavers and zeawant (wampum) were all-important. Pot and pearl ashes, so important in the trade of Harme's son at the end of the century, had not yet become standard items of barter. Throughout the colonial and Revolutionary periods, specie was rare. By 1744, Harme was doing business enough to open direct correspondence with London, through a merchant named John George Liebenrood. Liebenrood also served as agent for other Albany merchants, including Jacob Van Schaick and an unknown trader whose account book is in the New York State Library. Only five letters between Liebenrood and Gansevoort, the earliest one in Dutch, the rest in English, have been preserved. In 1764 Harme must have parted company with Liebenrood, for in a single letter to one John Goddard in London he hoped that this new connection might be happier than the last.

Harme's store was launched on a rising tide of prosperity which continued to run, with a few intermissions, for the rest of the colonial period. Immigrants were coming to Albany County in increasing numbers. After remaining almost unchanged for ten years, the population of the county rose from 10,500 in 1749 to 17,500 in 1756 and zoomed to nearly 43,000 in 1771, just before the Mohawk Valley settlements were set off as Tryon County. Imports into the entire colony also increased phenomenally in value in this period, from £126,000 in 1737 to £630,000 in 1759. That Harme prospered in this expanding economy is indicated by two tax lists from the 1760's which show him to have been one of the seven largest taxpayers in the city. His brothers, though nowhere near as heavily assessed as he, paid amounts large enough to show that they too had considerable fortunes.

In 1740 Harme married Magdalena Douw, a great-granddaughter of his grandfather's one-time employer and fellow Lutheran, Volkert Janse. The Douw family, like the Gansevoorts, was on its way into the Albany patriciate. Volkert Janse had bought land at Kinderhook as Harmen Harmense had bought land at Catskill. This land had descended to his children, who as substantial farmers (but by no means landed aristocrats) were part of a ruling group in Kinderhook analogous to the Albany patriciate, and for that reason henceforth to be called the rural patriciate. Petrus Douw, a grandson of Volkert Janse, married a daughter of Hendrick Van Rensselaer of Claverack. To marry any Van Rensselaer was certainly an advantageous marriage for a Douw, but it must be remembered that the Claverack Van Rensselaers were a younger branch of the family, who owned less land to begin with than the patroons, who shared it among more descendants, who often disagreed with their cousins of Rensselaerswyck when they were not opposing some common enemy, and who generally behaved far more like rural patricians than like landed aristocrats. On the strength of this alliance, Petrus Douw built himself a comfortable country house at Wolvenhoeck on the east side of the river and won election to the assembly in 1724–31, one of five Albany County representatives from outside the city (the others were from Schenectady) in the entire colonial period. His eldest son, Volkert P. Douw, became a merchant in Albany and married patrician Anna De Peyster; his daughter Magdalena married Harme Gansevoort, and ten years later another daughter, Maritje, married Johannes Gansevoort. The brothers-in-law worked together in business and civic affairs, and all three were among the most active of the new patricians. In 1752 Pieter Gansevoort married Gerritje Ten Eyck, a sister of Jacob C. Ten Eyck, and Elsje Gansevoort was engaged to their brother Barent Ten Eyck at the time of her death in 1753.

The point at which the Gansevoort family entered the Albany patriciate is a good place to pause and examine the patrician way of life. To indicate the standard of living which they thought appropriate, there remain a few pieces of Leendert's silverware, a tankard, a can, and two spoons. In that age of no banks and few secure locks, the safest way to store specie was to have it made up as plate. Each piece was stamped with the mark of the maker and usually deeply engraved, as was Leendert's tankard, with the monogram of the owner. A thief would have to melt down his loot to keep it from being recognized. The two silver tablespoons, inscribed "Nieu Yaars Gift aen Leendert Gansevoort, 1757," suggest an aspect of Albany social life. Among the Dutch it was customary for children to receive visits from St. Nicholas on December 6, while Christmas itself was a strictly religious observance and New Year's was an occasion for general visiting and the exchanging of gifts among adults. Many recipes remain for the cakes, cookies, and punches which housewives wore themselves out preparing for these festivities. Who presented the spoons to Leendert at this gay season we do not know; they bear also the initials M. G., but besides indicating any one of several of Leendert's relatives then living, these letters might have been on the spoons before or added later.

There are also in existence portraits of Leendert and Catarina, of their infant daughter Sara, who died at the age of twelve, of a young man named Pau de Wandelaer, who was probably a nephew of Catarina's, and of Magdalena Douw as a girl. All of them were painted at unknown dates by anonymous amateur itinerant artists called limners. The current consensus of folk-art specialists is that Sara was painted in 1721, that Leendert, Catarina, and Pau were all painted by the same artist about 1730, and that Magdalena was painted by another artist sometime before her marriage in 1740. Like other local painters of the same period, the "Gansevoort limner" depicted his subjects in costumes and poses imitated from mezzotints of English court portraits, but unlike some of them he also possessed common sense, unquenchable honesty, and a sense of humor. Leendert and Catarina chose to be depicted wearing their own dark hair rather than powdered periwigs, and sober brown broadcloth rather than figured damasks and colorful brocades like some of their more ostentatious neighbors. The limner managed his palette of earth-tones admirably, depicting his subjects as solid and substantial but by no means dull. One concession to convention he did make was to envelop Catarina in a peculiar windblown piece of drapery presumably intended to imitate a court lady's silken scarf but looking far more like her own serviceable brown woolen shawl. Insofar as personalities can be estimated from portraits, Leendert emerges as a man shrewd, silent, and reliable, while Catarina shows far more competence than beauty, and perhaps even an edge of shrewishness.

In the background of these portraits the limner filled in conventional pastoral scenes, behind Leendert a pond with several white swans—or were they supposed to be geese?—and behind Catarina a body of water with a small castle and a boat, indicating a ferry or ford. The conclusion seems inescapable that the artist intended a rebus on "Ganse-voort." Pau de Wandelaer has an interesting background, a recognizable view of the Hudson River in the Catskills, with a boat on the river which may very well have represented part of the boy's inheritance or symbolized his family's position as traders. Magdalena Douw's portrait, from another hand, does not share the still beauty by which the style of the Gansevoort limner is identified, but its background is a view of the Hudson Valley which may very well represent the environs of Wolvenhoeck. These portraits with their backgrounds of landscape reproduced in faithful detail may possibly look back to the great portraits and altarpieces of the medieval Flemish masters (although it is by no means certain that the limners were Dutch, the traditional taste of their Dutch clients could have influenced them) and unquestionably look forward to the Hudson River School of American landscape painters in the nineteenth century.

It is significant that when the Albany Dutch began to surround themselves with luxuries they bought silverware and pictures rather than books. Inventories of estates, especially in the seventeenth century, often included several valuable pictures and no books of any importance except the Bible. Leendert Gansevoort's huge Dutch Bible is still in existence, but we do not know that he possessed any other books. His contemporaries bought Bibles, manuals of devotion, and schoolbooks, but other forms of reading matter do not seem to have interested them. In a century and a half in America they produced very little writing among themselves, in contrast to the Pennsylvania Germans, who by the 1740's were supporting two German newspapers and a thriving market in other printed materials. Even the Dutch ministers, unlike their contemporaries in New England, felt no pressing urge to submit their sermons and theological controversies to the reading public. Gradually the Albanians learned to speak and write English, although at the beginning of the eighteenth century they had to send children to New York for that purpose. By the 1750's, leading Albanians were bilingual, though they preferred to speak Dutch among themselves. Harme Gansevoort wrote it fluently enough to correspond with English merchants and to hold the office of city clerk, being the first Dutchman to fill that position. But learning English did not make the Albanians bookish, although Pieter Gansevoort, who had studied in Boston, later had "the reputation of a classical scholar." [7] He was one of a very few;

Mrs. Grant noticed that the Albanians of his generation owned great quantities of religious pictures and few books, and lamented that education was difficult to acquire there.

The preference of the Albany patricians for religious books and pictures is only one of many indications that religion was as central to their way of life as it had been to the medieval Dutch. The Dutch church from the beginning was as important an institution as the magistrates' court. Domine Godefridus Dellius, in particular, participated in public affairs, taking a leading part in the Schuyler group's resistance to the Leislerians, and working with them to secure the friendship of the Mohawks by missionary activity; he baptized over a hundred Indians during his ten-year pastorate. For the first half of the eighteenth century Domine Dellius' successors were content to make their church a pillar of orthodoxy, in many respects the center of Albany Dutch tradition as local government and trade responded gradually to English influence. In 1712 the burghers rebuilt and enlarged their square church at the main crossing. Their Calvinist convictions did not prevent them from eventually embellishing it with stained glass windows bearing the coats of arms of the patrician families—some if not most of them assumed in the New World.

This building was barely finished when Governor Robert Hunter granted the Anglican church a lot in the middle of the wide, steep principal street halfway between the Dutch church at the bottom and the fort at the top. The burghers were furious at this interference with their privileges and the common council forbade the building of the church on the ground that even the governor had no right to grant land within the charter limits. There were only a few Anglicans in Albany to object—mostly members of the British garrison—but Hunter believed that he was properly exercising his prerogative powers on behalf of the English ecclesiastical establishment. He was further supported by the recently organized Society for the Propagation of the Gospel, which wanted to found an Anglican mission among the Mohawks —an undertaking supported by Queen Anne herself, who donated a silver communion service for the Indians' use. Hunter therefore insisted that the church be completed, and the common council had to give way. The rectors of St. Peter's Church were soon accepted into the community as the garrison had been, although they did not usually marry into Dutch families, but their church had little influence in Albany before the French and Indian War.

The Dutch in the New World were quite as prone to religious controversy as those in the Old. In the early eighteenth century some of them began to think that their church government would be more effective if it were independent of the Classis of Amsterdam, while others feared that such a change would open the way for unorthodoxy in doctrine. The proponents of an independent American governing body called it the Coetus; its opponents supported a body called the Conferentie, subordinate to the Classis of Amsterdam. This dispute was further complicated by pressure from the younger Dutch of New York City to have services conducted in the English language and resistance from their elders who feared that familiar doctrines and ritual would suffer by translation, a problem which did not arise in the Albany church until the time of the American Revolution, when the language was changed without upheaval.

At the same time there arose a controversy over theology which was, quite in the Dutch tradition, far more a dispute over the application than over the truth of familiar doctrine. Throughout the 1720's and the 1730's when Domine Theodorus Frelinghuysen won wide support from laymen and opposition from his fellow clergy by his vigorous preaching in New Jersey, the Albany congregation had no recorded disagreements with their notably orthodox pastor, Petrus Van Driesen. Then in 1745 Frelinghuysen's son, also named Theodorus, was called to the Albany charge and the church was soon rent by schism. This was certainly in part a reflection of the bitter rivalry between old and new patricians, but like his father, Frelinghuysen was outspoken and anything but tactful, and the doctrines in which his father had trained him had proven in New Jersey to be highly explosive.

The elder Frelinghuysen adhered fervently to pietism, the seventeenth-century manifestation of the tradition of Thomas à Kempis and the preaching friars. Through his sermons he tried to

44

induce in his hearers emotional experiences of the love and fear of God that would prompt them to practice piety in their everyday affairs. This approach was familiar among the Dutch and in some German sects, but when applied to audiences of the English-speaking religious traditions by preachers like Frelinghuysen's friend Gilbert Tennant and English evangelist George Whitefield, who like John Wesley was influenced by the pietistic Moravians, it provoked the explosion of enthusiasm known as the Great Awakening. The younger Frelinghuysen brought to Albany his father's interest in an American-trained ministry and in the Coetus, his concern for practical piety and his insistence on moral discipline within the church. By 1759 when he went to the Netherlands on business connected with the Coetus he had made himself so unpopular with some of his flock that an English observer believed he had been driven from the city. After he was drowned on his return voyage he was succeeded by Eilardus Westerlo, a brilliant and tactful young divine from the University of Grö-ningen, who healed the schism in the church so effectively that the common council awarded him the freedom of the city a year after his arrival. Ten years later in 1771, when Westerlo and Elder Harme Gansevoort attended the meeting which finally resolved the Coetus-Conferentie dispute in the whole Hudson Valley, the Albany schism was so far in the past that they were denoted "neutral brethren."

For a broader perspective on mid-eighteenth-century Albany, it is helpful to turn to the description recorded by Peter Kalm, a Swedish naturalist who visited the city in 1749 and 1750. Since the purpose of Kalm's tour, which carried him from the Swedish settlements on the Delaware to Canada, was to search for American plants that might profitably be introduced into Sweden, he wrote first and in greatest detail about the trees, herbs, and climate of the upper Hudson Valley. Then he described the physical appearance of Albany, with its square stone Dutch church at the foot of the steep principal street, its dilapidated and indefensibly located fort at the head of the same street, and its small stone Anglican mission church between them. Near the Dutch Church he noticed "a fine building of stone, three stories high" with a

45

steeple and bell, the Stadt Huys or city hall, which five years later was to be the birthplace of the Albany Plan of Union. Surrounding the town there was a palisade in a state of extreme disrepair.

Kalm found that the most conspicuous feature of the Albanians was their Dutchness. "The inhabitants of Albany and its environs are almost all Dutchmen. They speak Dutch, have Dutch preachers, and the divine service is performed in that language. Their manners are likewise quite Dutch; their dress is however like that of the English [colonists]." [8] He noticed their Dutch houses with gable ends to the street, and entered to find fireplaces decorated with Dutch tiles and Dutch cupboard beds. Their Dutch diet emphasized bread, dairy products, and salad—a Dutch specialty, introduced into England by Dutch immigrants in the time of Shakespeare—rather than the beef and beer of the English, which Kalm found more satisfying. Between the difference in nutritive elements and the thrift of Dutch housewives who prepared just enough food for the meal "and sometimes hardly that," Kalm sometimes thought they did not give him enough to eat. Nor did they drink as much liquor as the English—except on public occasions, such as elections and funerals, when drunkenness was considered no disgrace.

The most conspicuous feature of Albany was of course its trade with the Indians, whom Kalm believed the Albanians usually cheated, with the Canadians, in spite of prohibitions of smuggling by both English and French authorities, and with New York in wheat, lumber, and produce. Of the Albanians' business practices, Kalm was highly critical.

The avarice, selfishness and immeasurable love of money of the inhabitants of Albany are very well known throughout all North America, by the French and even by the Dutch, in the lower part of New York province. If anyone ever intends to go to Albany it is said in jest that he is about to go to the land of Canaan, since Canaan and the land of the Jews mean one and the same thing, and that Albany is a fatherland and proper home for arch-Jews, since the inhabitants of Albany are even worse. If a real Jew, who understands the art of getting forward perfectly well, should settle amongst them, they would not fail to ruin him. For this reason nobody comes to this place without

46

the most pressing necessity; and therefore I was asked in several places
. . . what induced me to make the pilgrimage to this New Canaan.
. . . they either fixed exorbitant prices for their services or were very
reluctant to assist me. . . . However, there were some among them
who equalled any in North America or anywhere else, in politeness,
equity, goodness and readiness to serve and to oblige; but their number fell far short of that of the former. . . . I cannot in any . . . way
account for the difference between the inhabitants of Albany and the
other descendants of so respectable a nation as the Dutch, who are
settled in the lower part of New York province. The latter are civil,
obliging, just in prices, and sincere; and though they are not cere-
monious, yet they are well meaning and honest and their promises
may be relied on.[9]

This passage must be taken with a liberal allowance of salt, because Kalm believed himself to be overcharged in an isolated
community where he had expected prices to be low, and because
the Albany Dutch, with their limited education and narrow horizon, doubtless did not welcome him with the understanding and
consideration expected by an eminent foreign scientist who had
been the honored guest of Swedish colonists, American natural-
ists, and the French government in Canada. Nevertheless, it is
evident from his statement that constant competition with each
other had honed the Albany merchants' acumen to a very sharp
edge indeed.

The general tenor of Kalm's observations depicts Albany
Dutch patrician society as isolated, suspicious, and ingrown until
its members could not even get along with each other, although
when Kalm passed through New Brunswick, he noticed a whole
street of Albanians living by themselves and having little contact
with their neighbors. On his return from Canada in 1750, he
wrote

Discord had taken a firm hold among the inhabitants of Albany. Although they were very closely related through marriage and kinship,
they had divided into two parties. Some members of these bore such
strong aversion to one another that they could scarcely tolerate the
presence of another member, nor could they even hear his name mentioned. If a visit was made at the home of one of them, you were then

47

hated by his opponent, even though you had visited him previously. It was interpreted that you were not satisfied with his friendship alone, but also wished to enjoy that of the other or that you liked him better.[10]

These two parties, in 1750, would have been the old and the new patricians; the twenty years of struggle between them since Cosby's administration, of which Kalm had no way of knowing, amply explain their animosity. They, of course, did not separate the political, social, and economic aspects of this conflict; commercial advantage, political power, and social prestige were still mutually interchangeable goals of ceaseless stubborn competition for family advancement, waged with whatever resources were available. By 1750 the general merchants, including the Gansevoorts, had fought their way to patrician power, but no amount of competition would compel the fur-trading patricians to accept them as equals. Only a common effort against an external enemy could accomplish that.

III

Awakening to Empire

Geographical and social isolation and political and economic communal independence by no means prevented the Albany Dutch patricians from nurturing imperial ambitions. Their ancestors had come from the Netherlands during its Golden Age of commercial leadership, although it is unlikely that those ancestors would have described that leadership as "imperial"; in the seventeenth century the word usually referred either to the dominion of the Holy Roman Emperor or to the authority of a king who ruled over more than one realm. Since the Dutch had no king or emperor, they did not think of their network of forts and trading posts as an empire, nor did the English and French begin to consider their mercantile colonies as imperial entities until the middle of the eighteenth century, when they fought large-scale wars using European troops to defend these colonies. The concept of "economic imperialism," in which large business organizations dominated the imperial policies of their governments, developed from events of the late nineteenth and early twentieth centuries.

The imperial ambitions of the Albany Dutch, which are in all probability more clearly visible to us than they were to themselves, were first, last, and always centered around commercial supremacy rather than conquest, acquisition of territory, or extension of rule over other peoples. From the beginning, New Netherlanders were by no means behindhand in the general European competition for Indian alliances and trade, which

49

quickly became associated with other issues of intercolonial rivalry. It was taken for granted throughout the seventeenth century that colonial governments often covertly permitted or even prompted their Indian allies to take advantage of other colonies in ways for which they publicly disclaimed responsibility. The participation of the Dutch in trade wars—which to the Indians were often a good excuse for going on the warpath—throughout the Connecticut, Hudson, and Delaware Valleys was by no means checked by the English conquest. Instead it became intensified during the 1680's, as French exploration brought to light the rich fur reserves of the Ohio Valley and traders from several English colonies sought routes through the Appalachian barrier. The Albanians sat squarely across two such routes, one directly west by the Mohawk River and the other north by Lake Champlain and west by the St. Lawrence, but when traders from newly settled Pennsylvania lost no time in exploiting alternative routes through the Delaware and Susquehanna Valleys, they became alarmed. They recognized particularly that the Pennsylvanians, by supplying the Indians who lived in these valleys with firearms and encouraging them to assert their independence, threatened the whole structure of Indian relations which the Albanians had built up by providing the formidable Iroquois with a plentiful supply of weapons.

Governor Dongan was as alarmed as the Albanians, though for somewhat different reasons, and the combination of Dongan's vision of imperial authority with Dutch commercial organization produced countermeasures so effective that they provoked immediate resentment and eventual retaliation from the Albanians' principal competitors, the French and the Pennsylvanians. When Dongan granted the Albanians' traditional Dutch request for a local monopoly of the fur trade, he included in it a monopoly of Indian relations on the northern frontier which the Albany traders immediately began to exercise. In 1686, the very year of the Dongan Charter, they sent to the Great Lakes a carefully organized expedition which invited the Far Indians all the way to Michilimackinac to bring their furs to Albany. The French took up this challenge at once, intercepting a second expedition in

1687, confiscating its valuable cargo of trade goods, and incarcerating most of its leaders in Montreal jails. The traders, perturbed by the loss of their goods, petitioned Governor Dongan to reimburse them and became extremely impatient when reimbursement was not forthcoming; some of them or their close relatives became Leislerian leaders two years later. During the Leislerian upheaval a group of Pennsylvania and New Jersey traders went overland to the Ohio Valley and made contact with the powerful Shawnees, some of whose kin lived in eastern Pennsylvania. Word of this probably reached the Albanians through the Mohawks, who wished to control the trade of the Shawnees; in response Arnout Cornelisz Viele, an outstanding Albany interpreter, went on a similar expedition, explored the Ohio River, and returned in 1694 with the friendship of the Shawnees and much beaver.

Exploitation of Viele's accomplishment was prevented by a general war which started in Europe and immediately set off hostilities involving colonists and their Indian allies all over eastern North America. It began when the Glorious Revolution placed Louis XIV's implacable foe, William III, upon the throne of England, making open war between England and France inevitable. The Albanians' participation in this war, in contrast to their imperial mercantile ambition, was notably local and particularistic. Their efforts at self-defense were frustrated by differences between Leislerians and Anti-Leislerians; the Schenectady massacre might not have been successful had the exhausted French and Indian attackers found the townsmen alert and united instead of unguarded and at odds with each other. After this disaster, the Albanians were eager for revenge but most unwilling to cooperate effectively with the intercolonial expedition Leisler organized for that purpose. When the expedition, plagued by disease and transportation difficulties, bogged down in the uninhabited wilderness between Albany and Lake Champlain, a party of Albanians and Indians under Pieter Schuyler's youngest brother Johannes dashed down the lake and burned the French settlement at La Prairie, which local retaliation for the Schenectady massacre was the only action of the campaign. For the rest of the war the significant fighting was between the Mohawks on the

British side and their kinfolk the Caughnawagas or Praying Indians, Iroquois who had been converted by French priests and resettled in the St. Lawrence Valley. Since the Iroquois in general were the most feared warriors in the Northeast, this internecine conflict was even more destructive than Indian wars usually were. The Albanians, their settlement sadly depleted by flight as well as by destruction, backed their allies with guns, goods, and the power of religion; it was at this time that Domine Dellius made his notable effort to welcome Indian converts into the Dutch Reformed Church.

After a decade of this vicious warfare, in which a quarter of the European population of Albany County left it by death or flight and the Indians on both sides were decimated, everyone had had enough. William III and Louis XIV made peace, temporarily, at Ryswick in 1697. The exhausted Indians buried the hatchet between themselves in 1701 and beseeched their white brethren not to ask them to take it up again at the behest of rulers beyond the seas. So, when news of the outbreak of the War of the Spanish Succession reached Quebec in 1701, highly placed French officials contacted the Albany traders then in the city and suggested that the colonists remain aloof from the European conflict, continue trading in spite of mercantile restrictions from both mother countries, and restrain their Indians from raiding. Two of the traders who were aldermen, David Schuyler and Wessel Ten Broeck, reported all this to the common council, which passed it on to the governor. In the meantime, the Albanians saw many reasons for accepting these conditions. They had not shared the French ravaging of their homeland in 1672—which prompted another epic Dutch defense successful only by the desperate device of cutting the dikes, and made their countryman William III the implacable foe of Louis XIV. Trade with an enemy's colonies in wartime was a conspicuous feature of the Dutch tradition, being considered an excellent way of depriving the enemy of profits which could then be used to furnish the Dutch with the sinews of war. To the mutual cessation of Indian raids the Albanians had nothing to say but "Amen!" and raids along the New York frontier did cease.

But the French Indians also had enemies, both red and white, in New England, with whom their white brethren had no tacit agreement; the present-day Mohawk Trail is reputed to follow a route they took through the Berkshires to fall on such Connecticut Valley settlements as Deerfield in 1704. The New Englanders, comparing Albany's safety with their own peril and resenting the Albanians' insistence on their privilege of monopolizing the fur trade on the northern frontier without fulfilling their responsibility for conducting effective Indian relations over the same wide area, developed a hatred of Albanians and of the Dutch in general which continued in full force as long as the Dutch were a recognizable ethnic group. As a matter of fact, trade was the Albanians' only means of exerting any influence whatever over the Indians, and in protecting the New York frontier from attack they exerted that influence to the utmost. Attempts which Pieter Schuyler did make to mitigate the attacks on New England only served to endanger such security as the Albanians had already acquired.

In the course of this war successive British governors recognized, as Leisler had done, that the Hudson-Champlain waterway was the most obvious route for the invasion of Canada. Various expeditions for this purpose were projected before Lieutenant Governor Robert Ingoldsby actually started in 1709, only to spend the whole summer waiting at the head of Lake Champlain for word of a British fleet expected in the St. Lawrence. When word finally came that the fleet had been sent elsewhere, it was too late for a campaign and the army disbanded. The Albanians contributed to this expedition primarily by enlisting Indians for it, in spite of their agreement with the French and the Indians' treaty with each other, and by providing supplies. At the same time, however, they demonstrated their military zeal and prowess —and the objects for which they were most willing to exert it— by sending an expedition westward under Pieter Schuyler to destroy a French trading post among the Onondaga Indians.

Pieter Schuyler was indeed his generation's moving spirit in the Albanians' cooperation with the British Empire. This imperial consciousness, like many other things about the Schuylers, was at this time exceptional among the Albany patricians; it is possible

53

that he acquired some of it from his brother-in-law, Robert Livingston. Certainly Schuyler, who had accepted many government contracts and was a public creditor for large amounts, learned from Livingston's protracted difficulties in settling similar debts, which had finally made it necessary for him to go to London in 1695 to collect them. In 1710 Schuyler, having extended much credit to the 1709 expedition, made a similar journey to London. With him he took, as tangible proof of his services, five Iroquois sachems to be presented to Queen Anne. The "American Kings" promptly became the sensation of London, feted by the great, followed through the streets by the mob, cheered at the playhouses, and toasted in the clubs. Richard Steele described them in his periodical, *The Tatler*, and the following year Joseph Addison made their (supposed) opinions of London and Londoners a starting point for some of his satirical essays in the *Spectator* and so, as it turned out, enshrined them in the English literary tradition. Schuyler, in the meantime, inconspicuously made arrangements with the British government for a more effective expedition the next year, to which it was hoped that the Indian "kings," impressed by the wonders of civilization and their personal introduction to Queen Anne, would lead their "subjects," and, doubtless most important to himself, collected the payments due him. He and the sachems returned to Albany without mishap or delay, but the expedition which was to follow them was less fortunate. Nor were the Indians as enthusiastic as the planners at Whitehall had hoped; their Canadian kin had already begun to retaliate for their breach of neutrality in 1709. So the 1711 expedition foundered, as had all the others, on the overwhelming difficulties of moving a large force across the hundred and fifty miles of trackless wilderness which separated Albany from the enemy.

In 1714, the Treaty of Utrecht ended the European war and ushered in thirty years of peace. The Albanians immediately pressed the trade with Canada in the face of official restrictions by the French, measures which only prompted Montreal merchants to buy their British goods in Boston or England rather than Albany. Nevertheless, in spite of the occasional arrest of Albany traders as smugglers, the Canada trade remained profitable. The only British attempt to restrain it was Burnet's 1721 act to tax it out of existence. The Albanians' response to this attack perhaps shows that they had learned something from Pieter Schuyler's account of his trip to London, for they prompted their mercantile correspondents in London to put pressure on the Board of Trade to disallow the law. The evident impossibility of enforcing it probably weighed more in the Board's final decision to do so than the Albanians' objections, but the incident demonstrates that they had learned how to apply the power available to them when they wished to influence an imperial decision. It also shows that, at least in commercial matters, the Albanians' isolation had not totally prevented them from thinking with imperial scope and range.

The Albanians participated only tangentially in the long struggle between governors and assemblies which shook the southern, more populous, more Anglicized part of the colony in the same period. Albany County was represented in the assembly, of course, usually by city patricians, but no provincial leaders came from Albany between Pieter Schuyler, who was a member of the council until his death in 1724, and Philip Schuyler, who was elected to the assembly in 1767, nor did Albany delegates often initiate important measures. They cannot be affiliated consistently with any of the factions which have been identified during this period; the only consistency which emerges from the chronicle of their service is consistency to the self-interest of the city of Albany, which is exactly what would be expected of their Dutch tradition. The Albanians did seek for support in the assembly during their dispute with Cosby, but his prompt interference with their elections apparently convinced them that by this course they only hurt themselves. When Lewis Morris, leader of the assembly faction which opposed Cosby, complained to high officials in London about a number of Cosby's transactions including his treatment of the Albanians, he aroused some righteous indignation in their favor, including, it was rumored, that of King George II, but since Cosby's wife was a sister of the influential Earl of Halifax and a first cousin of the even more powerful Duke of Newcastle, no action followed. For the rest of the colo-

55

nial period the Albanians sought less obvious but equally effective ways of evading the governor's authority when they chose to do so.

These local and provincial conflicts were drawn directly into imperial conflicts when another war broke out between England and France in 1744. This war, whose European phase was a half-hearted afterthought of the War of the Austrian Succession between Prussia and Austria, with whom respectively France and England were allied, was the beginning of a worldwide conflict between the two great maritime empires. This conflict continued in the colonies, with intermissions, until 1783, and then, after the French Revolution, broke out again as part of the general European resistance to Napoleon. The colonial part of this war was fought in India and the West Indies as well as in the Thirteen Colonies. Indeed, the few American events of King George's War (1744–48) appear quite insignificant beside the far-reaching diplomatic and military campaigns of Robert Clive in India in the following years, campaigns which reached a triumphant climax in the English victory at Plassey in 1757, when the decisive American war was only beginning to take shape.

Nevertheless, King George's War came home to the Albanians, for in 1745 French Indians massacred their relatives and friends at Saratoga, thirty miles above Albany on the upper Hudson. Governor George Clinton then found the obvious necessity of organizing provincial defense an excellent occasion for attacking Albany's Canada trade; his first move was to strip the Albany magistrates of their power in Indian affairs, which power had already much diminished with the removal of the Indians from the vicinity of Albany and with the collapse of the Albany fur-trading monopoly. As soon as possible he replaced the mayor, leading Canada trader Cornelis Cuyler, with general merchant Jacob C. Ten Eyck. By such maneuvers he hoped also to break the influence of the Schuyler–Van Rensselaer–Livingston group in the county because it commonly aligned with his opponents in the assembly.

In all of these ventures, Clinton had the encouragement and

support of a newcomer to the upper Hudson Valley named William Johnson. Johnson came to New York in 1737 from Ireland, the nephew and protégé of a British admiral named Sir Peter Warren who acquired lands in the Mohawk Valley and married a sister of James De Lancey of Westchester, in the 1740's and 1750's the most powerful single figure in the colony. De Lancey held various high administrative posts, notably those of Chief Justice and Lieutenant Governor, and was recognized as the leader of the dominant assembly faction in that generation. He and his followers usually supported Governor Clinton, receiving in return practical influence in many appointments to office, but sometimes they quarreled with him and Clinton then used his powers of patronage to seek support elsewhere. William Johnson, who had taken up lands near Sir Peter's in the Mohawk Valley and become an Indian trader, worked in provincial affairs with this "in" faction, to which he was connected by family ties, and therefore opposed the considerably less coherent "out" faction with which the Albany patricians cooperated.

William Johnson struck most directly at the Albany patricians by his evident determination to wrest from them the control of Indian trade and Indian affairs. The Albanians had always insisted that the Indians come to Albany, or at least to some subsidiary established post like Oswego, so that the community could enforce its regulations for the orderly conduct of the trade. Johnson went out and lived among the Indians, learned their language and adopted their customs, took an Indian wife, and became accepted by the Indians as a brother. Thus he won their trade, their confidence, and also their lands, all of which the Albany patricians considered their rightful monopoly by custom if not by law. Most of the fur-trading patricians therefore detested Johnson, and did not detest him any less because other Albanians, including the old patrician Cuylers and some of the new patrician general merchants like Jacob C. Ten Eyck and Sybrant Van Schaick, found it worthwhile to cooperate with him. The appointment of Ten Eyck as mayor in effect announced that Clinton and Johnson had moved from a moderate attitude toward the Albany

57

traders to an all-out attack on them, an attack sustained by Clinton's subsequent policy of appointing new patricians to all offices which fell vacant or could be vacated.

One of these offices was the inconspicuous but pivotal Albany city clerkship, technically the three posts of Town Clerk, Clerk of the Court of Sessions, and Clerk of the Court of Common Pleas. In 1674 Robert Livingston, then probably the only Albanian sufficiently bilingual to participate in town affairs in Dutch and keep the public records in fluent English, was appointed to all of them by Governor Andros. Also appointed by Andros as secretary to the Indian commissioners, Livingston took pains to secure a confirmatory appointment to the latter office from the Crown itself when he was in England in 1696. After his death his son Philip Livingston succeeded him in all of these offices, and like his father took the precaution of having the Indian secretaryship confirmed in London. In 1748 Clinton moved against the Indian commissioners—and against the Livingston family—by dismissing Livingston from his clerkships for flagrant dishonesty and notorious land frauds against the Indians. In his place Clinton appointed John Colden, son of provincial secretary Cadwallader Colden, who received all the fees, and to whom Clinton offered the offices themselves when the younger Colden died in 1750. When Cadwallader Colden refused, Clinton gave the Indian secretaryship to Edward Holland, now a member of the council, and, at Holland's suggestion, gave the Albany clerkship to Harme Gansevoort. In making these appointments and others like them, Clinton was struggling to build up a following of his own to set against that of James De Lancey, with whom he had quarreled; therefore Harme was in no way bound to or involved with William Johnson.

The De Lanceys struck back at Clinton for this assertion of independence by working with Thomas Pownall of the Board of Trade, a leader in a group of English politicians who were trying to undermine Clinton's influence in London derived from his brother's marriage to a sister of the Duke of Newcastle. One day in May, 1752, an English placeman named Peter Wraxall, one of

Pownall's followers, appeared in the Albany Mayor's Court with a royal commission as its clerk and demanded to be sworn into the position. The dumfounded mayor and aldermen informed Wraxall that they already had a clerk and hastened to write to the governor and the attorney-general for advice. Harme, who was still an alderman as well as clerk, absented himself from the meetings until the matter was decided. The course they finally followed was that suggested by their counsel, to swear Wraxall into the office in order to give him a legal ground for complaint, and then to leave the matter to be decided by the courts. But they refused to give him the city records and left no doubt about where their sympathy lay, "by no means intending to convey or transfer any Right thereby [by swearing Wraxall] other than what is consistent with Law or to prejudice the right of the said Harme Gansevoort."

Wraxall based his claim to the clerkship by royal commission on the precedent of Livingston's royal commissions as Indian secretary, and on the custom that all these offices had been held in plurality. Furthermore, the charter of Albany did state that the recorder and the clerk, being officers of the king's courts, should be appointed by the king, while the mayor was to be appointed by the king's governor. In practice the governor, acting as the king's agent, had made all local appointments under the charter; the possibility of a difference between the king and his agent had never before created any practical problems. Now the De Lanceys and Pownall, working together, sought to undo Clinton's appointment of Harme Gansevoort to an office of profit and prestige in his own community in order to make trouble for the governor on the highest levels in England. Harme recognized that the real struggle was far over his head and thought for a time of withdrawing, but when he conferred personally with Clinton about it, Clinton urged him to remain and promised to support him. The governor was as good as his word; although Wraxall had complained to his friend Lord Halifax, president of the Board of Trade, and the Lords of Trade had thereupon written to the Lords Justices that in their opinion Clinton ought to be censured and Gansevoort ousted, when Clinton returned to England in 1753 he exerted his own influence at Whitehall, which had begun to tell about 1750, and the matter was apparently dropped.

Such a conclusion of the affair was by no means satisfactory to Wraxall, who waited for two years for administrative action in his favor but finally, in 1754, lost patience and entered upon the trials and expense of a lawsuit. His charge was that Harme had obtained his office by purchase, on such evidence as a deposition by Edward Collins of Albany, who asserted that Harme had publicly declared that he had paid £300 for his post to the governor and £30 to Edward Holland. At the trial, Edward Holland, called as a witness for the plaintiff, admitted that

Defendant Gansevoort told him that Mr. Stevenson had offered by a gentleman in town £320 pistols for the Commission and 20 pistools to Ayscough, but it would not doo. He gave his note to pay the governor £300 and paid 30 pistools to Ayscough he made the agreement with Ayscough and paid the governor the money.[1]

The difference between Harme's and James Stevenson's offers to Dr. John Ayscough, Clinton's secretary, does not appear to be a sufficient reason why "it would not doo," especially as Stevenson offered Clinton himself more than Harme did. Very little is known about Stevenson; perhaps he was associated with William Johnson, with whom Clinton was temporarily at odds when this appointment was made.

Wraxall's counsel, John Murray, seized this opportunity to plead the Statute of 5–6 Edward VI, against buying or selling of offices of trust or profit, including those "which shall Concern or Touch any Clerkship to be occupied in any Manner of Court of Record wherein Justice is to be Ministred." [2] Harme's defense against what appears to be conclusive evidence of bribery was on several levels. His lawyer spent his time proving that Clinton was empowered to appoint officers of justice, that Harme had been properly commissioned and sworn under this power, and that he had exercised the office properly ever since. After Holland's testimony nothing was said about a deposition Harme had executed to the effect that he had not bribed Edward Holland; that, on the contrary, Holland had undertaken to act for him in the matter because he was a friend and a relative. Any family relationship must have been between their wives, and their friendship was evidently of the sort described by their contemporary in New York politics, Daniel Horsmanden: "No Friendships are so strongly cemented as those carry'd on by mutual Interest and Services; Nay indeed the very nature of Friendship is such." [3]

Wraxall believed that the turning point of the trial came when Harme's lawyer

said in open Court that for what we knew Mr. Clinton might have paid this money to *The King*, which passed without any notice from the Judges on the Bench, and when Mr. Murray my Council took notice of the Absurdity and Indecency of the Reflection, One of the Judges on the Bench (Mr. Chambers also one of the Council) said *if not to the King, yet* perhaps *to some of his Ministers*.[4]

Wraxall offered this remark as evidence that Justice John Chambers, like Holland one of Clinton's protégés, was biased in Gansevoort's—or Clinton's—favor; it certainly indicates that Chambers was more aware of political realities than juridical principles. The jury did not attempt to decide the point of law, but brought in a special verdict, that if judgment should be given for Wraxall he should receive damages of £42 10s. and costs—the sum representing the salary of the Albany clerk since May, 1752—and that if judgment be given for Gansevoort, then he "did not assume upon himself in manner and form as the said Peter Wraxall above against him hath declared." [5] Since no further decision can be found, perhaps Wraxall was forced to drop the proceedings for want of funds, or perhaps a compromise was reached. Gansevoort retained the Albany clerkship, but Holland apparently yielded the Indian secretaryship to Wraxall, who held it, much to the satisfaction of his superior, William Johnson, until his death in 1759.

The Wraxall case throws some light on the deep-rooted conflict between English and Dutch which Peter Kalm asserted that he observed in Albany just before Wraxall came there.

The hatred which the English bear against the people at Albany is very great, but that of the Albanians against the English is carried to a ten times higher degree. This hatred has subsisted ever since the time when the English conquered this section, and is not yet extinguished, though they could never have gotten larger advantages under the Dutch government than they have obtained under that of the English. For, in a manner, their privileges are greater than those of Englishmen themselves. . . . They are so to speak permeated with a hatred toward the English, whom they ridicule and slander at every opportunity. This hatred is said to date back to the time when the English took this country away from the Dutch.[6]

From the context it is evident that Kalm did not distinguish between animosity between Albanians and Englishmen from England and from New England; his examples describe ill feeling engendered by Yankee suspicion of the Albanians' neutrality in the early eighteenth-century Indian wars. Furthermore, it should be noted that Kalm's principal associate in Albany, Colonel John Lydius, was a Johnson supporter whom most of his fellow burghers detested, and that Kalm himself had enjoyed in New York the hospitality of Cadwallader Colden, who combined enthusiasm for botany with antipathy toward the Albany Dutch. Kalm's information was therefore certainly one-sided, and as a matter of fact the Albanians' resentment of Englishmen (distinguished from Yankees) before 1750 was in all likelihood resentment of obnoxious individuals or of interference with the city's privileges rather than ethnic antagonism for its own sake. Albany Dutchmen like Harme Gansevoort did not hesitate to trade with England, work actively with the British government, learn the English language for public and commercial purposes, and teach it to their children, who used it for domestic purposes as well. Individual Englishmen settled in Albany, married into Dutch families at all levels, and participated without prejudice in the city's economic and social life. Only rarely were they elected to the common council, but this was more a division of labor than an exclusion from civic affairs, for Englishmen connected by marriage with patrician families often held appointive offices requiring familiarity with the English language and legal system.

Nevertheless, a number of incidents occurred in the years following the English conquest which might have given rise to a tradition of ethnic antagonism. Although ethnic tensions were insignificant beside conflicts over trade and status in Leislerian Albany, it was quite true that stubborn Scotsman Robert Livingston and the English soldiers in the fort were on the same side, and that it was Livingston who called in troops from Connecticut and went to New England for further help against the majority of the Dutch burghers. Then in 1714 Governor Robert Hunter and the city magistrates clashed over the governor's power to grant land for an Anglican church. In spite of these instances of friction, in general the Dutch and English worked together harmoniously until 1733, when some of the Albany Dutch and their English relatives cooperated with Cosby in his attack on the city in order to gain profit and prestige at the expense of their local rivals. In this community schism, there were still Englishmen with Albany connections on both sides; for example, the Collins family allied with the old patricians while the Holland family aligned with the new. The appearance of William Johnson, related by blood to a rising family in Great Britain and at the same time closely and actively connected with the dominant faction in provincial affairs, extended this rivalry to a new level and gave the Albanians reason to detest not so much the English as an ethnic group but that particular form of the English political tradition which was defining itself during these very years of "Whig supremacy." It was against the intrusion into their Dutch tradition of this new English political system, built upon the patronage of members of the post-1688 English nobility and their personal followers, that the Albany patricians struggled from the administration of William Cosby until the American Revolution.

This local and provincial conflict suddenly took on imperial importance and immediacy with the outbreak of the French and Indian War. The war, eventually a worldwide war involving England, France, and all their colonies and allies, began in 1754 in the Ohio Valley when Colonel George Washington and a body of Virginia militia marched toward the Forks of the Ohio to destroy Fort Duquesne, now Pittsburgh, only to be ambushed and forced to surrender by the French and their Indian allies. England, already deeply involved with France in India, accepted this challenge and in 1755 sent an army of redcoats under General Braddock to complete Washington's mission, but this army too was ambushed and annihilated. In 1756 the war finally reached Europe, as the great powers rearranged their alliances and France, Austria, and Russia attacked Frederick the Great of Prussia, who promptly joined forces with England. Thereafter English gold paid Frederick's army, the most formidable military machine on the Continent, as it held the armies of its adversaries at bay in a series of classic campaigns until Russia wearied of the war and France was defeated by British naval and amphibious campaigns on the seas and in the colonies.

In the meantime the colonists took some measures to cooperate in their own defense, one of them being the Albany Congress of 1754, at which delegates from seven colonies tried to reach a common understanding with the Iroquois, and Benjamin Franklin presented his famous but premature plan for intercolonial union. The Albany patricians, who had been completely superseded by Johnson in Indian affairs, played no conspicuous role in this conference or in the negotiations by which Johnson secured the active and effective support of the Mohawks for the English cause. In 1755 an intercolonial expedition under Governor Shirley of Massachusetts arrived at Albany on its way to capture Fort Niagara, but like most intercolonial expeditions it suffered from inefficient organization and ineffective discipline, and was unable to advance beyond Oswego. In the meantime Johnson and his Mohawk allies marched northward and defeated the French advance guard under Baron Ludwig Dieskau at Lake George. This victory, two months after Braddock's defeat, was so conspicuous that Johnson was rewarded with the title of baronet—the first such title to be granted in the Thirteen Colonies. Sir William Johnson thenceforth was able to use politically the weight of his rank, his military glory, and, after the war, the votes of the tenant farmers he settled on his Mohawk Valley estate, and so brought to bear directly upon the Albanians the full resources of the new English system as well as the pressures which New Yorkers had formerly applied to each other.

As soon as the war spread to Europe, the British government

decided to attack Canada via the Hudson-Champlain Valley with an army of British troops. It was prompted to this decision by the recognition that the French had a small but highly professional army in Canada, under the command of the Marquis de Montcalm, and that they had defended the several approaches to their colony with great stone fortresses in the best tradition of Vauban, the famous engineer of Louis XIV. Although Fort Frontenac, at the outlet of Lake Ontario, Forts Ticonderoga and Crown Point, on Lake Champlain, and Fort Louisbourg, on Cape Breton Island, were hardly finished, their formidable batteries and bristling outworks were not to be assailed by any tactics known to the provincial militia. But it took time to assemble a sufficient army and send it to America, and soon after its commander, the Earl of Loudoun, arrived with the first contingent, he learned that the French at Fort Frontenac had sailed across Lake Ontario and captured Oswego.

It is generally accepted that Loudoun and his successor, General James Abercrombie, attained their commands more by their influence than by their very moderate abilities, but any commander would have had difficulties in the situation which faced them. Somehow they had to weld into an effective fighting force British troops used to fighting against European armies and provincial troops used only to fighting Indians and already demoralized by the Oswego disaster. They had to supply their army, in an era when armies commonly lived off the country, in a region whose total population—about 17,500 people in Albany County in 1756—was less than the size of the army and its camp followers. The 3,000 people of Albany were overwhelmed by the avalanche of soldiers. At one time 1,400 men were quartered in the homes of the citizens, but most of the troops encamped in the fields of Rensselaerswyck on both sides of the river. It was in this encampment that Dr. Richard Shuckburgh, supposedly observing some provincial troops while sitting on the well-curb in the patroon's yard, is said (erroneously) to have written "Yankee Doodle." The well, the yard, and the patroon's home, Fort Crailo, now on a quiet street in downtown Rensselaer, are open to the public as a museum which ought to be better known for its fine

65

representation of the Hudson Valley Dutch tradition. The region as a whole was entirely agricultural, with no manufacturing and no commercial center outside Albany. Everything the army needed, except food, had to come all the way from England; military supplies, parts and replacements for weapons, and men trained to use and repair them were especially hard to find in the colonies. Transportation as far as Albany was fairly well developed, but beyond Albany there were few roads and no vehicles or men with experience in transporting large numbers of troops with large quantities of heavy freight to the points which had been designated as military objectives.

Loudoun therefore took a year to organize his base at Albany, and then decided that an attack on Louisbourg, where he could have naval support, would have more chance of success. While he and his best troops were away on this maneuver, the French attacked Fort William Henry on the site of the battle of Lake George, prevented all relief from nearby Fort Edward on the upper Hudson, and finally were unable to restrain their Indians from massacring the garrison after it surrendered. After this disaster Loudoun was replaced by Abercrombie, who in 1758 assembled some 6,000 British regulars and 9,000 provincial troops and transported them and all their supplies by water routes which brought them safely within ten miles of Ticonderoga. At that point the second in command, the able and popular Lord George Howe (whose younger brothers Admiral Richard Howe and General William Howe served in New York during the Revolution), was killed in a skirmish. Shaken by this misfortune, alarmed by a report that the defenders were about to be heavily reinforced, and apparently bewildered by the problem of approaching the great stone bastions bristling with cannon, guarded by ditches and palisades, and fringed by a maze of felled trees, Abercrombie rushed his infantry onto the fort without waiting to bring up his artillery and blast paths through the obstructions or silence the enemy's guns. The troops struggled gallantly through the impenetrable mass of treetops and brushwood, but the French cannon mowed them down and sharpshooters picked off those who escaped the shot and shell; the stubborn persistence of the 42nd Regiment, the "Black Watch" Highlanders, who returned to the charge until they lost two-thirds of their men, was particularly noteworthy. After a full day of such devastating losses Abercrombie retreated hastily to Albany, where Lord Howe was buried in the Anglican church amid widespread lamentation.

In England, in the meantime, undisputed direction of the entire war effort had settled in the hands of William Pitt, who planned a coordinated series of campaigns to drive the French out of Canada and promoted effective commanders to execute them. In 1758, as Abercrombie marched on Ticonderoga, a British fleet took Louisbourg, the gateway to the St. Lawrence Valley. The following year, an amphibious expedition under General James Wolfe sailed up the St. Lawrence to attack the central citadel of New France at Quebec. To meet this invasion, Montcalm had to draw in troops from the other gateway fortresses. When Colonel John Bradstreet marched from Albany to Fort Frontenac in 1758 and General Jeffrey Amherst renewed the attack on Ticonderoga in 1759, they therefore fell with anticlimatic ease. Then Wolfe discovered a way to climb the cliffs which defended Quebec and on September 13, 1759, defeated Montcalm's army on the Plains of Abraham. This series of successes in North America was only a part of a chain of military and naval victories in such widely scattered areas as India, Germany, and the Atlantic coast of France which so astonished the English themselves that they called 1759 "Annus Mirabilis," the year of miracles. Even with the help of Frederick the Great in Europe, the military victory outside Europe of England, with eight million people and a conspicuously unmilitary tradition, over France, with twenty million people and a society organized since the time of Charlemagne for supporting warfare as the quintessential expression of ethnic identity, was a turn of events at which the English had good reason to be astonished.

The English, the French, and the American colonists were soon enough to discover that the developments which made these victories possible had also changed the whole nature of the British Empire. In a sense they called it into existence, for though British merchants had been very much aware of colonies with which they traded, Parliament had occasionally legislated to regulate that trade, and the Crown had taken measures when necessary for their government and defense, there had never been any coordinated policy for all of England's overseas possessions and Englishmen were not in the habit of thinking of them as a unified empire. It was Americans seeking recognition as equals rather than inferior "colonists" who particularly promoted the idea that the British colonies, taken together, should constitute an Empire equal in status to the mother country. This concept made more sense in England after Pitt's worldwide coordination of major military campaigns, but Pitt fell from power soon after his campaigns were over, and this idea of empire remained a minority opinion even among English statesmen until after the American Revolution. There is some justification for the claim of the United Empire Loyalists of Canada that it was their ancestors, exiled from the new United States, who showed the British where loyalty to a united empire might lead.

All of these developments were still in the future when Amherst's army finally marched away from Albany in 1760 to capture Montreal and occupy Canada, to the great relief of the Albany patricians. For five years they had been overwhelmed by soliders who lived in their homes, introduced new manners and fashions, and created inevitable tension by conflicts of custom and breaches of hospitality. For example Anne Grant, the daughter of a Scots officer who spent several years of her girlhood in Albany and experienced much kindness from such Dutch patricians as Philip Schuyler's aunt, Margareta Schuyler, recalled that the Dutch were shocked when some British officers presented a play and incensed when a certain patrician young lady discovered that she had relied not wisely but too well on a British colonel's promise of marriage. Mrs. Grant believed that a serious cleavage developed between parents and children, as had certainly happened in New York City a generation earlier over similar questions of manners and customs. In view of the central im-

68

portance of the extended and continuing family as the primary unit of communal organization in Albany, it is also likely that some Albanians of all ages feared that their whole way of life was threatened, while others wanted at all costs to follow the English mode.

Mrs. Grant remarked further that the Dutch church divided over the morality of English manners. She believed that the conservatives united behind Domine Theodorus Frelinghuysen and the rebels against him, until the church fell into a state of schism and Domine Frelinghuysen was driven away. Here her observation was more correct than her analysis. In the absence of detailed church records for this period—many of them were destroyed by fire in 1938—it is impossible to tell exactly how the schism in the Albany church was related to religious controversy in the Hudson Valley as a whole and to what extent it developed from purely local family and commercial rivalry, but it certainly exemplified a persistent Dutch tradition and accentuated cleavages within the community which long antedated the war. Nevertheless the coming of the British army evidently did reinforce Domine Frelinghuysen's devotion to the Dutch tradition and detestation of all things Anglican—although he himself had no Dutch blood, his father being German and his mother French Huguenot, and his wife was the daughter of an English officer. It also seems likely that Frelinghuysen shared his father's beliefs that pastors had a sacred responsibility to discipline their flocks, and it is quite probable that his concern was shared by parents who found it difficult to discourage their children from adopting English fads and fashions. Such tensions were doubtless brought to a head by the play, a comedy then popular in London, which contained some risqué passages and in which, in the absence of actresses, feminine parts were taken by officers dressed in women's clothes. Some of the Dutch patricians were entertained and others, including Domine Frelinghuysen, were shocked into vigorous protest. The anonymous hint to depart which Mrs. Grant recalled that he subsequently received was in all probability a pointed practical joke of a sort common in Albany since Maritje Gansevoort had been called into court to testify against some

69

jokers who went too far; Domine Frelinghuysen, who had been accustomed to controversy all his life, doubtless took it for what it was worth.

Both the dissension in Domine Frelinghuysen's congregation and that in the community at large had another dimension which Mrs. Grant was not in a position to observe. She saw nothing of the ruthless competition between the Albany Dutch merchants and the swarms of sutlers and speculators who followed the army. In the early years of the war Albany merchants, particularly the Cuylers, provided supplies for the provincial forces, but the main contracts for the major British expeditions were let in London or New York and in any case the Albany merchants did not have the resources or the facilities to handle them. From such opportunities as fell in their way they squeezed every last penny of profit; in one venture Harme Gansevoort's brother-in-law, Volkert P. Douw, received the following warning from the Deputy Quartermaster General's office:

It will be necessary you take Some Care that you do not issue more Clothes, than he [the captain] can Produce able men for. The return you made to the Governor of the number is 62 But if by desertion Death or any other disappointment they Should be Lessened You are only to Furnish Such as are left.[7]

But there was also profit to be made by supplying the personal needs of the soldiers and camp-followers. Harme Gansevoort extended little credit to such customers, although there is nothing to indicate that he refused to sell to them for cash, but other Albany merchants were less cautious, and all of them resented deeply the intrusion of British traders who came to Albany with the avowed intention of making their fortunes by war profiteering.

Against these intruders the Albany new patricians organized all the resources of the entire community. The assessors saw to it that the newcomers paid in their taxes for the privilege of doing business in the town. The magistrates haled them into court for minor infractions of disused ordinances which native Albanians disregarded with impunity; when the cases were tried, Albany juries became notorious for their partiality in punishing newcomers and letting established residents go free. John Macomb, one of them who stayed in Albany until he was driven out as a Tory twenty years later, described his experience:

To confirm the general dislike the Dutch have to the Europeans here, in aplotting the contingent money for the Citty of Albany they have acted the most partially anyone could imagine. Dutch merchants, who are known to be worth from 15 to 30,000 pounds are charged from 6 to 10 pounds when we trifling pedlars (I may say in comparison to them) are charged from about 10 to 30 pounds each and as there is no redress to be hoped for from any other qtr than from that universal good man Genl Amherst, I understand application has been made to him for that purpose. I hope you'll lend your helping hand, and endeavor to set the affair in a proper light to the Genl. Ever since I came here, we have been charged above double our proportion of all public charges—this we tamely bore with, but their behavior now obliges us to cry out for redress. Upon my applying to the chief magistrates I was told that I must pay whatever sum the taxers charged me with, and that it was not in my power to have any redress made me from any person whatever.[8]

William Corry, another newcomer, wrote of the same incident:

The good people of Albany has taxed our new merchants smartly, they have only made 4 of them pay a hundred pounds the 12th part of the taxes of this city—the merchants deneyed paying the tax, they distrained their goods, the merchants petitioned the Gen'l that as followers of the army they were oppressed by the Albanians, they have not yet rec'd an answer—the mayor said in the street, he thought to resign his mayorship, but he would keep it one year to pleague the Irish—well said, Mr. Mayor. [Sybrant Van Schaick] [9]

In spite of this appearance of a common front, the Albany patricians were far from united. The old and new patricians still distrusted each other, and over the question of relations with the English each of these groups had in turn split. The old patricians divided as usual between Schuylers and Cuylers; the Schuylers affiliated with the Hudson River gentry and the Livingston faction, while the Cuylers associated themselves with Johnson and the De Lancey faction. The new patricians also split; Sybrant Van Schaick associated with Johnson while Volkert P. Douw went over to the Livingstons when they won control of the assembly in

71

1761 and was rewarded with appointment to the Albany mayoralty, succeeding Van Schaick, in September of that year. Douw's brother-in-law, Harme Gansevoort, followed him and was soon participating in Mohawk Valley land grants with members of the Livingston family.

Just before Douw became mayor, Harme's possession of the city clerkship was challenged by another English placeman. From the viewpoint of Harme's opponents, the Albany clerkship as well as the Indian secretaryship had been vacant since Wraxall's death in 1759. Since the Albany magistrates no longer had any voice in Indian affairs, Johnson was quite willing that the two offices be separated; his candidate for the Indian secretaryship was the songwriting surgeon, Dr. Richard Shuckburgh. But in May, 1761, an English career official named Witham Marsh arrived in the colony with a royal commission for both offices. Shuckburgh met Marsh soon after he landed and found him ambitious and avaricious; he doubted that the offices would prove profitable enough to keep him in New York very long. On further acquaintance, Johnson found Marsh incompetent as an Indian secretary, in spite of his previous experience recording conferences in Maryland, and undeserving of respect for any other reason. Nevertheless he responded with unfailing tact and patience to Marsh's steady stream of querulous, self-exculpating letters and backed him unreservedly in a long legal struggle for the possession of the Albany clerkship.

In September, 1761, Marsh presented himself to the Albany Mayor's Court, produced his royal commission, and demanded that he be inducted into the clerkship. The court refused, declining to compromise their stand by permitting Marsh to read his commission or by entering the matter in the minutes. Marsh thereupon lost his temper. No record of what he said has been preserved, but undoubtedly he touched upon what were to become his favorite themes, the offense to the King's Majesty implicit in such disrespect to the bearer of his commission, and the treasonable attitude of the Albanians, who as Dutchmen could not be expected to be loyal subjects anyway. The court's reaction to this may be imagined. Its members were the dignitaries of whom Mrs. Grant wrote:

the people, little acquainted with coercion, and by no means inclined to submit to it, had, however, a profound reverence . . . for the families of their first leaders; whom they had looked up to merely as knowing them to possess superior worth, talent and enterprise.[10]

Their own tempers had already been rubbed raw by the many changes the war had brought to Albany; now this explosive individual appeared to insult them and all they stood for to their faces. It is no wonder that they united in righteous indignation and thenceforth backed Harme Gansevoort without reserve.

Marsh then appealed to the council, which ordered Harme to surrender the city records. Harme refused, asserting that he held his office during good behavior, under a royal commission under the Great Seal of the Province, and that unless and until he were ousted from it by due process of law it would be a dereliction of duty for him to give up the records. He added that Marsh had initiated a lawsuit against him for the possession of the offices and he did not doubt that the council would await its determination. Beyond this document no record remains of Harme's side of the cause. Practically all that is known of it comes from Witham Marsh's letters to Sir William Johnson. At first Marsh thought that the courts were prejudiced against him, though perhaps the strength of Harme's defense came rather from the previous decision in his favor:

My cause was to've been tried next Term; but I don't know how it happens, my attorney says, *we are somehow in the wrong!* For my part I think I'm in the right *upon both commissions:* but *I was not born in this Province.*[11]

In the fall of 1762, while passing through Albany on his way from Johnson Hall to New York, Marsh met Colonel John Bradstreet. After serving in Albany during the war, Bradstreet had bought an estate near the city limits and built a home he called Whitehall. He and his neighbor Philip Schuyler were good friends, but many of the Dutch merchants resented his high-handed actions as Amherst's supply officer. In particular, the consistory of the Dutch Reformed Church sued him for damage done by Amherst's army to a pasture they owned. Bradstreet thought of defending the suit by attacking the city charter, through which

73

the church derived its title to the pasture, but his lawyer, Attorney-General John Tabor Kempe, dissuaded him:

Now as to my attacking the Charter of the City of Albany as a publick Officer in order to defeat the Title of the Dutch Church to these Lands, I cannot think it right, unless other Reasons can be given than that if it was granted nowadays it would be informal nor do I think I ought to attack the Charters of any Publick Body unless I am ordered to do so, by those who have a right to command me.[12]

Bradstreet was full of this scheme when he met Marsh, and equally full of sympathy for Marsh's cause. As Marsh wrote Sir William:

. . . Col. Bradstreet told me, He had heard when I presented this King's commission in the Mayor's Court, that chick Cope Ten Eyck [Jacob C. Ten Eyck] had the assurance to say they (the Dutch) knew no such man as George the third. I told him he must be misinformed, tho too much was said in Court, as would appear by affadavits I had in Albany which I would shew him. . . . he read the Depositions with pleasure, assuring me, that as the bulk of the Dutch people were Rascals, he would give me any assistance in his power. . . . All this surprised me much, as you may well imagine, because I was scarcely known to him. He added, "I think I've sufficient matter to break the Charter; if I have, I will assuredly do it." [13]

In the same letter, Marsh expressed his opinion of his antagonist in his usual colorful manner:

There's strange news relating to my affair. All the English and many of the Dutch tell me that my Business will certainly be terminated to my advantage, and that Ganse is now really frightened. He looked shockingly black this day. No letters from my Lawyers! I have now only to make you my unfeigned Thanks for your very kind favours and which to my sorrow I am afraid I shall never be able to return unless the D—l will take away Ganse, or his precious Lawyers.[14]

When Marsh did hear from his lawyers, a few days later, he seized upon the opportunity they offered him to create further unpleasantness for Harme:

Two days before I left Albany, a writ was brought me against Ganset. I preemptorially ordered Mr. Sheriff to serve it, hoping to catch him

74

Tardy, for which I would have swing'd him severely, but he disappointed me, and did his office orderly; yet when he gave me the writ, *returned properly,* He doggedly left me, and looked like a R—l. My Lawyers have done all in their power last Term, to procure a mandamus. Father Horsmanden (my Countryman) either misunderstood the matter of the motion, or was Boggled by the opposite Council; but we intend to have a Riot next Court for the Mandamus besides working Ganse with the new action [a civil suit for £500 damages]. A friend of mine is lately come from England. Mr. Sec. Pownall still preserves his Friendship for me, as do two greater men, the Earl of H[alifa]x and Lord Londes. The usage of Mr. Mayor, and the Court last year, has made a great Noise at home, and what I shall now write will make much more.[15]

The case finally came before the Supreme Court in January, 1763; while Marsh was waiting for it to be tried Johnson wrote him, with a tact and sense of humor which he did not use in describing Marsh to other correspondents:

. . . I fear (by the Stile of your letter) that you take things too much to heart, and perhaps but few comforters, which to one in your situation are very necessary. Cheer up your Spirits, don't give too much way to Reflection nor to your disorder [gout] and you will find a benefit thereby. I am sorry for the death of Chief Justice Pratt on two accounts, the one as he was your friend and might be of service to you in your present unprecedented struggle with [Gansevoort, probably—Ed.] of whom I doubt not in the least but you will get the better, and that with credit; the other, as he was an Englishman and a good man etc. I should Imagine that the General or the Governor on a proper representation of the affair would use their interposition, as the King's prerogative is opposed and grossly abused. However you will be better informed there of the propriety of such a step. All I can say in the affair is, that I most sincerely wish you to triumph over your Enemies, and have the pleasure of perusing that inestimable treasure and stock of knowledge and learning which you are now refused, but which I hope a thundering Mandamus will put you in peaceable possession of.[16]

As it happened, before this missive was even written, Marsh had sent off a triumphant account of his day in court and of the overthrow of Harme's defense:

75

On the 21st Instant my Council moved for a Mandamus to deliver to me the Records of Albany County etc. etc. Young [William] Smith violently and, indeed, virulently opposed it, as it was for his Majesty's service. Mr. [John M.] Scott on this occasion exerted himself with great oratory, and, as He had the best side of the question, the Judge [Horsmanden] allowed his motion; upon which Mr. Banyar said to Mr. Will: Livingston *Now you are gone:* meaning Gans—t must lose the whole, as his cause was pre-judged by granting the mandamus. All agreeable to Law! In open Court, my Countryman [Horsmanden, from Kent—Ed.] asked me to Dine with him, and all the Lawyers, with which I thought it my Duty to Comply, as it was some Honour confer'd on me, in presence of a numerous audience.

Van Schiet has offered me Terms of accommodation, but they are such as I will not accept; besides my Council, tells me now, as I am sure of having full possession of the office (if I live) they will not permit me to agree with Him, on the most advantageous conditions, since he opposes, with a true Republican Spirit, the Royal Mandate! Had I not been here, I should have been put back Six months longer. A man cannot have his business completely done, but by himself.[17]

Marsh's enthusiasm was somewhat premature. Harme's lawyers tried to compromise, offering Marsh possession of the records if he would permit Harme to be his deputy and receive half the profits.

Yes, and if I was fool enough, I suppose he wou'd take t'other half too—the D—. I doubt his Dutch Modesty, as well as his Albany Honesty—They are both pretty much alike.[18]

In the spring Marsh came up the river with his mandamus, only to discover, as Sir William seems to have tried to tell him, that Albany was not New York. After attempting to enforce his judgment, he communicated sadly:

Had not Jerry Renslaer made a great mistake about executing the mandamus, and sent an Express in my absence to York, I should have set out from hence on Tuesday, tho' yet very lame. . . . I am fearful, Sir, we are a-back about my affair, for Jerry seems afraid to act. . . . The moment I had your letter about not continuing Van Frog, I appointed Jerry because I will never do anything contrary to your Judgment; and therefore wish that you and Mr. Scott would terminate the [matter] as I am really tired, and by fretting have hurt my constitution.[19]

But in spite of the danger to his gouty constitution, Marsh did not drop the suit. Harme and his lawyers avoided complying with repeated court orders, made Marsh another offer of compromise, again including the provision that Harme should become Marsh's deputy, and found some occasion to move for a new trial—"And God preserve us from an Albany Jury!" [20] wrote Marsh in December, 1763. Nevertheless, Harme's legal maneuvers were in vain. At the end of May, 1764, Marsh was back in Albany, writing "This Day, or tomorrow, finishes the affair about the Records— Ganse looks like a Devil." [21]

Marsh had what he wanted, after going to great trouble and expense and making himself thoroughly hated by those who opposed him and thoroughly despised by those who supported him. Still he was not satisfied. The clerkship proved, as Shuckburgh had predicted three years before, too lean for his avarice. In September, 1764, he was ready to sell it—provided his successor should be "no cursed Dutch republican, by reason he would ruin every Englishman, or at least bring the Titles of their Lands in question." [22] By November he was back in New York, reporting that his deputy, a respected Albany lawyer named Peter Silvester, had still been unable to get all of the records from Mayor Douw, but that he no longer cared. Greener pastures called him in the shape of £20,000 left to a lady of his acquaintance in Maryland, whom he evidently expected would find him irresistible. But this opportunity appeared too late. Two months later he was dead, leaving an unsigned will, a considerable debt to his lawyers, and affairs generally so entangled that Sir William refused to act as his executor. The last word on his lawsuit was written a quarter-century later by Harme Gansevoort's son, applying to the post-Revolutionary government for appointment to his father's post:

Permit me . . . to remind you that our Family have always considered that they have an equitable claim to this office, from the Circumstance that my Father had a Commission for the office *during good* Behavior, and was divested of it by what was deemed but a *Quibble* in Law, vz *the Demise of the Crown.*[23]

Incidents like the Marsh case disillusioned the Albany patricians with the new British Empire. To them, the campaigns which led to the victories of 1759 meant that invasions of their isolation and interferences with their privileges which had been sporadic and disconnected now became a constant and organized attack on their way of life. It is important for modern readers to notice that although their struggle to preserve this way of life was often carried on through government officials and court actions, it was only tangentially what we would call political. Although Albany's assemblymen were involved in it, the matters at issue in Albany were not the issues which attracted most attention in the assembly in the mid-eighteenth century, and though provincial factional leaders watched the Albany situation with interest and interfered when they thought it worthwhile, the conflict in Albany was not closely tied into any province-wide agitation for party votes. The Albanians' contests for the clerkship, the mayoralty, and the county offices in the governor's gift were rather for appointment to administrative posts which controlled the day-to-day implementation of local government, about which ordinary citizens had nothing whatever to say in either English or Dutch eighteenth-century traditions. Local elections for the common council, to judge by their results, still in effect consisted of co-optation among the patrician families.

The Albany patricians regarded civic offices, when they acquired them, as opportunities for promoting the advantage of their families and protecting the privileges of their community. For individuals such as the British merchants, attracted by the war, who chose to live in that community without being of it, there was no place in their system. When these newcomers then proceeded to organize into a rival community constructed according to the current tradition of Great Britain, the Albany Dutch closed ranks and fought back. Against Johnson, the newcomers, and a few ambitious Albany patricians like the Cuylers, the old and new patricians began to unite with each other and cooperated ever more closely with the Livingston faction in the province. The Livingstons, dominant from 1761 to 1768, backed Albanians like Volkert Douw and Harme Gansevoort in their struggles to acquire or retain public offices and encouraged them to share in land grants competing with Johnson's in the Mohawk Valley. But then when the Livingstons fell from power in 1769, the new patricians had to take the consequences of this alignment, for the victorious De Lancey party soon prompted the governor to replace Mayor Douw with Abraham C. Cuyler, the son of former Mayor Cornelis Cuyler. Young Cuyler was only twenty-eight; his extreme youth for such an exalted appointment suggests that the De Lancey faction may have had some difficulty in finding an Albany patrician willing to accept the mayoralty from them. All the other appointed officials were newcomers, and both old and new patricians were soon confined to a minority of the common council. Thus, after 1770, a very few Albany patricians tried to rule the city by the new British imperial system, while most of them, flung from power by external interference, reflected instead that their awakening to empire had indeed been rude, since it had deprived them of those pecuniary profits and communal privileges which, according to their Dutch tradition, it was the function of imperial authority to protect.

IV

Revolution Strikes Home

The very idea of revolution was foreign to the Dutch tradition of the Albany patricians. Their plebeian ancestors in the Netherlands had sometimes participated in revolts which seized the existing institutions of local government but had stood stubbornly behind their patrician leaders in their long war to prevent the King of Spain from changing those institutions. Patricians and plebeians together in Dutch towns regarded their traditional form of government as the foundation of their communal independence, the most cherished of their particular privileges, that which made possible the exercise of all their liberties, for which reason it would hardly have occurred to them that even the people could or ought to have a right to alter or abolish it. Factions within the community, usually organized for this purpose as for every other in Dutch towns around complexes of continuing families, sometimes assumed control of this government by extralegal processes including violence, but to overthrow it and replace it with some other kind of government would have been to destroy the very basis of the community's identity. It is therefore hardly surprising that the Albany patricians showed little understanding of the American Revolution until it burst upon them.

"The Revolution" in their understanding was the English Revolution of 1688, which had no relevance to their tradition except that it had provided an occasion for Leisler's Rebellion. The supremacy of Parliament, the Protestant succession, the toleration of dissenters, and the dominance of mercantilism were all

80

revolutionary departures in England, but similar in their effects on the colonies to traditions long practiced by the Dutch. The revolutionary parliamentary party system, which had originated in the 1670's and 1680's when King Charles II had used his powers of patronage to attach individual members of Parliament to his interest, thus creating an "in" or Tory party and an "out" or Whig party which seized power by force in 1689, became under the uninterested Hanoverian monarchs a multifactional system dominated by a few great lords, like the Duke of Newcastle, who gained access to the king's patronage and distributed it among their friends, relatives, and followers. This system resembled the factional system of the Dutch with one major difference: its principal bond was patronage, supported by political indebtedness and family relationship, while Dutch factions were usually organized around continuing family groups seeking the mutual commercial advantage of their members. In the 1760's, however, King George III and a group of politicians dissatisfied with all the great Whig lords set about to rescue the English two-party system from the disgrace into which it had sunk between 1715 and 1745 because of the Tories' association with the proscribed Stuart dynasty. For twenty years the king used his powers of patronage and of selecting his ministers to keep the government in the hands of his own supporters, thus forcing the Whig lords and their followers to resume the original Whig role of His Majesty's loyal opposition. The resulting parliamentary maneuvering, which took place primarily over American colonial questions, made sense in the context of the English political tradition, but it often made colonists of British background impatient, and probably meant very little one way or the other to the Albany Dutch.

The Albanians' closest acquaintance with a parliamentary body was with the New York Assembly, which followed the example of its English parent by engaging in a long struggle for power with the king's representatives, the provincial governors. Before this conflict began in the 1720's, the assembly was simply a body of local representatives, responsive sometimes to local pressures and sometimes to the governor's demands, but as a body neither particularly coherent nor particularly self-conscious. Dur-

81

ing the administration of Governor Burnet, however, a number of issues arose on which the assembly found itself on one side and the governor on the other, and by Cosby's time the cleavage had become so serious that each side used all the resources at its command to break the power of the other. Cosby depended on land grants and the "King's prerogative," powers of patronage, appointment, and control of the administrative machinery, including the law courts. In order to control its own members and the electorate behind them, the assembly had to control the appointments of officials by whom elections were conducted and the electorate governed. For this purpose the assembly used the traditional English parliamentary weapon of "power of the purse," insisting on designating the exact purposes—and sometimes the exact persons—for which appropriations might be spent. The group of political leaders who finally won this battle during the administration of Governor Clinton came mostly from New York City and the lower Hudson Valley. Preeminent among them were the De Lancey family, particularly James De Lancey, who served as acting governor during the French and Indian War. The De Lancey faction was organized like an English faction of the same period, on the basis of aristocratic (landed) influence, political interest, and family advantage. It reflected those aspects of the revolutionary English system which were closest to the Dutch tradition, and leading Dutch families, particularly landed gentry from the lower Hudson Valley and ambitious merchants from New York City, had no difficulty fitting into it. But, perhaps because it was so successful in filling the political needs of those New Yorkers who wished to cooperate with the new British Empire, it was unable to provide for other New Yorkers with entirely different interests.

The Livingston family, perennial rivals of the De Lancey family and ambitious to supersede them in provincial affairs, grasped this fact in the 1750's. Although their home base was Livingston Manor in the upper Hudson Valley—they no longer lived in the city of Albany—some of them settled in New York City, the center of the most populous and most politically active part of the province. There they appealed to a class of citizens whose potential power no New York politicians had yet exploited, the ordinary voters with definite political opinions of their own. At this time most New Yorkers, like eighteenth-century English voters (to say nothing of Netherlanders who did not vote at all), usually voted in accordance with the wishes of community leaders; differences were ironed out beforehand if at all possible, contested elections were rare, and it was taken for granted that contests, when they occurred, would be determined by the immediate material rewards which each candidate could offer the electors. But William Livingston was one of a very few New Yorkers in his generation who attended Yale College, which gave him an opportunity to see in action the New England town meeting system, where ordinary voters expressed opinions and balloted on issues. Community leaders won election to town offices on the basis of their positions on such issues as well as their family relationships and financial standing.

Livingston found this system, which derived from the same seventeenth-century Puritan tradition as that which in England produced the Long Parliament and the Commonwealth, particularly useful among the large proportion of New England voters who had settled in New York City and on Long Island. In 1753 he and some of his associates began an appeal to this electorate by attacking the attempt of the Anglican Church to control New York's own new institution of higher education, Kings College. The issue was shrewdly chosen to unite the Yankees, whose tradition included a definite thread of legislative support of non-Anglican education, with their usual enemies the Dutch, who cared very little about higher education but who feared Anglican interference of any sort with their churches and social customs. In Albany, Domine Frelinghuysen took up the bait at once, expressing himself with great vehemence in opposition to Anglicans and all their works. Some of his congregation were quite willing to accept all the nonreligious implications of this agreement with the Livingston party; others, associated for business and political reasons with Sir William Johnson, were much less enthusiastic. Doubtless this disagreement had something to do with Frelinghuysen's unpopularity.

In the meantime, the Livingstons set about perfecting a new political system in the southern part of the province. They started with a New York Assembly faction, organized in the same manner as but in opposition to the De Lancey faction, among a few important individuals and families who attached supporters to themselves by patronage in the revolutionary English manner. This faction the Livingstons placed consciously and coherently atop a foundation of independent voters whom they expected to have opinions of their own and to vote on issues in the New England manner. To hold the top and the bottom of this party together, the Livingstons depended on a new kind of professional politician, who was one of the faction either by family relationship or by participation in the patronage system, and at the same time could express the faction's struggle for power against its opponents in terms of issues which would win the support, and the votes, of individual electors. By 1758 they had so far succeeded that they were able to win control of the assembly from the De Lanceys.

The Livingstons' new system made no sense at first in Dutch Albany, because voting and elections were a minor part of the Dutch tradition, and voting on issues no part of it at all. But the Livingstons, seeking assembly backing from all possible sources, encouraged Albanians who disliked Johnson to support them for that reason if none other. In the course of the association which followed, an Albanian named Abraham Yates, an ambitious former shoemaker turned lawyer, became one of their professional politicians and began to introduce their new techniques into Albany elections. A remarkable letter written by Yates to his patron Robert Livingston, Jr., describing the Albany County Assembly election of February, 1761, shows the complicated tensions which existed among the Dutch and between the Dutch and the English before the new system had any appreciable influence. In this election the incumbents, Jacob H. Ten Eyck and Volkert P. Douw, both new patricians, were known to be "at such Variance that they went In Different Sloops down to New York to avoid Each others company." [1] Several leading Albanians, mostly old patricians and including former Mayor Cornelis Cuyler, sought to take advantage of this division among their opponents by encouraging the plebeian Yates to run against one or the other of them. Yates had barely announced his candidacy when Ten Eyck and Douw resolved their differences, "the Scheme of Ten Eyk in Joining with Dow to Stop Breadstreet (who is a Particular friend of Dow) from being against him."[2] Bradstreet then intervened in the election.

He Treatned some that he would Never pay their accounts Others that he would take their horses some People have Kings horses on fodder from them, and Others he woud Declare war against them, and more of the Like wild Expressions.[3]

Yates and his friends fought back with equally equivocal tactics.

The Next Day we met and voted Untill 12 O:Clock when I Desired them to Shut the Poel and give my opponents Joy—they with their party Expressed their obligation to me for telling them timely as it would have Brought them to voast Expense if it had Continud Longer.[4]

In conclusion, Yates suggested to Livingston:

You Now may Possibly have an opportunity to Settle with Sr William before the Next Election as you will see that he is not at all Inclinable to Ten Eyck or Dow. . . . I Conceive I have reason to think that Sr William will put up some one Next time Macomb or any Strangers I am afraid it would not Go down but was he to put up any two Inhabitants here with the Junction of you and Ten Broek [the Rensselaerswyck representative] no matter who they would carry it.[5]

In this election Yates had no chance, but in 1763 he won election to the common council from the third ward—the Gansevoorts' ward—and continued to be reelected for the next ten years. His real opportunity came after 1770, when Mayor Cuyler and the newcomers took over the city government and pushed the old and new patricians into a corner. Yates must have organized a party quickly and effectively, for in 1771 his cousin Robert Yates was elected to the common council, and in 1772 another cousin, Peter W. Yates. The sight of the three Yateses sitting simultaneously, one from each ward, so roused the patricians that they rallied all their forces and defeated Abraham Yates for alderman in

85

the third ward in 1773. Yates and his running mate, William Winne, immediately challenged the validity of the poll, and the common council heard evidence indicating widespread fraud on both sides before it finally accepted the original result. The Gansevoorts were in the forefront of this battle; one victorious candidate, John Ten Broeck, was Harme Gansevoort's son-in-law, and the other, Thomas Hun, was his next-door neighbor. Harme and Peter Gansevoort were charged with having visited an Albany tavern to influence voters during the election, but it could not be proven that they had given them any money. In this same contest, Leonard Gansevoort, Harme's twenty-two-year-old son, who despite his youth had exchanged uncomplimentary notes on politics with one member of the Yates family four years earlier, was elected assistant for the third ward in an unchallenged poll. Between this upheaval and the next election the common council laid down its first specific catalogue of residence requirements and other qualifications for voters.

In the meantime the Livingston party, having won undisputed control of the assembly in 1761 and enjoyed the pleasures of office for seven years, was decisively displaced by the resurgent De Lancey faction in 1769. Only seven assemblymen adhered to the Livingstons, and the victors even found ways to debar members of the Livingston family from taking seats to which they had been elected. Leadership of the opposition devolved, for the first time in the colonial period, on an Albany County member, Philip Schuyler, who replaced Volkert P. Douw in 1768. Douw said that he was retiring for the sake of his health, but since he continued to be mayor of Albany until the De Lanceys replaced him in 1770, and since Sir William Johnson was known to be "not at all Inclinable" to him, it seems likely that his ailments included Sir William's disapproval. Schuyler retained his seat until 1775, in spite of Sir William's increasing dissatisfaction with his Livingston affiliation, primarily because Sir William could find no one more suitable who was willing to run. Schuyler had a foundation for his independence in his old patrician standing and his friendships with Governor Moore and other British officials, dating from his service in the French and Indian War; but his Albany colleague, new patrician Jacob H. Ten Eyck, found it desirable to vote with the De Lanceys on many occasions.

As a result of their rather rude exclusion from the assembly, the Livingston party turned to revolutionary agitation, particularly among the self-conscious and articulate New York City electorate. In the 1770's, they built up a following among ordinary citizens who responded to their warnings of the dangers of parliamentary and royal tyranny and their calls for resistance to it. Some of the more active citizens became Sons of Liberty; others attended the mass meetings and participated in the mob violence which became features of New York City politics in this period. The Livingston leaders were certainly not responsible for all the actions of these groups, committees, and mobs, but they were unquestionably the most deliberate single force behind their organization. With this kind of political activity the Albanians had little to do until the Revolutionary War actually broke out. In January, 1766, they produced a belated Stamp Act riot, but it really had very little to do with the iniquitous behavior of Parliament. What happened was that when Douw and Ten Eyck returned from the assembly with reports of violence over the issue elsewhere in the province, it occurred to a crowd of young patricians to attack a half-dozen merchants, all newcomers or known supporters of Johnson like Philip Cuyler and Jacob Vanderheyden, who were suspected of having applied to become stamp agents. Some property was damaged, notably Postmaster Henry Van Schaack's sleigh, which was burned, but there were no attacks on persons and the whole escapade sounds much more like the pranks traditionally attributed to groups of Albany Dutch youths than like the grim, resentful violence of the Sons of Liberty in New York and Boston. In the 1770's there were Sons of Liberty in Albany; Philip Schuyler, who was involved with the New York Sons through the Livingston party, was aware of their existence, though perhaps not formally a member, but their activities did not attract much attention.

In this period, therefore, the potentially revolutionary party in the province of New York acquired three groups of backers among the Albany Dutch, all more or less at odds with each other, and all, like the Livingston party itself, out of power. Philip Schuyler was related to the Livingstons by family and factional ties on the provincial level, and brought with him a personal following held together by family relationship, political interest, and community influence in the mid-eighteenth-century Anglo-Dutch system originally defined by the De Lanceys. The Douws and the Gansevoorts, representing the new patricians of Albany City with their following organized in the traditional Dutch manner, joined them in the 1760's for value received in their struggle to maintain the independence of their community and assert it against Sir William Johnson and other intruders from the British Empire. Abraham Yates joined them for the sake of a future as a professional politician, and created a following by applying the new Livingston system to hitherto-neglected Dutch plebeians and non-Dutch plebeian immigrants to Albany City and County. These three groups built up their strength in a veritable political vacuum. A few Dutch patricians followed the Cuylers in their attempt to rule the city with the backing of the De Lancey party and the newcomers, but many more seem to have taken refuge in silence, affiliating with no faction, attending to their business, and declining to run for office. One result of this was that when the American Revolution finally did break out, its leaders in Albany included, besides some experienced dissidents, a remarkable number of very young men, among them Leonard Gansevoort, his brother Peter, and their cousin Leonard Gansevoort, Jr., all of them in their twenties.

Sometime before August, 1774, Abraham Yates and his brother-in-law, Jacob Lansing, became active on the Albany Committee of Correspondence, of which Yates was elected chairman on January 1, 1775, when its surviving minutes begin. At first this committee was secret and entirely plebeian, including both Dutch and non-Dutch members. (On the basis of presently available information it is impossible to tell what proportion of the "English" plebeians in the city were from the British Isles and what proportion from New England.) After the battle of Lexington it came into the open by calling a public meeting on May 1 and asking the whole community to elect representatives to a new, expanded committee. The burghers responded by choosing eighteen members, over half of them patricians, representing all shades of opinion from Yates himself to Mayor Cuyler. Although the meeting was held at the third ward market house—that is, in the broad street right outside the Gansevoorts' front door—none of the Gansevoorts were elected. A few days later, however, after young Leonard Gansevoort had demonstrated his zeal for the cause by canvassing the third ward for contributions toward supplies for Ethan Allen's troops at Ticonderoga, he was chosen to fill one of the vacancies created when committee members were designated to attend the Provincial Congress. Very soon after his election Leonard was appointed treasurer of the board, in which position he remained until he in turn was sent to the Provincial Congress in November, 1775.

The young Gansevoorts' enthusiasm was notable in a city which was proceeding into revolution with characteristic Dutch caution. Leonard's elder brother, Peter Gansevoort, quickly accepted a lieutenancy in his ward's militia regiment and hurried to ask his uncle, Volkert P. Douw, now vice-president of the Provincial Congress, to get him a provincial commission, but other officers appointed by the Provincial Congress refused, and General Philip Schuyler had to ask the Albany committee to find suitable candidates from the area who were willing to serve. Some patricians reconsidered when disputes over rank were adjusted, but others simply did not care to become involved. The eager Peter, who was only twenty-six, was finally commissioned a major in the Continental Army. In the meantime Schuyler had exerted his personal influence on prospective officers to some effect, so that by the time he reached Albany in July, on his way to invade Canada, he brought a fairly completely organized army with him. The extent of his support among the burghers was revealed when his formal entry into the city was ridiculed in an anonymous broadside. The citizens—quite possibly the young patricians—assembled in a tumult of indignation, forcing the committee to investigate and to discover that the squib had been written by one of its own members, Peter W. Yates. Yates apologized, but only his resignation would satisfy the aroused people. Then, having shown the Yates that popular enthusiasm could be mobilized against them as well as in their favor, the young patricians marched off with Schuyler. Leonard Gansevoort described the enthusiasm, aroused by their departure, in a letter to Peter, who was already in the field:

General Schuyler has Yesterday been in the Dutch Church and desired the Prayers of the Congregation for himself and the Army under his Command which he received, and I sincerely lament that you were not present that you might have heard it. Mr. Westerlo's prayer was so very pathetic and so well adapted that he drew Tears from the Eyes of almost all there present. May God grant that a happy Reconciliation take place upon Constitutional Principles and prevent the further Effusion of Blood.[6]

It was hard for the Gansevoorts who stayed in Albany to take a realistic view of the war in the fall of 1775. The army marched quickly to Lake Champlain, was transported by boats to its northern end, and soon captured Chambly. Leonard chided his brother for not writing, although two hundred miles of wilderness separated them. He gave way to anxious solicitude when word reached Albany that Peter had succumbed to the disease which swept the unsanitary camp at Chambly, and would have rushed off across the wilderness to his brother's bedside had his own wife not objected. Before Leonard could possibly have arrived, Peter was on his feet again, participating in the army's successful assault on St. John's. After this victory, Leonard expected that the spring would bring "an accommodation"—encompassing, of course, a full triumph for the Revolutionary principles which raised him to heights of zealous eloquence. Instead, the winter made the situation of the Canadian army desperate. Schuyler had fallen ill and returned to Albany; the army, under General Richard Montgomery, whose wife was a Livingston, settled in at Montreal, where Peter's duties were primarily concerned with controlling dissatisfaction and desertion among the soldiers. At the end of 1775 Montgomery went to Quebec with part of the troops to meet Benedict Arnold's expedition from Maine. In an unsuccessful attack on the city on the last day of the year, Montgomery was killed and Arnold wounded, but their army continued to besiege Quebec until British reinforcements arrived by sea in the spring. Peter was sent to join this wretched remnant after he recovered from another illness, but he only arrived in time to help it prepare to retreat from Canada altogether. In March, 1776, at the height of these preparations, he was promoted to lieutenant colonel.

As Schuyler's pestilence-ridden Continentals retired from Canada and General Guy Carleton's British regulars followed them to St. John's and began building boats to traverse Lake Champlain, the American cause suffered further reverses elsewhere. Washington's success in driving the British out of Boston only made it possible for them to attack some other part of the coast, and after being expected in many places, Admiral Richard Howe's fleet carrying General William Howe's army appeared off New York City in August. The Provincial Congress, in which Leonard Gansevoort was sitting, had left the city about the first of July, just before the Continental Congress published the Declaration of Independence, and throughout the summer a steady stream of citizens left Manhattan Island for safer locations. Washington's army came to New York and tried to defend it, but since it had no naval support the loss of the city was inevitable. But Washington refused to give it up without a fight, engaging the British on Long Island and afterwards extricating his outclassed army by a masterful maneuver, engaging them again at Harlem Heights on upper Manhattan, warning them to stay within reach of their fleet by defeating their vanguard at White Plains, and then, after losing Fort Washington to amphibious attack, slipping away across the Hudson into New Jersey. The British army followed him until he turned upon them at Trenton and Princeton at the end of the year, and the fleet did not at this point try to penetrate the defenses of the Highlands and sail up the Hudson to Albany. Nor, in the north, was it possible for Carleton to gain undisputed control of Lake Champlain until he defeated Benedict Arnold's hastily-constructed freshwater navy at Valcour Island on October 11, after which it was too late in the season for him to march on Albany. For the moment the city was safe, but with the British fleet in the lower Hudson its trade was utterly cut off, and

91

for the first time in its history it became, as it remained for six years, totally isolated from necessity rather than from choice.

The Gansevoorts took all of these great events as part of the day's work. Leonard took his seat in the Second Provincial Congress on December 6, 1775. He was immediately appointed to two *ad hoc* committees and thereafter participated faithfully but not conspicuously in the Congress's activities. At first, of course, these principally concerned the defense of the city of New York, but the Congress was also concerned about the security of the rest of the province. In July, 1776, with the ink scarcely dry on the Declaration of Independence, with Howe expected at any moment off New York, and with Carleton hovering at the north end of Lake Champlain, the Congress received disquieting reports that Generals Schuyler and Gates were engaged in a dangerous dispute about the limits of their respective commands. General Horatio Gates had been appointed by the Continental Congress to replace Montgomery as commander of the Canadian army, now at Ticonderoga rather than in Canada, while Schuyler remained in charge of the defense of the entire Northern Department. On July 22 the Provincial Congress appointed Leonard Gansevoort and his wife's brother Jacob Cuyler—not to be confused with his second cousin, Mayor Abraham C. Cuyler—a committee to deliver a letter to Gates, and incidentally to report "a candid state of our military operations in the Northern department" and to investigate "whether proper harmony prevails amongst the officers, and subordination among the troops." [7]

Caught between Schuyler and Gates was Colonel Peter Gansevoort, since June commanding at Fort George (Lake George). As at Montreal, his greatest problem was morale, which suffered with the perilous plight of the American cause elsewhere. To encourage the troops he could keep from deserting, Peter was generous with furloughs and frequently held military ceremonies. Gates, when he inspected, considered furloughs a sign of slack discipline and ceremonial salutes a waste of desperately needed powder, and objected further to formal irregularities in the written reports and returns sent him from Fort George. These points and similar disciplinary technicalities over which he took issue with

Peter may have been wisely raised, but his manner of calling Peter to account was fussy and fault-finding. Peter, who was fully aware that Gates was also striking through him at Schuyler, objected to Gates' attitude as a slur upon his military honor. This tension was at its height when Leonard and Jacob Cuyler visited the northern forts in August. Leonard first tried to play the peacemaker, explaining Peter's position to Gates when he saw him at Ticonderoga and suggesting to Peter afterward that he would be wisest to cooperate, but when he told the story to Schuyler he changed his mind and wrote Peter that Schuyler was "exceedingly happy at your spirit and the appearance of the rectitude of your Conduct." [8] The quarrel between Peter and Gates was smoothed over in September, but Gates continued to complain to him until November, when Schuyler ordered Peter and his command to Fort Saratoga, out of Gates's possible jurisdiction. Leonard and Cuyler duly reported to the Provincial Congress, but the quarrel between the two generals was not settled until it was eventually carried to the floor of the Continental Congress.

When Leonard returned to the Provincial Congress, which was frequently moving about among such mid-Hudson Valley villages as Kingston and Fishkill, he became active on the Committee for Detecting and Defeating Conspiracies. At the beginning of July, 1776, as the Congress left New York City, this committee had been formed by consolidating a number of others dealing with Tories, Tory plots, and rumors of Tory plots. Leonard, who had been a member of one of these committees, became active on the new committee as soon as he returned from Ticonderoga and by December was serving as its chairman. The Committee for Conspiracies had to deal with one of the most serious problems of that critical year, for many New Yorkers had been reluctant revolutionaries and no one knew how many of them might take up arms in the British cause as the British army approached. In September and October, as Howe occupied New York City and Carleton advanced as far as Crown Point, upper Hudson Valley Tories refused militia duty, "skulked" mysteriously in the woods, and assaulted and even murdered patriot leaders. Some were supporters of the king, but many more were motivated by hatred of

93

patriot landlords or local leaders, and some simply saw in the general unrest an opportunity to get away with robbery and other crimes. To curb this anarchy, Leonard's committee had its own intelligence networks and express riders and could call on troops if necessary. In four months it handled over five hundred cases and banished many leading Tories to New England. Then in February, 1777, it was replaced by a full-time commisssion of three men who were not members of the legislature.

While Leonard Gansevoort was helping to deal with Tories from all over the province, the Albany committee had to deal with serious Tory problems nearer home. In the city of Albany, Mayor Abraham C. Cuyler's cooperation with the committee had been of short duration. In the summer of 1775 he had been intercepted on his way to Canada, ostensibly on fur business, and had been sent politely back to Albany, since which time the Albany patriots had increasingly ignored him and his common council and absorbed the functions of the city government into those of the extralegal committee. Cuyler and his British newcomer associates responded by reiterating their loyalty to the king, and finally underscored it by toasting His Majesty publicly on his birthday, June 5, 1776. This was the last straw for the Albany patriots, who arrested Cuyler and a number of other prominent Tories the next day, and after shipping them about to various places of imprisonment for two years, finally banished them. Mayor Cuyler and his brother Henry, who was also arrested, did not take their restraint quietly; they bombarded the committee with requests for special treatment or, better yet, release, and frequently tried to escape. After their banishment Abraham C. Cuyler served with the Loyalist troops and eventually, having discovered that he would by no means be permitted to return to Albany, settled in Nova Scotia. He and his brother were the only Albany Dutch patricians actually banished as Loyalists, although several others, including the mayor's wife's brothers Jacob and Cornelius Glen, saved themselves only by taking the prescribed oath at the very last possible moment. The other residents of the city who were banished or otherwise punished as Tories were mostly new-

94

comers such as John Macomb, Recorder Stephen De Lancey, and Postmaster John Monier.

Elsewhere in Albany County, particularly on the Livingston and Van Rensselaer manors, districts with a history of tenant unrest against landlords who were now patriot leaders, were the scenes of considerable "Tory" activity. Even more serious, however, was the situation in Kinderhook, where the rural patriciate of substantial farmers clung obstinately together in refusing to join the patriots of the city and county. These Dutch farmers had some typically Dutch reasons for thus maintaining their independence. One, of long standing, was fear of encroachment on lands and interference in local affairs by patriot Van Rensselaers on the manor to the north and in Claverack to the south of Kinderhook. Another was fear of inundation by patriot Yankees pouring over the Berkshires; in the quarter-century before the Revolution this movement of population had helped to cause boundary disputes between New York and Massachusetts and tenant discontent on the manors east of the Hudson as well as tension in Kinderhook, whose eastern portion, Kings District, was by the Revolution largely peopled by immigrants from New England. Even in Kinderhook proper, along the river, the established Dutch families still controlled the government but were very nearly if not absolutely outnumbered by Yankee newcomers.

These Dutch families, notably the Van Schaacks, were unable to make common cause with the Albany patricians in the same position because they had chosen to associate their ambitions with Johnson and the De Lancey party—quite possibly out of distaste for alignments with the Van Rensselaers. In the 1760's, Henry Van Schaack became an Albany merchant and accepted the office of postmaster, in which capacity he was attacked during the Stamp Act riot; his sister Jane Van Schaack married Peter Silvester, the Albany lawyer who became Witham Marsh's deputy when he finally secured the city clerkship from Harme Gansevoort; their brother Peter Van Schaack became a lawyer in New York, where he laid the foundations of a brilliant career with the assistance and encouragement of the De Lancey leaders; and two

95

other brothers, Cornelius and David Van Schaack, remained at home in Kinderhook to support the family's position there. Peter Van Schaack was by no means unsympathetic to the principles of the New York City Revolutionary leaders, many of whom were his personal friends, and even served on some of the early civic committees which protested parliamentary measures, while his brothers were elected to represent Kinderhook on the Albany committee as soon as it asked the county towns to send representatives.

The Albany committee was unfortunately already suspicious of the Kinderhook patriciate. In its secret days it had had to reassure some nervous communities in Massachusetts that Kinderhook did not intend to attack them; the Continental Association found few adherents in Kinderhook and the Van Schaacks constantly discovered new reasons for refusing to force their neighbors to sign it; and, most important, there was a group of Dutch plebeians in Kinderhook who were eager to proclaim their patriotism, unite with the Yankees, and seize control of town affairs. With the backing of the Albany committee and presumably the enthusiastic support of the Yates group, who were using the same revolutionary means to come to power, the followers of Major Isaac Goes used the militia to control local elections in their favor. The Albany committee in turn refused to recognize any Kinderhook representatives except those sent by the Goes clique. The committee then proscribed the Kinderhook patricians as Tories and traitors, but the Van Schaacks resisted, insisting that refusal to acquiesce in Kinderhook's being governed by the Albany committee did not necessarily constitute disloyalty to their country.

Peter Van Schaack, in particular, argued cogently that a revolution ostensibly in the name of liberty should recognize the liberty of individuals to refuse to participate actively in it so long as they gave no aid and comfort to its enemies. His interpretation of the nature of liberty was a remarkable combination of Dutch tradition and post-Revolutionary English political and legal education, for his ideas about the rights of individuals to liberty certainly derive from his reading of John Locke, while his ideas about the ways in which individuals should use their liberty equally clearly derive from the Dutch conception of liberty as a communal privilege. His views gained him much sympathy among such highly placed patriots as his friend John Jay, who not only appreciated the brilliance of his reasoning, but also understood the situation in Kinderhook, and was at the same time having difficulties of his own with Abraham Yates and other plebeians who were just as anxious to take over the province as Isaac Goes's group had been to seize local power from the Van Schaacks.

But with British armies invading the Hudson-Champlain Valley from both ends and "Tories" of all sorts disrupting it in the middle, the Revolutionary patricians were too desperate to risk alienating their plebeian supporters. His former New York City friends gave Peter Van Schaack, who during this time was enduring many personal difficulties including incipient blindness, the lingering fatal illness of his wife, and the loss within five years of six of their nine children, such private assistance as they could inconspicuously, but they were powerless to prevent him and his brothers from being subjected to house arrest and eventual exile. Leonard Gansevoort, who knew the family only as they had been associated with the Cuyler party in Albany, did not sympathize with them at all; when all the important Kinderhook Tories were finally banished to the British lines in a body, he wrote to Peter:

The infernals at New York are in the greatest consternation. Doctr. Van Dyck, H. Staats, Van Schaacks, Thurman etc. etc. will be much surprised I fancy when they arrive there to see the length of their Friends faces—they are put down by the Commissioners for refusing to take the Oath prescribed by the Legislature. It goaded them much to be told as the Act says that they had acted from poverty of Spirit and an undue Attachment to Property, asserting they had acted from principle.[9]

While the Committee for Conspiracies and the Albany committee struggled to bring the Tories under control in the winter of 1776–77, Colonel Peter Gansevoort came back to Albany to recruit for his depleted regiment. He found that the Albanians had

97

lost most of their enthusiasm for the war, which was hardly surprising, since the British fleet at New York cut off all but local trade. Peter found recruits hard to find and hard to hold, writing:

I am under some apprehension that the men will be gone before I might find others, there appearing so great a reluctance in the young gentlemen in and about Albany to engage in the service; many of Col. Van Schaick's officers having, as I am informed, declined to accept their appointments.[10]

Then it became known that General John Burgoyne was assembling an army in Canada for a major invasion of the Hudson-Champlain Valley in the coming campaign season. In March, 1777, Peter's reconstituted regiment, the Third New York Continentals, was ordered to hold Fort Schuyler at the western end of the Mohawk Valley against British forces cooperating with Burgoyne.

Fort Schuyler had been built during the French and Indian War, when it had been named Fort Stanwix for a British general. Although the patriots officially rechristened it for General Schuyler, it continued to be commonly known by its original name, was remembered as Fort Stanwix by the Gansevoorts, and will be called so henceforth in these pages. Its function was to guard the eastern end of the Great Carrying Place, across which goods and boats had to be portaged between the Mohawk River and Wood Creek, which led eventually to the Oswego River and Lake Ontario. After Sir William Johnson made the Treaty of Fort Stanwix with the Indians in 1768, defining the boundary between Indian lands and white men's lands in central New York, the fort fell into disrepair. Peter's men found it in a tumbledown condition, but expecting Burgoyne to send a wing of his army around by Lake Ontario and the Mohawk Valley for a flank attack on the Hudson Valley, they hastened to repair it. They worked feverishly, but the timber and turf walls, the four bastions, the deep ditch, and the sharply-pointed palisades were hardly defensible and the barracks were far from complete when on June 26, 1777, two of the garrison were shot and scalped by Indians.

This scalping, the first overt act against the American cause by any of the Iroquois, opened a devastating civil and racial war in the Mohawk Valley which patriot leaders had been trying for two years to prevent. Sir William Johnson, who in 1771 had succeeded in having his part of the Mohawk Valley separated from Albany County and organized as Tryon County, had died in 1774. His son and successor, Sir John Johnson, with his associates Colonel Guy Johnson and Daniel Claus, fell heir to Sir William's estates, influence with the Indians, and imperial ambition, but not to his political and diplomatic tact. There was never any question but that Sir John would remain loyal to the Crown, nor that his father's recently settled Scots and Irish tenants would support him with armed force. General Schuyler and the Albany committee worried about the Johnsons from the beginning of the war, particularly when delegations of Indians began visiting Albany to inquire what the fighting was all about. Schuyler and the committee, falling heir to this function of Pieter Schuyler and the Albany magistrates, assured them that the patriots did not intend to disturb them and tried to persuade them not to participate in the war. The Iroquois promised to remain neutral, but as the Johnsons' activities became more distinctly warlike, the Albanians came to fear that it would be only a matter of time before that promise was broken. Under the pressure of desperation in 1776 they disarmed Sir John's tenants, arrested his family, and forced himself and his armed supporters to flee to Canada. With them went a menacing number of Indians, particularly Sir William's especial friends, the Mohawks, under the leadership of his Indian widow Molly Brant and her brother Joseph Brant. When Peter's two soldiers were found scalped, the patriots of the Mohawk Valley, who had just finished expelling these Tory neighbors, understood perfectly well that neither the Tories nor the Indians were willing to accept their expulsion as final.

In the meantime, Burgoyne's army sailed up Lake Champlain and invested supposedly impregnable Fort Ticonderoga. General Arthur St. Clair perhaps neglected some possible defensive measures, but perceived quite correctly that the monumental fortress was much too large and complex for him to hold with the forces at his disposal. He therefore abandoned the fort without a fight, wisely, though somewhat awkwardly, withdrawing his army to reinforce Schuyler's slender force in the Hudson Valley, but also undermining the confidence of the people in the Continental Army and discouraging even patriot leaders. Schuyler, with a genius for making the best of the means at his disposal, wrote off Ticonderoga as the white elephant that it was to a small army of citizen-soldiers, abandoned all attempts to dispute Burgoyne's control of the extended Champlain waterway, and put his troops to work obstructing the paths and creeks by which Burgoyne's army must travel when it left the lake behind.

In planning this defense, Schuyler depended on the forces of nature to supplement his inadequate army in the traditional Dutch pattern followed by both William the Silent and William III when the Netherlands were in desperate danger of foreign invasion. In a mountainous wilderness there were no dikes to cut, but when Schuyler's men had finished cutting trees instead—at which they had certainly had much more previous experience than at fighting battles—the effect on Burgoyne's army was remarkably similar to the effect of the Dutch defense on the armies of Philip II and Louis XIV. When the Dutch let in the sea to defend themselves their polders became shallow lakes too wet for armies to maneuver or camp in but not deep enough for boat or naval operations—a confusion between land and water which seldom failed to bewilder their attackers. Now Schuyler saw between Lake Champlain and the Hudson River a low valley between mountains, in which were several creeks, lakes, and swamps. These waterways were passable for canoes, though not for large boats; the paths alongside and between them were designed for foot travelers, not for vehicles. When Schuyler ordered his men to block these creeks and paths with felled trees, a delicate balance between land and water was upset which the British army upset further when they tried to clear away the obstacles, uproot some of the stumps which held the soil, and build a road solid enough for their wagons and cannon. To their consternation, they found themselves in effect bridging a swamp twenty-three miles long, too wet to maneuver or camp in but not deep enough to transport their supplies by boat—a confusion between land and water which did not fail to bewilder them. Behind Schuyler's army the Hudson Valley Dutch people prepared to cut their dikes in earnest; Mrs. Schuyler set the example by firing the family's growing crops with her own hands before she abandoned their estate at Saratoga, while the Albany committee made plans to sink the city's fleet of sloops should the British approach from either direction. But New England representatives in the Continental Congress, seeing only the retreating armies, remembering the number of Hudson Valley Tories, distrusting the Dutch in general for many reasons, some going back to the early eighteenth-century Indian wars, fearing that Burgoyne might strike New England from the rear, and probably not appreciating—especially from such a distance—the staying power of a last-ditch Dutch defense, became exceedingly impatient. As John Adams despairingly wrote his wife, referring to Schuyler's abandonment of Ticonderoga, "I think we shall never defend a post until we shoot a General." [11]

Under these circumstances great consequences turned on Peter Gansevoort's determination to hold Fort Stanwix against the British soldiers, Tories, and Indians under Colonel Barry St. Leger, whom Burgoyne ordered to attack him from Canada by way of the St. Lawrence and Lake Ontario. Should Fort Stanwix surrender, there would be nothing to stop this force from marching down the Mohawk Valley to take Schuyler's army in the rear, in which case Burgoyne's campaign would undoubtedly succeed. Peter and his family were fully aware that he was for a few weeks at the center of decisive events. On July 9, Leonard wrote to him: "Ticonderoga and Mount Independence are in the possession of the Enemy. Your Fellow Citizens put great Confidence in you and your Father flatters himself that you will Conquer or die." [12] Another friend, who had just escaped from Ticonderoga with only one shirt, penned a note of warning: "I am in pain for you not because you will not fight but lest your impetuosity should carry you too far." [13] Peter's fiancée Caty Van Schaick showed herself to be of a proper temper for a soldier's bride by writing, "All my fear is that you will be blocked up in the Fort and will be forced to surrender for the want of provision and left to the Mercy of those brutes." [14]

Throughout July, a steady stream of Indian attacks heralded the approach of St. Leger's army. To meet them, Peter had about five hundred Continentals and supplies for three weeks. Two hundred militia came in for a few days to repeat Schuyler's Dutch defense by felling trees across the waterways along which the enemy must approach. When that work was finished, they went home. On July 28, Peter sent to Albany the sick and wounded and the soldiers' families—except for eight intrepid wives, one of whom successfully gave birth to a daughter after being seriously wounded by a piece of shell late in the siege. On August 1, 250 men from Massachusetts marched in to reinforce the garrison. When their supplies arrived the next day, the soldiers hastened to unload them, and had barely secured six weeks' supply of food within the fort when they were attacked in force by Indians.

St. Leger's army arrived that night and the next morning paraded under the eyes of the besieged Patriots. This was too much for Peter and his officers. While some of them counted the force the enemy so obligingly revealed to them, others concocted a flag out of odds and ends of red, white, and blue cloth and ran it up the flagpole. It was the first American flag to fly in the face of the enemy. After this mutual show of defiance, both armies settled down to the business of the siege. Peter had 750 men and food for six weeks, but he was short of ammunition. St. Leger had about 700 regulars and Tories, including Sir John Johnson's followers, and about 1,000 Indians. He was joined on August 5 by his eight small field pieces. On August 6 the Mohawk Valley militia under General Nicholas Herkimer tried to relieve the fort, but were ambushed by the Tories and Indians at Oriskany, six miles away. Although St. Leger and the British soldiers stayed at Fort Stanwix to watch the garrison, they were not strong enough to interfere when a party of 250 Continentals took advantage of the opportunity to raid the Tories' and Indians' camp. This sortie, led by Lieutenant Colonel Marinus Willett, seized supplies, weapons, and records which gave Peter valuable information about the besiegers.

The following day, as the mauled militia were retreating from Oriskany, Peter received a visit from three of St. Leger's officers, who demanded the immediate surrender of the fort. They told Peter that Burgoyne was already at Albany—which of course was not true—and that the Indians, inflamed by the attack on their camp, would assuredly devastate the valley if the fort prolonged its resistance. Peter and his officers heard the message silently, in a candle-lit room whose windows had been covered to prevent the envoys' observing the defenses. Peter refused to surrender the fort, but, distrusting his abilities as an orator or perhaps fearing ridicule for his Albany Dutch accent, he delegated Willett to reply more fully. Willett, an enthusiastic and fluent Son of Liberty from New York, informed them in no uncertain terms that the threat of Indian retaliation on civilians was a message "disgusting for a British officer to send, and by no means reputable for a British officer to carry." [15] In subsequent correspondence, St. Leger laid all the responsibility for this unfortunate suggestion on his Indian allies. Like his countryman, William of Orange, Peter replied with the silence that speaks louder than words, only reiterating his determination to "defend this fort to the last extremity." [16]

Peter took advantage of the cease-fire which accompanied this parley to send Willett and a companion down the valley with a report of his true situation and a plea for help, if any could be found. Then he and the garrison settled down to resist to the last man, or rather to the last charge of their small stock of gunpowder, without much reason to expect any relief. On August 11 the British diverted Wood Creek, cutting off the fort from its water supply. Peter immediately had the men reopen some old wells inside the fort and detailed a dozen Negroes to keep the fort "sweet and clean," cleanliness, both of the camp and of the men's persons, being one of Peter's major concerns since his illness in the filthy Canadian army. In the meantime the British bombarded the fort with their eight guns, which did little damage at first. Peter's artillerists collected shot and unexploded shells and fired them back to their owners. But the British were also digging regular siege works to bring their guns closer and converting four mortars into howitzers so that they would be effective at short range. As soon as their trenches were done the British would be able to bring a formidable battery to bear on a single point in the

103

fortifications, blast a breach in the turf and timber walls, and rush through to overwhelm the garrison in hand-to-hand fighting. On the night of August 21, when it was obvious that another day or two would complete the British preparations, four of Peter's men deserted.

It was at this desperate point that help finally arrived. General Schuyler, digging in near Saratoga to make a last stand against Burgoyne, heard of the battle of Oriskany and decided, over the objections of his officers, to take the chance of weakening his own inadequate force by sending help to Peter. So Benedict Arnold marched up the Mohawk Valley with 1,300 Continentals, gathering members of the defeated and leaderless but still belligerent militia along the way. They met Willett, who reported that the fort had plenty of food and, knowing the numbers of the enemy, suggested that they wait for as many militia as possible. Willett of course did not know about the siege approaches and had no way of guessing how much damage the eight field pieces might be made to do. Arnold therefore advanced cautiously, as he had every reason for doing two weeks after the Oriskany ambush, and made use of psychological as well as conventional weapons. In the hope of discouraging the Indians, he sent a supposed turncoat among them with a story designed to play upon their superstitions. The ruse worked. The Indians decamped in panic and St. Leger, deprived of his screening force, was compelled to abandon his all-but-finished trenches and his menacing little cannon and retreat with them.

Peter first learned of these movements from a British deserter who came into the fort at noon on August 22. He reacted cautiously, first bombarding the British trenches and then, when there was no reply, sending out scouts. Only when they reported that the enemy had in fact departed did Peter send out a sortie to recover the baggage. Arnold's column arrived the next day. Arnold agreed that Peter had been wise to send no pursuit after a force so well able to set an ambush. Neither of them had any way of knowing that St. Leger's army hardly stopped until it got back to Canada. Arnold stayed until it was certain that the British would not return; then he went back to the main army. Peter turned over his command to Willett and went down the valley, presumably to report to Schuyler. He found that Schuyler had been superseded by Gates; the Continental Congress had at last lost patience with the Dutch defense, although John Adams wrote when he heard of Peter's victory, "Gansevoort has proven that it is possible to hold a fort." [17]

While great events thus reached a climax in the west and still greater approached their climax in the north, the Dutch in Albany swiftly and efficiently prepared to withstand a siege themselves. The danger from the north was far more menacing than that which still threatened from the south; it had been rumored that Sir William Howe was supposed to come up the Hudson to meet Burgoyne, but instead he had embarked for Philadelphia, and Washington's army had marched overland from New Jersey to meet him. The battles of Brandywine and Germantown were over the horizon for the preoccupied Albanians who only noticed that Sir Henry Clinton made no effort all summer to come up the river from New York. Perhaps they did not seriously expect that he would do so, for many of them sent their womenfolk down the river to Kingston for safety. In a letter written at the end of July, which reached Peter after being captured by the enemy and recaptured during Willett's sortie, Caty informed him that she was on the point of departure. "I am sorry to leave this place," she concluded. "I hope it is for the best." [18] On the day that Peter's men were beating the woods for the stragglers of St. Leger's retreat, Leonard snatched time from his public duties to take his pregnant wife to Claverack and the city records to Kingston. Ironically enough after these precautions, it was Kingston, the patriots' temporary capital, which Clinton eventually burned.

Meanwhile, inhabitants of outlying areas fled to Albany for protection. Such civic leaders as had not been arrested as Tories or gone to serve in the state government or the army set aside their personal, political, and family differences and worked together to preserve as much order as possible. Domine Westerlo conducted daily services of prayer for preservation from the hand

105

of the invader. Members of the committee kept their heads amid a multitude of cares, providing for the refugees, rounding up Tories and sending them out of the county, collecting and forwarding supplies for the army—including the lead weights from the burghers' window sashes—along with such mundane matters as mending roads and providing for local elections. When Clinton and the British fleet at last did sail up the Hudson in October, burning Kingston and Robert R. Livingston's home at Clermont, thirty miles below the city, they were ready to burn the city's shipping, but Gates did not think it necessary, and in fact the campaign ended a few days later.

While the Albanians were readying themselves for a siege, Gates confronted Burgoyne on the heights of Saratoga, supported by a rising tide of New England militiamen encouraged by John Stark's victory at Bennington and alarmed by the well-publicized massacre of Jane McCrea. With an army several times the size of that which Schuyler had held together to impede Burgoyne's advance, as large as the army that Abercrombie had marched up the valley to attack the French at Ticonderoga, Gates was able to stop Burgoyne, to surround his army, to subject it in turn to a siege, and finally to force him to surrender it. Thus a Dutch defense turned into a Yankee victory, which was fair enough in view of the fact that New England had undeniably started the war and had far more to fight with than the upper Hudson Valley. But Burgoyne, defending himself before Parliament, later picked out the most remarkable factor in his defeat when he observed that the Loyalists did not rise. Tory activity in Albany and Tryon Counties in 1776 had certainly been sufficient to give him a reasonable expectation of a rising; and the Tories had a whole campaigning season in which to plan and carry one out. But the Albany County committee kept its Tories well in hand, and the people of Tryon County ran even ahead of their committee in driving them away. Leonard Gansevoort and his Committee for Conspiracies showed the way for this tightening of loyalties and silently demonstrated another aspect of a Dutch defense at least as important as Schuyler's silent ingenuity with small means and Peter Gansevoort's silent stubbornness under fire. In a broad

106

sense, the whole of Burgoyne's campaign was a siege of the whole upper Hudson Valley, against which patricians and plebeians together organized a traditional Dutch defense—for even when revolution struck home, it was outside their tradition to be revolutionary.

V

Founding the Empire State

While the Dutch tradition of the Albany patricians provided them with no precedent of revolution in the English sense, it did contain examples of revolt by which plebeian groups forced patricians within particular cities to include them in the government. In the medieval Netherlands these plebeians were usually artisans, in the great clothworking cities of Flanders often master artisans employing hundreds and even thousands of weavers who formed a preindustrial proletariat, organized in the form of craft guilds. The master artisans used civic disorders perpetrated by discontented workers as occasions to force their way among the merchant patricians and sometimes to gain control of the city councils, although the workers themselves were unable to think beyond outbreaks of sometimes savage violence to the positive problems of governing the community. It is at this point that the Albany Dutch tradition diverges decisively from that of the Netherlands, for although Abraham Yates and his associates forced their way among the patricians exactly like Dutch plebeian leaders, they did so as politicians rather than artisans, and their followers were not guilds of ignorant Flemish weavers but articulate American mechanics and farmers educated by a generation of revolutionary agitation and held together by common political concerns. The Yates party founded its very existence upon the American political principle of gaining and holding power by winning popular votes in elections fought over issues—in short, by the success of professional politicians in formulating and expressing the opinions of majorities of individual electors—but throughout the Revolutionary period it used this power within the framework of the Dutch tradition of Albany and the Anglo-Dutch tradition of the province of New York.

The Yates group came into existence as a wing of the Livingston party, which in turn came into existence for the purpose of opposing the De Lancey faction in the assembly. As a result of their close cooperation with the new British Empire, with which many New Yorkers besides most Albany Dutch patricians were dissatisfied for numerous reasons, the De Lanceyites found themselves forced out of power all over the province by a combination of local and revolutionary forces. In many cases, as in Kinderhook, it was the localities which slipped out from under them into revolution and forced them into overt Loyalism, although often, as in Kinderhook, local pressure was not sufficient to proscribe them or drive them away without revolutionary support from elsewhere. But the Livingston party did not immediately rush into the vacuum the Loyalist De Lanceyites left behind. Instead it broke up under the strain of a task for which it was never intended.

That task was governing the province without a king. The Declaration of Independence assured the colonists that George III was a tyrant who was unfit to rule over them, but very few colonists—and very few eighteenth-century Europeans—had any practical idea of what a government without royal authority would be like. Besides appointing unpopular ministers and permitting them to levy unconstitutional taxes and impose oppressive punishment on a sister colony, the Crown was the source of commission for administrative officials at all levels and the ultimate court of judicial appeal. Ambitious colonists like Harme Gansevoort were sure that they could execute the duties of these offices as well or better than incompetent English placemen like Witham Marsh and render justice more adequately and appropriately to the needs of the colony than English judges, and probably they were right. But few of them had thought through the advantages of having a single indisputable source of appointments, or realized that confusion was certain to ensue when administrative and judicial appointments became political footballs in an elective assembly unrestrained by any royal prerogative. The scramble for office by Patriots in the early days of the Revolution, which shocked some New Yorkers, was inevitable in a province in which the very reason for existence of all the pre-Revolutionary factions had been, like English factions, to influence the disposal of executive (royal) patronage.

Parliamentary supremacy therefore had its pitfalls, as the Livingston party discovered as soon as Governor Tryon fled the state and left them with full responsibility for administering the revolution they had begun. Making no discernible effort to form a coherent government, the Livingston faction seems to have immediately split into its component parts, each of which seized upon such offices as lay within its reach in the assumption that possession of offices would in itself insure an orderly transfer of power and all the other blessings of liberty. For a time the necessities of the war compelled all these local and factional groups to work together in the common defense, but whenever the question of constructing a new form of government arose, their differences and ambitions reappeared in full force. The complexity of this situation was somewhat reduced by the British occupation of the southern part of the state, containing over half its people, and by Sir John Johnson's flight from the Mohawk Valley, but cleavages within the upper- and mid-Hudson region that was left—of all the regions of the state the most persistently Dutch—were deep and serious. One of the most important of the splits was that between patricians and plebeians in the city of Albany, which had come to light in the third ward election of 1773 and was now carried into the deliberations on the state constitution by two of the original adversaries, Abraham Yates and Leonard Gansevoort.

Leonard had expressed his animosity to the Yates family even before that election, when, at the precocious age of eighteen, he had exchanged acrimonious notes on politics with Christopher N. Yates. In spite of what was from all indications a feud between the two families for control of the third ward, Leonard's Revolutionary enthusiasm, his father's fortune, and his own evident political ability made him welcome and influential on the Albany

110

committee. After his first period of service in the Provincial Congress it was he who made the decisive motion in that committee, on May 9, 1776, that Mayor Cuyler be compelled to choose between signing the Continental Association and being disarmed as a Tory, and that the committee seize the city records. After his chairmanship of the Committee on Conspiracies there was no question of his place among the leaders in the Provincial Congress (after Independence, the Convention). But Abraham Yates, chairman of the Albany committee, was also a member of the Convention, and it was he who became chairman of the committee to draw up a state constitution. Another member of the Convention from Albany County was Matthew Adgate, a Yankee from Kings District who worked consistently with Yates and in all probability was close to the clique of Yankees and Dutch plebeians who overthrew the Kinderhook patriciate. These two men represented the new political system the Livingston faction had created in its out-of-office days, basing its power on swaying the opinions of the electorate. But now many of the original Livingston leaders, beyond all hope and expectation installed in the seats of the De Lanceyites, with no likelihood of their opponents' return, were less tolerant of their former allies, whom they now saw—as they were—as competitors for offices. Adgate's demand from the convention floor that the constitution committee begin its work by drawing up a bill of rights was therefore a specific appeal for support from a specific group of outside supporters, and was the opening gun in a battle between two political systems for control of the new state which spilled out of the committee into the Convention and out of the Convention into the constituencies themselves.

This was a silent battle. The Yates group pressed to hurry through a constitution providing for a form of government whose personnel would be professional politicians whom they could control by their influence over popular opinion at election time. A patrician group, led in the committee by Robert Livingston, held back in hopes of getting a form of government whose personnel would be gentlemanly statesmen with independent means like themselves and administrative appointees controlled, as in the

111

colonial system, by their influence and interest. Of this struggle Abraham Yates later wrote:

A diversity of opinion soon took place in this Committee, not whether the government should be of the republican form partaking of monarchy, aristocracy and democracy, but what proportion of ingredients out of each should make up the compound.[1]

On the other hand, Robert Livingston recalled, responding to an account of the adoption of the radical Pennsylvania constitution, "You know that nothing but well timed delays, indefatiguable industry, and a minute attention to every favorable circumstance could have prevented our being exactly in their situation."[2]

Chairman Yates and his supporters produced several drafts suitable to themselves and in all probability to a majority of the Convention, but the Livingston group, unable to do more, managed to block the committee from reporting for several months.

This impasse made observers outside of the committee, and even outside of the Convention, impatient, although it seems unlikely that it puzzled them very much. In September, 1776, the Albany committee, doubtless well informed by Yates and Adgate, tried to prod the Convention with the wishes of the people; Jeremiah Van Rensselaer—a member of the Claverack family, not the manor family, and a consistent supporter of the Yates group—pushed through a motion pressing the Convention to act on the constitution. Leonard Gansevoort, who was at this meeting, was appointed with Van Rensselaer and three others to a subcommittee to draft formal resolutions which never reported, but the day that Gansevoort returned to the Convention Yates's committee was ordered to meet every day until it was prepared to report, a requirement which it eventually evaded by finding an excuse to request another postponement. Then General Schuyler, concerned by the effects of delay in organizing the government on the war effort, began to prod from the other direction. In response to this pressure Yates announced that a draft would be ready by December 20, and then postponed presenting it although it was known to be completed. Finally, when the house reconvened at the beginning of March, 1777, it was Leonard Gansevoort who moved that the committee be asked to report, which it did on March 12, and Leonard Gansevoort was president pro tem of the Convention on April 20, the day the constitution was finally approved; therefore he signed the certification of its passage and the order for its publication. His first act under the new government was to secure for himself appointment to his father's post of City and County Clerk, which he lost almost immediately.

The cleavage among the Revolutionaries heralded in the constitutional committee by the split between the Yates group and the Robert Livingston group reappeared on a state-wide level in the gubernatorial election of 1777, when plebeian George Clinton defeated patrician Philip Schuyler. Clinton proved to be an effective leader of the whole Revolutionary effort, but his supporters, controlling the Council of Appointment provided by the new constitution to keep the governor from misusing the power of patronage as his colonial predecessors had done, filled every available office—including the Albany clerkship—with plebeians.

In the meantime, the local government of Albany was adjusting to Independence. In April, 1778, the state assembly elected under the new constitution confirmed the city charter and designated a mayor, John Barclay, grandson of an early Anglican rector, and a common council to serve until the usual time of elections in September. When these elections were held, the victorious candidates included patricians and plebeians, some of them non-Dutch, who had been active in the Patriot cause. Among them was Leonard Gansevoort, Jr., son of Johannes and a first cousin of Leonard and Peter, who was chosen assistant for the third ward. These Patriots immediately began to run the common council as they had run the Revolutionary committees; instead of meeting once a month, passing an ordinance or two, and adjourning, like the colonial common council, they met at least every other day and worked by means of subcommittees appointed for every conceivable purpose from auditing the municipal accounts to drawing up an ordinance against breaking the Sabbath. In 1780 Leonard was appointed recorder and thereafter

113

the two cousins frequently worked on the same committees. Their first joint effort was an address to Governor George Clinton, who was to be presented with the freedom of the city.

Early in 1778 Leonard, Jr., who was only twenty-four, was also appointed secretary to the County Commissioners for Detecting and Defeating Conspiracies, established by state law to supplement the work of the state commissioners. Their primary tasks were putting down bands of "Tory" robbers who assaulted patriots on the highways, attacked their homes, and rescued other Tories who had been arrested, and enforcing an act for banishing dangerous Tories, under which the Van Schaacks and their friends were exiled. Leonard, Jr., who had studied law with Peter Van Schaack before the war, had more sympathy with that unfortunate neutral than did his cousin; he enclosed Van Schaack's order of banishment in a cheerful letter reminding his mentor that he had been petitioning for an opportunity to go to England for medical attention for some time. Van Schaack, depressed by his many difficulties, took this message amiss, replying reproachfully, "Leonard, you have signed my death warrant, but I appreciate your motives." [3] This prediction was inaccurate, for after six years in England Van Schaack returned to Kinderhook and lived there for the rest of his long life, resuming many old friendships including that with Leonard Gansevoort, Jr.

After the State of New York provided itself with a constitution, its next necessity was to defend itself against invasion and subversion. The Saratoga Campaign, which was going on as the new constitution was put into effect, was managed by the Continental Congress, but after Burgoyne's surrender most of Gates's army went to reinforce Washington's, the New England militia went home, and New York was left to defend itself as best it might against local raids by Tories and Indians. A few Continentals remained in certain strategic locations, among them Peter Gansevoort's regiment at Fort Schuyler, of which post Congress voted him Colonel Commandant in recognition of his victory. Peter was not entirely satisfied with this reward; as he wrote to his congressmen, William Duer and Gouverneur Morris:

114

Congress has done me the honor of appointing me Colonel Comman- dant of Fort Schuyler. I should esteem it a favor if you would inform me whether I am to receive any pay for that commission, other than as Colonel of the Third regiment of New Yorkers; and if not, I should be glad if you would endeavor to get something allowed me, as my present pay will not reimburse my table liquors, which you may well conceive to be something as a commanding officer. I am not solicitous to make money on my commission; but I could wish not to sink by it as I am obliged to do now. The commission which congress has sent me as commandant of Fort Schuyler subjects me as much to the command of my superior officers as my former one. If that was the intention of Congress, the appointment is nugatory. If not, I wish Congress to alter the commission.[4]

Peter's letter conveys a Dutch mercantile attitude that in or- der to be real a reward had to have material value, and a patri- cian conception of the social responsibilities of a commanding officer. For his disappointment there was nevertheless some justi- fication, for in European military tradition the title of Colonel Commandant of certain forts carried with it special honor and perquisites, while in America, where there was no military tradi- tion, such titles carried no particular prestige and in fact the glory which Peter had fairly earned was quickly overshadowed by the inflated reputations of General Herkimer and Lieutenant- Colonel Willett. Both Herkimer and Willett were good officers and fought bravely, but it is often forgotten that Herkimer's Bat- tle of Oriskany began as a mistake and ended in a rout, and that Willett's sortie was a minor part of the defense, most of which took place after he left the fort to seek reinforcements. Herkimer's heroic death captured the imagination of his neighbors, many of whom had also been bereaved by the battle or were to become so by the raids of the next two years. Schuyler further suggested that Arnold publicize Oriskany as a victory to encourage the re- maining militia to fight again; the misconception that the militia drove away St. Leger has persisted ever since. After the war, Wil- lett returned to New York City politics and made as much politi- cal capital as he could out of his own exploits. It is likely that only Arnold's subsequent treason prevented the growth of a similar legend that it was he who stopped St. Leger single-handedly. Undeniably the fort would have been lost without the assistance of all three, but it is equally certain that it would have been lost without Peter Gansevoort, who put it in repair, organized its defenders, repelled its attackers, and stubbornly, silently refused to surrender it. He deserves to be more widely known by the sobriquet which attached to him in Albany, "The Hero of Fort Stanwix."

The winter after the siege of Fort Stanwix was a quiet period in the war in New York, though Washington's army enduring it at Valley Forge found it anything but quiet. Peter spent the winter in Albany honeymooning with Caty, to whom he was married on January 12, 1778, but late in May he returned to his post for a tense summer marked only by the sudden snap of concealed rifles or bowstrings and the sudden howls of scalpers. The endless waiting poised to receive a sneak attack that did not come was even more wearing than open warfare. But the Tories and Indians, who in 1778 descended on the Mohawk Valley in earnest although there were no British troops to support them, bypassed Fort Stanwix to fall upon isolated settlements and undefended clearings. This was a war for the militia, who had to and did fight it out by themselves; there was nothing the garrison could do to help them except to hold the fort and receive any refugees who succeeded in fleeing there.

In the meantime, Peter's messengers passed safely up and down the valley, keeping open his communications with Albany and, most important to him, with Caty. She, like many other Albanians, was terrified by the possibility of Indian attack. When Peter relayed a rumor of another invasion like St. Leger's to her early in July, Caty expected an immediate interruption of their correspondence, and was so agitated that she signed her letter with her maiden name. But even as she was writing, Peter sent word that the Indians were going to the Susquehanna Valley and were unlikely to besiege Fort Stanwix, which proved true. Some word of the Wyoming Massacre, which these Indians perpetrated, may have reached Caty by the time she wrote Peter again:

116

Luke Casada begs me every time when he comes, to write you that you must not come without him, he will guard you safe to me. I hope the enemy may have their fil[l] of inhumanity burning destroying and murdering the poor and inosent whose blood i doubt not but will seal the destruction of them.[5]

For the rest of the summer, Peter lived quietly at Fort Stanwix, fishing and sending Caty salmon for herself and all the rest of the family. In August he wrote her that he had recaptured and court-martialed nearly thirty deserters, but that the commanding officer of the department would not approve the sentences, so they could not be shot. Finally, after keeping them in prison for some time, he executed five of them on his own authority, and considered it a good riddance and a good example. Caty thought one would have been a sufficient example, but recognized that it was not fair to shoot one and let four others caught with him go free; still, she observed, "they are the first in your regiment punished with death may they be the last." [6]

That fall Peter's regiment was removed from the scene of its victory and replaced by the regiment of Caty's cousin Colonel Goose Van Schaick. After being stationed at Schenectady and Saratoga for the winter, Peter's regiment was ordered in the spring of 1779 to join in the Clinton-Sullivan expedition to punish the Iroquois who had devastated the Mohawk Valley as far east as Cherry Valley. General James Clinton's portion of the expedition proceeded up the Mohawk to Canajoharie, portaged south to the head of Otsego Lake, and rowed to the foot of the lake, the present site of Cooperstown. Finding the Susquehanna River too shallow for their boats, they dammed the outlet of the lake to back up the water and then, when all their boats were ready, cut the dam and floated downstream on the crest of the flood. After journeying down the Susquehanna to Tioga Point, where the Chemung River enters from the west, on August 22 they met General John Sullivan and his army, who had come from Pennsylvania and had just destroyed the Indian town of Chemung. The combined force immediately moved against the Indians, defeated them in the battle of Newtown on August 29, and spent the following three weeks marching through the Iroquois country

117

around the Finger Lakes, destroying villages and devastating crops, meeting no further organized resistance although individual soldiers were captured and tortured.

Unlike many other officers in this expedition, Peter did not keep a diary, and since they were far beyond the reach of postal or courier service he wrote no letters, so his particular role in the campaign remains unrecorded. On September 20, however, when the army had finished its mission and returned as far as Konadaseya, Sullivan detached Peter with a party of one hundred men to return to Albany by way of the "lower Mohawk Castle" at Fort Hunter, to seize the few Indians living there, to collect the army's baggage at Albany, and to take the Indians and the baggage to rejoin Washington's army on the lower Hudson. Peter obeyed these orders, but when he reached Albany he encountered serious criticism for taking the Indians into custody. The common council, which still claimed this tract of the Indians' land in the event that they should wish to leave it, defended their right to stay there as long as they chose. General Schuyler pointed out that Sullivan had been mistaken in thinking the Indians hostile, and informed Washington that they were in fact friendly. Eventually Washington overruled Sullivan's order, but by that time the Indians were scattered and the common council had provided for the division and sale of the land.

In the meantime Peter, who was suffering from a recurrence of the disease he had contracted on his first campaign, collapsed at home and did not rejoin the army all winter. By the spring of 1780 he had recovered and joined Washington's army. In July, when his regiment was stationed at West Point, Caty and their ten-month-old son Herman came down for a visit, as did many other officers' wives. "Bring a bed and Tea cups and saucers, plates, knives, forks, etc. . . . also my glass decanters,"[7] wrote Peter as she prepared to leave home. After this sociable interlude ended and Caty returned to Albany, Peter was placed in command of the York Brigade, an assignment he considered "not only Honorable but advantageous." His headquarters was Orange Town, of which he wrote: "This is as pleasant a Country as ever I was in in my life. We are encircled by old acquaintances from

New York and the inhabitants are all Dutch people from whom I can git every think by speaking Dutch to them." [8] In the fall he applied to be stationed near Albany and was assigned to command at Fort Saratoga, where he remained until January 1, 1781, when his rank was eliminated in a general reorganization of the army. His men, with whom he had always been popular, were sorry to see him go; under their new commanders they carried the regimental flag to Yorktown. Peter accepted the rank of brigadier general in the militia, succeeding General Abraham Ten Broeck.

When the war was over, all three of the Gansevoorts turned their principal attention to restoring the family fortune. Leonard's profession was the law, but he gave up his practice first for politics and then to carry on the family mercantile tradition. During the war he engaged in a speculation in merchandise with a cousin, John de Wandelaer, and joined his brother-in-law Jacob Cuyler, Deputy Commissary General of Purchase for the Northern Army, in a partnership to provide beef and flour for the troops near Albany. He invested in Continental securities and in houses and lots around Albany, apparently not confiscated Tory property, which he rented for specie—his faith in Continental currency evidently having its limits. As soon as the Revolution was over, Leonard and Jacob Cuyler started a store. As a Yankee visitor observed when the news of the Peace of Paris arrived:

No place on this continent which is so far from the enemy is so immediately affected as this, shut out from any seaport trade, this dependence entirely stagnated and the most affluent families reduced to poverty.[9]

The whole upper Hudson Valley was starved for manufactured goods when Cuyler and Gansevoort's store opened its doors in the summer of 1783 "at the house of Leonard Gansevoort, between the Dutch and English churches." [10] It offered, "Wholesale Only," an assortment including:

Teneriffe wine, Madeira wine, Bordeaux Claret, Jamaica Spirits, Holland Geneva, Rock Salt, Bar iron, Shear molds, German Steel, French and Holland Window Glass, Bristol grindstones, Bath coatings and Broadcloths fine and coarse, and other Dry Goods.[11]

119

The variety of commodities accepted in exchange is suggested by another advertisement which informed enterprising storekeepers that Cuyler, Gansevoort & Co. had

just received in the last vessels from London, an Assortment of Dry Goods, suitable to the [winter] season, which they will Sell by wholesale, for Cash, Country Produce, Public Securities, or Credit on good Security.[12]

In the fall of 1783, the partners became involved in an affair which eventually brought the firm to disaster. A brig from Europe, the *Maria Teresia,* belonging to a Dutch merchant named Jan Bronkhorst who traded from Croisie in France, came to grief in the Hudson River. Bronkhorst had a brother Jacob in New York, who was a friend of a friend of Cuyler and Gansevoort. When this mutual friend directed Skipper Roos of the crippled vessel to Cuyler and Gansevoort for refitting, the firm accepted the charge, had the vessel put back into shape at considerable cost, and sent it off for home. Jacob Bronkhorst was effusively grateful, but referred them for reimbursement to the head of the firm, his brother in France, upon which Cuyler and Gansevoort drew a bill on him for the amount they had spent and used it to pay one of their accounts. But the *Maria Teresia* never reached port; they learned afterwards that she had been captured by a British cruiser. Jan Bronkhorst had given her up and collected his insurance after the Hudson River disaster, and now refused to pay Cuyler and Gansevoort's bill. When Cuyler and Gansevoort sued him, Bronkhorst fled behind the protection of French law and the money was a total loss.

In the meantime, Cuyler and Gansevoort were caught in the general credit squeeze of the mid-1780's, as Americans discovered what it meant to do business without the support of the developed banking facilities and stable currency of England. A New York firm named Brothers Coster, who imported goods from the Netherlands, had been pressing them for payments since February, 1784. Cuyler and Gansevoort had used their bill on Bronkhorst for one such payment, but when Bronkhorst defaulted, Brothers Coster demanded that Cuyler and Gansevoort make

120

good the loss. The partners called in their debts, but the retailers were unable to pay, giving as their reason over and over again the scarcity of money for their customers to pay the debts due to them. So Cuyler and Gansevoort were unable to pay Brothers Coster, who thereupon sued them. Since their French suit had come to nothing, the partners expected to lose heavily, but Cuyler reported with evident relief when the suit was finally settled in March, 1788, that they did not have to pay a capital sum and might have suffered more. Nevertheless, the firm of Cuyler and Gansevoort quietly dissolved about this time. After his separation from Leonard, Jacob Cuyler continued as a merchant on his own account, but his credit collapsed with a resounding crash in 1790, when his houses and lots, his wagons, carriage and sleighs, his slaves and his livestock and his household furniture all were advertised for auction by Sheriff Peter Gansevoort.

Leonard, on the other hand, formed a new partnership with Stephen Van Rensselaer and his brother Philip. This enterprise was very different from Cuyler and Gansevoort. It imported its goods directly from England instead of dealing with American importers such as the Brothers Coster; there is no indication of any connection with Holland, and it sold largely by retail. The store, like the previous one, stocked everything—fabrics and ribbons, scissors and ironwork, wines and teas and notions. It accepted in payment pot and pearl ashes, then in their heyday as a medium of exchange, flax seed, peas, wheat, hides, and a single entry of furs, fifty-two marten skins. But the store was not the only iron Leonard had in the fire. He and Thomas L. Witbeck built a gristmill on a stream in Rensselaerswyck north of the city, which was completed in the summer of 1788. When it was done, a neighboring blacksmith wanted to use some of the excess waterpower from the millrace; Abraham Reynolds, the astute Quaker mill manager, related the advantages of the proposal, including that of having the mill's iron work repaired free, but added that they could put another mill there themselves "if Linnen manufactory should come to anything, also a paint mill." [13] An "Oyl Mill" for the production of paint soon entered their accounts, followed by an ice house in the fall of 1789.

121

While Leonard was carrying on the Gansevoort mercantile tradition in Albany, Peter was developing a lumber business at Snock Kill Falls near Saratoga. The Snock Kill is the first tributary to enter the Hudson from the west after the river leaves the Adirondacks at Glens Falls. It rises in a considerable range of hills which extend from Saratoga Springs to Ticonderoga, including Mt. McGregor and the mountains surrounding Lake George, and descends well over a thousand feet. At the point where it descends from the sand plain covering much of eastern Saratoga County through the clay bluffs which form the banks of the Hudson, it races down fifty or sixty feet of rapids in less than a mile; the force of the water has cut the falls over three miles upstream, leaving a gorge through which the stream rushes even in the summer and floods wildly every spring. This beautiful, useful, and dangerous stream was first exploited by a pioneer named Hugh Munro, who built a sawmill at the falls about 1770. His operations were interrupted by the Revolution, during which he fled to Canada and his land was confiscated by the Commissioners of Forfeitures. Peter bought it in 1783, having supposedly discovered the remains of Munro's mill and perceived the potentialities of the falls while he was commanding at Fort Saratoga (now Schuylerville) in 1780. He also had before him the example of his commander and friend, General Schuyler, who even before the Revolution had begun to develop the resources of Fish Creek, the next tributary downstream.

There were a few other settlers in the area, mostly on farms down by the river, when Peter came to Snock Kill in the spring of 1784, but his 1,500-acre tract on both sides of the falls was untouched wilderness. Its sandy loam supported a forest of white pine and hemlock, then the most valuable kinds of lumber. Like other exploiters of wild lands, Peter set up a saw in a rude frame next to the falls and put men to work chopping trees, sawing planks, and building a mill to house the machinery. A month later he began to record sales of board and plank in his personal daybook. He and his men lived in log huts near the mill. In 1787 he built himself a square two-story frame house, the "old yellow house" which, despite many alterations, still stands beneath its original elms at the head of Snock Kill Falls. That same summer he sent for millwrights from New Jersey to build a new sawmill, and the next year he made an agreement with Arie Lagrange of Albany to market his lumber. This arrangement may have been made necessary by the dissolution of Cuyler and Gansevoort; that Leonard sold some of Peter's lumber could be indicated by a complaint from an Albany neighbor that his view of the river was obstructed by lumber piled on Leonard's wharf.

By 1785 Peter's workers formed a community large enough to warrant the establishment of a general store by the firm of Gansevoort and Fondey. Which Gansevoort was the senior partner is not recorded, but the most likely candidate would be Dr. Pieter's eldest son Conrad, who at twenty-four was of an age to go into business for himself. In addition to this store, Peter set up a grist mill in 1788 and two years later another sawmill. He also cleared the brush and scrub from the land around his mill, grubbed up the stumps, and enclosed fields to form a farm of nearly two hundred acres which grew food for the millhands and fodder for the horses. But Peter always hired men to work this farm for him or leased it to tenants on shares; he himself had no experience as a farmer and did not try to become one. Instead, by 1790 he evidently felt that the mills themselves were a going concern which might safely be left in the hands of others. He accepted the office of Sheriff of Albany County, and sixty years later, old men remembered that he "moved back to Albany" and thenceforth returned only at the peak seasons of high water, when the mills worked night and day, and rafting, when the year's accumulation of boards, planks, and timbers was floated down the Hudson to market.

While Peter was developing his sawmill, Leonard returned to public affairs. After the war ended Philip Schuyler began to repeat the type of political activity with which he had begun his career by organizing opposition to Governor Clinton. In 1785 Schuyler drew together a patrician group in Albany County, including Stephen Van Rensselaer, Abraham Ten Broeck, and Leonard Gansevoort, which succeeded in electing its candidates to the assembly. The following spring Leonard and Van Rensselaer acted as campaign managers for this faction, which now extended beyond Albany County. Early in March, Schuyler asked his supporters in Albany to investigate some transactions of Peter W. Yates which were open to suspicion. Evidence must have been readily available, for only a week later John Tayler, another assemblyman, wrote to Leonard to thank him for helping to prove Yates's bad character. (Peter W. Yates must have been habitually maladroit, for in 1775 he was expelled from the Committee of Safety for writing an anti-Schuyler broadside, and in 1793 from one of Albany's Masonic lodges for revealing the secrets of the order.) Leonard's assembly mailbag also included letters from his distant cousin Leonard Bronk, representative from Coxsackie, who communicated personal news such as an explanation of why Leonard Gansevoort had been passed over for his party's nomination for the senate, and, much more eagerly, details of conviviality and excursions to the theater among their friends in a legislative boarding house.

Local leaders all over the upper Hudson Valley wrote to ask Leonard's backing and sometimes for more active help. Thomas Sickels of Walloomsac asked Leonard's support for his assembly candidacy, but a month later complained that the voters seemed to be confused about what office he was running for. The Van Schaacks were back from exile and busy in Kinderhook affairs; David Van Schaack sent in one report on conditions there which prompted Leonard and Van Rensselaer to visit the town within the week. The mayor of the burgeoning Yankee town of Hudson, founded only in 1783, sent in for approval the name of a candidate to replace a man who had been disqualified. But in spite of all this active management, Schuyler's party scored only a partial victory. The Yates party retaliated by seizing control of the administration of Albany; in the fall of 1786 the Council of Appointment replaced Leonard's uncle, Mayor John Beekman, by John Lansing, Jr., although Leonard himself retained his position as recorder until 1789, when he was supplanted by Peter W. Yates. In the meantime, the assembly elected Leonard a delegate to the Annapolis Convention, which he did not attend, perhaps because of his own commercial difficulties, and in 1788 elected him along with three other Federalists and two Anti-Federalists to the Continental Congress.

The continuing tension in Albany between Schuyler's faction and Yates's party came to a head over the ratification of the Federal Constitution. The Gansevoorts were eager supporters of this new form of government; Leonard, Jr., wrote to Leonard in January, 1788, "I believe that if the Legislature do not order a Convention that we will have one without their interference" [14] and encouraged informal campaigning at "Several Dinners since your Departure some altogether Federal others with a little alloy." [15] The assembly, which was hostile to the Constitution and hesitated to place it before the voters, finally gave its consent to the calling of a convention on February 1, but even then another month passed before there was much action in Albany. On March 3, two letters appeared in the *Federal Herald,* one nominating thirteen relatively obscure Anti-Federalists for Albany County's seven Convention seats and the other, signed by "Mercator," presenting seven leading Federalists and castigating the opposition as "demogogues." On March 8 there appeared in the *Albany Journal* another Anti-Federalist slate, this one containing the names of leaders of the party.

On March 14 the Albany Federal Committee at last selected their candidates, naming Peter Gansevoort and Jacob Cuyler among their seven delegates for the Convention and Leonard Gansevoort one of seven candidates for the assembly. The next day the Anti-Federalists chose their slate. All of these nominations appeared in the *Journal* for March 17, the latter list over a manifesto which Leonard, Jr., forwarded to Leonard with the comment:

Whigs and Torys during the Revolution were hardly more inveterate against each other than the present Partys are. . . . I enclose yesterday's Journal. It contains a piece which wounds deep. I have not yet seen our Friend Cuyler but imagine he must feel exceedingly hurt.[16]

The criticisms leveled at the Federalist nominees were indeed personal. The Anti-Federalists proclaimed that they had excluded from nomination (among others)

125

Every person suspected of being interested in the establishment of a constitution, which holds out an impunity for peculation, and a total oblivion for all sins of that nature—persuaded that the same disposition which first prompted an appropriation of the moneys entrusted to him, under the sacred function of an official oath, would endure a further sacrifice of the dearest rights of mankind, to secure his ill-gotten wealth. . . .

Every person who long conversant with military life, has imbibed an opinion and not hesitated to declare that the Will of One is much preferable to the *Liberty of All.*[17]

The accusation of peculation thus leveled at Jacob Cuyler referred to his conduct as Deputy Commissary General of Purchase; the attack upon the Hero of Fort Stanwix is by comparison mild. Both were similar to charges leveled at their opponents by Anti-Federalists in Dutchess County and elsewhere, and their rhetoric evidently reflected deep-seated prejudices of the electorate to which the Anti-Federalists wished to appeal.

Despite this assault on his dignity, a week later Jacob Cuyler believed the situation of Cuyler and Gansevoort to be more precarious than that of the Constitution—this was just before the decision in the Coster suit. Leonard, Jr., also took time off from politics to send his cousin a crackling "I-told-you-so" about an indiscretion involving the congressman with a lady. But at the end of March spectacular events in the campaign reduced such personal matters to their proper proportions. Leonard, Jr., reported a tricky bit of manipulation by the "minority" which resulted in the selection of Anti-Federalist election inspectors. Even more exciting was Yates's action in suing George Metcalf, editor of the *Federal Herald,* for libel in connection with an attack which appeared in his paper. As Leonard, Jr., was writing this story to Leonard,

Just now under my office window the Mayor [Anti-Federalist John Lansing, Jr., once Leonard's law partner] and the Sheriff [Leonard's brother-in-law John Ten Broeck] have had a sparring about those Bails, Mr. Lansing insisting upon knowing the names of the Bail taken by the Sheriff in those Suits and the Sheriff as positively refusing to gratify him in this instance. They were both very passionate and after exchanging Several warm Expressions they parted.[18]

On April 5, Jacob Cuyler, though still concerned about the reluctance to pay evinced by the firm's debtors, was considering how these obligations could be used to press those who owed them to vote for the Constitution. He was much less hopeful than two weeks before, but thought that time was in the Federalists' favor. In the meantime, Leonard inquired of Stephen Van Rensselaer whether he should come home to help campaign or stay in the Continental Congress to guard against moves by Abraham Yates "who is not wanted here at all," [19] dispatched some copies of the *Publius* letters, and announced some appointments in order to prompt the appointees to more vigorous campaigning. After all this labor, when the ballots were counted the city stayed with the Federalists, but the country districts deserted the perilous balance of 1786–87 and voted the whole upper Hudson Valley overwhelmingly into the Anti-Federalist camp.

Their defeat in this election meant that the Gansevoorts and the Albany Federalists had no voice on the floor of the Poughkeepsie Convention, but this was very far from meaning that they had no voice there at all. Schuyler's son-in-law, Alexander Hamilton, in any event the party's leading spokesman, was a delegate from New York City, and when the convention opened Schuyler, Leonard Gansevoort, and other Albany leaders were there as observers even though they could not vote. The Anti-Federalist Albany delegation, which included Abraham Yates, was alarmed with good reason by their appearance, for they knew perfectly well that these Federalists intended if they could to reverse the results of the election by the exertion of family and commercial influence. Their persuasion, exerted on doubtful delegates formerly attached to them at one time or another by a wide range of political favors, commercial accommodations, and family relationships reaching back for years and even for generations, could touch on strings far beyond the reach of the plebeians, backed by the immediate opinion of crowds of voters which men of long-range experience often believed to be fickle and untrustworthy. This silent pressure exerted by these Albany Dutchmen, as much a part of the political tradition of New York State as it had been of that of New York Province, must surely be counted among the

127

forces which eventually brought some Anti-Federalist delegates to accept the Constitution. The Albany County delegates knew it too well to give in; two of them from country districts probably left before the decisive ballot, but Abraham and Robert Yates and John Lansing, Jr., remained to vote "Nay" to the very end.

In the meantime, tension remained high at Albany. Rival attempts by Federalists and Anti-Federalists to celebrate the Fourth of July with a parade resulted instead in a riot which claimed one life and left eighteen injured. Riots had become a conspicuous feature of Albany politics in the score of years since the Stamp Act riot, but despite their superficial similarity with the plebeian riots of medieval Flemish cities, these were specifically political in origin and were probably first introduced by the Yates party in imitation of revolutionary tactics developed in New York City. But when the Convention at last accepted the Constitution, the long-frustrated Federalists prepared a grand procession and banquet which took place on August 8.

From its order of march, the parade appears to have included almost all of the male inhabitants of the city. First came the Albany troop of light horse, in full uniform, with Captain Leonard Gansevoort at their head. Then, after a band of music, appeared the Constitution, "neatly engrossed on parchment, suspended on a decorated staff, and borne by Major-General Schuyler on horseback." [20] Next came the United States standard, carried by Colonel John A. Wendell, and the eleven states, represented by "eleven ancient citizens." These symbols of the Federal Union were followed by all the trades of the city and its hinterland, agriculture, artisans, accompanied by their apprentices and carrying the tools of their trade, merchants with their clerks, "preceded by Mr. Jacob Cuyler, carrying a white flag, in an escutcheon, one ship inward and another outward bound—supported by two sheaves of wheat, Motto, *May our exports exceed our imports*," and at the end the professions, including the schoolmasters with their scholars. The whole procession wound through the city to the top of the hill, where a pavilion had been erected for a great banquet, followed, as was customary on occasions of public rejoicing in Albany, by more than a sufficiency of toasts.

128

Thus the Albany Dutch patricians and plebeians together used their Dutch tradition to help transform a portion of the British Empire into the Empire State. By 1788 the Schuylers and Van Rensselaers had accepted the Gansevoorts, (patriot) Cuylers, and Ten Eycks without reservation as patricians like themselves; the distinction between old and new patricians came to mean as little as that between Anti-Leislerian and Leislerian fur traders after about 1710. They worked together as equals in politics and business affairs, regarded each other as close friends, and permitted their children to intermarry freely. But they all regarded the Yates, Lansings, and their associates as plebeians, although the Albany Dutch leaders of this group undeniably exercised patrician power in civic affairs and behaved accordingly, intermarrying with each other and pursuing the well-trodden paths of local ambition. The fundamental difference was that these newest patricians had attained their position by political activity in the American sense rather than by the acquisition of wealth in commerce. Dutch patricians and English gentry alike distinguished between statesmanlike service to the community, which they considered a responsibility of the wealthy and well-born, and politics, which they regarded as a disagreeable and somewhat dirty necessity. Factional and party activity, though sometimes unavoidable, was beneath their dignity, and the career of a professional politician unthinkably below them. The old and new patricians had furthermore had many commercial interests in common, and only political ambitions divided them; in the Revolutionary period the newest patricians had nothing in common with their predecessors except political opposition to De Lanceyites and Tories. Furthermore, their exploitation of the growth of the non-Dutch rural population of Albany County to attack the city's domination of the assembly delegation, however much justified from the point of view of the rural voters, was to the Albany patricians but one more instance of civic treason by burghers seeking outside help to gain power in the city itself.

These local conflicts, which in minds conditioned in the Dutch communal tradition loomed far larger than state or national considerations, help to explain the perplexing attitude of

129

Abraham Yates, who became a perpetual obstructionist in both the assembly and the Continental Congress. All his life Yates remained a plebeian, who compelled the patricians to recognize his political power, but was quite right in expecting that they would use their continuing influence, exerted by the silent, taken-for-granted communication of men who have worked together in many varied ventures over long years, to fight his temporarily devastating but fragile control of the electorate. For a generation he had won, claimed to win, or seemed certain to win election after election—the third ward election of 1773, the election to ratify the state constitution he unsuccessfully desired in 1777, the ratification election of 1788—only to see his opponents, who somehow always included his old local antagonists, the Gansevoorts, snatch his victories from under his nose and achieve their own purposes in spite of the expressed wishes of that people. It is no wonder that Abraham Yates came to believe that any statement which disagreed with his views on liberty was some form of covert attack, or that he defended himself under these circumstances with the same particularistic obstinacy that was the traditional defense of communal liberty in Dutch towns. His history of the ratification of the Constitution in New York seems absurdly conspiratorial when read as we now read the history of that period, looking down from the state and national level; looking up from the viewpoint of an Albany Dutch plebeian, who had seen the question decided by the patricians in defiance of the expressed mandate of the people, however, Yates's attitude is at least understandable if regrettably narrow minded.

Leonard Gansevoort's viewpoint was broader than Yates's, but still unshakably communal and particularistic. He would have readily agreed that the struggle for the Constitution was a matter of detecting and defeating conspiracies, and would have pointed out that well before that 1773 election Abraham Yates—to say nothing of the untrustworthy Peter W. Yates—had been proving himself a subtle and dangerous conspirator. The leader who had turned from what Leonard would have considered a fair and merited defeat in the third ward to organizing the secret Committee of Correspondence which probably introduced mob politics into

Albany might well be expected to start another such revolution after any defeat, and therefore, Leonard would have said, could not himself be trusted to abide by the results of the elections in which he ostensibly placed his faith. Leonard, in the meantime, was serving his community by engaging in trade, learning the real needs of the town by active participation in the commerce which was its reason for existence, and standing to suffer in his own fortune and that of his family if the public measures he advocated were not in the long run for the benefit of the city. Furthermore, coming of a family with a tradition of public service and connected by marriage with others like it, he had grown up in an atmosphere from which he could learn all the unwritten and even unspoken rules by which the city was governed in an era when local government was not a science with explicit laws but a highly traditional art. He had doubtless chosen his profession—and changed it, when Peter turned out to be a soldier rather than a merchant, and Leonard, Jr., grew up to be a cleverer lawyer than he—with reference to the advantage of the community as part and parcel of his own. He could bring Peter's particular talents, military reputation, and wide experience into civic affairs when they were needed there, and the rest of the time know that Peter was busy making his own fortune. All in all, Leonard could hardly have helped thinking that he and his family had a far better basis on which to decide what was good for the notoriously fickle Albany voters—whose votes he himself had helped to sway with promises and beer—than his old third ward antagonist, Abraham Yates. In all of this, he was a typical product of the Albany Dutch patrician tradition.

Philip Schuyler blended the Albany Dutch tradition with the eighteenth-century English tradition and made the combination tell on the state level. He and his Dutch—and some non-Dutch—supporters built in Albany a tough, enduring party based on the New York Anglo-Dutch tradition of control of patronage by continuing families with wealth at their disposal, and won with it the unshakable support of the city voters, who continued to vote quite happily as their betters suggested to them.

Meanwhile Yates's party looked for its backing particularly to the non-Dutch farmers in the county, appealing to them with the issues to which they were responsive, accepting the support of the disgruntled tenants on the manors when it could be had, and affiliating easily with other local Hudson Valley parties organized around agrarian issues. In the 1780's and 1790's the agricultural areas in Albany County were one by one set off as separate counties, until Albany County included only the city and the West District of Rensselaerswyck, and Albany City lost its administrative domination over the entire upper Hudson Valley. Nevertheless, the two parties, agglomerations of local factions, conflicting across county lines, their basic difference in tactics remaining although each borrowed and learned techniques from the other, continued into the party battles of the nineteenth century.

As a leader of his party Philip Schuyler, like his great-uncle, Pieter Schuyler, proved to have exceptional statesmanlike insight. He was able to see the relationship between the Dutch tradition of independent mercantile communities and the British tradition of a mercantile empire, and to perceive that in America, where no single economic or social tradition predominated, the best hope for the maintenance of a diversity of traditions lay in a strong central government. Showing English influence from early in his career by his willingness to act and become prominent as an individual rather than a member of a family group, he certainly learned much from the imperial ambitions of Alexander Hamilton. But he was also able to translate Hamilton's conceptions into the familiar political idiom of the particularistic Hudson Valley Dutch—such as Albany patricians who came to recognize that it was very difficult if not impossible for their community to carry on its own business without the support of centralized credit and communications facilities, which neither localities nor states could provide for themselves, and without continental supervision over interference with trade by other states and localities similar to that which the British Empire had provided. Perhaps they even saw in the future an Empire State which extended mercantile domination over its neighbors as the British Empire had dominated the colonies.

1. Albany Dutch Reformed Church, 1715–1806. Engraved after a drawing by Philip Hooker (1766–1836).

2. East side of Market Street (now Broadway), ca. 1805. Harmen Harmense's house is first from left; the house second from left was also purchased by him and formed part of the home lot. Watercolor by James Eights (1798–1882).

3 and 4. Leendert and Catarina Gansevoort. Painted by an anonymous limner, ca. 1720–30.

5. Tankard, bearing monogram of Leendert and Catarina Gansevoort on the lid. Made by Peter Quintard (1699–1762).   6. Funeral spoon presented to General Peter Gansevoort in memory of his mother, Magdalena, who died Oct. 12, 1796. Made by Isaac Hutton.   7. Gansevoort coat-of-arms from the front of the tankard.   8. Teapot owned by Dr. Pieter Gansevoort. Made by his brother-in-law Barent Ten Eyck (1714–92).

9. General Peter Gansevoort, ca. 1794. By Gilbert Stuart.

10. Catherine Van Schaick Gansevoort. B Ezra Ames (1768–1836).

11. Fort Stanwix. Photograph of model, 1897.

12. Leonard Gansevoort. Probably by Gilbert Stuart.

13. Andirons used by Leonard Gansevoort at Whitehall.

14. Maria Gansevoort in 1814.
Miniature by Anson Dickinson.

15. L. H. and Mary Ann Gansevoort. Miniatures by an unknown artist.

16. Herman Gansevoort's mansion at Gansevoort, N.Y. Built in 1813.

"The old yellow house," neral Peter Gansevoort's ginal home at Gansevoort. ilt in 1787 and frequently ered since; the white paint d the porch are certainly er additions.

18. Reformed Church of Gansevoort. Built by Herman Gansevoort, ca. 1841.

19. Parlor at 115, showing portraits of Susan and Peter Gansevoort over the fire place.

20. 115 Washington Avenue at right, home of Peter Gansevoort.

21. State Capitol, 1806–83. Designed by Philip Hooker.

22. Albany Academy, of which Peter Gansevoort was for fifty years a trustee.

23. Family party on the garden (rear) steps of 115, ca. 1867. Seated on steps: Kate Gansevoort and Anna Lansing; seated on top step: Peter and Susan Gansevoort, Sarah Lansing; standing: Abe Lansing.

24. Colonel Henry Gansevoort (seated second from left) and some of his officers, 1864.

25. Abe Lansing in his library at 115 Washington Avenue.

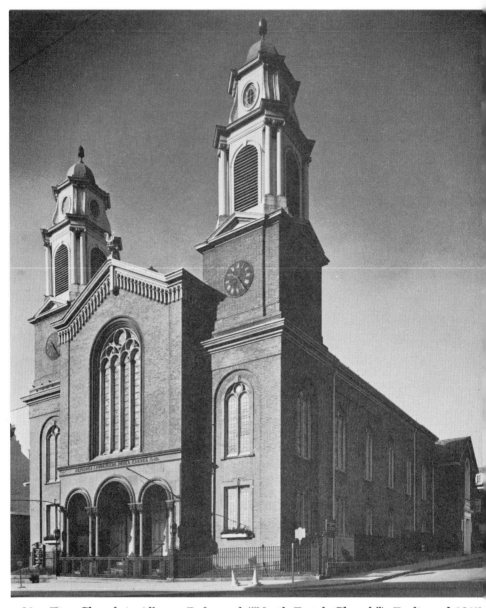

26. First Church in Albany, Reformed ("North Dutch Church"). Dedicated 1815.

27.   Albany City Hall; Pruyn memorial carillon in the tower. Designed by H. H. Richardson, 1883.

28. Stanwix Hall (1833–1932) as remodeled in 1876 (dome replaced by two upper stories in front).

29. Dedication of General Peter Gansevoort statue, Rome, N.Y., 1907.

30. Sites in Albany Associated with the Gansevoorts, ca. 1850: 1. Albany Academy (off picture); 2. Broadway; 3. Capitol; 4. City Hall (1832–80); 5. Clinton Square—Peter Gansevoort home (1833–38); 6. Delavan House, site of Gen. Gansevoort Mansion (1800–33); 7. site of Dutch Reformed Church (1656–1806); 8. Dutch Reformed Church; 9. Gansevoort home lot (1677–1800); 10. Maiden Lane; 11. St. Peter's Episcopal Church; 12. site of Stad Huys one block south; 13. Stanwix Hall; 14. State Street; 15. Washington Avenue—115 two blocks west on north side.

VI

Civic Fathers

The Albany patricians maintained another element of their Dutch tradition when they devoted some of their wealth, power, and prestige to the benefit of the entire community. Patricians in the medieval Netherlands contributed notably to public works, both through the city councils and in the course of their private business affairs. Some promoted such improvements as wharves, canals, bridges, and public buildings which simultaneously increased the profits of those patricians who built them and enlarged the trade and reputation of the city as a whole. Others endowed hospitals, orphanages, schools, and monasteries, and contributed largely to the building of churches. Still others patronized artists, commissioning portraits of themselves and works of art to embellish public buildings, particularly churches, and provided their cathedrals with great organs and also—in a tradition particularly associated with the Netherlands—with carillons whose bells were carefully tuned so that melodies could be played on them, in contrast to the rhythmic permutations of English change-ringing. Descendants of these civic-minded patrician families often left active trade but continued in the cities, living on their incomes from investments in the commerce of others and practicing such professions as law, medicine, or full-time public service in the city government and the States-General. Some of them purchased nearby country estates which they developed, building cottages and dikes and introducing improved farming techniques, with the same unremitting attention to detail, care for

133

profit, and concern for the common welfare that had marked their pursuit of business in the city. But even these patrician gentry remained associated with their cities of origin and with their relatives still in trade in a manner that English commercial families entering county society were quick to disavow.

In all of these respects the Albany patricians followed in the pattern laid down by their Dutch predecessors. The first patrician generation benefited the city primarily by procuring and defending its civic and commercial privileges—often paying for them in the first instance from their private resources and collecting reimbursement from the community later, sometimes much later. Then essential public structures had to be erected; the first was the original blockhouse church, built during the Dutch period, and the next was the town stockade, begun in 1670, to which all the burghers contributed, but, like their ancestors who built the massive walls of Dutch cities, the wealthier traders were expected to contribute more generously. The king's fort, first built in 1676 and rebuilt after 1700, was a project of the governor's rather than the town's, although burghers participated by furnishing supplies and labor. In 1712 the burghers themselves rebuilt and enlarged the Dutch church. The small stone Anglican church was constructed by the governor's order, over the patricians' objections, and they likewise had never had anything to do with the abandoned Lutheran church, which in the eighteenth century was apparently used for occasional meetings of non-Dutch sects. Finally, the common council built the three-story stone Stadt Huys, which lodged the city government in comfort and convenience and completed the Dutch contribution to the public buildings of colonial Albany.

The contributions of the Gansevoorts to these public works are not recorded, beyond the single entry of payment to Leendert in 1722 for beer supplied to men repairing the fort. Harme was the first member of the family to engage in notable civic benefactions, the most notable of which was the "Harme Gansevoort wharf," built about 1767. Before this time the tremendous masses of ice which blocked the river every winter and the overwhelm-

134

ing floods which swept the ice away every spring had deterred the Albanians from trying to construct any permanent waterfront facilities, ships being unloaded by small boats from their anchorages in the river. Finally, in a typically Dutch way of combining public and private enterprise, the city council and the merchants cooperated to build three wharves, of which "Gansevoort's" was one, and placed each under the supervision of a nearby wealthy merchant who was rewarded for his trouble by the privilege of collecting wharfage fees. Earlier in the same decade, while he was still city clerk, Harme acted as the city's agent in procuring a fire engine—its second—from London to supplement the four leather buckets which every citizen was required by ordinance to keep in his house and bring to the bucket brigade when needed; hooks and ladders for the whole community were kept in the Dutch church and later, as the city grew, in other convenient locations in each ward.

The "Harme Gansevoort wharf" and its warehouses descended appropriately to Leonard, who had his home and store a block or so from the family lot, on the north side of State Street between Broadway and Pearl, until his residence there was suddenly terminated in the fall of 1793 by a civic disaster. On the night of Sunday, November 17, fire swept the stables behind Leonard's home and raged on to destroy most of the homes and business establishments in the block and to threaten the houses on Pearl Street. It spread through combustible pine timber, the goods in warehouses, and the hay in stables, in spite of the efforts of the citizens, notably the Episcopal rector, the Reverend Thomas Ellison, who directed the wetting down of the houses on Pearl Street, and the crew of Edward Willet's sloop, who stopped the flames in another direction by chopping down a small frame building, until the driving rain turning to sleet finally checked the blaze early in the morning. Reports differ as to whether Leonard's house, which was built of brick, escaped destruction or not.

This fire was generally suspected to be the work of arsonists. The common council's investigation implicated three slaves belonging to other Albany patricians, two girls who admitted set-

135

ting the blaze and a man named Pomp whom they insisted had persuaded them to do it; one girl testified further that Pomp had in turn been bribed by a Mr. Bissbrown who had a grudge against Leonard Gansevoort. The girls' owners did their best to allay their terror by leaving chastisement to the law, but after their confession it was probably a foregone conclusion that an example must be made of them sufficient to deter any similar attempts in the future. Nevertheless the executions were postponed at the last moment when Pomp made a confession which seemed to exculpate the two girls, much to the disappointment of the crowd gathered on Gallows Hill, approximately the present site of the State Education Building. After further investigation, the girls were hanged on March 14, 1794, and Pomp a month later on April 11. The mysterious Mr. Bissbrown was not further identified, but a romantic tale grew up that the slaves had been prompted to commit the crime by a rejected suitor of Leonard's daughter Magdalena. Leonard and other sufferers from the blaze meanwhile petitioned the assembly for permission to recoup their losses by a lottery. The committee to which this petition was referred reported a bill for that purpose, citing the extraordinary circumstances and the resulting dislocation of commerce in the entire north and west of the state. But then other disaster-stricken communities began to submit similar petitions, which were all referred to the same committee, and after the bill received its second reading on February 6, 1794, no more was heard of it.

After the fire, Leonard and his family moved to the country house near Albany named Whitehall which Leonard had purchased, along with its 1,090 acres of farm land, in 1789. Built in the 1760's by General Bradstreet, Whitehall was used as a Tory hideout during the Revolution and afterward passed into the hands of General Schuyler's son, John Bradstreet Schuyler, from whom Leonard bought it. This estate was far grander than the Gansevoort home on Market Street, and even than Leonard's comfortable town house, but he was not content with it as it was and promptly added two wings to it, each larger than the original building. Thereafter, distinguished guests, who had traveled a mile and a half out of town on the road later known as the Delaware Turnpike before they entered the drive shaded by huge horse-chestnuts, approached an H-shaped mansion with double verandas which presented a frontage of 110 feet and revealed a depth of 70 feet. The hospitable double doors opened into a great hall which filled most of the center section of the first floor. Also on this floor were the grand dining room in one wing and in the other the family dining room, the library and the "dood-kamer," according to Dutch custom reserved for laying out the dead. In the basement was the kitchen; on the second floor were bedrooms and, over the large dining room, a ballroom which opened on the upstairs verandas. The principal rooms were paneled and furnished in mahogany, which formed a fitting background for Leonard's treasures of monogrammed crystal, fine porcelain, and heirloom silver. All of this magnificence was kept in perfect order by trusted and faithful slaves, and was partly supported by cultivation of the surrounding farm. It soon became famous for lavish social functions, some of them political and official entertainments during Leonard's terms as first judge of Albany County (1793–97) and state senator (1799–1803), but many of them prompted by the pleasure in conviviality and in seeing others enjoy themselves which Leonard had showed ever since his youth.

Leonard also carried on the Gansevoort tradition of service to his church. Harmen Harmense had begun it by his faithful support of the Lutheran congregation, but after Leisler's Rebellion his children joined the Dutch Reformed Church, Leendert in 1695. Available records tell nothing of Leendert's or his sons' participation in church affairs except that in 1771 Harme was the member of the consistory who accompanied Domine Westerlo to a convention to resolve the Coetus-Conferentie dispute among all the Dutch Reformed churches in the American colonies. Two years after Domine Westerlo's death in 1790, Leonard in his turn was called upon to serve on the consistory. He was most reluctant to accept, hesitating to become involved in contentions which had arisen between members of the congregation and Domine

137

Bassett, which seemed likely to produce another schism. As he wrote to Leonard, Jr., who had informed him unofficially of his election:

Be assured my Dear Friend that I have more dreaded than wished the Honor conferred upon me by the Consistory of our Church in electing me one of the officers. I feel myself so incompetent to the Arduous Task and the present distracted State of our Church appears to me so alarming that without divine interposition its destruction is inevitable. The concerted measures of some individuals which is so Conspicuous in some of the persons in the present administration I conceive augurs the prediction and from the idea I have of the new Elected Members I have no Reason to Loke for a melioration of Conduct, but may the Lord direct them so to conduct themselves as that all their doings may tend to their own peace of Mind and contribute to the Cause of true piety and the Glory of our heavenly Father, that the good of our Church my be promoted and *they* receive the divine benediction, of *well done thou good and faithful servants.*

In my present Ideas of this business I cannot persuade myself that I ought to accept the appointment for which I think I can offer abundant satisfactory Reasons, but as I shall not be officially informed till I arrive at Home shall reserve myself on the Subject that I may advice [sic] with my Friends and implore direction at the Throne of Grace.[1]

Leonard did, upon consideration, accept the office in question, served conscientiously, and was later remembered as the one of all the Gansevoorts who had contributed most faithfully to the church. A decade later, however, that church did split into the North Dutch Church, which built a substantial new edifice on North Pearl Street, now the First Reformed Church of Albany, and the South Dutch Church, which later became the Second Reformed and still later went out of existence by merging with other congregations. The Gansevoorts and most of the patricians supported the North Dutch Church.

In the meantime, Peter and Caty and their growing family— between 1779 and 1791 they had five sons and a daughter—lived next door to the original Gansevoort home in a two-and-a-half story Dutch house which Leendert had bought in 1734. As

138

Harme turned over more and more of his business to his sons, Peter became responsible for all the buildings crowded onto the home lot, which at this time measured 49½ feet across the front, 177 feet deep and 57½ feet wide at the rear. Along Market Street —now Broadway—were the old house and Peter's house; on the back of the lot, along the river, were the brewery, a stable, and a "chair" (coach) house. The brewery continued to operate, although Johannes Gansevoort died in 1781 and his son Leonard jr. apparently sold it to Peter. Peter himself kept the brewery books, bought supplies, and sold the beer for a year or so after his uncle died, but as soon as he began his enterprises at Snock Kill Falls he turned over these functions as well as the actual brewing to a series of partners. In the meantime, the neighborhood became entirely commercial. In 1799, after Harme deeded his property to his children in anticipation of his will—he lived until 1801—Peter bought another lot two blocks farther north on Market Street and built a three-story Federal mansion similar to those of other patrician families. Then he remodeled the two houses on the home lot and rented them as stores, and in 1807 demolished the brewery to make way for a livery stable.

Like most of the Albany patricians, the Gansevoorts used slaves for domestic service. In the 1790's Peter was paying for shoes for six or seven different Negroes at a time. One was Caty's faithful maid, Chris, who remained with her all her life and was remembered in her will. Others probably cared for or belonged to the children; in accordance with a Hudson Valley Dutch custom, Harme gave a boy named Claus to his namesake grandson, Herman, some time before he confirmed the gift by a bequest. After the children grew up Peter's establishment usually included a Negro man and woman. But Peter had a number of difficulties with slaves in the early 1800's. One died not long after she was purchased, another did not fit into the family so that Peter was glad to sell him, and still another was so unhappy that he was sold at his own request. Finally there was the tragic case of Prince, for whom Peter paid Thomas G. Whitbeck $250 in 1809. Prince had what was later described as "a ferocious appearance" and apparently developed a vicious temperament. After being

139

sent on two or three voyages as a common sailor, he had to be confined in the New York "Bridewell" for five months. It is not clear whether the reason was crime or insanity, but the Manumission Society interested itself in the case and put pressure on Peter to set him free. Peter preferred to sell him, but he could find no buyers; after Peter's death his executors sent Prince to New Orleans, where no one would buy him either and he finally died. After such experiences with slaves, it is not surprising that the Gansevoorts came to prefer Irish hired help. Some of their Dutch neighbors were less willing to part with their slaves, whom they usually treated well, when Yankee immigrants insisted that slavery be abolished as a moral evil. As Delaware County politician Erastus Root later colorfully recalled with reference to the gradual abolition law of 1799, providing that slavery would cease to exist in the state after July 4, 1827,

The slaveholders at that time were chiefly Dutch. They raved and swore by *dunder* and *blitzen* that we were robbing them of their property. We told them they had none, and could hold none in human flesh while yet alive, and we passed the law.[2]

The Gansevoort brothers both contributed further to the welfare of their community by their ordinary business activities, Leonard by his store and his investments in local shipping and mills, and Peter by his developments at Snock Kill Falls, whose lumber came to the Albany market. Peter also purchased shares in enterprises designed by others for private profit and the public benefit. In 1792 Leonard, then in the legislature, suggested:

I would advise you to sell as much of your public Debt as will enable you to subscribe 50 shares to the Canal; you will certainly double your money in 6 weeks—keep this private but subscribe in single shares. The Bridge Bill is passed. £9450 is given to the Western District and the Bridge across the Mohawk near the Cohoos is a primary object. Our friend T. V. W. Graham I got appointed one of the Commissioners.[3]

The "Canal" was one of the two Inland Lock Navigation Companies which a group led by General Philip Schuyler was then promoting, the Western Company, which eventually succeeded in improving the route to the Great Lakes, and the Northern Company, which failed to construct a waterway from the Hudson to Lake Champlain; the Albanians oversubscribed the stock of both companies as soon as the books were opened. The "Bridge . . . near the Cohoos" was built by the Cohoes Bridge Company, in which Peter held stock and of which he was elected a director in 1807. He also owned shares in several local turnpikes. In 1803 he was one of the founders of the New York State Bank. Since banks at this period were usually closely associated with political factions, it is interesting that the Federalist Peter had for co-directors several leading former Anti-Federalists.

Peter also sought out public offices which might lead to further private profit. In 1788, the Confederation Congress nominated him Indian Commissioner, a post which Leonard, then a congressman, urged him to accept because

It occurred to me instantly that if I could procure your Name to be added to the number, it would serve as a Basis to my future operations and designs. . . . You will easily perceive the good use that can be made of it. . . . We shall not be precipitate in this Business. It is necessary that it should mature but we have promised each other not to lose sight of the object and have no doubt but we shall eventually succeed. As I mentioned to you upon a former Occasion public Life is the Road to Preferment.[4]

The exact line of Leonard's reasoning is not entirely clear, but the "object" was probably to extract from Congress some substantial though belated reward for Peter's services in defending Fort Stanwix. Peter did accept the post, and in 1790 made a journey to the Indians in connection with his duties. One unanticipated result of this trip—or perhaps of some similar but unrecorded one— was the establishment among the Seneca Indians of a family named "Gansworth" who claim to this day to be descended from him. Later in the same year Leonard tried to get Peter the city clerkship; it was on that occasion that he reminded Schuyler of the circumstances under which he and his father had lost it. In

1790 Peter accepted the office of sheriff of Albany County after the resignation of his brother-in-law, John Ten Broeck, and served in it for a year.

Peter's principal opportunity for peacetime public service came ten years later, when his Revolutionary comrade, Henry Dearborn, once an officer of the Sullivan expedition and now Secretary of War under Jefferson, appointed him U.S. Military Agent for the Northern District. The duty of military agents was to forward supplies to army posts, which duty Peter discharged faithfully for seven years. His Revolutionary service enabled him to understand military necessities, while his commercial operations provided him with the experience and the credit necessary to move large quantities of goods over great distances. Most of the work consisted of providing transportation for clothing, hospital supplies, and Indian subsidies of dry goods, farming utensils, and gunpowder from Albany through the Mohawk Valley and the Great Lakes to Fort Niagara and the other forts in the Indian country beyond. The supplies came by sloop from Philadelphia to New York and up the Hudson to Albany. Then they had to be forwarded by the waterways through the Mohawk Valley, which was fairly well settled, and the wilderness beyond, which was only beginning to be opened. There were no roads beyond Canandaigua, sixty miles east of the site of Buffalo. Buffalo itself was a few huts by Black Rock Creek, Cleveland another cluster of huts by the Cuyahoga River. There was nothing between them but Fort Erie and nothing beyond them but Fort Detroit, to which "the track of the road [was] scarcely discernable." [5] Beyond Detroit, across three hundred miles of trackless wilderness, was the post of Michilimackinac and, after 1804, Fort Dearborn at Chicago. Nearly all communication between these posts was by rowboats, canoes, and a few sailing ships. In 1803 there was no mail beyond Niagara, although by 1806 the Canadians north of the Lakes had monthly postal service to Detroit.

All this time Peter continued to be active as a general in the New York State militia, inspecting at training days and confirming the sentences of courts-martial, many of which arose out of political disputes between officers and men or among cliques of officers. Then in April, 1809, he was appointed brigadier general in the United States Army, which had been increased to ten regiments by an act of 1808 in response to threats of war with England. Peter became commander of the Northern Department, including the coast defenses of New England and New York, the border defenses of the Great Lakes and the St. Lawrence Valley, and the central barracks at Carlisle, Pennsylvania. His troops were the Fourth, Fifth, and Sixth Regiments, one third of the entire U.S. Army, hastily and recently raised, officered by political appointees, and manned by the scourings of the streets. To further lower morale in this makeshift army and make discipline hard to maintain, the thrifty Jeffersonian government did not forward their pay regularly and the civilian population distrusted them, thinking the militia sufficient for defense and any regular army an instrument of tyranny—especially when it was ordered to enforce the unpopular Embargo Act. Therefore an important part of Peter's duties was to review the sentences of regimental and general courts-martial. Regimental courts-martial tried cases of desertion, mutiny, neglect of duty, and drunkenness among the men; general courts-martial tried charges against officers, which could include stealing the men's rations, striking them, and the catch-all, "conduct unbecoming an officer and a gentleman." Such charges were often based on rumor or spite, and many cases resulted in acquittal.

Peter was also called upon for special duties, notably to preside at the court-martial of General James Wilkinson at Frederick, Maryland, in the fall of 1811. Wilkinson's activities in the Mississippi Valley, particularly his contacts with Spanish officials in New Orleans before the Louisiana Purchase, had been raising suspicion in many quarters for years, but it was hard to find anything definite against him. Now he was charged with conspiracy with Spain, complicity with the plots of Aaron Burr, and neglect of the welfare of his troops, but it proved impossible to convict him of any of them. Historians have since discovered that he did indeed take money from the Spaniards, but at that time the incriminating documents were hidden in Spain, their very existence unknown to the prosecution. It was irrelevant to try Wilkinson as

143

Burr's accomplice in 1811 since Burr had been acquitted of treason at his own trial four years earlier. The incident which gave rise to the charge of negligence grew out of misunderstandings and shortages of supplies for which the War Department was at least as responsible as Wilkinson—and the members of the court had had many similar experiences with the War Department. Furthermore, it was well known that much criticism of Wilkinson originated with politicians whose real purpose was to embarrass and discredit the Madison administration. After hearing voluminous evidence, the court voted Wilkinson "not guilty" and adjourned on Christmas Day.

Peter hurried home through the winter weather, on the way catching a cold from which he never recovered. One illness piled on another through the spring of 1812; in May he was believed to be on his deathbed, and on July 2 he died. His funeral was a public and patriotic event; in the first flush of enthusiasm for the War of 1812 the burghers celebrated it with all the military pomp that Peter loved, and the whole community turned out to watch the solemn parade which accompanied him from his mansion to the family's new burial vault on Swan Street, at the crest of the hill. It was the Hero of Fort Stanwix' last and perhaps his most conspicuous moment of glory.

In the meantime, General Gansevoort's sons had been growing up to the patrician tradition of civic responsibility. A serious problem arises at this point because these sons, three of whom will be prominent in the remainder of this narrative, were named for relatives who have been important in the earlier part of it. It has therefore been necessary to devise a few conventions for telling them apart. Henceforth, General Peter Gansevoort will always be referred to by his military title. "Peter" will always refer to his youngest son, Judge Peter Gansevoort (1789–1876). The General's eldest son, Herman (1779–1862), may be distinguished from his ancestors Harmen and Harme by the use of English rather than Dutch spelling—which usage was his own. Another son, Leonard (1783–1821), distinguished himself from his uncle Leonard (1751–1810) and his cousin Leonard, Jr.

(1754–1834) by the middle initial H.; this distinction is not sufficient for modern readers, who will find him regularly referred to
below as "L. H." H. and L. H. Gansevoort will be used, as Herman
and L. H. themselves used it, to refer to their partnership in the
Snock Kill Falls lumber business from 1809 to 1817.

Herman early became associated with the lumber mills at
Snock Kill Falls. He later recalled that he visited them with his
father when he was a boy, not more than twelve years old, although the family never spent their summers there, preferring
such resorts as Ballston Spa. In 1801 Herman took up permanent
residence in the General's yellow house and began acting as his
agent. The General made agreements—usually oral; it was exceptional for them to be written down—with the mill foremen and
with the tenants on the cleared farm land. Herman's responsibility was to make sure that these agreements were carried out in
between the General's visits at peak lumbering seasons. Like his
father, Herman was much more interested in mills than in farming. The sawmill "was run when there was water; it was doing all
it could," [6] but Herman soon became convinced that the gristmill
was obsolete and in 1804 persuaded his father to build a new one
with three run of stones.

In 1809 Herman was joined in the yellow house by his
brother, L. H., whose mercantile career had been nipped in the
bud when the Embargo Act of 1807 cut off American trade with
the belligerent powers of Napoleonic Europe. Before the passage
of this act, L. H. had worked as a clerk for James and Archibald
Kane, then the leading merchants in Albany. When in 1805 he
formed a partnership with James Lagrange, his father remodeled
the "ancient family mansion" [7]—Harmen Harmense's house—to
serve them as a store, the whole family invested in the business,
and the Military Agency made many purchases through it. After
this partnership was dissolved, L. H. served on his father's staff in
the militia and acted as clerk to the Military Agency. He was
appointed military agent in his father's place in 1809, but the
Madison administration had political friends of its own who were
eager for office and the senate refused to confirm the appoint-

145

ment. After this discouragement, L. H. and Herman and a third brother, Wessel, decided to lease the Snock Kill mills from their father for a term of twelve years.

Wessel (1781–1863) was the problem child of this generation, clever and charming but unstable. He is first heard of as a schoolboy at Williamstown, Massachusetts, who went through more pairs of shoes in a year than any of the rest of the family. After attending Williams College for one year, 1795–96, he served on his father's staff and accompanied one of the Military Agency's cargoes to Niagara. He studied law; when he came to Snock Kill Falls he opened a law office and had for a clerk Esek Cowan, who eventually became a judge in Saratoga County. But Herman and L. H. soon discovered that Wessel was not interested in the large-scale lumbering which was their reason for leasing the property. Late in 1809 they bought out his interest in the lease for $1,000. Wessel then opened a store, but it was becoming sadly evident that his instability was too much for him. The love of a good time which he shared with the rest of the family led him to inordinate drinking, to carelessness with money and chronic indebtedness, and to quarreling with the neighbors. When he came to the end of his own funds he did not hesitate to borrow on the family's credit, and to use his ingenuity and charm to persuade his relatives and friends of his intention to mend his ways if they would pay his debts. General Gansevoort lost patience with Wessel's promises in 1811, when he added a codicil to his will replacing Wessel's share of his estate with a small fixed income. In the same year the General was in severe financial straits which could possibly have been caused by Wessel's debts. Simultaneously he was exerting his influence to have Wessel appointed an officer in the army; his lieutenant's commission came through three months before the General died, but service in the War of 1812 completed the ruin of Wessel's character. After the war the family extricated him from the army and then wondered what to do with him. He had made himself thoroughly unwelcome at Snock Kill Falls, but it was obvious that he would get into less trouble in a rural district where he was known than in

Albany or some other locality where he could obtain credit. He was therefore boarded around with various neighbors, but was never again permitted to reside with his family although he sometimes visited them.

In the meantime, H. and L. H. Gansevoort hustled the family timber on the market. After their father's death and their mother's subsequent severe illness, they exchanged their long-term lease for an annual one, by which they were to pay $700 rent, taxes and repairs, and seventy-five cents for each of the five hundred saw logs they had permission to cut. In spite of the restraint thus suggested, men who worked for them later recalled a headlong rush of activity. The brothers searched out the trees "wherever they could find them," [8] had them cut, and fed them to their two voracious mills which sawed for as much of the year as there was water for power, and day and night in the peak winter season. They built roads and stripped the great white pines from the eastern portion of the General's tract; they bought more land to the north and south of it, and other lots as far away as Luzerne in Warren County. They sawed pine planks and boards, hemlock timbers, piles and dock logs, ash blocks and hickory handspikes for use in ship-building. The timbers and logs they floated down the chute-like gorge of the Snock Kill. The boards and planks, which were not sturdy enough for such rough treatment, they piled by the mill until winter, when they loaded them on ox sledges and hauled them a half-mile eastward to the Beaver Meadow. There they were built into rafts which the lumbermen floated down the little beaver stream into the Snock Kill below the falls and then piloted down the Hudson as soon as the ice went out and the crest of the flood passed by, usually about the first of May. The boards and planks were usually sold at Albany; the timbers went on to New York, where rapidly expanding commerce required ever more wharves and waterfront facilities. In their peak year, 1817, H. and L. H. Gansevoort sawed and shipped 70,000 board feet of all kinds of lumber. But that peak year was also the last year of their partnership. They surrendered their lease, their mother paid them $3,500 for their improve-

147

ments, and in 1819 L. H. moved back to Albany, where, after serving as Sheriff of Albany County in 1820, he died of tuberculosis in December, 1821.

After L. H. moved away, Herman continued to saw and market hemlock timbers, piles, and dock logs, although the white pine was exhausted. He also formed partnerships with neighbors, notably Captain Sidney Berry, to buy more timberland at Luzerne and other places. After the Champlain Canal was completed in 1823 he began sending his sawed lumber to Albany on canal boats, one of which was appropriately named the "General Gansevoort"; the timbers still went to New York, to which in 1830 he rafted 17,081 board feet of hemlock timber and 644 dock sticks. But though Herman's lumbering was still his principal business, it was by no means the whole of the Gansevoort mills. From the beginning the gristmill had been important in providing both food for the mill hands and a service to neighboring farmers. The patent mill which had been built in 1804 was worn out by 1820, and it cost Herman $460 to rebuild it. The following fall he erected a new sawmill. He also built a carding and fulling mill which served the neighborhood's household cloth-makers, as did similar mills on many streams at this time. By 1828 he had added a dyehouse and was expanding his operations when the whole cloth mill was swept away by a fall freshet. Nevertheless, he immediately rebuilt the carding and fulling mills and resumed operations. In 1832 it was again necessary to rebuild the gristmill.

In these same years, Herman also devoted much attention to his home and its surroundings. In 1813 he built for his bride a mansion which, like the yellow house, is still standing, although the interior has been much altered. One approaches it across a piazza with six white pillars, and enters the hallway by a hospitable wide door. The parlors, sitting rooms, and dining room on the first floor have been remodeled beyond recognition, but the tiny second-floor chambers, hardly big enough for a bed and chest, are unchanged, as is the empty attic, where the beams are a foot square and held together entirely by wooden pegs. Down in the basement, reached by a separate door where the ground slopes away at the rear of the house, is the modernized kitchen, and behind the kitchen the storage cellars, where the rugged stone foundations stand as sturdily as the day they were built. Behind the house the hill falls away to the Snock Kill; in front of it a curving drive sweeps graciously to meet the quiet main street of the village of Gansevoort. From the upstairs windows one looks across the level Hudson Valley to the bold profile of Mount Equinox and the Green Mountains.

In 1813 this house stood, rough and new and smelling of fresh white paint, in the midst of a booming lumber camp. In May, 1818, Herman got around to transplanting some elm trees in front of the house, put five men and a yoke of oxen to work hauling out the pine stumps in the door yard, and had the space thus cleared plowed, dunged, and planted with potatoes, corn, and beans. Nine years later David Austin was employed for weeks drawing several hundred more stumps around the house, cleaning them off, and getting them ready to make into stump fences. In 1829 Herman had sycamore, elm, maple, and basswood trees set out in front of his home; some of them now tower over it. Major renovation in the summer and fall of 1835 employed ten to fifteen men who raised the mansion on screws four feet off its foundation, built the foundation up to meet it, and "renewed" both outside and inside.

By this time Herman's mansion was the center of a fair-sized community, in whose civic affairs Herman had been a leader almost from the beginning. In 1798, three years before his arrival, the area around Snock Kill Falls had been formed into the town of Northumberland. In 1803 Herman was elected town clerk, an office he held for three years, and in 1807 he was elected supervisor for the first of four consecutive annual terms. He was appointed a justice of the peace in 1804, in which year L. H. wrote that he had won the respect of his neighbors "by his virtues [?even] more than by his talents." [9] In 1815 and 1835 he was again elected supervisor. He was by far the largest taxpayer in the township; in the first years of the century, the Gansevoorts were sometimes called upon to pay $100 in taxes and to contribute 100 days of labor on the roads. In 1827 Herman was

149

assessed for about 10 per cent of the town's total taxes and the
next highest taxpayer, the Fort Miller Bridge Company, paid only
a third as much as he. In 1817 and 1821 he represented Saratoga
County in the assembly, but his opposition to the Constitutional
Convention of the latter year appears to have ended his political
career, although in 1821–22 he served as brigadier general for the
county in the militia.

In the meantime the General's youngest son, Peter, was maintaining the family's patrician position in Albany. Peter received
more formal education than any previous Gansevoort. He attended the Dutch Church Academy with his brothers and sister
and prepared for college with the Episcopal rector, Thomas Ellison, and, after Ellison's death in 1802, with John MacDonald. It
was in Ellison's school that Peter became acquainted with James
Fenimore Cooper, with whom he remained friends throughout
Cooper's life although they rarely corresponded. Whenever Peter
had occasion in later years to mention Cooper, he always expressed the warmest friendship toward the author and the greatest respect for his works. In the fall of 1804 he entered Williams
College, but one year there was enough for him. The following
winter when he wrote to L. H. from Princeton, he congratulated
himself on his escape from Williams and characterized it as a sink
of iniquity into which he had been in danger of slipping.

The reason why I came off with so few vices I cannot attribute to
anything but that pride which would not allow me to commit an
act which was beneath a Gentleman; for when I saw them at their
Card Tables with their liquor before, swearing like so many enraged
Sailors, I immediately took such a disgust to their Card Parties that
I never touched a Card while at that place, neither do I at present
know how to play a game at Cards.[10]

He acknowledged, nevertheless, that had he stayed at Williams
the desire to be sociable might have led him astray. His moral indignation probably had two sources: the necessity of reassuring
his family about the innocent nature of the secret Cliosophic Society, to which he had just been elected and for whose dues he
later in the same letter requested money, and the desirability of

dissociating his good times from Wessel's extravagances, which if Williams was at all as Peter described it, might have received some encouragement during his student days.

In his reply, L. H. was very anxious to impress his younger brother with the responsibilities to himself and his family which he accepted along with the privileges of higher education.

I expect a great deal from you—and all the family—they have a right to. You are the only one now of us who will have a liberal education. In case of difficulty you will be the greatest support to the family. We may one day much need the sound Judgment which your education is now preparing for you. We have at present but few young men in this place of any extraordinary abilities and especially at the Bar. I anticipate with pleasure at a future date to see you there not only adding respectability to yourself but also to the family. You may rely upon that at the present time the only Road to preference or respectability is by knowledge and the way to knowledge is by perseverance. I shall forever regret my not having received a liberal education.[11]

These remarks of L. H.'s, which proved to be a remarkably accurate prediction of Peter's contribution to the family, represent a very great change in Hudson Valley Dutch attitudes toward education since Peter Van Schaack had been in 1765 the first of them to graduate from any college. Nevertheless, the spirit of admonition and envy of his younger brother's opportunity did not prevent L. H. from appreciating some of his difficulties. Though he reminded Peter to be sure to send an account of expenditures when asking for money "as you know papa wishes it," he also suggested that Peter apply to him if their father, probably made cautious by Wessel's example, kept him on too short an allowance "to support you as a gentleman." [12]

Two years after Peter graduated from Princeton in 1808, he went to Litchfield, Connecticut, to spend a year at Judge Tapping Reeve's law school. The contrast between Dutch Albany and Yankeedom struck him on all sides; of the monstrosity of a house where he first boarded he concluded:

I am a lover of antiquity and this room just hits my fancy. It looks like a remnant of the ark of Noah. . . . I imagine myself sometimes seated in the castle of my ancestor Baron von Gonsevort—and a large Pond which I view from my window with the Cackling of old Baldwin's Geese confirms the idea.[13]

This whimsy obviously owes much to popular Gothic romances, but certainly also refers to the scenes in the background of Leendert and Catarina's portraits, although at this time the Gansevoorts knew nothing at all about their possible ancestors or connections in the Netherlands. Later in the winter Peter changed his lodgings, finding that his "ancestral" room was cold and Mrs. Baldwin's housekeeping deplorable after Albany housewives' tidiness.

I would rather dine in Baker's stable [on the site of the Gansevoort brewery] than in her kitchen—yea much rather, for Baker's stable is cleaned daily, her kitchen not even annually. Now my squeamishness and good old Dutch habits, being accustomed to as clean a Kitchen as a Parlour, could not brook this.[14]

In April Peter observed the Connecticut election and wrote his father a full description. Peter's religious sensibilities were offended by the Yankee practice of holding political meetings in the church and prefacing them with a sermon, which custom he attributed to the "priest-ridden" habits of Connecticut. But he went on to observe:

I was surprised at the order and regularity preserved at the Election, so different from our tumultuous Elections. Here was no quarrelling, and what I remember as more unusual out of so great a number, I saw no man intoxicated. They generally bore the marks of Industry and Honesty. I am convinced that we have a very erroneous opinion of the Yankees—we see none but their dregs. They send the rascals out of the State and keep the Honest men at Home.[15]

He was more critical of some of the political theories already under discussion in the state which two years later was to see the Hartford Convention:

These are Federalist, but they are illegitimate children, or at least prove themselves such, if they act contrary to the interests of our beloved Country. I am a Federalist, but my principles are founded in the Purest Patriotism—as long as Federalism is animated by the

principles of the Revolution I enlist under her Banners—but I disdain
her acquaintance when she disregards the precepts of Washington.[16]

When Peter returned to Albany in 1811, just before his
father's death, and began to practice law, he found that the
Dutch tradition was being overwhelmed by a Yankee invasion.
The Dutch themselves had already abandoned the language of
their fathers for public purposes, including church services after
1788, although General Gansevoort's generation continued to
speak it in their homes and Peter's generation spoke it to their
parents. But the Yankee merchants who came to Albany to supply
their fellow Yankees pouring through the city on their way to
western lands saw many opportunities for immediate improvements. In the first decade of the nineteenth century, they won
enough power in the city government to compel the Dutch city
fathers to accept many basic changes. One which aroused much
resentment among the Dutch was a fundamental alteration in the
city's drainage pattern. Although Albany was built on a steep hill-
side, its streets, like those of flat Dutch cities with their network
of canals, had always been paved with a single gutter in the
middle, in lieu of a canal. Runoff from the high roofs with their
stepped gables was conveyed to the gutter by overhead waterspouts which projected several feet over the right-of-way. This
system was convenient enough for a small town where everyone
walked, but the waterspouts and central gutters impeded vehicles. A group of Yankees led by Elkanah Watson started a newspaper war on the issue and eventually secured ordinances outlaw-
ing waterspouts and providing for gutters at the sides of the
streets, which directed the water toward instead of away from the
houses, spilled it into the burghers' cellars, and antagonized their
tidy wives. But the Yankees were adamant on this and many
other matters, and in the face of such determined opposition the
next generation of the Dutch families, hopelessly outnumbered
anyway by a tremendous expansion of population in the city, left
local government to the Yankees and devoted themselves to their
businesses and professions or lived on their inherited wealth. The
Yankees, for their part, learned from the Dutch how to conduct

an Albany election and continued this part of the city's political tradition among the Irish who were flooding into it. In the third ward, the opening of the Erie Canal was the decisive factor, which rendered obsolete the political and social structure within which members of the Gansevoort family had won election to the common council. In 1820 several branches of the family still lived there and a number of them were active in the city government; ten years later they had all moved away, and Peter was unable to secure election as alderman in 1831 and 1833 although he was in those years an elected member of the legislature.

Peter Gansevoort reached the height of his career in state rather than local politics. He began as a follower of De Witt Clinton, serving as Clinton's private secretary and winning appointment as Judge Advocate General of New York State when Clinton as governor controlled the Council of Appointment in 1819. But there was at this time great dissatisfaction with the Constitution of 1777, particularly with its provisions concerning appointments; after this constitution was revised in 1821, the obnoxious Council of Appointment was abolished and many formerly appointive offices made elective, and Peter and many others were removed from their posts. Although he was out of office, Peter continued to participate in the conflict of factions which swirled through legislative Albany, but like his uncle Leonard his greatest contributions seem to have been in the form of personal contacts which by their very nature left no records. Occasionally he appeared at a public meeting, like that on January 25, 1822, which passed a crackling resolution condemning Vice-President Daniel D. Tompkins and the federal senators from New York (Martin Van Buren and Rufus King) for interfering with the appointment of Solomon Van Rensselaer as Albany postmaster. In this major patronage imbroglio, President James Monroe successfully asserted his right to appoint whom he pleased (Van Rensselaer) in the face of the senators' insistence that offices should be given to their political followers as they directed. In the same year Governor Clinton sent Peter to the towns along the Canadian border to investigate notorious frauds by hunters claiming the bounties offered by town, county, and state governments for the extermination of wolves; later the legislature limited the total amount which might be paid in bounties in any one town in a year. Finally, in 1828, Clinton died suddenly and his faction dissolved.

In the meantime the Constitution of 1821, with its multiplication of elective offices and its provision of universal manhood suffrage, had in fact rendered obsolete factions like Clinton's, which attempted to control public affairs by the old Anglo-Dutch system of exerting personal or family influence upon a limited body of electors or the appointing power. Instead there developed a new system, based fundamentally on the ability of professional politicians to formulate issues in terms that would attract the votes of the majority of a wide electorate. It was frankly based not on the reasoning of the wise, the wealthy, and the well-born, but on the feelings of ordinary men; as Martin Van Buren, one of its major architects, observed:

In this matter of personal popularity the working of the public mind is often inscrutable. In one respect only does it appear to be subject to rule, namely in the application of a closer scrutiny by the People to the motives of public men than to their actions. When one is presented to them possessed of an ardent temperament who adopts their cause, as they think, from sympathy and sincerely regards their interests as his own, they return sympathy for sympathy with equal sincerity and are always ready to place the most favorable constructions upon his actions and slow to withdraw their confidence however exceptionable his conduct in many respects may be. But when a politician fails to make this impression—when they on the contrary are led to regard him as one who only takes the popular side of public questions from motives of policy their hearts seem closed against him, they look upon his wisest measures with distrust, and are apt to give him up at the first adverse turn in his affairs. The process by which they arrive at one or the other of these conclusions is not easily described. Feeling has of course more to do with it than reason, yet, tho' sometimes wrong, it must be admitted that they are much oftener right in their discriminations.[17]

This system, and all that went with it, was anathema to patricians and aristocrats; as General Pierre Van Cortlandt, like Peter forced out of office in 1821, later confided to him:

155

Is it not to be lamented that such a reptile as R . . . . r I . . . . n without talents, respectability of Character or Scarcely the Appearance of a Man, so filthy that he ought not to be touched by a Gentleman only with a pair of Tongs, the sycophantic Pick Spittle of Mat Van Buren, should be the prime mover of the Legislature of this State.[18]

Nevertheless, after Clinton's death Peter, like many other Clintonians, joined Van Buren's Albany Regency. It was not an entirely unfamiliar system, for the organization of the Albany Regency, which became the organization of the national Democratic Party and the prototype of standard American party institutions, bears distinct marks of its principal architect's Dutch origin. Martin Van Buren was a Kinderhook plebeian, proud of six generations of unadulterated Dutch ancestry, related to that Major Isaac Goes who had led the Kinderhook revolutionaries, and a consistent opponent of the Van Schaacks, who, Tories or no, returned to their position as rural patricians almost as if no revolution had happened. Van Buren had great respect for Peter Van Schaack, in spite of enduring differences between them, but the rest of the family, he wrote, "were persons of much reputation and distinction, but they were all ardent politicians, and some of them very violent in their feelings." [19] He soon moved from Kinderhook to Hudson, the new center of Columbia County affairs, where, like Isaac Goes thirty years before, he made common cause with the Yankee newcomers against the Dutch rural patricians. His party, combining Yankee voter appeal with Dutch voter discipline, soon gained control of the county and reached out to join hands with similar plebeian parties including those the Yateses had been forming in other upper Hudson Valley counties and Aaron Burr had been forming in New York City. These parties had an uphill struggle while the 1777 Constitution was in force, for although the patricians and aristocrats were divided into many personal and family factions, they were still in a position to influence the limited electorate and to nullify the effect of elections by their influence on appointed officials.

To counteract such influences, Van Buren and those around him developed a concept of party discipline that was very similar to the Dutch concept of community loyalty. The party, like the

156

town, was the unit of civic participation; it acquired "privileges" (= liberties—i.e., any form of favorable legislation) for its supporters by using their "wealth" (in votes) to "buy" legislative majorities. These privileges were acquired by the party as a whole for the benefit of the party as a whole, rather than for any individual within it; they were exercised in behalf of the whole party by a small group of leaders who were rewarded for their acquisition of a large "fortune" (in votes) by elevation to offices of trust, profit, and public service. These democratic patricians then held onto their positions as long as their "wealth" held out, and perpetuated their power not by marriage alliances with other families, but by political alliances with similar machines from other localities. Thus professional politicians elevated themselves to peaks of status in localities, states, and the nation comparable to the heights attained in their own cities by wealthy Dutch patricians. It should be noted that mechanisms of all sorts are as typically American as the continuing family is typically Dutch; the irresistible vision of these politician-patricians as faces on machines (like an Artzybasheff cartoon with its absurd structural resemblance to the crowd scenes of Pieter Breughel) conveys a profoundly significant analogy.

Therefore, although he had been fighting the Albany Regency for ten years, Peter Gansevoort found his transition into it easier than he might have expected, and in time he became as loyally attached to Van Buren's party as he had been to Clinton's highly personal faction and as he remained to the city of Albany. In 1829 he was elected to the assembly. Soon after his election he and two colleagues attended the Virginia constitutional convention then meeting in Richmond and stopped on the way home in Washington, where they visited Secretary of State Martin Van Buren and dined with President Andrew Jackson and his cabinet. On his very first day in the assembly, January 5, 1830, Peter was appointed to the committee sent to inform Governor Enos Throop that the House was ready for business, and also moved that local clergy be invited to open each session with prayer. A year later, he felt it necessary to introduce a resolution condemning theatrical satires on the House and its members as "a breach of privileges and of dangerous tendency," [20] which motion was immediately tabled. After his reelection in 1830 it was suggested that he run for speaker, but as his friend James Stevenson wrote him some months later from Washington, "I am afraid your Regency friends were not true to you. I *know* they were neutral at least, with the exception of [Edwin] Croswell." [21] Peter's most substantial legislative contribution was on committees, such as one to study poor laws and insane asylums, for which purpose he visited insane asylums in several states. His most important assignment was the busy committee on banks, to which in 1830 and again in 1831 thirty-two new banks petitioned for charters and seven or eight existing banks for renewals. This committee was very sensitive politically, since no bank could operate without a charter and charters were often granted or withheld as political favors.

In 1832, Peter was elected to the New York State Senate. There he also did most of his work on committees, including state prisons, incorporation of cities and villages, public health, militia, public buildings, asylums for insane paupers, and for three years "literature," which covered all of the state's various activities in support of education. On May 26, 1836, at the end of his term, Peter's colleagues elected him president pro tem for his final session. According to the formal procedure, two senators were delegated to inform the governor and two to inform the assembly. Peter concluded his legislative career with a gracious little speech which was entered in the journal:

Senators:

I present my thanks for the honor you have conferred upon me, and entertaining a grateful sense of this additional evidence of your kindness and consideration, tender to you the assurance of my intention to discharge faithfully impartially and to the extent of my ability the duties which belong to this station.[22]

While Peter was involved in the state government, he was nevertheless still fundamentally concerned with the community of Albany. He remained active in its nonpolitical civic affairs, serving as a bank director, a trustee of schools and charitable foundations, an organizer of civic banquets and other public cere-

monials, and even as chairman of a committee to erect a mausoleum for De Witt Clinton in newly redeveloped Clinton Square.
The Clinton family consented, but the mausoleum was never
erected and for many years his remains reposed in the Gansevoort
vault in the Swan Street cemetery. Peter's legislative service centered around matters of interest to Albany; his committee assignments on banking and social service institutions reflected typical
Dutch patrician concerns; his use of his political position to gain
appointments to office for as many of his relatives as possible fell
within the Dutch patrician tradition. But although Peter Gansevoort could fit comfortably on top of Martin Van Buren's party,
which welcomed him because he brought with him inherited
wealth, status, and community leadership which it could use although it could not attain them by its own efforts, he could never
appreciate the aspiration which motivated the plebeian leaders of
that party who had thrust themselves up from below. Martin Van
Buren, indeed, like the Yateses, had gathered plebeian power to
make himself a patrician, and because he was Dutch and it was in
the Dutch tradition for plebeians to become patricians by gaining
enough wealth (or in this case, votes) he did eventually become
one. But the non-Dutch politicians who used Van Buren's Dutch
form of party organization to achieve their own non-Dutch ends,
acquired wealth, power, and prestige (in votes), and used them
to defend and extend the liberties of the party-community, did
not automatically become patricians. Instead, the American political system which they built with Van Buren's devices eventually
pushed patricians like Peter Gansevoort aside, even in the city of
Albany.

VII

Mothers and Matrons

Unquestionably women played a far greater part in Dutch patrician society than has been directly recorded. Most histories of that society—as indeed, most histories of any kind—rely primarily upon public archives and therefore describe those activities customarily carried on by men, in which women, if they are interested parties, ordinarily employ either a male relative or a professional man to represent them. Furthermore, the education of all the Dutch was far more practical than literary, and though patrician women could read, write, and keep accounts, they did not as a rule cultivate the arts of correspondence or journalkeeping. In the Netherlands, women's most important activities were carried on in the home, the shop, and the church; in order to assess their contribution to the Dutch tradition it is therefore necessary to consider the place of these institutions in Dutch society as a whole.

The home was the center around which the Dutch social system revolved. It was usually the family's place of business as well as its shelter, and patricians as well as plebeians lived behind or over their shops and on the same premises with their warehouses. Several generations of the family often lived under the ancestral roof, the son—not necessarily the eldest—who followed his father's trade living in his father's house until his marriage and, if his parents were getting on in years and his brothers and sisters few, bringing his bride and raising his own family there while his parents were still alive. When the other sons married and set up

160

in their own trades, they moved into nearby houses, but were quite likely to remain in the neighborhood. The home was therefore not only the place where most of the family's important transactions of every nature were planned and carried out, but also the center of a pattern of socialization characterized by frequent face-to-face contacts between relatives associated in a wide range of activities which in other societies may be but are not necessarily carried on primarily within the family circle. In such homes the wife was always present, always aware of what was going on, often the agent of other members of the family who had been called away from home for shorter or longer periods. It is inconceivable that such women should have been totally without influence in family decisions, even though these decisions were carried out by male members of the family; in matters in which a wife's own relatives were associated or in which her family had special experience, her influence must often have been paramount. Furthermore, in cases in which a man raised his status or an outsider entered a family complex by marriage, his wife cannot have done other than initiate him into the unwritten, often unspoken, traditions by which such social units governed themselves. The exercise of such feminine influence of course cannot be documented by conventional means, but some of the long-range effects of it might be discovered by a close study of the whole range of activities of a family with reference to the activities of the other families with which it was associated by marriage.

The activity of Dutch women in business was noteworthy to other Europeans, and was certainly associated with the close relationship between the family's domestic and business activities. Everyone in the family contributed in some way to the accumulation and distribution of the family fortune, which insofar as possible was kept together from generation to generation by the customary practice of investing individual inheritances in the business ventures of relatives. Sons and daughters shared equally in their parents' estates, usually receiving a part of their share as a marriage portion and the rest as a legacy. When the greater fortune invested in the family business was the wife's, her influence

161

—or that of her family—often determined major decisions about its management. In general the head of the family took the lead in administering investments and commerical ventures, made major purchases, and paid and collected bills, but his wife was responsible for using the household goods thriftily, for deciding what purchases were necessary, and for directing servants in making many items of household use which were produced within the family. When the husband was away on business, ill, or dead, his wife or widow was usually fully competent to administer his affairs or his estate in his absence.

The piety of Dutch women was, like their other characteristics, exceedingly practical and most important on the everyday level. Attendance at public worship was, as in medieval and early modern society generally, the central regular social act of the entire community, in which entire families participated. But men, except for members of the clergy, were as a rule too busy in their businesses for religious activities other than serving in the administration of the church or endowing its buildings and charitable foundations. Women had both better opportunities and more frequent occasion to engage in the equally important continuous maintenance of the tradition by religious education of children, "good works" to neighbors and the poor, and devotional reading and meditation. In the medieval Netherlands women joined religious orders—the most famous and most typically Dutch were the Beguines, or Sisters of the Common Life—for full-time participation in these activities, but after the Protestant Reformation they had to engage in them privately or in informal association with like-minded relatives, friends, or members of their congregations. Pre-Reformation Dutch religious art shows a notable interest in the Holy Family and in incidents of a family nature from the lives of the saints and from Scripture. It is furthermore most interesting that a recently published early medieval Dutch musical drama, the twelfth-century "Maastricht Easter Play," chose for representation the discovery of the empty tomb by Jesus' female disciples. In all of these areas, Dutch women carried out the same attitude toward religion that was expressed by the greatest Dutch religious writers such as Thomas à

Kempis, who found that his mystical experiences of the love of God helped him to maintain a spirit of Christian love toward his brethren in the tight, closed, often petty community of a monastery, and Erasmus, who directed his incomparable scholarship toward determining the most accurate text of the Holy Scriptures so that eventually they might be translated for all men and women to read. As Erasmus wrote:

Christ wishes his mysteries published as openly as possible. I would that even the lowliest women read the Gospels and the Pauline Epistles. . . . Surely the first step is to understand in one way or another. . . . Would that, as a result, the farmer sing some portion of them at the plow, the weaver hum some parts of them to the movement of his shuttle, the traveller lighten the weariness of the journey with stories of this kind. . . . Why do we restrict a profession common to all to a few? [1]

The scanty evidence available about Albany Dutch patrician women indicates that their contribution to their community was along similar lines. It was most extensively described by Anne Grant, who believed that early marriage and "the reverence which children in particular had for their parents, and the young in general for the old, was the chief bond that held society together." [2] She went on to describe how young couples, particularly those who found it necessary to marry in haste, moved in with one set of parents or the other and often continued to live with them from choice long after they could support themselves. She also noticed that marriages usually took place within "companies" of young people who had played together since childhood, which companies were encouraged by the parents and "had a strong rivalry with each other. . . . they regarded the company most in competition with their own with a degree of jealous animosity." [3] Mrs. Grant could offer no explanation for these groups, but it seems logical to associate them with the family complexes which determined most associations among the burghers.

Mrs. Grant said little about the women of Albany as businesswomen, but she was very much interested in their patient care for their children—and their gardens. ". . . not only the training of

163

children but of plants, such as needed particular care or skill to rear them, was the female province." [4] She found children industrious but spoiled.

. . . affection restrained parents from keeping their children at a distance, and inflicting harsh punishments. . . . The children returned the fondness of their parents with such tender affection, that they feared giving them pain as much as ours do punishment, and very rarely wounded their feelings by neglect, or rude answers. Yet the boys were often wilful and giddy at a certain age, the girls being sooner tamed and domesticated. [5]

Girls and their mothers spent much time knitting and sewing clothing for the family and slaves, for though fabrics were plentiful, ready-made clothes were expensive. They also learned the spic-and-span cleanliness which Peter Kalm observed in Albany Dutch women who scrubbed their floors religiously every Saturday, and cookery thrifty but substantial for every day and astonishingly elaborate for special occasions. As Mrs. Grant recalled:

Tea here was a perfect regale, being served up with various sorts of cakes unknown to us, cold pastry, and great quantities of sweetmeats and preserved fruits of various kinds, and plates of hickory and other nuts ready cracked. In all manner of confectionery and pastry these people excelled; and having fruit in great plenty, which cost them nothing, and getting sugar home at an easy rate, in return for their exports to the West Indies, the quantity of these articles used in families otherwise plain and frugal, was astonishing. [6]

In the 1750's girls learned to read the Bible and religious works in Dutch and to speak English more or less, but a girl who could read English was accomplished; only a few learned much writing.

This confined education precluded elegance; yet, though there was no polish, there was no vulgarity. . . . At the same time these unembellished females had more comprehension of mind, more variety of ideas, more in short of what may be called original thinking, than could easily be imagined. [7]

Of one of the products of this tradition, her friend and patron Margareta Schuyler, the "American Lady" of her title, Mrs. Grant said:

164

. . . her reading was not very extensive; but then the few books of this kind that she possessed were very well chosen; and she was early and intimately familiar with them. . . . Whatever she knew, she knew to the bottom; and the reflections, which were thus suggested to her strong discerning mind, were digested by means of easy and instructive conversation.[8]

The piety of Albany Dutchwomen entered Mrs. Grant's observations frequently, particularly with reference to religious instruction of children. She summarized it succinctly:

Their religion, like their original national character, had in it little of fervor or enthusiasm [i.e. revivalistic emotionalism]; their manner of performing religious duties was regular and decent, but calm, and to more ardent imaginations might appear mechanical. None ever doubted of the great truths of revelation, yet few seemed to dwell on the result with that lively delight which devotion produces in minds of keener sensibility. If their piety, however, was without enthusiasm, it was also without bigotry; they wished others to think as they did, without showing rancor or contempt toward those who did not. In many individuals, whose lives seemed governed by the principles of religion, the spirit of devotion seemed to be quiescent in the heart, and to break forth in exigencies; yet that monster in nature, an impious woman, was never heard of among them.[9]

This account of the Albanians' religious tolerance hardly accords well with the schism in their church at this very time and with Domine Frelinghuysen's detestation of Anglicans; perhaps she considered these upheavals social rather than doctrinal. She also noticed many religious pictures in patrician homes. Some of these pictures, perhaps imitated in color by local limners from engravings in Dutch Bibles, have been preserved. Their subjects emphasize the practical, everyday aspects of Christianity and family relations recorded in Scripture; particularly popular subjects seem to have been Christ with two ordinary disciples on the road to Emmaus and the Adoration of the Magi. Another family scene which was repeated was Isaac blessing Jacob—and one cannot help wondering if the shrewd Albany fur traders perceived the ironic comparison between Jacob's sleight-of-hand with pelts on this occasion and their own?

165

The very little that is known about the colonial Gansevoort women brings out other elements of this picture of the feminine side of the Albany Dutch tradition. The experiences of Harmen Harmense's wife, Maritje, were typical of what is known of the frontier women of pre-patrician Albany. Like them, she did not hesitate to appear in the local court in her own person, and to plead not only her own cause but also that of her husband. In the farm suit, she effectively employed her maternal concern for the welfare of her home and the security of her children. Adverse witnesses pointed out that she wished the farm to be sold because labor was unavailable to make it support the family and because schooling for the children was inaccessible. Five years later, Maritje appeared in court as a witness in an action brought by her next-door neighbor, a widow, against three youths who broke into her house, taunted her with obscenities, and tormented her with practical jokes. Maritje became involved when she heard the uproar and came over to investigate. The perpetrators of this instance of juvenile delinquency were found guilty and fined.

Of Leendert's wife, Catarina, no record remains beyond her shrewd, strong-featured portrait and her grandson's recollection, written sixty years after her death, that

She was one of those extraordinary women whose like we seldom see. I have heard her described as a tall genteel very handsome woman, her eye keen and penetrating, a strong mind which manifested itself in all her domestic concerns, but more particularly in the management of her husband's business. It lay with him to earn money, with her to place it at interest and dispose of it advantageously in the purchase of real estate. She kept her husband's books of account, regularly posted them, and yearly called upon those who owed for pay.[10]

Catarina, the trader's daughter, initially superior in community standing to her brewer husband, was evidently the Dutch businesswoman who understood commercial affairs as well as those of her household. But the extent to which she in fact dominated her family cannot be determined from this statement, which depicts her as she appeared to a child at the very end of her long life. No documentary evidence, such as letters or books in her handwriting, survives to support it. A possible parallel might be Jeremias Van Rensselaer's observation concerning the business talents of his wife, the daughter of a brewer:

I have taken up brewing, and this for the sake of my wife, as in her father's house she always had the management thereof, to wit, the disposal of the beer and helping to find customers for it.[11]

Furthermore, though she may have been an active partner in Leendert's business she certainly did not follow him to the common council.

For most of her life Catarina's energies must have been largely absorbed by her household which included her mother-in-law, her unmarried sister-in-law Maria, her ten children, of whom five survived to maturity though only three to marriage, and at various times possibly widowed sisters-in-law, nephews, and cousins. For example, Pau de Wandelaer, who is mentioned nowhere in the Albany records, was probably her nephew, a son of her deceased brother Andries of New York, another of whose sons was in 1721 a ward of her brother Johannes of Schagticoke. Since there is not even a record of Pau's death—only his portrait, obviously from the same hand as those of Leendert and Catarina, it is probable that he left Albany after he came of age.

Of Harme's wife, Magdalena, even less is known than of Catarina. She too was of higher social status than her husband, her father being a landholder and a former member of the assembly while his was merely a craftsman and a member of the Albany common council, not quite though almost patrician. Magdalena's brother, Volkert P. Douw, and her husband became merchants in Albany at about the same time, entered the patriciate together, and worked together in civic affairs for the rest of their lives. Magdalena herself once sent a message to her son, Colonel Gansevoort, exhorting him to take care of his clothing and to send home—from Canada!—any garments he did not need. In 1788 she wrote a very brief note to Leonard reminding him of his religious duties; quite possibly Leonard's life-long service to the church was a result of his mother's piety and religious training.

167

Otherwise Magdalena was one of those silent figures who contribute most to their tradition by inconspicuously performing its everyday activities.

Caty Van Schaick Gansevoort is much better known to us than her predecessors because it was in her generation that the Gansevoorts began to write personal letters. The Revolution separated them just at the time when postal service was becoming widespread and fairly reliable. Furthermore, the bilingual balance of the upper Hudson Valley was settling decisively in favor of English, which both young men and young women of the Revolutionary generation read and wrote fairly easily, although they still spoke Dutch to their parents. Sixteen-year-old Anna Gansevoort, writing to her brother Leonard in 1769, commented:

I hope wen You right to me again you will right as I do haf dutch and haf Engleis. I don't no the meaning of haf the words. I have no time to right You any more.[12]

Caty had much less language trouble in the letters she wrote to Colonel Gansevoort in the field. His were more studied than hers, in one case an elaborate declaration of affection being repeated word for word after a six-month interval, which perhaps suggests the extent to which he used the English language primarily for formal written communication.

Caty's correspondence with her fiancé became much freer after their formal engagement in the winter of 1776–77. Their letters were interrupted by her family's flight from Albany and by the siege of Fort Stanwix, but were resumed in November, when the Colonel wrote to beg Caty to marry him at Christmas. This letter was delayed, and Caty did not receive it until the middle of December, which left her and her mother very little time to arrange a wedding. After a frenzied family consultation which lasted until the wee hours, Caty finally composed herself to write—though not very grammatically—that her lover's impetuosity was in fact impractical haste:

. . . which I a most willingly would do to your Satisfaction as well as my own. I could wish you had acquainted my Superiours before your Departure from here what your Intention was after your return, but for all I hope through the Blessing of God to comply with your Proposel. I expect not so soon as the Letter end of this month which time you propose or expect to be down.[13]

The eager bridegroom was further restrained by the weather; winter travel in the Mohawk Valley was by sleigh on the frozen river, but though there was plenty of snow at Fort Stanwix there was none farther down the valley. Nevertheless, Colonel Gansevoort was able to arrive in Albany in time to be married to Caty on January 12, 1778, ten days after his sister Anna married his comrade in arms, Colonel Cornelius Wynkoop of Kingston.

For the rest of the war, Colonel Gansevoort consistently sought to be assigned tours of duty in or near Albany whenever it was possible. Early in the summer of 1778 he wrote Caty from Fort Stanwix:

It is impossible for me to express to you how much I long to see you. Often before marriage did I think it hard to be from you, alas how much greater is the anxiety now; as I cannot consistently with my Honor in my present situation leave my post to pay you a visit.[14]

She answered immediately:

Dear Peter, I must tell you i am anxious to see you, but can it not be, consistently with your honor and the good of the Post to you entrusted, I must with you refer it till a good opportunity offers, and then I hope you will be cautious of your Scalpen enemy on the road, for how much happyer am I to expect you, then I would be when forced to forget you.[15]

But ordinarily their letters dealt with domestic details—she sent him groceries, notably sugar for his punch, and he sent her fish and furs for herself and his and her sisters—and family affairs, such as the impending wedding of "Miss Polly Gansevoort." Caty spoke of Polly as "your sister," but since both of Colonel Gansevoort's sisters were married she was probably his twenty-five-year-old cousin, Maria, Dr. Pieter's eldest daughter, whose home was only a couple of doors from the original house. Apparently her wedding never took place, for though "Aunt Polly" was occasionally mentioned in family letters in later years, she remained single until her death in 1841.

Leonard Gansevoort's two daughters were the most conspicuous women in his family. Leonard and his wife Hester Cuyler lost three children before Magdalena was born in 1777 at the height of Burgoyne's campaign, and had no more until Catherine arrived in 1789. For Magdalena, who was therefore for twelve years an only child, Leonard was lavishly solicitous, providing her with every luxury and the best education. He was particularly proud of her accomplishments on the spinet, and of the letters in which she informed him of her music teacher's praise. In 1792, when she fell ill while attending school in New York, where her father was in the legislature, he wrote to Leonard, Jr.:

The indisposition of my Child has for many Days marr'd all the Pleasure Comfort and enjoyment which can result from the agreeable Society of Friends and even the happiness anticipated from once more abandoning public Life and a determined resolution to seek for temporal bliss only in domestic Life, but thanks be rendered to the supreme dispenser of Events, he has reanimated me by restoring the Health of my Daughter and thereby has multiplied the concatenation of Obligations which his manifold Bounties have laid me under, and Oh! that my Heart was but sufficiently susceptible of their importance and that he would add but one more, to wit, his Grace to enable me rightly to adore his Name and manifest the gratitude which I feel for his undeserved favors—[16]

After her marriage to Jacob Ten Eyck in 1795 she and her husband lived at Whitehall, which, along with the Gansevoort wharf, they inherited when Leonard died in 1810. His final concern in his will was that his daughters, the younger of whom was barely of age and as yet unmarried, should not quarrel over their inheritance:

to remember *they are Sisters* and that their Father loved them alike and that it was always the wish of his Heart and firm Determination to do them equal justice, that nothing is more [distant?] from him than the Idea of preferring one to the other and therefore he sincerely prays that a Division of that portion of Earthly Goods which the Lord has vouchsafed to bless him with may not be the means of alienation or of friction between his children as then they love justice as they fear their creator God and Reverence the Memory of their Father he

170

instructs them to be mutually forbearing and let every thing be done in sisterly affection.[17]

This passage was probably prompted by the long and complex law suit between the heirs of Harme Gansevoort and of Volkert P. Douw which dragged on for years after the deaths of those two venerable merchants in 1801.

After three decades of inconspicuous Dutch wifehood, Caty Gansevoort emerged into full view after the General's death in 1812. She was his sole heiress and executrix, and until her death in 1830 the General's fortune in lands and lumber was administered in her name and under her general direction, although her sons ordinarily represented her. Her relationship with the mills at Snock Kill Falls was to receive the rent that Herman and L. H. paid her, along with presents of lumber, firewood, and agricultural products. Once in awhile she made the two- or three-day journey to Herman's home for a visit, but with the details of his business she did not concern herself. She was much closer to her son Peter's management of her houses and lots in Albany, western lands which had come to General Gansevoort as veteran's bounties, and frontier lands in New York State left her by relatives of her own. Peter found tenants, received their rent, dunned them when they did not pay, and evicted them when they fell too far in arrears, but she expected him to keep her informed about all these matters in her absence. Peter also made major household purchases and paid the bills, but when Caty was out of town he closed the house, dismissed the servants, and boarded with the legislators at the Eagle Tavern.

In the years of her widowhood, Caty's health was always poor. Some of her constant worry about it was certainly justified, but when she visited Boston in 1816, she forgot all about her doctors and diets and seemed to be much better than usual. Three years later, however, Peter had to advise her against giving way to excessive depression:

You have with an eye of observation viewed this world for about sixty years—have experienced its variety of pleasures—its variety of cares—what *have* you lived for? . . . Again I ask—what *do* you live for? . . . And what has this experience taught you? . . . You will find it [such meditation] better for body and soul than the composition and fostering of factitious evils.[18]

She found some relief for her misery in religious devotion, expressing it practically by subscribing to the *Christian Visitant* and by contributing to a theological chair at Rutgers College. Much more frequently, however, she depended on her children to raise her spirits, and therefore visited them often.

Caty caused Peter much concern by trying to travel by herself, accompanied only by her faithful slave, Chris. Peter thought it both unwise and undignified for her to journey unescorted by one of her sons, and once, when she expressed such a determination at a time when it was inconvenient for him to forestall it by dropping everything to fetch her, addressed her very firmly on the subject:

My dearly beloved Mother,

A few days since I replied to a letter from Herman, which contained an expression of your wish that I would go to New York on Monday last for the purpose of attending upon your return to this City. I could not disguise my perfect astonishment in receiving such an intimation at a time when the state of the weather precluded any rational determination as to the time of your return and every pulsation of a heart of any Gratitude to him by whose Providence you have happily been spared to gain affectionate children and friends must have reminded you of the sinfulness and danger of a rash exposure to the present vicissitudes of the season.[19]

He promised to come for her as soon as his business permitted, but in the meantime cautioned her "*by no means* come upon me by surprise." In the summer of 1829 she hardly arrived at Herman's home when she wanted to come back again. Peter sent the carriage as she requested, but warned her, "I expect by all means that Herman will accompany you. He certainly will not permit you to leave his house unattended." [20]

Especially close to Caty was her youngest child and only daughter, Maria, who was born in 1791. In her childhood, Maria went to Mr. Merchant's Academy, like her brothers, and also attended dancing school—as did her children and grandchildren after her. She learned enough needlecraft at an early age to execute a large embroidered picture of a young lady grieving over a tomb, in the shade of a weeping willow. Some such samplers, like her cousin Hester Ten Eyck's needlework picture of her home at Whitehall, were solidly worked in colored silks, but Maria's was confined to black on white and the background was filled in in water color. Her special accomplishment was music; her father imported a piano for her from London about 1800, when the piano was just becoming a popular keyboard instrument, and she took lessons once or twice a week from then until her marriage in 1814. She was less enthusiastic about literature, although she enjoyed novels, which at that time were primarily sensational and sentimental romances and Gothic tales. Her brother Peter cautioned her against reading too much fiction and suggested that she devote some attention to "important and elegantly written" works such as Robertson's *History of Scotland*. At the same time he criticized one of her letters, resenting her neglect to put it in an envelope, which permitted it to get very dirty in the pocket of the stage driver who carried it. He also reminded her that letters should be dated, that a "neat ladylike hand" was preferable to flourishing script, and that affected coyness of expression was neither "cute" nor "cunning." The style of these comments of Peter's, however, was quite as open to criticism as Maria's, being as conspicuously influenced by the conventions of oratory as Maria's could have been by those of sentimental fiction.[21]

Maria's education thus provided her with the accomplishments then considered suitable for a lady. Her mother also instructed her in the domestic arts of the Albany Dutch tradition, in which thorough housecleaning and good cooking were particularly important. She was further knowledgeable about clothes, which she always insisted must be of the best materials and the most fashionable design. As General Gansevoort's daughter she was of course the object of admiration to all the young officers who surrounded him, and mingled with a wider circle at such civic social events as the grand ball in honor of Commodore Perry, the victor of Lake Erie, in November, 1813. But one thing

Maria's education did not include was helping with her father's business. Her grandfather retired from trade long before she was born. When she was ten her father left the brewery and Gansevoort's wharf behind and moved to his fine new dwelling. There he sometimes paid off his lumbermen after the rafting season, and there he later added a small office for his military business, but after 1800 General Gansevoort's enterprises were usually carried on outside his home. His wife seldom visited the mills at Snock Kill Falls; there is no record that his daughter ever did. Instead, Caty and Maria accompanied the General to the then-renowned health resort of Ballston Spa for a summer change of scene.

Sometime during the unhappy years 1811–13, which included illnesses of her own, her father's death, and her mother's nearly-fatal illness, Maria became acquainted with Allan Melville. Allan's grandfather, who was related to a landed family in Scotland, had come to Boston before the Revolution. His father, merchant Thomas Melville, reached the rank of major in the war and served for many years in the Boston Custom House. Allan himself, the fourth of eleven children, received a gentleman's education, including a Grand Tour of Europe, before he entered the importing business in Boston. He and his partners' concern for importing dry goods from Napoleonic France, to which Allan Melville made several visits, was put out of business in 1811 by the British blockade. Traveling up and down the Atlantic seaboard in search of a new place to establish himself, he came to Albany and met Maria Gansevoort.

Maria considered this acquaintance most fortunate. Melville, as she always called him, was very different from Albany boys like her brothers. Herman's mind was always on his mills, L. H.'s on his ledgers, Peter's on his lawbooks, but Melville had learned the manners of a gentleman in the refining atmosphere of Paris. Nine years older than Maria, distinguished and attractive, he liked to read and exercise his imagination fashioning elegant compliments and delicate attentions. His family background was good, his father's fortune ample, and his father's Revolutionary service honorable, though as Melville himself was the first to acknowledge, it was not to be compared with the heroic career of

General Gansevoort. He had the reputation of a sound businessman, although at the moment he was between two enterprises; to
Albanians, his decision to engage in the wholesale dry goods
trade in their city would have been additional evidence of his
perspicacity.

Melville had reason to consider himself equally fortunate.
Maria was a lady, beautiful and accomplished, who thoroughly
understood the arts of making a house both a home and a social
center. Both he and she appreciated fine possessions. She was less
interested in books than he, but it was only in Boston that ladies
were expected to be literary. She was the daughter of a leading
family in a town which he believed to be a profitable location for
his business. She was heiress in her own right to a considerable
fortune and further closely related to established Hudson Valley
merchants and Albany bankers. Maria's marriage, which was
celebrated in the Dutch Reformed Church on October 4, 1814,
was therefore eminently suitable on both sides. It was furthermore from beginning to end, and ever thereafter in Maria's memory, a marriage of sincere affection. Her husband never tired of
praising her in his letters, both to her relatives and his own.
When, after three years of marriage, he left her for a business trip
to Europe, he grew more and more homesick the longer he was
gone. On the eve of his return he wrote her:

Believe me Maria you have a Husband who duly estimates your
Worth, admires your virtues, and is more than ever enamoured of the
chaste warmth of your heart, the cool discretion of your mind, and
the unspeakable graces of your Person.[22]

Maria's honeymoon took her to Boston to meet her husband's
relatives. They welcomed her into a family group as generous and
warmhearted as her own. Nevertheless, Maria remained especially close to her mother, to whom Melville wrote during their
honeymoon with elegant yet tender irony, "Indeed Madam she so
often talks of you, and desires to be with you again, that I sometimes tell her she will make me jealous." [23] For the first two years
of her marriage Maria and her husband lived in her mother's big
house; Melville paid his mother-in-law $75 a month as board for

175

himself and his servant, and helped her with her business affairs. Their first two children were born there and baptized in the Dutch Reformed Church.

After three years in the wholesale dry goods business at Albany, Melville decided that the location was less ideal than he had believed. In May, 1816, he wrote his father that Albany was suffering from a superfluity of merchants and a general postwar depression which had descended the year before. Not anticipating the building of the Erie Canal and the tremendous expansion of trade which followed, he thought that there would be no future in wholesale trade so close to New York, and was debating removal to either Boston or New York. Maria preferred Boston, though her mother urged that New York would be more accessible. They accordingly did move to Boston, but the removal proved unsatisfactory and by the end of 1817 Melville definitely decided to settle in New York, giving as one of his main reasons the wishes of Maria and her mother. But first Maria and the children returned to her mother's home while Melville went to France in the spring of 1818 to renew his contacts and select goods. On his departure Peter assured his brother-in-law, "I will not only be to her the kind and affectionate brother and sincere friend, but will feel the sacred responsibility of a father to her children." [24]

Both Maria and Melville found separation a strain. He, in particular, bridged it by long, elegantly composed letters which Maria preserved carefully, forwarding to his relatives as he asked those in which he described his journey to the Melville family seat in Scotland. He visited his great-grandfather's grave and proudly traced his lineage to a Sir James Melvil who had been knighted in 1580, but the high point of his Scottish tour was his cordial reception by the Earl of Melville and Leven, to whom he was distantly related. Thus he demonstrated an awareness of ancestry which the Gansevoorts, proud though they were of the General's Revolutionary exploits, did not at this time possess. After he left Scotland Melville's letters to Maria contained much less general information and many more personal messages. In the Netherlands he initiated inquiries into the Gansevoort family history, since

my mother-in-law being most enthusiastically attached to the *father-land* speaks dutch in preference to english and is very desirous to obtain the above information.[25]

He was particularly appreciative of Maria's matter-of-fact acceptance of his absence. To Peter he wrote:

I am not surprised that Maria should sustain my absence with her characteristic fortitude, for her natural firmness of mind and instinctive sense of propriety, shape the course of her actions, and make her all that is lovely in Woman, all that a Husband and a Brother could require.[26]

To Maria herself he was more explicit:

I rejoice, my noble Wife, that you should have exhibited during my absence that strength of mind and accommodation to circumstances which render you more than ever lovely in my sight, and commands my respect and admiration. I fully approve of your having generally accepted invitations, and that you have endeavoured to appear as cheerful as possible. This was precisely what I wished, truly becoming your Character as a Wife and Mother, and makes me more than ever proud of a Woman, whose own native good sense dictates the propriety of her conduct in every possible situation.[27]

Although Maria was not experienced in business, Melville's respect for her judgment led him to confide his affairs to her and sometimes to use her as his emissary to communicate matters too delicate for paper to her family. After a rather unhappy first winter adjusting to New York—neither of them had ever lived completely apart from their families, and neither was used to the expense of living in New York—they settled down to running a wholesale business in fine dress goods, a fashionable and sociable home, and a regularly increasing family which eventually included eight children. Maria quickly found that social position in New York depended far more on conspicuous consumption than it did in Albany, where family relationship was all-important, or Boston, where Maria noticed that families like the Melvilles used inexpensive Scotch carpets and no curtains instead of the Brussels carpets and damask drapes she found in New York parlors. Many New York merchants were Yankees like her husband, newly rich but without roots in the community; they practiced cutthroat competition in business while their wives carried it into the social sphere. It was they who created the society described twenty years later by James Fenimore Cooper and Francis J. Grund, in which fortune was the sole criterion of social acceptance and conformity in possessions and behavior the condition of social success. The principal way for newcomers to rise above this social pressure was to marry into old New York families, many of which, though no longer active in trade, were not unwilling to accept successful young merchants as husbands for their daughters—but since Melville already had a wife, and an Albany wife at that, he could not acquire capital and connections by marrying one of these heiresses.

In various business vicissitudes through the next decade, Melville relied on Maria's relatives as well as his own to loan him money. Soon after he went to New York, Peter Gansevoort and his cousin and closest friend, James Stevenson, invested in a half-share of one of Melville's cargoes, but the goods moved slowly and they did not repeat the speculation. Through the 1820's Melville borrowed money through Peter from the Albany banks where he and Stevenson had influence. In 1827, when other attempts to raise $10,000 in capital for a new venture failed, he called frantically on Peter to tide him over. With Caty's consent, Peter advanced the money, which represented part of Maria's eventual inheritance, but neither they nor Herman, to whom he also applied, were enthusiastic about including a scheme concerning which Melville had told them very little among their investments. When Melville indicated that he wanted to keep half the money for three years instead of the six months for which he originally borrowed it, Peter reluctantly acquiesced, but sent word by Maria that the other half must be repaid when it was due, which Melville did with the help of a loan from his father. In all of these ups and downs, Maria's attitude was more down-to-earth than her husband's. When retrenchment seemed inevitable in 1823 he thought the necessity disgraceful, but Maria wrote Peter:

Mr. — difficulties, with a reduction of the establishment, and the closest economy, will I hope be in some degree more easy. Nothing can this year be saved in rent but next year a house and large yard and garden may doubtless be had at Brooklyn for a trifling sum in comparison with what is now paid. After all this world has little to offer and I think a pleasant house at B— would be much more agreeable through the year than a house in town, where one is in daily dread for four months in the year of being driven from home [by typhoid fever or other summer epidemics]. You have kept all communications on this subject confined to your own breast. Mr. — delicacy on this subject is greater than you can imagine.[28]

Through her years in New York, Maria and her mother remained close. Trips to Boston were rare, because they meant either an arduous and jolting ride by coach or a long voyage through Long Island Sound and around Cape Cod, both confining and difficult for children. But nearly every summer Maria, the children, and their nurse and governess fled unhealthy, unsanitary New York by stepping on the Hudson River steamboats which docked near their home in the evening, going to bed, and arriving at the Van Wies Point landing in the morning; from the landing, a few miles below Albany, it was a short and pleasant ride to Grandmother's big house. In return, Caty paid many visits to New York, particularly for her daughter's confinements but also often in between. Melville valued her company as much as Maria did, even cheerfully turning his home into a hospital when she required surgery in January, 1825. She did not recover easily or fully, and Maria wrote Peter three months later, "Mother requires a person of good sense and some judgment to be with her constantly." Nevertheless, Caty was mentally alert, concerned because Peter had not written about her business affairs, and two weeks later she was anxious to return to Albany as soon as Peter could come for her, perhaps because of the outbreak of scarlet fever among Maria's children.

Caty's death in January, 1831, left her son Peter without a home. Peter, who was forty-two and unmarried, had once been engaged to Margaret Stevenson, sister of James Stevenson, and his second cousin, but in one tragic swoop in the fall of 1817, death claimed Margaret's grandmother, her mother, and herself. Peter reported to Herman that her death was Christian, tranquil, and happy, and Maria expressed her grief and disappointment, but otherwise the Gansevoorts never mentioned her. Peter, busy caring for his mother, practicing law, and engaging in state and local politics, remained unmarried as long as his mother lived, though as a distinguished and eligible bachelor he was undoubtedly sought after by every matchmaking hostess and ambitious coquette in Albany. Then in the spring of 1831 he finally allowed himself to be captivated by black-eyed, seventeen-year-old Mary Sanford, daughter of former Chancellor Nathan Sanford.

Nathan Sanford had grasped and held power, prestige, and profit in the treacherous and slippery politics of the New York City area. Martin Van Buren, himself one of the wiliest politicians of the period and one of Sanford's antagonists, spoke of Sanford with prudent respect and an undertone of distrust. He had served as speaker of the assembly—in 1811 he was the last speaker to preside in a cocked hat—U.S. District Attorney for New York, in which position Thurlow Weed believed he had laid the foundation of his fortune by dubious means, and U.S. senator. In 1830 he retired from public life but not from politics, which brought him to Albany during the legislative seasons of 1831, 1832, and 1833. Sanford's home was in Flushing, Long Island, in a huge mansion which his heirs finally, after much difficulty in finding a purchaser, sold to a lunatic asylum. He had six children by three marriages, of which Mary was a child of the second, but took little interest in them and left them to be brought up by servants.

Perhaps as a result of this neglected childhood, Mary grew up quickly. In 1830, when she was only sixteen, she managed her father's household while his third wife, who was very little older than she, was preoccupied by the birth of a son. At eighteen she was helping with her father's political entertainments, and describing them to her favorite brother, Edward, with the skill of an experienced reader of novels. The following vignette suggests the

180

strains placed on political hospitality by the emergence of "Jacksonian democracy":

We have had two dinners and a soiree, the latter of which was highly amusing. The people are invited as usual for seven o'clock, and accordingly at a few minutes after, a week ago yesterday, all the Yahoos of the members arrived, and seated themselves around the rooms, with their feet crossed, a red bandanna handkerchief spread upon their laps, and two kinds of cake one upon each knee, together with a cup of coffee as causy [sic] as you please, and we could hardly persuade them to give their seats to the ladies. One of them remarked that he wished they would give him a glass of beer instead of whiskey punch, as he much preferred it. Another said that he would take some of that stuff what shook, and a variety of other equally queer speeches were made much to the amusement of the whole company. There were but 2 ladies here owing to the night's being so severely cold.[29]

These members, so grotesquely out of place in Mary's patrician drawing room, were doubtless astute enough on the floor where they perhaps represented the roadless districts in which bounties were still given for the extermination of wolves. In such a mixed social milieu, Mary Sanford was very much aware of the necessity of maintaining appropriate distinctions. Later in the same letter she reported having danced with a local retailer, but "I have henceforth determined never to go to his store and not to speak to him again as it was very impudent in him to ask me and very wrong in me to do it."

It must have been during this year that Peter began to pay Mary particular attention. After she consented to marry him, he wrote of their courtship:

My love for you, is pure and holy—there is not a particle of interest in its composition—I had never found a recipient for my heart. My dear Mary, you gained it before you knew it. Do you remember, that about two years since, I had the honor at table of being seated between your excellent Mother and yourself. . . . Do not be surprized when I tell you, that from that moment, I purposely avoided you—and that it was not until I had reason to hope that I was not indifferent to you, that I suffered the least manifestation of my strong partiality.[30]

181

In this rhetorical effusion of feeling, Peter seems to have been carried somewhat beyond the facts. Mary, who knew James Stevenson well, must have heard of "sainted Margaret," but after fourteen years she doubtless considered her lover's lapse of memory pardonable. If he indeed wooed her by avoiding her until she gave evidence of having fallen in love with him, it seems rather strange that a young woman of Mary's independence and awareness of what was due to her would ever have done so, but this statement must be read with reference to a context of social intrigue at least as bitter as the political intrigue in which its participants were simultaneously engaged, against which Peter's restraint indicates shy pride, courteous dignity, and chivalrous reluctance of a middle-aged man to overwhelm a young girl.

Despite the disparity in their ages, Mary loved Peter deeply and sincerely. He was kind, affectionate, and generous, especially after her querulous father, who at this time "has been as cross as a bear to poor Mother during his stay in town altho pretty good to me." [31] She feared that he might object to her marriage, but he did not and they were married on June 4, 1833, in a very small wedding to which only the immediate families were invited. After a honeymoon to Niagara Falls and down the St. Lawrence to Montreal, they moved temporarily into General Gansevoort's home, which since the opening of the Erie Canal was in a rapidly decaying neighborhood. Before her marriage, Mary asserted to her brother, "G. is going to sell his house as I will not live there," but it did not move quickly, and in September James Stevenson wrote Peter from Paris, "I am glad to hear you are going into the old mansion, it shows the good sense of your better half." [32] The following spring Peter and Mary rented a new house in recently redeveloped Clinton Square, across the corner from the new North Dutch Church which had been completed in 1815.

For three or four years Peter and Mary were blissfully happy, regretting only brief separations which they bridged by long and affectionate letters. Their first child, named Henry for a deceased brother of Mary's, was born in 1835; a daughter, also named Mary, was born in 1836 only to die in infancy. Then in the fall of 1837 Mary went to Flushing to help care for her father, who after years of living with arrested tuberculosis was suffering from a renewed outbreak of the disease, from which he soon thereafter died. Under the strain and excitement of his unwilling departure for the Bahamas in search of relief, Mary narrowly avoided a miscarriage. The child, Catherine, was born on April 12, 1838, but Mary never really recovered from the birth. In hopes of improving her health, Peter bought a new home in a suburban location, 115 Washington Avenue, on top of the hill west of the Capitol. Mary did feel better there until another pregnancy terminated prematurely with the birth of Herman in February, 1840. The baby was "a beautiful child and will resemble his dear mother"[33]— evidently in constitution as well as appearance, for he was weak and puny and clung feebly to life. After this event Mary did not recover at all. That summer she traveled to various health resorts, but finally collapsed completely at Sachem's Head on Long Island. After Peter brought her home she failed rapidly until she finally died of tuberculosis early in February, 1841.

Mary's death, expected as it was after years of pain, weakness, and wearying decline, shook Peter to his uttermost foundations. To her stepmother, who wrote at length urging him to Christian resignation, he replied graciously and tactfully, but confessed "I am only beginning to realize the heart-rending thought that she has gone from me forever,"[34] and indicated that conviction of the benevolence of God was a state of mind he hoped for rather than expected in a somewhat distant future. Perhaps it was at this time that he dropped formal religious affiliation, though he left no written record of it beyond the odd fact that he became a member of the Dutch Reformed Church in 1857, although his children later remembered attending services there as a family throughout their childhood. Not surprisingly after such a long period of strain, Peter's grief and despair were heightened by illness of his own, and by serious financial difficulties which came to a crisis at the same time. Under all of these pressures, Peter came very close to collapse. A year after Mary's death, Herman warned him that rumors were circulating "that Peter Gansevoort was broken down and not worth anything and that he was in the habit of frequent if not daily inebriation,"[35] which rumors, fortunately, turned out to be untrue.

Under these circumstances, his own and his wife's relatives

descended on the grief-stricken father, each with a different plan for reorganizing his motherless household. There were only two children now, six-year-old Henry and three-year-old Kate; the frail Herman had succumbed to whooping cough two months before his mother's death. But to all hints of this kind, Peter replied firmly that he had not the slightest intention of giving up his home or farming out his children. Finally, after nearly three years of being a widower, Peter married Susan Lansing in December, 1843. She was a grand-niece of that John Lansing, Jr., who had once been Leonard Gansevoort's law partner, and later a leading Anti-Federalist, chancellor of the state, and finally the victim of a mysterious disappearance in which foul play was strongly suspected. Her grandfather, Abraham G. Lansing, had married Susanna Yates, thus uniting two leading plebeian families, but by the 1840's the Albany Dutch were so outnumbered by non-Dutch Albanians that these plebeian families were accepted without question by the patricians. When Peter married Susan she was a spinster of thirty-nine, fifteen years younger than he. Unlike Mary, she was matter-of-fact rather than sentimental, domestic rather than social, local rather than cosmopolitan. She kept Peter's house in the old-fashioned Dutch manner and brought up Henry and Kate in the way that Albany Dutch children were expected to go. But she was like Mary in being generous, open-hearted, affectionate, and devoted, and Peter found the thirty years of his second marriage as satisfying, in an entirely different way, as the eight years of his first. This satisfaction was avowedly expressed on both sides through the common activities of everyday; when Peter went to Europe with a lawyer friend in 1853, Susan wrote him:

The hope of hearing from you is now the only comfort I have in my lonely situation for it is truly so to me. I miss you my dear Gansevoort more than tongue can tell and feel more determined than ever that I never can consent to being separated from you again.[36]

Nor did she, until her own death in 1874.

All of these Gansevoort women maintained the Dutch tradition of keeping their homes as the center of their families' existence. For the first four generations they lived in the original

184

Gansevoort house, under the same roof with the family store and adjoining the family brewery. Leonard and General Gansevoort were the first generation to move away from their places of business, but although Leonard's store was downtown and General Gansevoort's mills in another county, both still used their residences as headquarters for their political and military affairs. Peter moved to new houses twice in ten years, both times for the convenience of his non-Dutch wife, although altering neighborhoods and financial difficulties also probably influenced his decisions. Maria Melville and her Yankee husband, in New York, also moved frequently, prompted partly by the demands of competitive conspicuous consumption and partly by the requirements of their rapidly increasing family. All of these homes were distinctly removed from the place of business which supported them, and so reflected the nineteenth-century differentiation between home and work which ran particularly contrary to the Dutch tradition.

Maria, Mary, and Susan were prepared by their education to be ladies unfamiliar with their husbands' professions rather than helpmeets in their trades. They all kept their houses and directed their servants with the thoroughness and efficiency characteristic of the Dutch tradition, and participated conscientiously in the affairs of the church, particularly the religious education of their children. But their attention was especially drawn to the practice and maintenance of all the complicated social usages which became customary in "good society" in the nineteenth century. Among the Albany Dutch this general social tendency toward recognizing consequence by conformity to certain standards of behavior rather than by birth took a peculiarly Dutch twist which amounted to a belief that the way in which a fortune was spent was as important as the fact that it had been acquired and maintained. Women like Maria and Susan became experts in the selection and use of fine goods, and thought no expense too great for the appropriate embellishment of their persons and their homes. Except in times of economic stringency, their husbands encouraged them and even pressed them to employ the family wealth in this manner, until shopping became one of their major occupations; when Peter took his family to Europe in 1859–60, his wife and daughter divided their time about equally between stores and museums, with his entire approval. It should be noted that the goods these women selected were uniformly chosen for quality, durability, and usefulness; they purchased no works of art as investments and few shoddy items simply because they were fads or fashions. In this way, since under eighteenth-century conditions the head of the family made most major purchases, it might almost be said that the Albany patrician women, thrust away from one side of the counter by social pressure, came back with increased force to the other.

The Albany matrons furthermore remained central to that vast web of noneconomic, nonpolitical relationships which still united the Albany patricians. Although they practiced the general nineteenth-century genteel customs of large formal receptions, balls for three to five hundred people, and weekly "at-homes," the heart of the Albany patricians' social system was still their informal contacts with their relatives. Peter's and his daughter's diaries record constant meetings with a wide range of more and less distant cousins through afternoon calling, visits for tea, supper parties planned and unplanned, men dropping in in the evening, and gala holiday celebrations. Birthdays and anniversaries of all sorts were made occasions for affairs of this kind. The old Dutch customs of New Years calling and New Years gifts were kept up, although the increased size of the city made them unwieldy; in the late 1820's Peter made a list of over 150 New Years calls, which must have kept him busy far into the evening even if in most cases he merely left his card in the box hung outside the door for that purpose. The men were included in this social activity when they were not at work, but all the planning and preparation for it, as well as the whole responsibility for maintaining the network of "calling" and tea parties, fell upon their wives and daughters. Furthermore, this social fabric was used not only to maintain the underlying patrician family structure, but also to further contact with the families of men concerned in the husband's business or political ventures. All such entertaining was far more important in a day when there was no telephone to replace much face-to-face contact, few clubs and organizations to

186

promote and further acquaintances, and few opportunities for public entertainment, than it is today.

Finally, the Albany matrons contributed to the stability and endurance of the Albany Dutch tradition by providing their husbands and children with a still center of emotional security. As a rule their homes were happy homes, in which husbands were cherished and supported and children were welcomed and loved. There were, of course, exceptions, but so far as information is available, the family history of the Dutch patricians is not one of runaway marriages (except for some of Philip Schuyler's daughters, who seem to have done so primarily because they thought it romantic), broken homes, adulterous affairs, sexual perversions, parental tyranny, filial rebellion, and similar evidences of family instability. Their family letters indicate uniformly that the Gansevoort men both loved and respected their wives and were loved and respected by them. Having been brought up in the same tradition, each appreciated and was prepared to meet the demands and respond to the needs of the other, most frequently without even the necessity of verbal communication. Of the Gansevoorts, Maria and Peter married outside of the Dutch tradition, and both found themselves facing problems of everyday adjustment as well as romantic bliss which were not part of the pattern of their ancestors. Both Melville and Mary came from families of which other members were notably emotionally unstable, and both suffered from internal tensions which drove them eventually to nervous and physical collapse, susceptibility to infection, and early death. But despite all these difficulties, and the additional problems of coping with their children who inherited these unstable personality traits, Maria and Peter remembered their spouses with continuing devotion. Thirty years after Melville's death, Maria wrote; exactly as one would expect of a Dutch matron,

Oh the loneliness the emptiness of this world when a woman has buried the husband of her youth and is left alone to bring up their children, without a loved father's care and experience in the training them to fulfil life's duties and to point the way to heaven by his Christian example.[37]

187

VIII

The Wheel of Misfortune

The Albany patricians followed another Dutch tradition in generally avoiding disastrous failures of any kind; as *The Spectator* observed in 1711,

When a Man happens to break in *Holland,* they say of him that *he has not kept true Accompts.* This Phrase, perhaps, amongst us would appear a soft or humorous way of speaking, but with that exact Nation it bears the highest Reproach; for a Man to be mistaken in the Calculation of his Expence, in his Ability to answer future Demands, or to be impertinently sanguine in putting his Credit to too great Adventure, are all Instances of as much Infamy, as with gayer Nations to be failing in Courage or common Honesty.[1]

Nevertheless, there were crises which cautious Dutch traditions of particularism and privilege were unable to meet. Patrician families in competition sometimes drove one another out of business and sometimes manipulated and interfered with civic institutions to gain advantages over their rivals. Plebeians whose interests were not served by the patricians in power rebelled violently, causing civic disorder. Towns asserting or defending their privileges against other towns were sometimes defeated and even subjected to their neighbors. After the Netherlands became independent, the States-General, organized for the protection of particular privileges, proved cumbersome and ineffective in national emergencies. In the seventeenth century the republic turned to the leadership of the Orange family whenever war broke out; in the eighteenth century it came to rely upon them in peacetime as

188

well until, in accordance with the practice of nearly all European countries in that century, it became virtually a monarchy. The States-General was finally permanently overthrown by revolutionary French armies in 1795, after which Napoleon incorporated the Low Countries into his empire; when the Congress of Vienna restored the independence of the Netherlands, it was as a kingdom under the rule of the dynasty of Orange.

After Albany became the capital of the Empire State in 1797, its civic career settled quickly into what was becoming the American pattern. The Dutch tradition of particularism and privilege which the Albany patricians had created and maintained over a century and a half was simply irrelevant in a rapidly expanding city to which politicians and lobbyists flocked from all over the state, and through which migrants poured westward from all over the Northeast. Albany's Dutch economic tradition of local monopoly also became irrelevant when the opening of the Erie Canal confirmed Albany's position as the natural gateway to the Great Lakes Basin and made the city a key node in the nationwide transportation system. Opportunities expanded illimitably westward, but so too did possibilities of failure. In the nineteenth-century American business world of quick gains and quicker losses, swift booms and sudden busts, sensational profits and shattering panics the slow, sure Dutch processes of fortune-building over several generations could find little basis for security.

One of the greatest risks nineteenth-century merchants faced was the danger of widespread, snowballing collapses of the entire structure of credit. Such nationwide financial distress indeed swept the United States almost before it was a nation, when the Revolutionary War ended and thirteen mutually suspicious states tried to construct some substitute for the credit and currency system of the British Empire. Continental currency was generally regarded as practically worthless, and the failure of the Bank of North America ended for the time the possibility of a central credit system like the Bank of England. The states, supporting their currency and their credit by taxation, collection of state tariffs, and sale of western lands, were somewhat more successful, but not entirely so. Merchants trying to trade with England and other countries could not collect hard money in America to pay their debts abroad because no one had any, and so long as England prevented them from selling American foodstuffs in the West Indies there were few opportunities to earn it elsewhere. Furthermore, in some states debtors, distressed by the scarcity of money and sudden fluctuations in the value of currency, put pressure on highly democratic legislatures to pass "stay laws" granting delays for paying all debts. Under these circumstances merchants failed all over the United States in the 1780's; Cuyler & Gansevoort at Albany were by no means unique. The worst of this depression was over by 1786, but commerce remained very risky indeed until the next decade, when Alexander Hamilton instituted his famous measures for consolidating the national debt and organizing the First Bank of the United States, and John Jay concluded a commercial treaty with England. It was in the midst of this depression that proud old Harme Gansevoort, writing to his son Leonard in a pathetic Dutch note, the last that survives from his hand, was forced to beg assistance in meeting some minor demands for cash:

Regarding my petition for relief of taxes, other circumstances have obliged me to accept money from Mr. Coenraet Gansevoort [Dr. Pieter's eldest son, a merchant] in order to fulfill my obligations. I have not sought one penny from my other friends to support my credit.[2]

Another member of the Gansevoort family who endured repeated misfortunes, though from somewhat different causes, was Leonard, Jr. After the Revolution, he settled down quickly and unspectacularly as a lawyer in Albany, at which profession he worked hard and, although he was willing to put in some time on political activity, refused on at least one occasion to go junketing to New York. Although he was a double first cousin of General Gansevoort and Leonard, his personality was totally different, perhaps partly the result of a motherless childhood, but also probably partly from living under the shadow of his wealthy and prominent cousin, and undoubtedly being mistaken for him on innumerable occasions. Leonard, Jr.'s intelligence was the keenest of

190

the three, and also the readiest to cut friend and foe alike; it expressed itself fluently and even wittily in written words. But Leonard, Jr., quite often felt sorry for himself, and quite easily permitted his temper to turn bitter. His bitterness came out most frequently in a prickly Puritanical censoriousness which his cousins, whose sense of humor was more prominent than his, did not permit to sour family intimacy; as Leonard wrote in 1792,

I was going to request you if you do not conceive it improper to tender my Love to Mrs. Gansevoort and Children, if you do, make it my regards Esteem Compliments or anything else so you do but impress their Minds with the friendship I feel for them.[3]

Leonard, Jr., had much heavier family responsibilities and much more limited financial resources than either of his cousins. He never had anything to do with the brewery, which he or his father's widow—his stepmother—must have sold back to Harme or General Gansevoort soon after Johannes' death. He may have inherited property at Wolvenhoeck, his grandfather Douw's home, from his own mother. His wife's father, one of those Claverack Van Rensselaers who had always had smaller fortunes and larger families than the manor clan, died in 1781, leaving his estate to his nine children. From these inheritances and his own earnings, Leonard, Jr., derived a comfortable income sufficient to support the nine of his thirteen children who survived early childhood, but no fortune comparable to that of the other Leonard and no landed estate comparable to General Gansevoort's. About 1797 Leonard, Jr., moved from Albany to Wolvenhoeck, and soon after was appointed First Judge of the newly created Rensselaer County.

Leonard, Jr.'s children were the source of most of his misfortunes. His eldest daughter, Maria, who in 1795 broke the heart of a young lieutenant on General Gansevoort's staff by her engagement to wealthy, middle-aged Abraham Hun, lost her husband to tuberculosis in 1812 and died of it herself a year later. Her parents thereupon gave up their home in Rensselaer County and moved into the Hun house, next door to the ancestral Gansevoort home, to bring up their two surviving Hun grandchildren.

191

Thomas, the eldest, studied medicine at Philadelphia Medical College and in Paris, and as an Albany physician tended a number of his Gansevoort relatives; his sister Elizabeth died in early womanhood. Leonard, Jr.'s next daughter, Harriet, had some sort of mental or emotional difficulty which required her to lead a very quiet life; she could write perfectly sane and intelligent letters, and once in a great while was taken to church for communion, or to visit the home of one of her sisters, but the least excitement upset her. Three other daughters, Betsey, Eveline, and Rachel, married disappointing husbands who failed repeatedly in business and expected their father-in-law to loan them money for dubious schemes to recoup themselves or at least to support their children. Catherine became the third wife of her cousin John De Peyster Douw, and lived an exceedingly busy, practical, and normal life at Wolvenhoeck with him, their four children, and his several children by previous marriages. Elsie, the youngest, married a grandson of a former Schoharie Valley Tory and moved to Canada, where she too established a flourishing family.

Leonard, Jr.'s two sons were even more disappointing than some of his daughters. The elder, John, became a lieutenant in the U.S. Artillery in 1806 and was stationed for several years at Fort Niagara, where he served as assistant military agent during General Gansevoort's agency at Albany. During the War of 1812 he distinguished himself in the battle of Queenston Heights, but after the war he left the army and went into business, in which he failed at least twice, seriously diminishing his father's fortune and dragging down at least one of his brothers-in-law. He served as police justice of Albany from 1821 to 1825, during which time he failed again, lost his wife in 1830, left his five children with his sister Eveline in New York while he looked for another opportunity elsewhere, and dropped out of his family's knowledge. The forthright Eveline, who had a none-too-successful husband and several children of her own, and was further at the same time caring for the deceased Betsey's eldest son, whose unfortunate father had sent him to the city to seek his fortune for himself, was shocked to discover that some of John's children had never even been baptized—a deficiency she promptly had remedied—and

192

thoroughly disgusted when their father made no effort to contribute to their support. Eventually John's three daughters came back to Albany, where all of them married and left families, but his two sons were of notably weak character; Hun served as a naval officer until he drowned at sea in 1843, and John Maley lived out a long, obscure life as a clerk in a drugstore. When Leonard, Jr.'s widow died in 1842, she left a special legacy to the three girls, but conspicuously overlooked both John himself, whom the executors could not even locate, and the two boys. Leonard, Jr.'s other son, Rensselaer, became a physician and started practice in Albany. "He will be a credit to the family," [4] wrote Maria Melville after he visited her home in 1823, soon after John's second failure. Unfortunately in 1825 Rensselaer became involved, possibly through John, in financial difficulties out of which his father had to assist him by selling a tract of land. Then he irrevocably offended the puritanical Leonard, Jr., by eloping with another man's wife to Louisiana, where he lived until his death in 1839. Once his heartbroken father drafted a letter pleading with him to leave the woman and return, but instead of sending it he filed it with the obstinate annotation:

part of a letter I would have wished to send to Rensselaer but having declared that I would not again write to him until I heard that he was rid of —— I did not send the letter.[5]

Under all these misfortunes it is hardly surprising that Leonard, Jr., was more weary and embittered than ever when in 1831 he wrote his memoir of the family—the first attempt by any Gansevoort to record information about their ancestry, accurate enough in describing people whom its author knew personally, but recounting utterly unreliable traditions for the more remote generations. Three years later, at the age of eighty, he died.

Herman Gansevoort had no children to bring him misfortune, but his brother Wessel involved him in a great deal of trouble. In addition to Wessel's debts there were Wessel's quarrels with the neighbors, particularly one Ephraim Osborn. Ephraim Osborn owned a farm south of the Gansevoort tract, but sometimes worked as a lumberman for General Gansevoort and later for H.

and L. H. Gansevoort. About 1811 the Gansevoort brothers secured a judgment for debt against Osborn, in satisfaction of which they tried to seize his farm. When Osborn stated that he no longer owned the farm, having sold it to Captain Sidney Berry and leased it back, H. and L. H. Gansevoort insisted that the sale was not bona fide. This suit was rendered personal by the charge that Osborn was perjuring himself and further embittered by another suit which Osborn brought against Wessel, who was his brothers' attorney. The records in this suit have disappeared, but the other Gansevoorts were much afraid that Osborn might bring up in court matters which would reflect against the family. They were relieved when the jury gave little credit to Osborn's testimony and, though it decided the suit in his favor, awarded him only nominal damages. Before this case was decided Wessel received his army commission and left both law practice and Saratoga County. Osborn also went away and tried to make a new start further west.

When Ephraim Osborn left Northumberland his sons continued to live on the farm, but it remained unclear who had title to it. In the spring of 1814, Osborn came back. After an unsuccessful attempt was made to settle the matter out of court, in order to permit him to declare himself bankrupt, the Gansevoorts obtained two or three writs of ejectment, which one after another were proven to be directed against the wrong party. In 1821 the question of title was finally settled by the court. Herman then tried to dispossess the Osborns forcibly, but when the posse arrived the family barricaded themselves in their house and could not be removed without tearing the house down. This the Deputy Sheriff thought would be too dangerous, and Herman agreed that it would be too extreme, so the Sheriff retreated and waited to catch the Osborns off guard, which proved to be easier to propose than to do.

The Osborns now resorted to violence in their turn. The next spring they set fire to a house belonging to Herman one night while he was away, and continued to harass him until he had to write Peter in January, 1823, that he dared not leave for a visit to

Albany "on account of the Osborn villainy." [6] Two weeks later there was a threatening incident which Herman took sufficiently seriously to record it in detail in his ledger:

About dusk of this evening I was standing on my front Piazza when I observed persons passing viz the 2 younger sons of Ephraim Osborn who were before a woman and Boy which I took to be Isaac Wilson's wife and her son, when nearly opposite to my house one of the young men said there is old Hunks on his stoop—I want to ketch him out so as to have a shot at him—and more such language only parts of which I heard—the woman may have been Eli Velzy's wife and her son—one or other of the young Osborns have for some time past carried a Gun with them on all occasions.[7]

Two days after this menace to his life, Herman wrote Peter that Osborn was ready to surrender the farm, but was trying to buy another in the area. Herman immediately tried to forestall the move by purchasing the land himself, but the owner, knowing the situation, raised his price with true Yankee shrewdness and perhaps a touch of wry Yankee humor. Simultaneously, Osborn's son-in-law was annoying Herman with small lawsuits.

The Osborns evidently had some support in the neighborhood, since Herman feared the effect upon public opinion if he should turn them out of their home in midwinter. But when spring came he suffered further annoyance: "My spring and piazza was last night besmear'd and the spring in a measure filled with Human Ordure—supposed to be done by the fiend old Osborn's wife." [8] The following day the sheriff went to the Osborns'; two days later the family departed. Herman cleaned his spring out at once and protected it for the future with a spring house, but one cannot help wondering whether the violent fever which put his wife to bed a couple of weeks later was connected with the incident. Fear of reprisals deterred tenants from occupying the Osborn lands, but on April 19 an old employee of Herman's moved into the house. The Osborns immediately had a writ of ejectment served on him, and one night in June four hundred hills of his corn were uprooted. The tenant thereupon had Mrs. Osborn arrested, but late in the summer more corn was pulled up and

195

fences let down. Under such circumstances it is hardly surprising that Herman's wife protested violently when he had to go to Albany in November to do some urgent business.

But even the ejectment of the Osborns did not end the dispute. Four years later Ephraim's son, Aaron Osborn, claimed the land. "He has some standing, is a religious man by profession, and will no doubt if a witness go great lengths," [9] Herman wrote. He hoped Osborn would settle out of court, for which purpose he offered him another tract of land in a distant county, but he was not sure that Osborn would accept it. It was not until four more years had passed that Aaron Osborn finally gave up his claim to his father's land, and five years later still, Herman had trouble with one of Ephraim Osborn's sons-in-law over the boundary between their farms.

This quarrel, as bitter in its way as any produced by the anti-rent agitation, had nothing to do with rent. Ephraim Osborn was not a tenant of the Gansevoorts, but owed them money. H. and L. H. Gansevoort made it very clear that they distrusted him because his efforts to evade repaying it cut too far into the area of sharp practice. Osborn, on the other hand, had some grievance with Wessel in which the law was on his side, and may also have had the sympathy of neighbors who disapproved of Wessel's behavior on moral and religious grounds. In view of Wessel's known habits, it is by no means irrelevant that his former partner, Esek Cowan, was instrumental in founding a very early Temperance Society in Northumberland in 1812. With the Osborns' legal resistance to the Gansevoorts' suits no exception can be taken. Their pressure on their opponents by means of extraneous suits was perhaps less defensible, though Herman brought similar pressure to bear on them when he tried to buy the land to which they proposed to remove. But their reprisals in the face of defeat were inexcusable; by contaminating wells and deliberately destroying the property of others they made themselves a menace to the community as well as to Herman.

In the meantime, Maria and Melville were also undergoing misfortunes. He started business in New York during a general depression which drove him almost to the wall before it finally ended. After doing well for a while, he, along with many other New York merchants, was hard hit by the increasing popularity of the auction system of wholesaling. In 1823, after it nearly ruined him, he adopted it himself, disposing of his silk dress fabrics, Leghorn hats, artificial flowers, feathers, and furbelows to the highest bidder as soon as they arrived instead of keeping them in his warehouse until storekeepers came to buy them. He was well satisfied with the change at first, but in 1827 he gave up importing on his own account altogether, went to work for another merchant, and relied for the rest of his income on a silent partnership in a wine and dry goods store—this partnership being the "scheme" into which he pressed the unwilling Peter Gansevoort's capital. In 1830, in spite of Peter's insistence that the $5,000 of his money still invested in the silent partnership be repaid, Melville decided to return to business on his own account. He rented a store, but his creditors were less confident of his solvency than he was himself and forced him into bankruptcy.

When this blow fell, Melville took his family to Albany, called upon his father to help him meet his most pressing debts, and spent the summer and fall trying to rebuild his shattered fortunes. After considering other possibilities, he decided to undertake the reorganization of a fur-cap factory in Albany which belonged to a recently bankrupt client of Peter's named Denison Williams. He intended at first to live in New York and handle the firm's business from there, but Maria's desire to remain with her dying mother and his own inability to raise the capital he needed in New York determined him to remove to Albany. He installed his family in a house on Market Street a few doors from the Gansevoort mansion, borrowed money for their immediate necessities from his father and Peter, and set about putting the fur factory on a firm foundation. In his anxiety to recoup his fortunes he overworked, suffered a nervous collapse, and contracted an infection from which he died in February, 1832.

The disaster which thus overwhelmed Melville, Maria, and their children was closely related to Melville's expectations for his family. His pride in ancestry had some meaning in Boston, where his progenitors had lived for three generations, and more in Al-

197

bany, where Maria's had lived for five, but to his competitors in New York, Yankee newcomers like himself, it was totally irrelevant. Among the old families of New York, who regarded Albanians with traditional hostility and New Englanders with traditional distrust, it could only have provoked resentment. His distant relationship to a Scottish peer was of no more advantage to him; although his noble cousin politely invited his correspondence and he wrote Maria that the connection "will perhaps be of future consequence to my Children," [10] the Earl of Melville and Leven never felt it necessary to answer the letter which Melville carefully composed. Melville's expectations of himself as the head of his immediate family were equally elevated. He tried to put into practice not only the values of a merchant, to whom "Money should be the substratum of success," but also the code of a gentleman, to whom money should be no object. It was essential to his pride, as well as to the conduct of a business which, it should be noted, depended more than most upon the acceptance of his goods by the leaders of fashion, that his wife and children should conform to the current standards of conspicuous consumption, regardless of fluctuations in his capacity to support them. Maria always valued quality and style in goods and she kept up appearances whenever it was possible, but neither the threat nor the fact of a reduction in circumstances ever drove her to nervous collapse. To maintain this exalted combination of standards Melville spared neither himself nor the family he dearly loved and in which he expressed his pride on every possible occasion.

When Melville died, he left Maria with a promising brood of eight children ranging in age from sixteen to two. All but the toddlers were in school, most of them with several years of education ahead of them, and none of them were ready to earn a living. Nevertheless Gansevoort, the eldest, whose scholastic ability had impressed influential gentlemen at Harvard on one of his visits to Boston, left the Albany Academy to take his father's place managing the fur factory. Thirteen-year-old Herman, not to be outdone, left the Academy likewise to take a clerkship in the New York State Bank, of which Peter Gansevoort had recently become a director. At this time Maria's sons were not compelled by economic necessity to support her, since her own fortune, which by the terms of her mother's will was entirely at her disposal after her husband's death, was ample for her needs. Nevertheless, Gansevoort insisted on acting as head of the family. Backed by his mother's fortune, his uncle's advice, and the memory of his father's experience, he worked hard at the fur factory and ran it successfully until a nationwide collapse of credit, the Panic of 1837, undermined it along with thousands of longer established businesses. As conscientious as his father, considering even the possibility of a temporarily overdrawn checking account disgraceful, Gansevoort's bankruptcy at the age of twenty-one, which swallowed up Maria's entire fortune, distressed him so deeply that like his father he suffered a nervous collapse. After his recovery he returned to New York and began a more normal career for his age by studying law, which led him into politics and eventually to London on a diplomatic appointment, where he died on May 12, 1846. Even in England his first concern was for his family. He sent his mother his savings and insisted that his younger brother Allan make regular contributions from his income as a fledgling lawyer, reassuring his mother: "I again write to Allan on the subject of the monthly family payment, insisting that that shall be promptly and religiously met, even if every other payment should be dishonored." [11]

While Gansevoort was trying to fill his father's place by remote control, Maria's misfortunes mounted. She had to give up her fashionable home on Clinton Square, two doors from Peter's, and moved instead into an inexpensive house in Lansingburgh, on the north side of Troy. She sold everything she could sell, including some of her silverware, but her creditors still pressed her and on at least one occasion threatened to foreclose on her furniture. She called on her brothers to help her, but Peter and Herman could spare her only a few dollars at a time—much less than she needed. Her children tried to help, but young Herman Melville could not find a steady job in a period of widespread unemployment, and finally in desperation became a common sailor. Young Allan began to study law with Peter, but when he and his uncle proved incompatible his brother Gansevoort helped him find a more congenial place in a New York law office. Tom, who was still a little boy, in due time went to sea and eventually became a captain in the merchant marine. The girls helped their mother at home and went to Boston on long visits to their parents' relatives and friends. Finally in 1847, when Herman, who had begun writing books about his experiences at sea, and Allan, who had established himself as a lawyer, both married, the two young couples rented a house in New York large enough for the whole family and invited Maria and the girls to share it with them.

In April, 1832, only three months after Melville's death, fire broke out in Teunis Morrell's carpenter shop and destroyed the hundred-fifty-year-old buildings on the Gansevoort home lot in Albany. Herman hurried down from Northumberland to help Peter assess the damage. The lot had become a valuable commercial site which they considered selling, and of which they did sell the back portion where the brewery had stood. On the site of the old home they decided to erect a new business building. This building was constructed of stone faced with blue Quincy granite "like the Tremont House in Boston," and was divided into three sections. The principal one, which fronted on North Market Street, was topped by the shining tin-roofed dome that Albany Dutchmen promptly dubbed "old Harme Gansevoort's brew kettle turned upside down." [12] It contained a restaurant in the basement, shops on the street floor, offices on the second story, and a grand ballroom on the third and fourth under the dome. In the center and rear sections were more shops including a bakery, a drill hall, "large rooms for societies, and convenient parlors and bedrooms for single gentlemen." [13] The total cost of construction was over $74,000, and Peter later estimated that they had put well over $100,000 into the building. As it neared completion in the spring of 1833, a delegation of citizens approached Peter and Herman with a testimonial complimenting them upon their addition to the city, and suggesting that it be named Stanwix Hall in honor of the Gansevoort family.

The circumstance that the ground on which it is erected, is derived from your ancestors, and the solidity and the durable character of the edifice seem to render it desirable and proper to give it a name, which while it refers to an important event in the revolutionary war, will be a lasting monument of the skill and bravery with which your father defended Fort Stanwix.[14]

Stanwix Hall began accepting tenants as soon as it was finished in the fall of 1833. One of the first was William Whale, who leased the ballroom and its adjoining office and cloakrooms for $100 "as a professor of dancing" on Wednesday and Saturday evenings, with the privilege of subleasing the room on any evening except Sunday and Thursday, the day of the city assemblies, for "Balls, Assemblies, Cotillion Parties, Dancing School, Concerts, and the Exhibition of Paintings." [15] The tenants of the restaurant in the basement rented as well the supper room and pantry adjoining the ballroom. Various military organizations and a fencing teacher leased the drill room for one day or evening a week. Artists, doctors, and lawyers moved into the offices; Odd Fellows, Masons, and other organizations took the meeting rooms. A "school for young men and ladies" which met from 6 to 8 A.M. and 7 to 9 P.M.—before and after working hours—and a "writing academy" inhabited the building briefly, but their pupils disturbed the other tenants and Peter decided not to admit any more schools. Among the tenants of the stores were former occupants of parts of the burned buildings, the Canal Collection Office, the post office, and the new Albany and Stockbridge Railway depot. There were also transient tenants who exhibited pictures, a "statue of Cleopatra," a "new Rail Road invention," and "the Mysterious Lady."

At the same time that Peter was straining his resources to help build Stanwix Hall, he and his law partner, John J. Hill, became involved in land speculation through their political contacts. In 1835 or 1836, the partners were invited to join a syndicate which wanted Peter's support in the senate for their plans to develop Van Buren Harbor, the best natural haven on Lake Erie between Buffalo and Erie, Pennsylvania, as the western terminal of the Erie Railroad.Unfortunately for this syndicate, a rival group was promoting nearby Dunkirk. At the last minute Peter made a rather clumsy attempt to prove that the Dunkirk group had exerted improper influence among the directors of the company, and Hill, trying to support him, only succeeded in laying their own group open to the same criticism. After the company decided in September, 1836, that Dunkirk would be the terminal, the Van Buren syndicate tried to get a federal appropriation to develop their harbor anyway, in the hope of forcing the company to reconsider, but this attempt was unsuccessful. Then President Jackson issued his Specie Circular, banks failed all over the United States, a general panic spread and deepened, and the other members of the syndicate lost interest. Instead of a hundred acres of valuable lots in a boom town, Peter and Hill were left with a debt of $10,000 and a not very desirable farm.

The general contraction of credit which was the Panic of 1837 found Peter burdened with obligations. He owed $10,000 with Hill, over $20,000 for Gansevoort Melville's fur factory, and nearly $40,000 from the building of Stanwix Hall. The last debt was as much Herman's as his, but Herman could not help after severe losses in the great fire in New York in 1835, and in the failure of banks, transportation companies, and a venture called the "Steam Saw Mill." Their mother's estate could not be settled because various complications postponed completion of the Saratoga County surveys, and during the depression no one wanted to buy land for its full value anyway. Peter's creditors, struggling to maintain their own solvency, called upon him to pay his debts as they fell due; Peter managed to scrape up money to pay the interest, but he could not retire the principal. In the fall of 1840, as Mary lay dying, he called desperately upon her brother Edward Sanford to advance him something on Mary's share of her father's unsettled estate, but Edward could not raise money either. Two months after Mary's death, one of the Stanwix Hall creditors threatened to foreclose his mortgage. Peter found $1,000 of the $4,000 that was demanded, but wrote that he would have to give up if further time could not be granted him to pay the rest, to which the mortgagor reluctantly consented. In 1844, after business in general had improved, Peter converted Stanwix Hall into a hotel, which throve because it was convenient to the railroad station, but which gave Peter frequent difficulty when the tenants who actually managed it sought to alter or evade the terms of their leases, which they insisted were unrealistically stringent. In the meantime the family of L. H. Gansevoort had been having nothing but misfortune for twenty-five years. In 1809, L. H. married Mary Ann Chandonette, whose father was a French officer who settled in Philadelphia after serving in the Revolution, and whose mother, Mary Davis, was a member of a leading family of Poughkeepsie. Both of Mary Ann's parents died soon after her birth and she was brought up by her mother's sister, whose marriage to Guert Van Schoonhoven of Waterford was childless. Despite her French and English background, Mary Ann therefore grew up in one of the leading Dutch Federalist clans of Saratoga County, and her home at Waterford was not far from Van Schaick's Island, where lived a family of Caty Gansevoort's cousins. Mary Ann was noted for her beauty and charm; she inherited no property from her parents, but her uncle gave her a valuable piece of land as a wedding present. In the spring of 1809 L. H. brought her home to Northumberland, and for the first time in its twenty-two years the yellow house had a mistress.

L. H. and Mary Ann were very happy together and with their eventual seven children, but both they and the children were constantly subjected to severe and protracted struggles with illness. In 1812, when Mary Ann was expecting her second child, L. H. was summoned to his father's deathbed. Not daring to leave Mary Ann alone, he wrote:

I am distressed beyond the Power of Description—50 miles from my Father and he on the brink of Eternity—perhaps this moment expiring —my Wife on the eve of a most Perilous situation in the midst of a Wilderness with not one solatary Relative, not a Friend to assist her, should I leave her—In the last moments of agony and Distress should she call for my help, and expire for the want of it—how could I ever forgive myself—what atonement could I make, how ever regain my Peace of Mind—what an awful situation—Great God, what must I do————*I cannot leave her*——[16]

Four years later, Mary Ann exerted herself too soon to care for another child, and suffered complications which kept her unwell for months, on top of which she caught a severe respiratory infection and suffered a temporary loss of her memory. Before she recovered completely, an epidemic of whooping cough swept the neighborhood and invaded her nursery. The following winter, L. H. developed an inflammation of the lungs which eventually proved to be tuberculosis. In the face of all this misfortune, when some time not long before his death L. H. drew up an account of his resources, which he estimated at $66,645, about $15,000 in lumber and the rest in land in Saratoga and Warren Counties, he concluded it, "A Wife called Mary worth more than all the Rest and Children almost as much as Wife—Rich Indeed!" [17]

After her husband's death, Mary Ann lived in Albany for a while and then removed to Waterford to be near her foster parents, but often paid long visits to her mother-in-law and to Maria, who both depended on her cheerful gossip to relieve the depression which often accompanied their illnesses. She particularly noticed and recounted human details; for example, Allan Melville once hastened to help an old man off a coach, tripped, and fell painfully into a coal hole, after which he refused to see a doctor, but Herman, Maria, and Mary Ann, who like all the Gansevoorts were enthusiastic amateur practitioners, ministered to his cuts and bruises. Another time Mary Ann rearranged all her summer visits so that her maid, a Methodist, could have a week of vacation at the time of a camp meeting. She appreciated Peter's helpfulness to herself and her children, writing:

Accept of my grateful acknowledgements for your kindness this morning and permit me to add, that the reluctance I feel in asking repeated favors, is invariably done away by the delicate and prompt manner in which they are always granted by my kind Brother.[18]

During the cholera epidemic of 1832 it was she who pressed him repeatedly to leave Albany, in which he stubbornly remained:

None of your age stand above you in a professional point of view; you never appear at the Bar, but you do yourself credit. In a political point, you know as well as I do that your increasing popularity, your honorable and gentlemanly deportment in all public business in which for the last several years you have been engaged, has been such as to excite the envy of some of your own party, you are independent, why should not life be dear to you? [19]

204

With her children Mary Ann had further misfortunes. The eldest, another Peter, was particularly disappointing. His father had wished him to pursue a military career, but he failed the entrance examination for West Point twice and, despite an intervening period in a military school, the commanding officer found him not only poorly prepared but also wanting in discipline. He was then sent to sea as a common sailor, at which time Maria wrote of him:

For my part I think it is the best thing that could be done with him. He does not appear to me to possess talents or inclination for study or improvement. He is obedient and seems to be anxious to please. I do not think we should be offended with him for not attending to his studies it was not his destiny. . . . Since his arrival which is nearly two weeks, I can say with truth that in my presence he has never been heard to say more, than answer yes, or no Sir to any question. He never even answers Gansevoort, who is an incessant talker with anything more than a kind good-natured smile. . . . I do not blame Peter but his Mother for her total want of ingenuousness on the subject.[20]

When Peter returned from this voyage his Uncle Peter exerted his influence to have him appointed a midshipman in the Navy; after he served for a time in the Brooklyn Navy Yard, his uncle urged the Secretary of the Navy to order him to sea for a long cruise. On his return in 1831 he wrote his uncle that he had reformed, that he needed money for clothes, and that he wanted to come home for a visit. When Uncle Peter sent the money but advised him to remain where he was, young Peter ingenuously replied, "I told one of the other middies I was reconciled to my uncle—he slapped me on the shoulder and said He doesn't know the half of it." [21] In all quarters grief was probably tempered by relief when young Peter drowned in a shipwreck the following March.

Mary Ann's next son Guert was much more promising. He was appointed a midshipman in the Navy in 1823 and went to sea, with Melville's enthusiastic approval and assistance in his outfitting, in October, 1824. In 1832 Guert was promoted to passed midshipman and in 1837 to lieutenant. In 1842 he was second in command of the training ship *Somers* when its captain, Alexander Mackenzie, decided to make an example of three midshipmen who had flouted naval discipline. The court-martial which tried them, over which Guert presided, thought that the evidence against them was a product of boyish mischief rather than serious mutiny, but Captain Mackenzie insisted that they review the case and impose the death penalty. Guert and the court very reluctantly complied—perhaps Guert compared the teen-aged offenders with his unfortunate elder brother—and the boys were solemnly hanged at the yardarm. Thereafter the ship seethed with unrest, and it was only by unceasing vigilance that its officers kept the situation under control until they reached New York. Then the fact that one of the boys who had been hanged was a son of the Secretary of War insured wide publicity for the affair. Public opinion condemned Captain Mackenzie for undue severity, but the Navy Department investigated and upheld him in the name of discipline. Guert was much distressed by this experience, and, though he refused to discuss it with anyone, even his family, they believed that it haunted him for the rest of his life. It also impressed his cousin Herman Melville, who soon afterward served as a sailor on a man-of-war, where the subject was undoubtedly much discussed, and nearly fifty years later used it as material for his story "Billy Budd."

The next of Mary Ann's children was her only daughter, Catherine, who married a lawyer, George Curtis, in 1836, had three children, and shared the family susceptibility to illness. The younger boys had notably poor health. Young Leonard, whose birth in 1816 was followed by his mother's protracted spell of weakness, went to sea as a merchant sailor and made two or three voyages before ill health—possibly the effects of rheumatic fever—compelled him to remain ashore, where he worked in the New York Customs House. Francis (Frances?) died in infancy in 1818. Herman Richard, born in 1820, was incurably ill for some time before he died in 1826. The baby, Stanwix, whose dying father had hoped that this son he never saw would be an especial comfort to his mother, was a perpetual problem. He attended a half-dozen schools before he became a midshipman in November, 1841, but the service was too much for his health and his character. After participating in part of the Mexican War and reputedly fighting a duel with the son of Stephen Decatur in the South Pacific, he resigned. At loose ends and suffering from arthritis, he rattled around aimlessly for several years. His ailing mother, to whom he always remained the baby of her widowhood, found him incomprehensible and unmanageable. Finally he came to rest near his sister's home in Glens Falls, where he lived in one room on the income of various legacies. No one considered him competent to manage his financial affairs, which Stanwix resented, but in spite of his frequent complaints that his brother-in-law George Curtis was cheating him, his uncle Peter named Curtis as trustee of the $1,000 he left his nephew in 1876.

In the 1830's, Peter and Herman managed all of Mary Ann's and Maria's financial affairs under the terms of their mother's will. After Melville's bankruptcy, Caty added a codicil setting off Melville's debts to Peter against Maria's share of the estate and placing the rest of it in trust for her children. L. H.'s share was likewise placed in trust for his children, and Peter and Herman were in both cases appointed trustees. When Caty died, therefore, they inherited not only their own shares of the Gansevoort fortune but also the responsibility of administering the rest of it until their nieces and nephews should come of age. Melville's death placed Maria in command of her own fortune, but like her mother she relied heavily upon Peter in the management of it. When she chose to back Gansevoort in the fur business, Peter supported her with his credit and influence at the bank, and eventually accepted the burden of a $20,000 note to save her—and himself as her endorser—from legal action. Mary Ann had little understanding of business. Under these circumstances, Herman and Peter left their mother's estate unsettled and continued to administer the family fortune as a unit, although they did divide some Albany lots and western lands in 1835.

In the meantime, Herman was trying to develop the lands in Saratoga County into a town. In 1835 the Saratoga and Washington Railroad began construction, only four years after the Albany and Schenectady Railroad, one of the first in the United States, began operation, and another railroad from Schenectady to Saratoga Springs was constructed. Gansevoort's Mills was on the di-

207

rect route between Saratoga and Fort Edward; the tracks eventually passed only a few hundred feet from Herman's mansion. Herman's employees then lived on nearby farms or around the sawmill on the west side of the Snock Kill; Herman now planned a whole new village on the east side, centered around a triangular green whose corners were the depot, his mansion, and the Empire Hotel. Leonard Street and Catherine Street ran northeast from the mansion, parallel to the tracks. Besides selling lots for homes and businesses, Herman gave land to the Dutch Reformed and Methodist churches and contributed to their buildings. A post office was established, and so the village of Gansevoort achieved independent existence. But then the railroad suspended construction in 1836, and was not completed until 1848. The village of Gansevoort became a liability instead of an asset, and agricultural land in the county declined sharply in value in the Panic of 1837. Herman's lumber was nearly gone, and in any case the price was low. His investments dropped in value; when he finally salvaged some of them the money was immediately swallowed up in other debts. On top of this the tremendous mortgage on Stanwix Hall burdened him as well as Peter.

It was just at this time that Mary Ann's children one after another reached the age of eighteen and became entitled to their inheritance from their grandmother. The boys at sea were out of touch with family affairs and did not press matters, but Catherine's husband George Curtis was anxious for his wife's share. He recognized that it was not only the low price of land at Gansevoort which prevented Peter and Herman from settling the estate. By the terms of the will they were required to pay the other heirs certain sums in lieu of their shares of the home lot, the General's mansion, which went to Peter, and Herman's own farm at Gansevoort. When Stanwix came of age in 1840, L. H.'s heirs agreed that there was no need for them to wait any longer, but the brothers did not have and could not raise large sums of cash while their other debts pressed them so closely. L. H.'s heirs accordingly sued them in 1841, and Peter and Herman took advantage of all the law's delays for five years, in the meantime selling some of the

Gansevoort property. When the Court of Chancery finally handed down its decision in December, 1846, it was found that after all debts and legacies were set off against each other, each of the heirs was entitled to about $17,000, less $1,000 which each was to contribute to provide for Wessel's small annuity—with true Gansevoort longevity he survived until 1863. Peter and Herman were each ordered to pay $16,000, but since Maria's debt to Peter amounted to more than her share, her inheritance was set against her indebtedness, and Peter was relieved of the necessity of making an immediate cash payment. The whole burden of paying L. H.'s insistent heirs, who had indeed been kept waiting far longer than Caty's will intended, fell upon Herman, who could not raise the cash.

Curtis, acting for Mary Ann, would wait no longer; he sued Herman, secured a judgment, and sent the sheriff to execute it. Thus Herman was brought by his own sister-in-law to the humiliation of a sheriff's sale. Almost beside herself, Herman's wife, Catherine, who had always prided herself on her relationship to one of the leading families of New York City, took up a worn-out pen and scratched off a barely legible letter to Peter

to inlist all the sympathies and humanity of your nature in behalf of your honourable and manly brother, whose suffering from wounded feelings must now be total. Yet I will make one remark. When alone with me then the strong man gives way and upbraids himself for injustice done himself and to me who left a thrice happy home to share with him the solitude of a then desert, and now when we have by every prudent exertion been enabled to erect two neat buildings for Public Worship to be degraded by a sheriff's sale, that is too humiliating, even to minds of much lower grades than ours. . . . the horrors of a sheriff's sale would I think be my last conflict.[22]

Curtis insisted that the sale must go on, while Peter pulled every string to have it put off until Herman could return from a last fund-raising expedition. When Herman was unsuccessful he assigned all his property to Peter, who finally arranged with Curtis to pay the legacy in four annual installments. He relieved Herman of his interest in Stanwix Hall for $5,000 and sold the real

209

estate in Saratoga County. It proved possible to satisfy the judgment and Herman's other debts without selling his home or the mills, which were released from the assignment in 1855.

But this was not the end of Herman's misfortunes. In 1851 George F. Munro, a grandson of the original Tory proprietor, returned from Canada and questioned the Gansevoorts' title. When the suit came to trial in December, 1855, right after Catherine's death, it was too much for Herman, who left the whole matter to Peter except for testifying when called upon. Munro tried to prove a flaw in General Gansevoort's title by demonstrating that his grandfather's attainder during the Revolution was not legal. The Gansevoorts insisted that this claim, even if justified in itself, which they denied, was invalid because they had occupied the land far longer than the statute governing adverse possession required. It was as evidence that their title was rooted in actual and continuous possession that most of the early history of General Gansevoort's mills was recalled and set down. At first Munro's title was upheld, but Peter appealed the decision, and finally in 1863, after Herman's death, the Gansevoorts' title was confirmed.

Thus the Gansevoorts flung their fortune into the gamble of American development and lost the larger part of it. The obvious reason was certainly incompatibility between the preindustrial Dutch tradition of accumulating a fortune by generations of commerce and the emerging American tradition, springing from both the Industrial Revolution and the frontier, of making a fortune— or losing it—overnight. The old sure investments were sure no longer, as ships, shipping routes, and cargoes underwent a transportation revolution and wild lands no longer gradually appreciated as orderly settlement approached them, but "boomed" and "busted" with the progress of internal improvements. The locations of roads, canals, and railroads were no longer determined primarily by the obvious dictates of geography, on which the promoters of Van Buren Harbor depended, but upon the shifting favors of the people's representatives influenced by special-interest lobbyists. The credit structure was in the hands of the people's banks, chartered for political purposes by those same legislatures, who expanded or contracted credit in response to the will of the people—or of the special-interest groups who claimed to represent it—without much reference to the written or unwritten laws of economics. In this expanding universe, the man most likely to succeed was the promoter, politician as well as shrewd trader, who had started from among the people and could convince them that he was trying to sell them something they wanted to buy already, or wanted them to invest in a scheme which he knew from his own experience to be something they wanted to build, and at the same time could convince the people's representatives that it would be to their political advantage to grant him whatever privileges he needed for success. The Dutch tradition, in which patrician families exercised the privileges of the community and regulated its trade for the communal benefit, was relevant only if and when a patrician could convince the people—and their representatives—that his slow, sure plans in fact forwarded their interests, of which in the nineteenth century the American people were often unwilling to be convinced, or else if he would risk his inherited fortune on the apparently least chancy of the thousands of investment gambles offered to him. This both Melville and the Gansevoort brothers did, and flung their family fortunes into the bottomless pit of American depressions, which were only seen a hundred years later to follow a definite—but different—pattern peculiar to the Industrial Revolution.

But the Gansevoort fortune was by no means entirely lost during the Panic of 1837 and its predecessors, and indeed Peter Gansevoort later restored it and left it intact to another generation. Therefore it seems obvious that part of the family's misfortune was due to weakness in its individual members, which cropped out almost simultaneously in several branches. There is too little information about Leonard, Jr.'s children to explain why so many of them found that everything they touched went wrong. Part of it may have been vocational and social misplacement; John was a good enough soldier, but a total failure as a businessman, and Rensselaer was a promising young doctor before he became entangled in business affairs that were possibly his brother's and involved with another man's wife in an era when divorce was not a practicable recourse. Nevertheless both of them, John's two

211

sons, and some of Leonard, Jr.'s daughters as well, seem to have been simply weak in character, as others were weak in health, which weaknesses may well have been partly hereditary. The same is true of L. H.'s disappointing brood of children, who inherited physical weakness from their father and quite possibly mental weakness from their mother, who was beautiful, charming, and lovable, but never keenly intelligent or acute about business, and on one occasion was actually mentally ill. Furthermore, Dr. Pieter's grandchildren, some of whom had removed to the town of Bath in Steuben County, also failed in business and in general disappointed the world's expectation of them. Maria Melville's children had a closer source of fragility in their intelligent, intense father whose relatives shared the nervous weakness which he passed on to them, but the possibility of a Gansevoort contribution to their highly strung, easily overset mental and emotional balance cannot be discounted.

In the absence of detailed information about the earlier generations no common source for these traits can be identified, but since they appeared in descendants of all of Leendert's children, perhaps it is significant that Leonard, Jr., recollected that Leendert was meek and mild, and just possibly Leendert's sister, Maria, who never in all her long life married, shared some of them. Farther back not even conjecture can reasonably go. It is interesting to note, however, that with a few exceptions these inherited weaknesses—if they were inherited—affected the men, particularly in the fifth and sixth generations, when they not only failed in business but also failed to marry and perpetuate the family name. Most of their sisters married, usually had large families, and carried on the tradition of the Dutch matrons as staunchly as ever.

Individual weakness does not completely explain the Gansevoorts' misfortunes any more than the then-unwritten laws of the American economic tradition. Particularly among General Gansevoort's children, who had among them the largest fortune of any branch of the family, ultimate disaster came about because family members disagreed with each other about the disposal of their fortune. Maria had definite ideas of her own about how her fortune should be invested, as a result of which she lost it, and Mary

Ann was willing to break up the family—which, after all, was her husband's and not her own—for the sake of that fortune. One cannot help wondering why Maria's formerly prudent brother encouraged her to pledge the whole of her fortune to support her inexperienced teen-aged son's fur factory, but in the 1830's Peter was not so prudent in his own affairs. In the years after his mother's death, when he sat in the senate, married Mary Sanford, built Stanwix Hall, and plunged into the Van Buren Harbor scheme, he piled his own obligations to dizzy heights in areas in which he had no previous experience. Nevertheless, when the crash came Maria understood what it was all about and endured her share of the family's straitened circumstances with "characteristic fortitude." But Mary Ann, and Mary Ann's son-in-law—neither of whom were Dutch—were unable to take the long view. In law, and perhaps in equity, they had a case, but as a matter of business they would have been wiser to wait until Stanwix Hall established itself and Herman's share of the profits enabled him to pay what he owed them. By forcing the matter they got their money but estranged themselves from the rest of the family and also estranged Herman from Peter. Both of these differences were more or less made up, the latter completely, but after *Gansevoort v. Gansevoort* the extended family for all practical purposes ceased to exist. Instead, many of its individual members flung themselves away from it and from the Dutch patrician tradition to face the problems of the nineteenth century alone.

IX

Escape from Tradition

In the middle of the nineteenth century many descendants of Dutch patrician families left the city of Albany, some to participate in state, national, and even international affairs, some to live on country estates, some to become merchants and professional men in other towns and cities, a few to join the army or go to sea. Those patricians who remained in Albany found their Dutch tradition swept out from under their feet by Yankee invasion and population explosion within the city and the pressure of main currents in nineteenth-century economic, social, and political development outside it. But at the same time the younger generation often deliberately turned away from aspects of the Dutch tradition to which they might have clung, notably its fundamental attitudes toward the acquisition and disposition of wealth and power, toward family relationships, and toward religion. In particular, Herman Melville and Henry Sanford Gansevoort experienced psychological as well as social conflict between the Dutch and American traditions.

To Herman Melville, who passed his childhood in New York with frequent visits to and from his father's Yankee relatives, his mother's Albany Dutch tradition was from the beginning only a part of his environment. He lived in Albany with his family for several years after his father's failure and death, dwelling two doors from Peter Gansevoort on Clinton Square and having frequent contact with him, and working in his brother's fur factory. After his brother's failure he sought other work, but he had quit

214

school before he was prepared for a profession, his experience as a clerk was a drug on the market in a depression, and his uncle's Democratic political affiliation was a positive hindrance to obtaining public employment after the Whig party came to power in the state in 1838. All the resources of the Dutch tradition thus failed Herman Melville and he was forced to go to sea as a common sailor, doing work suited neither to his social position nor to his mental ability, but meanwhile learning all there was to know about the small, particularistic, privileged, tradition-bound communities of ship's companies—as he subtitled *White Jacket* (1850), "the world in a man-o'-war."

When Melville came home, brimming over with his experiences, he poured out some of them into a South Seas adventure story, *Typee* (1846), which when published was quickly successful. It particularly appealed to Peter Gansevoort, who always preferred it to any of his nephew's later works; it is easy—and revealing—to see why. *Typee* is in many respects like a Dutch genre painting, for example, like some of Breughel's peasant scenes in a South Seas setting. Its situation and story, such as it is, are idyllic, but its geography, characters, and action are communicated by the piling up of hard, accurately observed facts, presented not as individual events deeply analyzed nor as flowing masses of indistinguishable incidents, but as groups of individual occurrences, each carefully delineated in its relationship to others of its kind and each possessing mass and specific gravity as well as dimensions. It should be noted further that both here and elsewhere in his works Melville's imagery was highly visual, and that when he utilized other kinds of sense impressions they were usually produced by something that could be seen, and presented with the spatial immediacy of a picture rather than, for example, the temporal flow of a piece of music. In *Typee*, therefore, Melville was concerned with the artistic ordering and presentation of observed facts, and not at all with abstract ideas. Such concepts as did appear in the work, most notably severe criticism of missionaries whose practice did not bear out their preaching, were moral rather than intellectual. In all of these respects *Typee* resembled Peter Gansevoort's own immense outpouring of busi-

215

ness and family letters and legal documents, in the tradition of
those original Hudson Valley Dutch settlers who,

being realistic business men, weighed their phrases as they did their
grains or cheeses, and the words they used referred to concrete things.
In their petition to the members of the Amsterdam Chamber these
worried men had nothing to say about the collapse of civilization or
even of the end of their own freedom: they wrote simply about the
flimsy hold their deeds gave them on their property.[1]

After *Typee*, Melville wrote *Omoo* (1847) and *Redburn*
(1849), drawing openly on his various experiences at sea but reorganizing them and transforming them imaginatively to a level
beyond direct autobiography. These books, though not as successful as *Typee*, were published in both England and America
and established Melville as a promising popular author. In 1847
he felt himself sufficiently secure in this new, utterly unexpected
but highly respectable profession to marry and settle in New York
with his brother, Allan, sharing with him and his wife both a
home and the responsibility for supporting his mother and sisters.
There he came into contact with other men of letters and began
to develop an interest in the dynamics of intellectual debate
which turned *Mardi* (1849) into an odd and utterly unsalable
combination of South Seas adventure, social and moral criticism,
and philosophical quest. Most readers found it unintelligible primarily because they were unfamiliar with Spenser, whose works
the boy Melville had found in his father's highly idiosyncratic library, and Rabelais, to whom his New York friends introduced
him. The narrator, Taji, a sort of Pantagruel in shining armor rid-
ing into the sunset in a Yankee longboat, reflected a point of observation of American life and thought not so far removed from
that of Peter Van Schaack. Taji personified liberty while Van
Schaack discussed the nature of it, but the debates of Taji and his
companions agreed with Van Schaack's arguments that liberty
was primarily a moral rather than a political quality, and that so
long as an individual's actions did not interfere with the liberty of
others or the activities of the community, his opinions, and more
important, his conscientious beliefs, were no concern of the community.

216

After the unfortunate experience of *Mardi* Melville wrote *White-Jacket,* another imaginatively autobiographical account of seafaring life, this time aboard a naval vessel. Then, the joint menage having become unwieldy with the birth of children to both his wife and Allan's, he and his family, including his mother and sisters, moved to a farm near Pittsfield, Massachusetts. There, while beginning yet another book about his experiences on a whaler, he became acquainted with his neighbor, Nathaniel Hawthorne, who encouraged him to develop his interest in probing to the psychological depths of moral dilemmas. Under this stimulus *Moby Dick,* like *Mardi,* turned into something more than an adventure story, becoming as well a study in the moral psychology of obstinate conviction which did not appeal to the mid-nineteenth-century reading public. *Pierre,* which Melville wrote to recoup this failure in communication, was an attempt to tell a popular melodramatic tale of innocent and guilty love and death in a Hudson Valley setting, but Melville was not really interested in telling this kind of story, and his readers were not at all interested in the moral and philosophical dilemmas in which the hero became involved. After this further failure to satisfy his audience, Melville wrote no more novels, although he continued to contribute short stories, anonymous articles and reviews, and a few poems to magazines.

In the meantime the strain of continuous confinement to his desk told on Melville's health, as, incidentally, happened to other Gansevoorts, notably his cousin Henry, and he began to develop symptoms of the rheumatic complaints which plagued many other members of the family and probably represented a hereditary weakness. Both of these physical pressures strained the delicately balanced nervous system he inherited from his father's family, and helped to produce frustrations and depressions which alarmed his family and interfered with his work. He was relieved of responsibility for two of his sisters when they married, and for the other two and his mother when they moved to Gansevoort to live with Uncle Herman after his wife died in 1855, but by this time Melville and his wife had four small children of their own. Needing an additional source of income—it should be noted that very few American authors in that generation were able to support themselves and their families entirely by the sale of their works—he tried for a diplomatic appointment like Hawthorne's consulship at Liverpool, but his writings included no campaign contributions like Hawthorne's biography of his school friend, President Franklin Pierce. Peter Gansevoort then tried to exert his influence in the nationally regnant Democratic party, but the Whigs were again in power in New York, controlling the more accessible state offices, and in any case Melville was at this time by a few miles a resident of Massachusetts. His abilities, his influence, his connections were all out of phase with the times, and the utmost that all his relatives and friends could ultimately do to help him support his family was to get him—and, in the age of the spoils system run rampant, to keep him—a minor position in the New York Customs House. Then, in 1867, his eldest son committed suicide, an event from which Melville never recovered, and after which he abdicated all attempts to act as head of the Melville clan and cut himself off increasingly from all of his family outside of his own immediate household. In these years, however, he did write one more major work, a long religious and philosophical poem entitled *Clarel,* for which Peter Gansevoort, once more commanding a sizeable fortune, offered to underwrite the cost of publication. It was perhaps just as well that Peter, by that time in his eighties, died before the book was ready for him to read, for it was not at all like his favorite *Typee* and he would probably have found Melville's concern with moral philosophy unintelligible. Certainly his daughter Kate complained that she could not understand even Melville's *Battle Pieces,* short poems about events of the Civil War.

Like many other geniuses, Herman Melville appeared to be a failure largely because his ideas were ahead of those of his audience. His interests anticipated those of literary scholars of the 1920's, who delightedly rediscovered his works. As changes in curriculum brought the books which inspired Melville into the background of readers, and scholars explored more thoroughly the areas with which he was concerned, his accomplishment in com-

218

pressing into a few volumes of imaginative discovery the intellectual investigations of three quarters of a century began to be appreciated. Literary critics have written extensively on his work,
stressing his perceptions of depth psychology, his moral interpretations of social questions, his criticism of the way of life and the
literary conventions of his time, his use of personal experience as
imaginative raw material, and his romantic questing for an un-
earthly goal. They have been unable, however, to fit his mature
works securely into any known literary tradition. This is hardly
surprising, since the literary and formal intellectual tradition of
nineteenth-century America was fundamentally English (notably
New Englandish) and Melville was only half Yankee. The other
half of him was Dutch, but since, as has already been demonstrated, the Dutch tradition was anything but literary, its influence upon his work has hitherto been undescribed. The relationship between Melville's vision and that of Dutch painting has
already been mentioned, but even more than in pictures the
Dutch tradition habitually expressed itself through everyday human behavior, often deliberately denying the reality of intellectual abstractions. As Erasmus wrote:

Another, perhaps even a non-Christian, may discuss more subtly how
the angels understand, but to persuade us to lead here an angelic life,
free from every stain, this indeed is the duty of the Christian theologian.[2]

Melville's Pierre faced exactly the same dilemma:

So the difference between the priest and Pierre was herein:—with the
priest it was a matter, whether certain bodiless thoughts of his were
true or not true; but with Pierre it was a question whether certain
vital acts of his were right or wrong. In this little nut lies germ-like
the possible solution of some puzzling problems; and also the discovery
of additional, and still more profound problems ensuing upon the solution of the former.[3]

Melville believed that decisions in such questions in fact were
and in theory ought to be made ultimately by conscience rather
than reason. He concluded *Clarel:*

219

Yea, ape and angel, strife and old debate—
The harps of heaven and dreary gongs of hell;
Science the feud can only aggravate—
No umpire she betwixt the chimes and knell:
The running battle of the star and clod
Shall run forever—if there be no God. . . .

But through such strange illusions have they passed
Who in life's pilgrimage have baffled striven—
Even death may prove unreal at the last,
And stoics be astounded into heaven.[4]

Melville's meaning here is likely to be mistaken by modern readers accustomed to think of the dichotomy between reason and emotion in psychological rather than religious terms. Like Erasmus, Melville's concern with religion was primarily with its function as a motivation of right human conduct, which in secular terms subordinated reason to conscience. This conscience, which reaches down from above, must not be equated with the unconscious, which wells up from below, nor confused with the superego, which is social in origin. For the conscience, though socially and traditionally conditioned, represents ultimately an eternal standard of values whose very existence scientific relativism denies. Therefore Melville's insistence throughout his works on the supremacy of the heart was no supremacy of fickle sentiment, but the supremacy of the God-given human conscience of mankind, to which authority Peter Van Schaack appealed in asserting his individual opinion against the whole collective weight of the American Revolution, and on which authority Martin Van Buren relied as the effective expression of the fundamental will of the sovereign people. This conscience, so obstinately Dutch in defending its particular privilege of independent judgment, and at the same time American to the extent that it occurred in individuals rather than in a community as a whole, directed itself primarily to those aspects of life which were fundamental to the Dutch tradition—fortune, family, and religion. It is most interesting that Melville's three mature major works dealt with precisely these subjects.

220

Moby Dick was especially concerned with the morality practiced by men seeking their fortunes through their work, although
Melville by no means equated fortune with pecuniary profit, and
Captain Ahab in particular passed before the story opened from
the pursuit of profit to the pursuit of power. In this connection,
however, the interconvertibility of profit, prestige, and power in
the Dutch tradition may well be remembered. The encyclopedic
information about whales and whaling which Melville inserted
into his narrative not only added weight, depth, and verisimili-
tude to the story, but also showed how the details of men earning
their living possess a dramatic value of their own which may be
used to forward the purpose of a work of literature. Time and
again Melville used a technological procedure as a framework for
placing a philosophical discussion or disquisition in perspective,
or for demonstrating some human relationship between the characters performing it. He explored every aspect of the shipboard
community, showing its development in time as well as describing it in space, and making clear how its common bond, the pursuit and processing of whales, held it together by his massive
inclusion of details describing the nature of that bond. Thus he
built up tremendous power which was released through the continuous surging action of the last quarter of the novel, in which
this small and self-sufficient community was destroyed when one
of its leaders became overwhelmingly ambitious. In this sense it is
a story that Abraham C. Cuyler and Abraham Yates—and even
Peter Gansevoort—might have read with profit, although undoubtedly they would have been unwilling to apply its lesson to
themselves.

Pierre, alone among Melville's works, dealt with the general
subject of family relationships, particularly with the havoc which
resulted when those relationships became confused with each
other, as might very well happen and sometimes actually did
when people took seriously the rhetoric of sentimentality. Pierre
was a teen-aged only child with no living adult male relatives,
whose widowed mother perpetuated her own youthful image by
encouraging him to call her "sister" and maintained her power
over him by a charm essentially sexual. Pierre therefore stood on

the verge of adulthood and marriage to Lucy, a fiancée of his mother's choice, with no clear-cut distinction between mothers, sisters, and wives. When Isabel, a mysterious orphan with strong sex appeal, convinced him that she was his illegitimate sister, he immediately broke away from both his mother and Lucy to elope with her, but he could not make up his mind whether to treat her as a sister or a wife, and never forgave her for not filling his mother's place. After his mother died of wounded pride, Lucy insisted on joining him as another anomalous sister-wife who did fulfill motherly functions and thereby roused Isabel's jealousy. Unable to cope with this menage and reprobated by Lucy's outraged relatives, representing public opinion, Pierre finally killed his only cousin, a rival who sought to take Lucy away from him, and with Isabel committed suicide in prison as Lucy died of grief.

This moral tale, which Melville's cousin, Kate Gansevoort, who idolized her brother Henry almost beyond the patience of her most patient fiancé, might well have taken as a cautionary exemplum, resembled in many respects the Shakespearean tragedies of family life, notably *Romeo and Juliet* and *Hamlet*, and Dante's *Inferno*, all of which it explicitly quoted. Its relationship to the Dutch tradition was far more implicit, partly through visual imagery reflecting Dutch popular demonology most familiar today through the paintings of Hieronymus Bosch, but much more fundamentally by Melville's specific evocation of the American Dutch tradition at the opening of the novel.

Consider those most ancient and magnificent Dutch manors at the North, whose perches are miles—whose meadows overspread adjacent counties—and whose haughty rent-deeds are held by their thousand farmer-tenants, so long as grass grows and water runs; which hints of a surprising eternity for a deed, and seems to make lawyer's ink unobliterable as the sea. Some of those manors are two centuries old; and their present patroons or lords will show you stakes and stones on their estates put there—the stones at least—before Nell Gwynne the Duke-mother was born, and genealogies which, like their own river, Hudson, flow somewhat farther and straighter than the Serpentine brooklet in Hyde Park.

Those far-descended Dutch meadows lie steeped in a Hindooish haze; an eastern patriarchalness sways its mild crook over pastures, whose tenant flocks shall there feed, long as their own grass grows, long as their own water shall run. Such estates seem to defy Time's tooth, and by conditions which take hold of the indestructible earth seem to cotemporize their fee-simples with eternity. . . .

But whatever one may think of the existence of such mighty lordships in the heart of a republic, and however we may wonder at their thus surviving, like Indian mounds, the Revolutionary flood; yet survive and exist they do, and are now owned by their present proprietors, by as good nominal title as any peasant owns his father's old hat, or any duke his great-uncle's old coronet.[5]

Thus Melville answered his friend Hawthorne's complaint and the similar observation of English travelers that there were no traditions in America in the Dutch manner, with a statement of indisputable fact. It is quite true that the future of this fact was very dim after the anti-rent wars of the 1840's, and that the Hudson Valley aristocratic tradition which Melville chose to compare with the aristocratic traditions of Europe differed somewhat from the Dutch patrician tradition whose values his story in fact embodied. Nevertheless, in the Dutch tradition in general his imagination discovered what it required, factual evidence of the existence of some tradition in the New World, which the main current of nineteenth-century American thought vociferously and insistently denied.

Melville needed this tradition as a fulcrum for the criticism of the then current sentimental frame of mind which was a major theme of his story. The stated values of the novel were those of the sentimental tradition—the country was a haven of bliss, the city a den of iniquity, the facts of love and death were unmentionable and idealizations of them wholly out of touch with reality, and "the two most horrible crimes . . . possible to civilized humanity—incest and parricide." Most shocked nineteenth-century readers, and some twentieth-century psychological critics, agreed that *Pierre* was about incest and parricide, though as a matter of fact no one in the book committed either. Instead, Pierre committed the crime of murder, prompted thereto by the sin of Captain Ahab, arrogating to himself the supreme power of

223

determining standards of right and wrong. These standards, in the Dutch tradition, were properly determined by the cumulative experience of many generations in a community, which cumulative experience may be equated in America with the voice of the people, and through them, with the voice of God. That Melville was following this tradition was evident from the crucial passage in which Pierre declared his independence by destroying his father's portrait and his other family relics:

It shall not live. Hitherto I have hoarded up mementos and monuments of the past . . . but it is forever over now. . . . all is done, and all is ashes! Henceforth, cast-out Pierre has no paternity, and no past; and since the Future is one blank to all; therefore, twice-disinherited Pierre stands untrammeledly his ever-present self!—free to do his own self-will and present fancy to whatever end! [6]

In the face of this avarice—the chief of the mediaeval Seven Deadly Sins—even Pierre's mother's fatal sin of pride sank to relative unimportance and lust, which Pierre in his youth and inexperience—and his sentimental readers in theirs—believed to be his greatest temptation, faded away to the periphery of the moralist's concern. Melville doubtless found much support for this traditional hierarchy of values in his reading, but his very unspoken reliance upon it as a basis of judgment indicates that it was ingrained in him as a part of his childhood religious training, not nearly so much in the doctrines set forth by his pastor as in the traditions handed on by his mother from centuries and generations of Dutch matrons teaching their sons and daughters the fundamental difference between right and wrong behavior.

The question often arises of the extent to which Melville modeled characters, particularly in *Pierre*, upon members of his own family. Many resemblances have been pointed out between Pierre's mother and Maria Melville, Lucy and Herman's wife Lizzie, Isabel and one of his cousins. Melville himself provided an explanation in introducing Lucy; after a few conventional lines describing her beauty, and two poetic pages conveying his conception of beauty—a spiritual quality—in women generally, he observed:

Never shall I get down the vile inventory! How, if with paper and pencil I went out into the starry night to inventorize the heavens? Who shall tell stars as teaspoons? Who shall put down the charms of Lucy Tartan on paper? And for the rest; her parentage, what fortune she would possess, how many dresses in her wardrobe, and how many rings upon her fingers; cheerfully would I let the genealogists, tax-gatherers, and upholsterers attend to that. My proper province is with the angelical part of Lucy. But as in some quarters, there prevails a sort of prejudice against angels, who are merely angels and nothing more; therefore I shall martyrize myself, by letting such gentlemen and ladies into some details of Lucy Tartan's history.[7]

The fact that the tiresome details which immediately followed resembled Lizzie Melville's history was proportionately a minor matter, as it is a minor matter that saints in Renaissance paintings of religious scenes incidentally resemble the models from whom the artist drew them. Melville's characters were intended to be representatives of types, not differentiated individuals as is usual in twentieth-century novels: What was important to him was that a certain sort of human being—a real person with a particular type of character; "angelical part" by no means indicates "disembodied spirit" from this practical Dutchman—when placed in a given situation would react in a particular way. The personal description and family history which readers insisted on finding might as well be copied from his own experience as from someone else's conventional novel. It is only necessary to read the letters of the relatives he used as models in this way to discover that the resemblances were primarily external and that the characters played out their roles in the story entirely independently of the personalities of their models.

Melville specifically expounded his ideas about religion in *Clarel*, whose subject was the conflict between religious revelation and scientific discovery which perplexed so many late-nineteenth-century intellectuals. *Clarel* followed the general format of *Mardi* in describing a quest, this time a religious pilgrimage specifically compared to that of Chaucer's *Canterbury Tales*, which provided a framework for philosophical discussions among the various pilgrims. As in *Pierre*, the central figure was a young man on the verge of adulthood, a theological student named Clarel who was troubled by religious doubt while visiting the Holy Land, where his tour followed the route taken by Melville himself in 1857. Clarel's particular problem was that of many Americans, including Mark Twain, who journeyed from the wide-open, well-watered spaces of the New World to the confined desert of Palestine. Their ideas of holy places, conditioned by American geography and Biblical imagery, accorded ill with the hot, stinking squalor of the Middle East. For example, Melville described Clarel's mental state in the Garden of Gethsemane in a manner startlingly reminiscent of the Bible pictures of the Hudson Valley limners:

> What frame of mind may Clarel woo?
> He the night-scene in picture drew—
> The band which came for sinless blood
> With swords and staves, a multitude.
> They brush the twigs, small birds take wing,
> The dead boughs crackle, lanterns swing,
> Till lo, they spy them through the wood.
> "Master!"—'Tis Judas. Then the kiss.
> And He, He falters not at this—
> Speechless, unspeakably submiss:
> The fulsome serpent on the cheek
> Sliming: endurance more than meek—
> Endurance of the fraud foreknown,
> And fiend-heart in the human one.
> Ah, now the pard on Clarel springs:
> The Passion's narrative plants stings.[8]

But this experience was interrupted by a monkish guide with an extended spiel about "the exact spot where" each event in the Biblical account occurred, by a tourist

> Spruce, and with volume light in hand
> Bound smartly, late in reference scanned,[9]

and by one of Clarel's own companions who, Clarel thought, was inappropriately amused by this tourist. Melville expressed the total attitude of disillusion he was describing:

226

> But ah, the dream to test by deed,
> To seek to handle the ideal
> And make a sentiment serve need:
> To try to realize the unreal! [10]

Falling in love—that nineteenth-century panacea—did little to resolve Clarel's religious doubts, which returned to him with redoubled force when he took a side trip to the Jordan with several companions. These formed Melville's favorite unit of the company or small community, and their moral encounters in the course of philosophical debate were his principal subject. Among them they presented the major post-Darwinian scientific and religious viewpoints, and gave Clarel a wide range of choice in his search for an image of a father which could also serve him as an image of God. This search was undoubtedly the other side of Pierre's idolization of his dead father: "Not to God had Pierre ever gone in his heart, unless by ascending the steps of that shrine, and so making it the vestibule of his abstractest religion." [11] Modern readers may need to be reminded that this is the sin of blasphemy, breach of the first and second commandments together, for the alleged commission of which Jesus was crucified; for practical purposes, the moralist was tacitly pointing out the danger of confusing sentimental and moral relations, the human and the divine. Though Clarel learned something from each of the older men on the pilgrimage, if it was only to avoid the example of several who had committed or were committing the sin of Captain Ahab, even the attractive figures, Rolfe, who drew him intellectually, and Vine, who drew him emotionally, eventually left him to face his own doubts and the additional loss by the girl's sudden death of his sentimental expectation of redemption through human love. But at this point Melville concluded in his own person:

> Unmoved by all the claims our times avow,
> The ancient Sphinx still keeps the porch of shade;
> And comes Despair, whom not her calm may cow,
> And coldly on that adamantine brow
> Scrawls undeterred his bitter pasquinade.
> But Faith (who from the scrawl indignant turns)

227

With blood warm oozing from her wounded trust,
Inscribes even on her shards of broken urns
The sign o' the cross—*the spirit above the dust!* . . .

Then keep thy heart, though yet but ill-resigned—
Clarel, thy heart, the issues there but mind;
That like the crocus budding through the snow—
That like a swimmer rising from the deep—
That like a burning secret which doth go
Even from the bosom that would hoard and keep;
Emerge thou mayst from the last whelming sea,
And prove that death but routs life into victory.[11]

Herman Melville thus escaped from the Albany Dutch tradition physically and intellectually only to return to it emotionally and spiritually. His cousin Henry Gansevoort had somewhat similar experience, although instead of being thrust out of the tradition by necessity Henry had to fight his way out at the cost of great distress to himself and his family. Henry's conflicts were undoubtedly partly the result of his insecure childhood, shaken by his mother's long illness and death and his father's grief. Peter loved his son dearly, but he was far past the usual age of fatherhood and had spent very little of his life in the company of children. Driven nearly to distraction by the loss of his wife, he probably never realized how overwhelming his torrents of affection and tempestuous rages would appear to a small boy—especially as Peter was, like a number of his close relatives, over six feet tall and stentorian in voice. After Peter's remarriage Henry further disliked his stepmother, whose quiet watchfulness was much harder to outwit than his father's frequent extravagance and inconsistency. As he grew up, furthermore, Henry came to resemble in many respects his grandfather, Nathan Sanford, who was known as a slippery, secretive, and selfish politician, and whose children disputed bitterly over his estate, quarreling further with Peter Gansevoort when he tried to arbitrate among them. It was quite possibly from the Sanford family that Henry acquired his moody, irritable, and erratic temperament, his intellectual quickness, and his disposition, both suspicious and capable of deliberate cruelty, which was quite unlike that of any other Gansevoorts.

After a few childish difficulties Henry generally did well in school, graduating from the Albany Academy at the head of his class in 1851. Planning to enter Princeton as a sophomore, in order to avoid the social indignities of the freshman year, he went to Andover for postgraduate study, but returned home after two months because the work he went for was not offered, and made a formal agreement with his father concerning arrangements for completing his studies at home. The terms of this agreement indicate areas of friction between Henry and his father that were to increase with the years. Henry's draft read:

That in staying home I will attend my recitations at the Albany Academy and study at my room applying myself vigorously to the prosecution of my studies, having an end in view and only a limited time to attend to it. And also if at any time, I should not fitly and intinsly [sic] apply myself to my studies and accord in my behavior taking fit and proper exercise in the afternoon I shall be compelled to attend the Albany Academy as a day scholar besides other proper punishment. In return I am to go to Princeton College to enter Sophomore. And besides I shall be fitted for the class in June next. (s.) H. S G. And that I shall go to the Commencement and attend examination in June.

To this Peter added some more specific conditions:

First—That you are not to go out in the evening unless I know where you are.

Second—If I ask you where you have been, I shall receive a prompt and truthful answer, not an indefinite reply.

Third. To make yourself pleasant about the house and agreeable at Table.

Fourth. That you will retire at 10 oClock [the family hour] and have your lamp out at that time.

Fifth. That you will attend your own Church regularly every Sabbath, with liberty to attend any other Church in the evening.[12]

Henry duly entered Princeton in August, 1852, and pursued a normal college career. He studied sufficiently to attain high grades, though not the very highest, as "confinement ill agrees with me," [13] enjoyed himself as much as possible, joined his father's secret society, and ran into serious trouble with the administration which at one point threatened to prevent his graduation. Like most students, including his father, he never had enough money, but Peter, perhaps remembering the General's parsimony to him, did not stint his son and Henry's requests for additional funds were moderate. Nevertheless, tension between him and his father continued and right after his graduation in July, 1855, exploded into a tempestuous disagreement about his future. There was no question in Peter's mind but that Henry would come home and enter his law office. Henry was equally determined that he would do no such thing. He therefore answered a newspaper advertisement and accepted a position as a tutor in the family of a perfect stranger from Memphis, Tennessee. This employer, impressed by Henry's family background, assured him:

You will be treated like a gentleman and as one of the family, we are all of liberal ideas of matters in general, but all Presbyterians but not afraid to eat a good dinner and drink a Bottle of wine at dinner. . . . We live two miles from the Town of Memphis, Tenn. 300 acres. You can have a Horse or a Horse buggy when you require it.[14]

The situation sounds somewhat like that of the Grangerfords who took in Huckleberry Finn; it is hardly surprising that Peter, with all his cherished plans for his beloved only son whose judgment was evidently less developed than his intelligence, should have absolutely forbidden Henry to go. By the end of the month the tempest was over and Henry had resigned himself to the study of law, but he flatly refused to have anything to do with his father's office, with any law firm in the city of Albany, or with the newly founded Albany Law School. Instead, he wanted to go to Buffalo for a year, study in some firm there, and then go to Harvard Law School, to which plan his father acceded.

In August, 1855, Henry accordingly went to Buffalo and became a clerk in the law firm of former President Millard Fillmore's brother. A month later his straightforward sister Kate reminded him "You must study hard dear Henry for a great deal will be expected of the only young Gansevoort in Albany." [15] Advice of this sort Henry much preferred to ignore. On his own for the first time, he neglected to write to his parents and then wondered why they wrote infrequently to him. At the same time he was interested in writing for newspapers, and at Christmas began an epistle in response to an invitation, received through a friend, to contribute to the *St. Paul* (Minnesota) *Times.*

Albany Jan. 4th 1856

Mr. Editor—
The excellent sleighing and the assembling of the legislature have forced our venerable conservative city to assume an unnatural air of excitement and activity. Albany is however not as slow a place as many are wont to believe. She has her seasons of depression but she has her periods of growth. Settled originally by the Dutch under Hendrick Hudson and situated on the banks of the noble stream which bears his name she has ever been noted as much for hospitality as for wealth. From a population in 1830 of twenty four thousand and in 1850 of fifty thousand she now numbers upward of sixty four thousand. Her growth has not been rapid but steady, her progress has not been sudden but certain. She has always been considered as the centre of New York politics. Here the pronunciamentos of the Federalists were wont to issue—here the Van Buren regency governed the state and here the Seward dynasty reigned in splendor. The Holidays are observed with much of olden formality. Christmas trees are hung with costly presents and New Years calls are regularly exchanged.[16]

The rest of the letter, of which this extract is about a third, described the factions in the legislature and included a puff for Stanwix Hall as "the finest [hotel] in the city." It is interesting to note that though Henry himself was fascinated by the opportunities of the West and anxious to get as far into it as possible, when he described his home town to Westerners he selected its most traditional characteristics—and its Dutch patrician characteristics, at that, although by this time only a small minority of Albanians would have seen their city from his viewpoint.

Henry's excursion into journalism was checked by the onset of ill health which plagued him for the remainder of his stay in Buffalo and at frequent intervals thereafter. He inherited from the Gansevoorts a large frame which required a great deal of outdoor

231

exercise to keep in condition and from the Sanfords a tendency to be susceptible to all sorts of infections. Emotional stress sometimes made him ill, and furthermore, Henry had discovered as a child that physical collapse was one sure way to evade his father's sometimes unreasonable expectations and turn his just anger into sympathy. Therefore Henry not only really was ill frequently, but made the most of it whenever it happened. During his year and a half at Harvard Law School, from September, 1856, to the spring of 1858, he was not kept from his studies by poor health, although he worked hard enough to do as well as he always did in school. But when he finally came home he was too unwell to confine himself to the routine of a law office. His father agreed to continue his allowance during a long summer vacation, which Henry spent boarding on a farm in the Poconos. The family's expectations of his benefit from this excursion were summed up by twenty-year-old Kate, who informed him, with her own devastating combination of her father's thunderous authority and her stepmother's ruthless honesty:

I hope you are enjoying yourself, and that your health will be improved by the air and exercise you take, and that meditation and reflection will make a man of you, and that when you return home in September you may be able to settle down and begin business. . . . Do you think that you treated Mother as you should when you were home? Think about it. I hope when you return to this your home, the home of your childhood and where you will *always* be welcome that you will treat *Father* and *Mother* with more *love* and *respect* and make yourself more agreeable.[17]

Henry's meditations, however, led him along somewhat different lines, resulting in a long letter to his father which started as an appeal for funds and turned into a general discussion of their relationship. Since his departure for Buffalo Henry had received a monthly allowance, and he now considered his father's wish to pay his vacation expenses as they arose an indication of distrust, which he attributed to:

my oppositeness of views on religious topics; my belief (credulity as you may perhaps term it) regarding various transactions [Henry was attracted by Spiritualism, at its height in the 1850's] and my conclu-

232

sions in regard to several facts. . . . I however value my own convictions of truth more than the approbation and affection of any individual and altho' I should not cease to regard him the less, I should continue to value them more.[18]

After this declaration of intellectual independence he acknowledged his need of material support until he should become established in his profession:

I assure you I look down on money. I would gladly if I could get along do without it but I only ask enough to live in a deacent [sic] respectable way with my fellows and peers. . . . I don't ask anything but what I consider fair and consistant and I do not seek aid, altho' I do advice, but for a short time longer.[19]

Upon receiving this disquisition, Peter sent Henry money for his next month's expenses, but he did not answer the bulk of the letter at all, which irritated Henry and throws considerable light on the differences between them. Henry's ten pages of argument were logical and well stated, but as Peter undoubtedly noticed at once, they ignored all the issues raised by Henry's previous equivocal conduct and made promises which Peter had learned by years of experience to consider no assurance of performance. What Peter did not recognize was that the issues Henry did raise were just as important to him as the ones he ignored. Henry was very different from his father, physically, mentally, and emotionally. He could grasp the structure of a problem far more quickly than his father could, but he was far less able than Peter to visualize how a theory would work in actual situations and far less precise in remembering and repeating details. It is quite understandable that the sustained desk work and constant pursuit of minutiae which went to make up Peter's idea of a man's work should have been both irksome and intolerable to a person with his son's constitution.

Henry's conflict with his father was also a conflict of traditions, particularly two differing conceptions of gentility. Peter always believed and taught Henry to believe that above all he must be a gentleman. To Peter and his contemporaries among the Albany Dutch patricians it was perfectly normal for a gentleman to support his family by commerce or a profession, although his wife and daughters, if they were to be considered ladies, no longer helped him in his shop as they had during the colonial period. But Peter married so late that his children's contemporaries were the grandchildren of his friends, who practiced an entirely different idea of gentility. Henry James, only five years younger than Henry Gansevoort and just such a grandchild of an Albany merchant (though not a Dutch merchant) described this new concept, which became widespread in late nineteenth-century America:

[Notable was] our sudden collective disconnectedness (ours as the whole kinship's) from *the* American resource of those days, Albanian or other. That precious light was the light of "business" only. . . . Our consensus, on all this ground, was amazing—it brooked no exception; the word had been passed, all round, that we didn't, that we couldn't and shouldn't, understand these things, questions of arithmetic and of fond calculation, questions of the counting-house and the market; and we appear to have held to our agreement. . . . The rupture with my grandfather's tradition and attitude was complete; we were never . . . guilty of a stroke of business.[20]

To Peter the attitude that the height of gentility was to be of no profession at all indicated immaturity and moral slackness; to Henry his father's insistence that he work even though he would inherit a large fortune was hard to understand. He certainly had no clear comprehension, such as Peter had acquired by the bitterest experience, of how nearly the Gansevoort fortune had been lost in the Panic of 1837 and how seriously it was at that moment threatened by the Panic of 1857; indeed, he still took its continued existence for granted ten years later when he wrote:

My great ambition is to settle down with an ultimate view of attending to literature and politics not as a profession but as a means of influence and position among my fellow men.[21]

At the end of his Slatington vacation Henry wrote a friend: "I shall . . . if possible locate in New York City. If I find it impossible to do so I shall leave for the West. Stay in Albany I shall not." He accordingly went to New York, where he worked the next winter in a law office in spite of recurrent bouts of illness. In the spring, his father invited him to join the rest of the family on a European tour. Henry had wanted to go to Europe for a long time, but he was not anxious to travel with his parents and sister. Nevertheless, after some hesitation and some tactful pressure from a family friend, he went. He was miserably ill on the voyage, and enjoyed very little that he saw in England except Byron's home at Newstead Abbey. Byron was all the Gansevoorts' favorite poet. Peter probably honored him for his contribution to Greek liberty, Kate certainly learned from his works of the devotion possible between sisters and brothers, and Henry found his poetry of lonely gloom compatible with his own emotional condition. Henry's identification with the poet was so complete that he spent the night following his visit to the shrine in a state of sleepless rapture, attempting to compose some appropriately Byronic stanzas in honor of the occasion. His genius, unfortunately, was not equal to that of Byron, nor was his poem very effective.

While his parents and Kate took a journey up the Rhine, Henry went directly to Paris for medical attention, where in between a painful course of treatments he enjoyed himself thoroughly. He rejoined them in Switzerland, but soon fell ill again, and after following them back to Paris insisted over their objections on going to a water-cure in the Swiss Alps. Under a rigorous regimen of baths, exercise, and simple fare, which seems to have been designed to restore health by shocking the system into expelling its ills, Henry at first grew weaker than ever, but then improved until when he rejoined his family in Italy in December he had achieved a state of well-being that he had not known for a long time. They in the meantime had been discovering the shops, museums, and churches of Paris, and waiting to see whether the situation in Italy would permit them to spend the winter there.

Italy was in 1859 in the midst of unification. Early in that year Giuseppe Cavour, the leading statesman of the kingdom of Sardinia-Piedmont, had persuaded Emperor Napoleon III of France to drive the Austrians out of the provinces they held in northern Italy. In June, while the Gansevoorts were sailing to England, Napoleon III defeated the Austrians at the battles of

235

Magenta and Solferino. Then, to Cavour's chagrin, he made peace at Villafranca in July although the province of Venetia still remained in Austrian hands. Nevertheless, Sardinia duly annexed Lombardy, and a number of smaller North Italian states hastened to join the new Italian kingdom. For the moment southern Italy and Rome remained under their old rulers, but revolutionary sentiment was growing, and in the new kingdom the professional revolutionary Garibaldi was preparing his Red Shirts for any eventuality. In November Peter Gansevoort finally decided that it would be safe to go to Rome as they had planned, but he warned that if the French garrison were withdrawn from the city they must leave at once.

The Gansevoorts spent their time in Rome, as did most tourists, visiting museums and churches, participating in the Carnival, attending services in St. Peter's, and finally observing the solemnities of Holy Week and Easter. Kate and her mother were particularly interested in churches and church services; they went to many together while Henry went out with his father or by himself. As a rule his family wished he would do more things with them while he wanted to go off on his own. Sometimes he took Kate to the theater or to entertainments that his parents did not wish to attend. She, in the meantime, was reveling in works of art and keeping a massive journal of the museum pieces which particularly impressed her. They all shopped freely—the family fortune had been reestablished once again, and Peter Gansevoort was determined that his wife and children should purchase anything they really wanted—and enjoyed social activities with other Americans in Rome, including twenty Albanians. Henry reported to a friend that all the family were much improved by the trip:

We find Rome rather dull, the air seems to agree with party. Father is growing young while I am growing old. His hair has grown under his chin and even hangs like icicles from his underlip. His step is firmer and his appetite better than it was same time last year, although he complains of the fare. Mother weighs a few pounds more than she did last month and seems to be in better humor and Kate is in the ambiguous transitional state which is the effect generally produced upon ladies of a delicate age by a voyage to this quarter of the world. She is intoxicated with sightseeing and has imbibed an appetite that I fear is too costly to be of continued gratification.[22]

But there were riots in Rome during Lent, and the beginnings of a revolution in Naples. As soon as Easter was over the Gansevoorts hurried out of Italy, crossed Austria and Germany, and went to the Netherlands, where Henry and his father investigated the history of the Gansevoort family and visited the home and grave of a medieval scholar named Johan Wessel Gansfort, whom they wished to believe was one of their relatives. Then, after spending ten more weeks in Paris, mostly shopping, they went back to the British Isles, hurried through the principal sights of Scotland, Ireland, and Wales, and returned to America at the end of August, 1860.

Henry then settled again in New York, where he went into partnership with another young lawyer. But Henry found little business for young lawyers in New York in that winter when one by one the southern states seceded. One of his amusements was drilling with the Seventh Regiment of the city militia, which after the capture of Fort Sumter the following spring was called into active service. After an inspiriting sendoff when enthusiastic crowds cheered the departing soldiers as they marched down Broadway, an unpleasant journey by sea to Baltimore, and a grim march into Washington when trains broke down, Henry was billeted with his regiment in the Capitol and wrote his father on official stationery of the House of Representatives. After the regiment returned to New York a month later, Henry was convinced that if he were to fight for the Union it must be as an officer. He therefore applied for a commission and asked his father to support his application with his political influence. Kate again relayed a consensus of family opinion:

Why do you ask for a commission in the regular army? It seems a great pity for you to throw away all the advantages you have received and become a wanderer for so a soldier's life seems to me. But I know if you really want it father will do all in his power to secure a commission for you—and I have no doubt will succeed—for our grandfather's name and his gallant conduct can never be forgotten—and if a soldier's lot you choose may his mantle of courage, bravery and patriotism fall upon his grandson. There is Henry a great deal to be taken into consideration before you enter the U.S. Army. The hopes of promotion are very small. I should prefer my brother's being a civilian than a soldier, but Henry you are of *age*, and know your own mind best. Think well before you take the step.[23]

When Henry continued to press his request, Peter did exert his influence and Henry was appointed a second lieutenant in the Fifth Regiment, U.S. Artillery. Henry's satisfaction with the artillery was greater than he had ever shown over any career. He liked the open-air living, the order and discipline of the service, the process of commanding men, and the complex science of gunnery.

The truth is that I never was made for continuous confinement and this open air work and practical, adventurous and romantic life combines mental activity with physical activity in just proper doses. This is no sinecure and if I never earned my bread as you have often told me dear Father before I do it now.[24]

Nevertheless, Henry soon became impatient, complaining that the other second lieutenants were his inferiors in age, education, and social standing, and asking Peter to exert his influence again to have him promoted or transferred. This time Henry had to abide by the fortunes of war, serving in a training camp until he was sent to the front during the Peninsula Campaign, after which he took part in the battles of Second Manassas and Antietam, where he commanded his battery for part of the day and was commended for his coolness and bravery under fire. When he received this news Peter could not restrain his pride. He showed Henry's hastily scrawled letter from the battlefield to his influential friends Judge Amasa Parker and Senator Ira Harris, and, much to Henry's annoyance, permitted it to be copied in the newspaper. To Henry himself he was equally overjoyed:

The graphick account of your position at the Battle of South Mountain on Sunday—the march on Monday and Tuesday, to the bloody field of Antietam, and the terrific scenes of that Battle on Wednesday—the fiercest and most important of the War, presented an accurate idea of

238

the heroic conduct of our brave men in that glorious struggle for the Republic. You must excuse me for suffering Judge Parker (who was delighted with your letter) to shew it to Judge Harris—who returned it, with a letter highly complimentary to you and saying he is proud of you himself; and prays that God may bless you, and preserve your life.[25]

The distinction which Henry thus earned made his desire for higher rank more attainable. The War Department permitted regular officers to be detached from their regiments to command volunteer troops, who were technically state militia mustered into federal service. Volunteer officers were therefore appointed by the state governors, so even though the national administration was Republican, Peter and his friends could make use of their influence in the Democratic state government at Albany. They finally secured for Henry the colonelcy of the 13th New York Cavalry, about half of which had been recruited when the Confederates invaded Pennsylvania for the Gettysburg campaign. Henry and four of his companies were hastily called into service, and in the confusion of the invasion the four companies were sent off to the field without their colonel, who was waiting for two more companies that were on their way from New York. Henry complained bitterly about this, but before his men could be returned to him—which, in the army's own good time, they were— he came down with typhoid fever and had to spend six weeks in bed in Washington. When he returned to his command, he found that the regiment had been organizing itself in his absence and that some of his officers wanted to displace him. When the regiment was finally fully recruited in March, 1864, these officers prompted their political friends in Albany to have Henry superseded on the grounds of youth, inexperience, and poor health. Henry alerted his father, who exerted pressure in various offices to expedite the issuing of Henry's commission until Kate wrote exultingly that

nothing can prevent your being Col. of the 13th N.Y. Cavalry. He [Peter] saw the Adjt. Genl. this morning, and intends *himself* to *see* your commission made out. . . . Your friends here have all been deeply interested in your cause. Do not forget to thank those who have done all in their power to assist you. Father, Judge Parker, and Mr. Coles (your Major's brother) and your friend A.[braham] L.[ansing] have been untiring in their endeavors to *watch,* and keep *all right.*[26]

Henry's regiment was stationed in northern Virginia to keep down guerrilla raids and help prevent the Confederates from attacking Washington. This duty was not very glorious, especially when General Philip Sheridan began his dramatic campaign in the nearby Valley of Virginia, but Henry had plenty to do. Many of his troops were raw recruits who did not know how to ride or care for horses, let alone to ride in formation, respond to bugle calls, and fight the enemy offensively and defensively. Men and horses had to be drilled together, a great deal of the men's effort going into training the horses. Although Henry once observed that it took two years to produce a really effective cavalry regiment, he was soon thirsting for action, considering the dismounted picket duty to which his men were assigned demoralizing—though until they were trained it is hard to see how they could have performed more complex assignments. Finally, after Henry had pestered his superiors for a year to order him on a real raid, in October, 1864, his commander, General Augur, called upon him to provide five hundred troopers for an expedition after the guerrilla John Mosby. Henry and his men soon encountered Mosby's force, which they scattered after a sharp fight, capturing four small field guns with which Mosby had been annoying Federal detachments for months. Highly elated, Henry's troops pushed on after Mosby himself, but the wily guerrilla slipped through their fingers. Then, after ten days of pursuit, Henry fell ill and had to return to his headquarters.

There he found that Republicans among his officers, some of whom had personal grudges against him, were letting it be known that he had improperly influenced his soldiers to vote for the Democratic candidate, General George B. McClellan, in the hotly contested presidential election of 1864. Henry, despite his Democratic background and his respect for McClellan as a soldier, considered it his duty to express no political opinions at all, and succeeded in clearing himself of any malpractice regarding the soldiers' balloting, but the incident did not endear him to the Republican War Department. Peter wholeheartedly approved of Henry's defense, writing him:

I am gratified by its perusal. It is straightforward, candid and pointed; and carries on its face intrinsic evidence of its truthfulness. It clearly states facts, which are conclusive, in your favor and ought to have silenced any further official inquiry in the matter, as regards yourself.[27]

Nevertheless, Henry had to deal with further investigation from Washington, and the upset cost him the command of his brigade, to which he had succeeded only a short time before. Then, in the spring of 1865, the war ended, all the volunteer regiments were disbanded, and Henry returned to his regiment of artillery, where he remained until just before his death in 1871.

Henry thus found that the outbreak of the Civil War broke the impasse in his relations with his family, less by permitting him to escape from their tradition than by making it possible for him to embrace an alternative form of it. The only thing that could reconcile Peter Gansevoort to his son's not becoming a lawyer like himself was to have him become a military hero like his father. Henry's service was certainly creditable, although it is hard to estimate his actual military effectiveness because most of the information about his army career comes either from his own records or from testimonials written to his grieving family after his death. Probably in the army, as everywhere else, he was often incapacitated by illness and always far quicker at grasping the theory behind any task than at acquiring practical experience in doing it. Nevertheless, officers under whom he served agreed that he was quick, eager, zealous, thorough—sometimes a little too thorough—in training his men and conscientious in his responsibility for them, and in general a good soldier. Like his grandfather he spent most of his career as a commander building and defending fortifications; unlike his grandfather he withstood no crucial sieges. The utterly different military conditions of the Revolutionary and Civil Wars preclude any other meaningful comparisons beyond the observations that both were the same age—twenty-six—when they went to war and both emerged from

241

it with the rank of colonel. Henry hoped to share his grand-father's ultimate rank of general, but though his father's friends procured him a nomination as brevet, or honorary, brigadier general, a Republican senate refused to confirm it.

After the war, Henry stubbornly pursued the profession of arms, putting both his family and the Dutch tradition firmly behind him except for occasional short visits which he deliberately made as brief as possible to avoid disagreements with his father and quarrels with his forthright sister Kate. He wrote to his father about possibilities of promotion and matters of business, and after he was stationed in isolated Pensacola in 1867 corresponded freely and extensively with Kate on a wide range of subjects, but as throughout his life Henry's attachment to his home increased in direct proportion to his distance from it. In his military profession, his political opinions, his ideas about the structure of society, and his continued contact with his family he did more or less continue its tradition, but in turning aside from the pursuit of wealth, declining to marry, and dropping all church connections he effectively dissociated himself from its fundamental concerns.

When Henry died he was thirty-seven years old, the age at which Herman Melville made his disillusioning pilgrimage to the Holy Land. It is possible that had Henry lived—and particularly had he outlived his father—that he, like his cousin, would have eventually returned to the Dutch patrician tradition. But as it was both of them were successful in their own time precisely insofar as they departed from that tradition. Melville in his earlier, more popular writings described and Henry in his Civil War service carried into practice an Albany Dutch form of the nineteenth-century American tradition of individual achievement. Both tried to found their ambition on the resources of their family in the Dutch tradition, but the circumstances of American development rendered the assistance their family could give them less effective than it had been in earlier generations. But it should also be remembered that the scope of both Melville's and Henry's ambition was commensurate rather with the promise of the American nation than with the resources of the Albany Dutch community. Both of them therefore required a broader base than their

242

inherited tradition of particularistic, privileged community could supply. Nevertheless, in the broader environments of the army and the open sea, both found their way to smaller communities within them, in which their patrician background helped them to aspire to and fulfill positions of influence and leadership. Consistently with the American tradition, however, both worked their way up to these positions from the lowest level, held them by the choice and the support of the ordinary people of the community, and gave them up when the people no longer desired their services. Therefore, although they acquired power—intellectual and military—with the support of the patrician tradition and exercised it in the patrician manner, they were unable to transmit it to another generation according to patrician custom, not only because neither had sons capable of exercising leadership, but also because the community of the American nation had developed a contradictory tradition of popular rule. This democratic tradition was intensified and confirmed by the Civil War, as the original American tradition of liberty had been forged in the Revolutionary War. To American liberty the Albany Dutch patricians had made valuable and continuing contributions based on their traditional Dutch understanding of liberty, but the Dutch contribution to American democracy was made by the plebeians, and by a few individuals who escaped from their patrician heritage.

X

Twilight of the Patricians

After the Civil War the Albany Dutch patricians lost nearly all of their distinctive characteristics. Only a few old people remembered when Albanians had habitually spoken the Dutch language, and except for a very few phrases, nursery rhymes, and endearments, the younger generation knew nothing of it at all. Civic affairs fell into the hands of bosses who controlled the votes of masses of Irish, and later Italian and Polish immigrants. The Dutch Reformed churches called pastors of non-Dutch ethnic origins, while non-Dutch residents became members and numbers of patricians affiliated with other denominations. Dutch families intermarried freely with Yankee Albanians and with outsiders from all over the United States, and younger members of these families often moved away from Albany. Family fortunes were divided by inheritance, lost in business failures and depressions, or diminished by comparison with the accumulations of wealth of the newly rich. The social customs which Albany Dutch families cherished gradually fell into disuse, until by the beginning of the twentieth century even New Years calling and Dutch funeral customs, which lingered longest, were only memories, and the Albany Dutch patrician tradition passed into history.

The twilight of the Gansevoort family commenced about 1860, when General Gansevoort's children began to pass away. Herman never recovered from the humiliation of his bankruptcy. A year after that event, Mary Ann wrote, after meeting him by chance:

244

He looks awfully—his nose was red as a cherry, and several great purple pimples on it, and all over his cheeks—Guert what does this mean? I cannot believe that Uncle Herman is *intemperate*—God forbid—and yet he looks like it—I know he is threatening with a cancer in his cheek, and I think perhaps it proceeds from that—I pray it may; I would much rather he should die of cancer than become a drunkard.[1]

The death of his wife in 1855, in the midst of Munro's suit to break his title to his remaining lands, shook Herman even more deeply. Catherine had a difficult personality which many people disliked, but she and Herman were happy together and Herman was desolated by her loss. He who never troubled to write down anything unnecessarily, recorded her death at length in his ledger:

Her soul sustained her in her final hour. Her tender sensibility and kind affection appeared unbounded during the nine days of her sickness and long before she was taken ill, would often after her daily private devotions, declare the blessed and happy mind she enjoyed in the love she felt for her neighbors and friends.

Her health and strength appeared to decline for more than a month before she was taken sick, and caused much sad and fearful apprehension . . . extreme enervation and the loss of energy and force was such as to sadden all who saw her.

On Saturday 20 engage sweeping the small sitting room she gave the broom to Margaret and took her seat on the sofa. . . .

On Wednesday the 24 made a bed in the Dinner room. She brushed the dust from the Bible, carried it into the room and placed at the head of the Bed . . . and was found lying down on the sofa. . . . She refused to take any medicine, as she was sure it could not help her, saying she was old could not live much longer, her mind might fail and not be as well prepared for her last hour. . . . All through her sickness her mind, when most alone was often engaged in Prayer (frequently audible).[2]

After Catherine's death Herman gave up what was left of his interest in the world and his own affairs, inviting his sister Maria Melville and her unmarried daughters Augusta and Fanny to live with him and leaving the entire management of the household to them. For awhile he pottered around the house and the mills, but the rheumatism which had twisted his huge frame for years finally confined him to a sofa, where he lay from morning till night, often dozing, never complaining, appreciating pathetically the comforts that Peter and his family sent him—wine and oysters, Dutch New Years cakes, a pair of embroidered slippers. After his death on March 18, 1862, Peter attended his funeral at Gansevoort and brought his body back to Albany to be buried with the other Gansevoorts in the Albany Rural Cemetery. Maria could not afford to buy new spoons to distribute to his relatives in the traditional Dutch manner, so she distributed instead pieces of silverware that Herman had owned, properly engraved with his name, the date of his death, and the name of the relative to whom the spoon was presented. In this manner, for example, Maria's daughter Catherine Melville Hoadley acquired a huge eighteenth-century ladle which had come down in the family from Caty's parents.

After Herman's death, Maria's children made the mansion at Gansevoort their summer center. Sometimes the sons and daughters came with, and sometimes without, their spouses and children. Often they sent the children by themselves. Maria was particularly partial to Herman's boys, for years her only grandsons. She appreciated the stylishness of Allan's daughters, but Herman's girls later remembered that she laughed at their homemade clothes. Her niece Kate, Peter's daughter, sometimes passed a week or two at Gansevoort, but she found the quiet "intense" and Maria's household regimen strict. "Aunt Melville has excused our evening toilette so that I might write this letter home," she informed her mother during one such visit. A typical afternoon she described as follows:

Dinner is over. Aunt Melville has retired for her afternoon nap. Cousin Helen and Kate are in their rooms, Cousin Gus putting her work basket in order and entertaining at the same time the three [Hoadley] children, Minnie, Lottie and Frank. Florence Melville [Allan's daughter] is writing home, and Tom Melville is lying in the hammock reading Harpers Magazine, and Fanny busy with the domestic affairs. Gus is the upper housekeeper and Fan has care of the Culinary Dept.

Aunt Melville looks quite well, but feels the want of regular exercise. She walks about the house, but has taken only one meal downstairs since October. She finds the noise of the family so fatiguing. The other morning I saw her breakfast served on a *salver* in the parlour—onions, cheek, bread rolls and tea—so you see Papa and Aunt Melville's tastes are alike! [3]

While they lived at Gansevoort, Maria and her daughters varied their family responsibilities with community participation. They were particularly active in the Dutch Reformed Church which Herman had founded. Augusta, the moving spirit of its Sunday School, frequently entertained visiting relatives by taking them to Sunday School picnics. Fanny preferred to give secret individual assistance to all sorts of people who needed it, to many of whom she eventually left individual keepsakes. Maria also attended public gatherings such as a camp meeting and a wartime Lincoln rally, both of which she found tiring, but not so tiring as to prevent her from making precise observations of the ladies' costumes. Two years later she missed an exciting joint meeting of the Reformed and Methodist churches which she nevertheless described vividly from Augusta's account:

It seems Dr. King is a red hot Radical. It was a fiery discourse. He said he would like to tear up our Constitution and write another, for our Constitution might have been written by infidels. He would impeach our President Andrew Johnson etc. etc., and thumped our poor Bible at a great rate, so that its friends feared for its safety. Many persons looked uneasy, uncomfortable, as if they could not agree with the noisy demonstrations and wild words of the speaker.[4]

In the following years Maria was more and more confined to the house, although like her mother she continued to travel on visits to her children's homes until she died at Tom's on Staten Island in 1872; Augusta and Fanny inherited the Gansevoort mansion, which they made their home until their deaths in 1876 and 1885, after which the house was sold and only the name of

Gansevoort on the map was left to perpetuate the memory of the family in Saratoga County.

A number of other Gansevoorts died in the 1860's, Wessel in 1863, L. H.'s son Leonard in 1864, and Guert in 1868. Guert's career included occasional successes and many disappointments. In the Mexican War, he won distinction as the leader of a landing party which attacked Vera Cruz in 1847. In 1855, the year following his promotion to commander, he brought the ship *Decatur* to the aid of the inhabitants of Seattle during an Indian attack. Not long thereafter, however, he was relieved of his command for drunkenness on duty. The officer who removed him observed that this breach of discipline was universal in the fleet, and army officers like Ulysses S. Grant, bored beyond endurance with the inactivity of frontier posts in peacetime, succumbed to it as well. Guert insisted that it was an exceptional instance, and with Peter's aid was assigned to more congenial duties at the Brooklyn Navy Yard. In the spring of 1862, after forty years of service, he at last received the command of a new sloop of war, the *Adirondack*. His delighted Uncle Peter reminded him to send for a dozen bottles of fine old Madeira that had been waiting for this occasion for thirty years. Six months later the *Adirondack*, on blockade duty in the Bahamas, ran on a rock and was lost. A court-martial cleared Guert of blame, but the blow to his pride was shattering. After returning for a time to the Brooklyn Navy Yard, he retired and went to live with his sister Catherine Curtis in Schenectady, where he died.

Thus by the end of the Civil War, Peter Gansevoort's family were the only Gansevoorts still busy and active in Albany, and Peter's son was away in service. Then in January, 1867, Peter suffered a paralytic stroke. Henry rushed home in answer to his family's urgent call, but after a short leave he had to depart for his new station at the isolated post of Pensacola, Florida. His sister Kate took it upon herself to communicate with him weekly, mostly describing the heartbreakingly minute improvements in their father's health.

We all live a very quiet systematic life here in Albany. . . . at 6 A.M. Sallie rings a small bell in the saloon to which there is a feeble

248

response and at 7 she makes another attempt to waken the sleepers and about that hour we begin to stir about. Mother partly robes herself and commences to wash and dress Papa and shortly after 8 A.M. Sallie brings up Father's breakfast and Mother and I descend to our morning meal after which we look over the Paper and by that time Father's room is in order and he returns to his armchair in Mother's room, having breakfasted in the Saloon. Then he smokes a pipe and Mother reads what news there is and after that either Mother or I walk—on the average three or five times about the rooms in the upper story. Papa then reads a little in the Argus for himself—he is beginning to understand what he reads—and then he again takes a walk. This takes until about 12:30 M. when he eats a cracker (and orange or grapes whichever he can get) and then takes another walk. The blinds are closed and the room darkened after this and for an hour he rests and sleeps if he can, and Mother usually goes out for a walk and stays about two hours. It is wonderful how she bears all this confinement and routine. After his nap Papa takes another walk and has his hair brushed and at 2:30 P.M. he dines. In the afternoon I usually take my exercise. . . . You don't know how everything interests Papa—he is well posted about the news of the day, city and political.[5]

Although Peter gradually learned to walk again, recovered some of the use of his hands, and managed to speak, though indistinctly, he refused to see any of his friends but demanded the constant company of his wife and daughter. Of this Kate observed:

I hope he will change as it will be very forlorn not to have any company this summer except when he is in his room and that after 8 oclock P.M.[6]

For the next eight years the Gansevoorts lived with this difficult and depressing situation. Peter, who had always moved quickly and often and poured forth his feelings in floods of words, found it terribly frustrating to be severely limited in both motion and speech, but he struggled to live with his limitations. He learned to walk downstairs, to stroll in the garden with his canes, and finally consented to ride out in the carriage. As his speech improved, he became more willing to see old friends and even to lie on the sofa by the fire and listen unseen to little parties. Nevertheless,

249

Papa is so determined, just as ever, and has everything his own way—
and Mother does arrange and manage everything so sweetly.[7]

It took all of Susan's Lansing diplomacy—several of her close
relatives were professional diplomats—to keep her patient reasonably contented, to master the details of his affairs, to communicate questions that he must decide to him, and to understand,
untwist, and sometimes imperceptibly alter the answers he gave.
He in turn depended upon her utterly, and Kate was divided between admiration of such constant lovers and an uneasy feeling
that three is a crowd. She was of course very much needed, especially after the doctor "said he must be carefully watched . . . so
without Papa's feeling a surveillance he is never left alone," [8] but
when Peter and Kate disagreed there was, as between Peter and
Henry, only one answer, and Kate developed a settled feeling of
frustration.

In the meantime, Henry's life at Pensacola was as confined as
his sister's, and though he did not write as frequently as she, he
was more willing than ever before to send her long letters developing his views on many subjects. For example, he agreed with
his family that it would be advisable for the Dutch Reformed
Church to change its name:

My reasons for the change are that any name which misleads or has
a tendency so to do is an improper name. This name most emphati-
cally does so. . . . People imagine that the services are in Dutch and
wonder what was the necessity of reform with such a sober decorous
people. Again I favor the change because the term Dutch tends to
preserve the distinctions of birth or descent and to prevent the Amer-
icanization idea which to be thorough should govern in the church as
well as the state. We are an original people no more like our Dutch
progenitors than a steam engine is like a windmill.[9]

Despite his dislike for "distinctions of birth or descent," he later
concluded:

I think more and more of family as the unit of government. . . . Our
hasty and jumbled development lacks stability for it honors and
rewards only individual success and even when it is the mushroom
growth of corruption hypocrisy or vice. . . . The custom of today
unfortunately teaches us that in almost every sense a man is better off

without a family at his back. Our President and legislators are selected (availability) because they hardly know who were their Fathers, our Railroad Kings are foundlings and the society of all our great places is chaotic. . . . A foundation of Govt. on family besides the stability it secures would give us statesmen instead of politicians, scholars instead of smatterers more morality and fewer divorces.[10]

Thus Henry viewed what his cousin Herman Melville called "the vast Dark Ages of democracy" [11] in roughly the same light as his contemporaries Henry Adams and Mark Twain, but came to conclusions about it which clearly reflected his inheritance of Dutch tradition.

During his years in Florida, Henry gave considerable thought to leaving the army and to founding a family of his own, the latter an event to which his relatives had been looking forward with breathless eagerness for years. But, though he wrote wistfully of matrimony, he observed to Kate upon the death of one of the officers' wives:

I have long since determined not to marry as long as I remain in the army or at least not until I am about to leave it. I never should expose any woman I loved to the trials and vicissitudes of climate and of the camp.[12]

To one of his friends, who was about to marry, he wrote:

It is not because I am unwilling. The proper subject has not been found and if I were to remain in this cast-away place I suppose I should be single for the rest of my life.[13]

He was more interested than his family in the possibility of his leaving the army, especially after Congress reduced its already inadequate pay scale and made it an instrument in Radical Republican Reconstruction politics, but his father said invariably, "Henry knows what I think of it. He needs an active life with a great deal of *out door exercise*. A sedentary life would destroy him." [14] Henry was determined not to go back to the law, writing to Kate:

With an appointive judiciary and an exclusive bar, I should once more feel proud of my state and forswear some of the disgust that at an early day so violently prejudiced me against the practice of the law.[15]

He wrote of foreign consulships and a quiet rural retreat, but since neither was within his reach, he remained a soldier. In 1869, looking back over his nine years of service, he commented:

When I entered the army it was with the intention of remaining for life but I am satisfied that the condition of an old officer is one not enviable. . . . Still I remain, for the excitement of the duty, the wild independence of the life, the "camaraderie" of the service have wooed me on. I know it is a false light, a fatal glamour which it sheds around but still I obey it. Oh that I could get in some reliable business and trim myself to the realities of life.[16]

But instead of doing so Henry took up a new station at Boston, where in the cold, damp climate his long-strained health gave way and he developed tuberculosis. He collapsed in September, 1870, returned home, and finally in December sailed for the Bahamas, as his grandfather Nathan Sanford had done thirty-three years before. Kate went to take care of him, but when he grew worse instead of better she brought him back to Albany; he died on the Hudson River steamboat a few hours before it reached the city.

Kate, who thus became the only living younger member of the Albany Gansevoorts, was thirty-two when her brother died. Her youth had been marked particularly by troubles in school; when she went away to a young ladies' seminary she was so homesick and had so much difficulty with the work that she became ill and had to leave after a single term. Henry, then in Buffalo, wrote his father:

Kate I am convinced needs something of excitement. Confinement essential to application in study is not exactly suited to her temperament unless varied frequently with pleasure and exercise.[17]

She then attended a boarding school in Albany from which she could visit her home frequently, and finished her education by traveling in Europe with her family. For Kate, Europe unfolded vast vistas of history and tradition. The past of which she had read in the poetry of Byron and the novels of Bulwer-Lytton now came home to her as she saw historic sites and memorable objects. Her five-hundred-page diary of her tour is a catalog of places visited and things seen; she recorded nothing of the people, institutions, or ideas of Europe, for her interest was in the material remnants of the past, particularly relics associated with memorable events and works of art. She and her mother also spent much of their time, wherever they went, in shopping for clothes and ornaments for themselves, furniture and household goods for their home, and presents for their friends, in selecting all of which they insisted that their purchases be pleasing to the eye, suited to their use, substantial in workmanship, and of the best quality materials. In this way Kate's observation of the tradition of past ages was immediately useful to her in the formation of her own taste.

Soon after Kate returned from Europe she was sought in marriage by Abraham Lansing. Abe, as everyone called him, was Susan Gansevoort's nephew and in their school and college days had been Henry's best friend. Abe graduated from Williams and the Albany Law School and worked in his father's law office until he was suddenly attacked by "inflammatory rheumatism." After a year in bed he was able to resume his practice, but he walked on crutches for several years thereafter. He became engaged to Kate in January, 1862, with the delighted approval of her father, but a bare month after Kate wrote in her diary

Abe came up with the "Grey horse named Mulligan" and we took a drive up to Lansingburgh—*a drive never to be forgotten*—and may *we never repent what passed between us,*[18]

she buried her hopes:

One word has changed my life into a vast regret. My dream has flown and my bubble burst. Oh why should *friends* thus part? [19]

She spent the next year regretting the explosion of temper which had wrecked her happiness, soon concluding that she had been mistaken, but the misunderstanding was too complex to be cleared up by any single explanation. Finally, after a number of meetings in the company of their families, Kate and Abe made up their quarrel and in 1863 again became engaged, but after various ups and downs and two refusals by Kate to set a date for the wedding, Abe terminated the engagement at Thanksgiving, 1865.

It was generally believed among their relatives and acquaintances that Kate's caprice was responsible for the uncertain course of this courtship. Some of them blamed her for it, as indeed she frequently blamed herself, but Abe was equally responsible. He was sensitive and delicately balanced, as was Kate, but while she expressed her feelings immediately, verbally, and often violently, he buried his in the depths of reserve and expressed them, if at all, in silent but decisive action. This reticence was based on principle as well as temperament, for he once concluded a few remarks about depression from illness and other disappointments, "such things do not look well on paper, and in fact ought not to find expression anywhere." [20] Kate, on the other hand, was accustomed to her father's explosive rages and equally effusive expressions of affection, so that three months before she finally married Abe, she could still write him: "Some men make love on paper as well as by mouth. Won't you be able to do so someday?" [21]

Furthermore, Kate's family, much as they approved her marriage to Abe, also got in the way of it. Quite possibly Peter Gansevoort, who when he retired from his law practice to go to Europe turned over his office and his library to Abe, had been wishing for it for some time. For his wife's nephew to become as well his son-in-law and the heir to his daughter's share of the family fortune doubtless gratified him greatly and, after Henry's stubborn wilfullness, relieved his burdened mind. But Kate wanted to be loved for herself, not as the heiress to the Gansevoort fortune or as her eminent father's daughter, and Abe's punctilious courtesy on top of common professional and family interests made him often pay as much attention to her parents as to herself. Susan's attitude was somewhat ambiguous. She loved both Kate and Abe and wanted them to be happy together if they really wished it, but she was also aware of the criticism which might be leveled at her for promoting a match between her own relatively impecunious nephew and her husband's heiress. Susan therefore played Devil's advocate, confronting Kate with all the objections to the match with her usual ruthless common sense, and refusing to take Kate's outbursts of emotion any more seriously than she took Peter's. Kate, like Henry, often found Susan's irony disquieting, and concluded that her parents were insensitive. About two months before Abe terminated the second engagement, she wrote:

I do not believe that my F. or M. care to have me with them, certainly they try and shun all companionship with me, and "call my life filled with enjoyment" when I have *no one* to confide in, no one to love.[22]

Henry also came between Kate and Abe. During the Civil War, Abe's poor health precluded military service, although he wanted desperately to enlist. In the meantime, Henry, after years of disappointing his family, became a dashing and successful officer, of whom Kate was as proud as her parents. To Abe, doggedly plugging away at the law, her enthusiasm must sometimes have been nearly intolerable; her very sensitivity to his physical misery, a characteristic she shared with many other Gansevoorts, would have reminded him, quite unintentionally, of the things he wished most to forget. Furthermore, in the tradition of their favorite poet Byron, Kate was romantically devoted to her heroic brother, and at the same time often considered the stable, undramatic Abe, with whose family she had freely associated all her life, in a light more brotherly than loverlike. Kate therefore suffered in a direct and practical way from the emotional confusion among family relationships which her cousin Herman Melville had criticized in *Pierre*. She and Abe became engaged once more after her father's illness, when Abe and his brother Will, as their Aunt Susan's nephews, in effect took over the male functions of the Gansevoort household, but at the same time Henry paid more attention to Kate than ever before, responding fairly often to her regular letters to him. Although she was thirty when she became re-engaged, Kate was still in no hurry to marry, waiting first for an improvement in her father's condition, then for Henry to be able to come to the wedding, and finally for Henry to recover from his illness.

In spite of her devotion to him, Kate and Henry usually quarreled when they met. When he returned from Boston in 1870, mortally ill, they disagreed so seriously that he refused to see her for a month, during which he grew steadily worse. Nevertheless, when he arrived at Nassau he was so weak that he was glad to have her come to him. This was Kate's first taste of independence. She traveled to Nassau alone, since none of her male relatives was available to accompany her—as her father and her fiancé thought proper—and nursed Henry as patiently as she and her mother had cared for her father. Henry, who by this time was weak enough to appreciate her attentions as never before, wrote home: "Kate has been all in all to me, and I have found out qualities and affections which I did not think she possessed." [23] His death, which she had never allowed herself to believe inevitable, set off an emotional reaction which assumed the proportions of a major nervous breakdown, taking the form of hysterical devotion to her brother's memory and insistence that someone should have prevented his death. She blamed herself for not caring for him properly, the entire family, particularly her father, for requiring him to remain in the army to the detriment of his health, the family physician for not informing her of the dangerous nature of his illness—none of which accusations were true—and even blamed Abe for refusing to blame everyone she did with the same degree of vehemence.

Everyone was patient with Kate, waiting for her storm of grief to blow itself out, but it did not blow over quickly or easily. Kate was physically worn out from her three months of nursing Henry, after years of nervous strain caused by her father's illness. She also found grief an effective means of self-assertion, both for retaliating upon her parents for what she felt to be long-term insensitivity to her emotional needs, and for attracting attention among her friends in a socially acceptable manner. Furthermore, Kate's frame of mind—which, consonantly with the Dutch tradition, was emotional rather than intellectual—had been set by her education in the sentimental tradition of the mid-nineteenth century, which dwelt upon and glorified all of the emotions connected with death. For the rest of her life Kate remarked the anniversaries of deaths with as much care as those of births, weddings, and other family events, and seldom failed to embellish such dates in her diary with an emotional effusion compounded of grief for the departed one and guilt over her own shortcomings

256

toward that person. These confessions served the same purpose, though directed toward a human rather than a divine object, of the self-humiliations found in medieval and post-medieval works of piety and mysticism, and perhaps represent a cumulative effect of the undocumentable habits of private devotion of generations of Kate's Dutch ancestors.

It is certain that Kate's excessive grief for Henry followed very soon after a period of religious turmoil which ended in her leaving the Dutch Reformed Church. Kate had been much impressed by the venerable churches and stately ritual she had seen in Europe, and thereafter found the matter-of-fact worship of her Albany Dutch tradition unsatisfactory. It is possible also that her emotional tendency toward enthusiastic religion was partly an inheritance from her non-Dutch mother, who had demonstrated a similar trait when in her last illness she received much consolation from a Methodist pastor. In any event, in 1869 Kate insisted on joining St. Peter's Episcopal Church, against her parents' wishes and without their consent but with Henry's support. Kate never discussed her feelings on this matter in a connected way, but the conflict of traditions which she experienced may perhaps be conveyed, in view of her great interest in art and architecture, by comparing the two church buildings. The North Dutch Church, finished in 1815, still stands on Clinton Square, across the corner from the site of the house where Kate was born. Solidly built of tan-colored stone with two towers, its rectangular sanctuary is simply ornamented, but the pulpit and shallow chancel are carved and highlighted with gilding; the windows are plain yellow stained glass. The effect is substantial and severe, but entirely different from the substantial severity of a Boston meeting house of similar date, for New England churches are gleaming, spotless white inside and out, while the Albany Dutch Reformed Church glows instead with the rich luster of old gold. St. Peter's on State Street hill, on the other hand, was rebuilt in 1855 at the height of the Gothic revival, with a brownstone exterior adorned by pointed arcades and a soaring campanile. Inside, the vaulted nave terminates in a deep chancel dominated by five complex pictorial windows, which, like the memorial windows in the nave, were specially designed in leading English studios. The effect is far more like the ecclesiastical architecture of Europe than any earlier Albany church. In the 1860's this church, unfinished as it then was, formed the background for the stately Episcopalian service as it was performed by the Reverend, later Bishop, William Croswell Doane, whose conception of what was fitting in worship was eventually embodied in the hymn "Ancient of Days, who sittest throned in glory."

All of Kate's relatives and friends agreed that the normal and natural antidote for her grief would be her marriage, but instead of marrying she flung herself into a project of publishing Henry's letters, with the enthusiastic assistance of her cousin Catherine Melville's husband, John Hoadley. Abe waited patiently for her for two years, while she postponed their wedding from time to time for one reason or another, usually connnected with duties she believed she owed to Henry's memory, but finally in the summer of 1873 put his foot down and insisted that she either marry him or terminate the engagement once and for all. At this point Kate capitulated, and the wedding finally took place in the Gansevoort parlor on November 26, 1873; the honeymoon was a journey to New York, Philadelphia, and Fortress Monroe, a pilgrimage to places Kate associated with Henry. When the newlyweds returned they settled into a three-story brownstone at 166 Washington Avenue, across the street and about a block away from Peter's home at 115. Kate, who had apparently taken little part in housekeeping before her marriage, was back and forth a dozen times a day for her stepmother's advice. She was particularly unsure of herself with respect to cooking, but Abe, who understood food and wines, was glad to help her with shopping, with specific instructions to be relayed to the cook, and with encouragement. Still, she always found the details of entertaining burdensome and often left many of them undone.

Kate and Abe had been married nearly a year when Susan Gansevoort suddenly died in her sleep on October 28, 1874, after a brief illness which was not considered to be dangerous. Kate was much distressed by the event, which she soon came to believe was hastened by malpractice on the part of her mother's physician; he, forewarned by her similar accusations of him with respect to Henry's illness, resolutely refused to discuss the subject with her. Then Kate got a taste of her own medicine when her distracted father, now confined to a wheelchair, began to blame *her* for not having prevented his beloved Susan's death. Kate insisted on moving in with him and Abe admitted that it was necessary. A year later Peter was visibly failing, and on January 8, 1876, nearly eight years after his first stroke, he finally faded away, at the age of eighty-seven, in the presence of his daughter and son-in-law.

Abe now expected that they would move back to their own home, but to Kate, unstrung by grief as had become her habit, the thought of breaking up 115 was intolerable. Her imagination structured itself upon material objects, and her whole idea of home was integrated with a specific building containing particular furnishings. It did not matter to Kate that her father had bought 115 after her birth and that it had been thoroughly remodeled at least once in her own memory; to her it embodied everything that the Gansevoort name stood for as surely as if it had been the little old Dutch house in which her ancestors had lived for four generations. To break it up would symbolize to her not only the breaking up of her childhood home, but also the extinction of the Gansevoort name, which was no longer hers, and the Gansevoort tradition as well. So, with the stubbornness of grief, Kate insisted to her husband that they give up their own home and take up residence in 115. He tried gently to persuade her, but no persuasion proved effective. For a while he used to walk over to his own house of an evening and read in his own library, but finally he rented it and resigned himself to sharing his wife with the ghosts of her ancestors. At the same time she quarreled bitterly with the Lansing family over the division of Susan's estate, and tried to make her husband quarrel with them as well, but with true Lansing diplomacy Abe remained his brother Will's law partner and maintained contact with the rest of his family in spite of his wife's attitude toward them.

At the same time that Kate cut herself off from the everyday practice of the Dutch tradition of family association by quarreling with her husband's relatives, she proved in her own person unable to perpetuate that tradition to another generation. She and Abe very much wanted children, but in June 1876, December 1879, and March 1881, when she was forty-four, Kate suffered miscarriages. Considering her age and her mother's history of difficult pregnancies, Kate was perhaps not so much to blame for her childlessness as she herself believed, but she never ceased to regret her lost babies and the lost heirs of the house of Gansevoort. Assured that she would have no children of her own, Kate then flung her family feeling into holding together her existing relatives. For many years she was especially close to the Melville cousins, whose early misfortunes had welded them into a proud, defensive clan. Allan died very suddenly in 1872, when Kate's kindness to his grief-stricken family drew her out of her own grief and earned her special commendation from Abe. His widow kept up correspondence with Kate for some years but gradually turned her attention to other interests, while his daughters quarreled with their stepmother and Kate lost track of them. Herman Melville remained closely attached to Peter Gansevoort as long as he lived, and Kate usually stayed at his home when she went to New York to shop, but Herman was poor, proud, and as touchy as she was. They had a difference soon after her father's death when Kate tried to press some money on Herman and he refused to accept it; finally, in November, 1879, they quarreled irrevocably. She never stayed with them again, and Herman found excuses to avoid coming to Albany, even for general family reunions like the Christmas party for which Kate assembled fourteen cousins in the same year. In 1868 Kate was a bridesmaid at Tom Melville's wedding to Catherine Bogart; the Sailor's Snug Harbor of which he was head was thenceforth home port for the Melvilles as Gansevoort had been for the ten years previous. But Tom died suddenly in 1884, his sister Fanny in 1885, Helen Melville Griggs in 1888, Herman Melville in 1891, and the last of the clan, Catherine Melville Hoadley, in 1905.

As the Melvilles drifted away from her, Kate tried to reopen contact with other branches of the family. She occasionally heard from the Curtises in Schenectady, but George died in 1884 and

Catherine in 1887. She hunted up Stanwix Gansevoort in Glens Falls and found him a lonely old man who delighted in writing her long letters reminiscing about his youth. Later still, in 1910, she welcomed to Albany the family of Ernest Sofio, a Curtis grandson. Robert Sofio, one of Ernest's sons, often visited Kate to deliver chickens he had raised. He remembers Kate's interest in his stamp collection—she eventually left him the stamps she had saved over the years—and her concern for his education, which she expressed in practical terms by making it possible for him and his brother to attend the Albany Academy. Josephine Sofio, Robert's younger sister, remembers Kate herself as "a compact dignified, agreeable, albeit firm person. 'All of one piece' is the way I think of her. . . . She had a way of talking that engaged my whole attention." She also remembers the house full of strange and curious things, the books lining the walls of Abe's library—"She told me . . . he never put a book onto the shelves which he had not first read"—and the charming little girl's sewing box, Kate's own, that she gave her.[24] Kate also found in an old people's home the old and ailing John Maley Gansevoort, a son of John Gansevoort and grandson of Leonard, Jr., and in another old people's home his equally old and ailing wife, who had never been separated before and were very unhappy. Kate provided for their admission to the same old people's home, where they lived peacefully and ever more feebly until she died in 1908 and he in 1910, at the age of ninety-five—the greatest age reached by any of the long-lived Gansevoorts. Kate also had occasional contact with some very distant cousins, descendants of Dr. Pieter Gansevoort, who lived in Bath, New York, but who did not carry the name beyond the sixth generation.

In the meantime, Kate and Abe were also active in Albany civic affairs. Abe's profession led him to such public offices as supreme court reporter, acting state treasurer, and corporation counsel for the city of Albany. In 1879 he was a delegate to a conference on international law in London, thus making his contribution to the diplomatic activities of the Lansing family, the most conspicuous member of which was Abe's distant cousin, Robert Lansing, Woodrow Wilson's secretary of state, whose wife's sister was the mother of John Foster Dulles. In 1882–83 Abe was a member of the state senate, where he promoted bills regulating railroads, abolishing canal tolls, reorganizing the "scientific departments," and establishing a state park at Niagara Falls. He also participated in many nonpolitical organizations, serving as a director of the National Commercial Bank, a trustee of the Albany Savings Bank, a trustee of the Albany Academy, a member of various city boards and commissions, and vestryman of St. Peter's Church. In 1880 he was one of the founders of the Fort Orange Club, which made its headquarters at 110 Washington Avenue, right across the street from his home. Kate encouraged him to go there in the evenings, where he enjoyed the company of friends whose favorite drinking song had the refrain,

> I'm a Van of a Van of a Van of a Van
> Of a Van of an old Dutch line.[25]

Kate's civic interest was in preserving Albany's vanishing past. When the famous elm tree at the corner of State and Pearl Streets was cut down in 1877 to prevent it from falling down, she mourned:

The news of the fall of the old Elm Tree was sad indeed. Who were the vandals who ordered its destruction? and had no Albanian the voice to Amen or oppose such a demolition of past years. It truly seems as if all the past was floating, and dear *old Albany* becoming a thing of the past.[26]

It should be recalled that at that time the whole complexion of Capitol Hill was being changed beyond recognition by the construction of the present Capitol, which went on for twenty years. To Kate, who lived within a block of it, the change was undoubtedly as overwhelming as the present South Mall development is to those who grew up in Albany before it was thought of. Kate also participated in civic celebrations, notably by loaning General Gansevoort's uniform and Henry's regimental flag to be displayed at the city's bicentennial in 1886. She was particularly concerned that her precious relics be properly cared for and appropriately exhibited. A friend recollected later how a member of the committee conducted her, with proper respect for the heiress of Gen-

eral Gansevoort's famous temper, to approve the location of
honor in which her grandfather's portrait had been placed, when
it was discovered that a printer's error caused the catalog entry to
read "#33: An old Dutch mug." [27] Kate was not amused.

In 1895 Kate founded the Gansevoort Chapter of the Daughters of the Revolution, but when this organization amalgamated
with the Daughters of the American Revolution in 1897, she resigned. She tried to join the Colonial Dames, but gave up in disgust when they declined to accept her Revolutionary grandfather
as a noteworthy colonial figure. A friend on the committee suggested that she submit an application based on the services of
Volkert P. Douw, but Kate pointed out indignantly that he was not
her ancestor and that even if he had been his claims to fame were
insignificant beside those of General Gansevoort.

She was also particularly interested in the National Mary
Washington Association, which sought to raise money to perpetuate the memory of George Washington's mother. In a public
appeal for funds she stated reasons for supporting this cause
which reflected not only the sentimentality of the generation
which established Mothers' Day, but also the habitual patterns of
reasoning of the Dutch tradition:

Your contributions will not certainly in the sense that they will minister to any physical need or misfortune, be a charity, but that they
will be for a purpose educational and beneficial in the highest degree,
it does not seem to be rational to question. To suggest that such an
undertaking is not practical, or is unnecessary or unworthy because it
will minister to a sentiment, and not to a physical need, is surely to
repudiate the influence and the example of lofty character and noble
deeds in shaping the civilization of our race. [28]

This busy life was cut off when Abe died of cancer on October
4, 1899. After the funeral Kate wrapped herself in a cocoon of
grief from which she never emerged. For a time she did not go
out except to take a daily drive to the cemetery; for nearly twenty
years she kept his room as he had left it, with fresh flowers on the
bed, and had a place set for him at the table, in accordance with
an old Dutch custom. In accordance with another custom, she
distributed funeral spoons to his relatives—the last recorded in-

stance of this practice in Albany. In the city, she became noted as an eccentric, who wore her clothes to tatters and clung to a certain bonnet long after it went out of style because Abe had liked it. She had her own ideas about her financial affairs, which sometimes got her into difficult situations and often caused headaches for her bankers, her lawyers, and, eventually, her executors. But to her main interest during her widowhood, the preservation and disposal of the Gansevoort heritage, she gave the benefit of her full attention, her soundest judgment, and the best professional advice that the Gansevoort fortune could command. First she erected monuments and memorials to her nearest and dearest, a window in St. Peter's in memory of Abe, a portrait to Harvard Law School in memory of Henry, a parsonage to the Reformed Church at Gansevoort in memory of her father and uncle. In 1907 she presented a statue of her grandfather to the city of Rome in honor of the defense of Fort Stanwix. For the dedication Kate provided a special train to take over a hundred guests from Albany, including the surviving relatives, and the Mayor of Rome addressed a gathering of citizens, school children, and patriotic societies—but for this occasion so important to her Kate very reluctantly bought a new dress, refused to have a new coat, and insisted on wearing the dilapidated little bonnet that Abe had admired.

At the same time, Kate began to sort and catalog the family relics, family papers, and historical and genealogical information she had been gathering for years. As early as 1877 she and Abe were considering depositing her grandfather's papers and General Gansevoort's portrait by Gilbert Stuart in the New York Historical Society. She also preserved her father's papers, Henry's and her own, and documents given or left to her by other relatives who hesitated to destroy them but did not want to keep them. With the assistance of a secretary, she prepared eight volumes of family letters and a number of other documents for binding. She also put in order and had bound invaluable albums of photographs, some of family members, some of family relics and landmarks, and some of the city of Albany in general. She published a collection of her husband's letters similar to her memorial to

Henry, encouraged the State of New York to publish General Gansevoort's military papers (an enterprise that was never completed), and in 1917 published a life and a translation of a work of Johan Wessel Gansfort, the medieval scholar to whom the family believed, without any proof, that they were related. So she finally insured that when 115 should inevitably be broken up, the Gansevoort family tradition should not be broken up with it.

In the meantime Kate aged into a frail old lady, more eccentric than ever. In December, 1917, she appeared at her bank, wasted and pale from an illness but otherwise quite herself, to sign her will. One of the witnesses was later asked:

And state whether to the best of your knowledge information and belief, she was under any restraint.
Hardly! I think she came down alone and acted perfectly free and with the customary independence of manner she always had.[29]

The peppery Irish maid who witnessed her signature to a codicil a month later testified:

The only thing I can describe was just her little temper, she had always a hot temper. . . . Her mind was perfectly clear and sound; she was able to take care of her own home until almost the last day, was her own housekeeper, gave her orders until she went to bed.[30]

After an illness of a week or ten days, Kate died at the age of seventy-nine on January 22, 1918. Her quiet funeral was very short, and only a few relatives were present; the short notice, the winter weather, and World War I travel restrictions made it impossible for her scattered cousins to assemble as had been customary at Albany Dutch funerals. The *Albany Evening Journal* published a brief obituary which was also an obituary for the Dutch tradition:

Mrs. Lansing was one of a group of representative Albany women who clung to the old ideals of Albanians and whose interest in patriotic matters and those of civic events of importance did not wane with the passing of the years, although of late she took no active part in public affairs.[31]

Kate's executors then had the task of distributing the Gansevoort family fortune, which amounted to about $350,000. About

265

$210,000 was invested in various securities, the largest single item being $90,000 of stock in the National Commercial Bank, of which Abe had been a director. There was also slightly under $140,000 in real estate, principally Stanwix Hall, valued at $95,000, the Gansevoort home, Abe's house, to which Kate had come as a bride, a farm at Gansevoort, and the ill-fated 100 acres at Van Buren Harbor, neither of which was under cultivation. Over half of this fortune was divided proportionately among numerous cousins, some so distant that the probate officials did not even list them as relatives. The closest was a second cousin, Charlotte Hoadley, who had been close to Kate in her last years and who eventually received about a tenth of the estate. Then there were considerable legacies to all of the local churches with which Kate and the Gansevoorts had any contact, scholarship funds for schools and colleges from which Gansevoorts had graduated, and contributions to local charities, notably hospitals, and to national patriotic and missionary organizations. The house at 115 and $20,000 for endowment went to the Albany Institute of History and Art, "provided that the same [house] shall never be used for commercial purposes." [32] Finally, like a tidy Dutch housewife, the last of the Gansevoorts left $1,000 to the cemetery for perpetual care of the Gansevoort lot.

When the executors came to assess the real estate, however, they found that in her last years Kate had not been very tidy. All of the buildings were so dilapidated that they could not be sold for anywhere near their real value. The house at 115, besides being out of repair, was stuffed from cellar to attic with furniture and household goods, two thousand books, innumerable papers, valuable collections of china and silverware, personal possessions and mementos, and junk. It took Kate's two servants and an additional caretaker a year and a quarter to sort everything, find the legal and business papers bearing on the estate, distribute the furniture, preserve everything of value, and dispose of the rest. The Albany Institute, which already had a building of its own a few doors away, tried to sell 115 to the Gansevoort Chapter of the D.A.R., which considered it too expensive, and finally did sell it to a Catholic order. In 1933, when they wished to sell, the neighborhood had become commercial, so the restriction in the will was broken by legal action; a short-order restaurant soon replaced the Gansevoort home, and has now been replaced in its turn by an insurance company. Stanwix Hall was also sold, with some difficulty, and in 1932 was demolished to make way for the massive white marble United States Post Office. The papers, relics, and objets d'art went to various museums. Kate's executors did not render their final accounting to the Surrogate's Court until November, 1941.

In Kate's time, the Albany Dutch patrician tradition was almost entirely a matter of social custom and of sentiment. During her young womanhood, the Dutch families with which she was associated still considered themselves active entities and maintained their tradition by habitual frequent face-to-face contact. During the Civil War years, Kate and her mother spent nearly every afternoon calling, usually visiting at least one relative and often staying for tea or even supper. They were especially close to the Lansings, Susan's own brother and sister, with whom they gathered for a meal at least once a week, and nearly always on special occasions such as Thanksgiving, New Years, birthdays, and wedding anniversaries. When she was at home Kate, who was an accomplished needlewoman, spent much of her time making gifts for the family occasions—notably births—of her friends and also making afghans and similar items to be sold or raffled for civic charities. As the years passed, however, many of these relatives died or moved away and Kate quarreled with most of those who were left. At the same time the other Dutch families developed other interests and left their tradition behind; when Kate hung out a basket for calling cards on New Years Day, 1880, after ten successive years' suspension in respect to one or another deceased relative, only a dozen or so cards were left where a hundred or more had been usual.

As the customs of her youth fell into disuse, Kate's maintenance of the Dutch tradition became a stubborn clinging to sentiment. In her diary she frequently recorded her awareness that she was the last of her line, and elaborated on the feelings of grief and desolation which she considered appropriate for a person in

267

such a situation. She furthermore lost no opportunity to remind others of the glories of the Gansevoort name, by placing monuments and memorials in every suitable location, and also by encouraging historians and genealogists to record the family's accomplishments. The account of her grandfather's Revolutionary achievements which she prepared was in general accurate as to facts, with a couple of minor exceptions, but was presented in a manner which modern taste finds excessively laudatory. Still, General Gansevoort did have one real heroic moment, and Kate's pride in it was quite justifiable—and quite in the Dutch tradition. "The laconic and determined reply which was made by him to the British colonel's demand for surrender, ranks in my view of it, as one of the most impressive incidents of the war." [33] Somewhat less justifiable was the attention she persisted in giving to medieval theologian Johan Wessel Gansfort, whom she always claimed as a member of the family although her father and brother proved fairly definitely while they were in the Netherlands that as a churchman he could not have been their ancestor. Although Kate scrupulously refrained from claiming him as such, in her genealogical contributions she gave him quite as much space as she did the General. Her favorite story about him suggests that, in accordance with a somewhat contrary Dutch tradition, the theologian himself might not have appreciated her ostentatious display of him:

It is related that he was asked by [Pope] Sixtus [IV, an old friend] what favor he could do for him, and in answer Wessel asked for a Greek and Hebrew Bible from the Vatican library. "You shall have it," said the Pope, "but what a simpleton you are; why did you not ask for a bishopric or something of that kind?" "Because I do not want it," replied Wessel. [34]

As the Gansevoorts' Dutch tradition at last became a matter of sentiment and sentiment alone, so too did the Dutch tradition of Albany. The general interest in history and tradition which developed in the United States after the centennial of Independence in 1876 prompted the founding not only of societies like the D.A.R. to promote patriotic tradition, but also ethnic organizations. That of the Dutch was the Holland Society of New York, founded in 1885. Kate could not be a member since its constitution permitted the admission only of men descended by direct male lines from settlers who had come to the Hudson Valley while it was ruled by the Dutch, but Abe joined very soon after the society was formed. The members gathered every year in New York to perpetuate the Dutch tradition by a banquet, speeches by students of Dutch culture or distinguished visitors from the Netherlands, and publication in their annual yearbook of historical and genealogical information including the colonial marriage and baptism records of the Albany Dutch Church. A similar organization, the Dutch Settlers Society of Albany, formed in 1924, does admit women and descendants by female lines of Albany Dutch families, and likewise preserves records and publishes research about the Albany Dutch in its yearbook.

In the mid-twentieth century, however, awareness of Albany's Dutch tradition is by no means confined to these societies, or to the descendants of patrician families who still participate significantly though inconspicuously in the city's economic development, social life, and civic improvement. School children study local history not only in their social studies classrooms but also by visiting such museums of the Dutch tradition as Fort Crailo, the Schuyler Mansion, and the Albany Institute of History and Art. School and community choruses sometimes sing the Dutch national anthem "Wilhelmus van Nassauwen"—in English—at civic events. Visitors to downtown Albany are reminded of its past by a large number of historical markers and the substantial fabric of the First Reformed Church. The Chamber of Commerce promotes the annual Tulip Festival, a community pageant which originated after World War II when the Dutch city of Nijmegen responded to the Albanians' contributions toward its relief and reconstruction with a present of thousands of tulip bulbs, whose flowering every May is the occasion for a typical American civic celebration. In 1959 the entire Hudson Valley celebrated the 350th anniversary of its discovery by the Dutch with a year-long series of events climaxed by the visit of Crown Princess Beatrix of the Netherlands.

The Dutch tradition has thus become an indispensable part of the city's image, an effective element of civic promotion; as the Ten Eyck Hotel, a downtown landmark, is demolished, Stuyvesant Plaza, a shopping center, becomes a new landmark—appropriately commercial—in a suburb not far from soaring Stuyvesant Tower on the Albany campus of the State University of New York. But perhaps the most typically Dutch of these present-day monuments to the Albany patrician tradition are the brooding statue of Philip Schuyler which stands in front of the neo-Gothic city hall built in 1884—appropriately with his back to the city hall and his face to the State Capitol—and the carillon over his head in the city hall tower. Donated as a memorial to Dutch patrician civic leader and statesman John V. L. Pruyn by his daughter and her husband, a student of the civic carillons of Flemish cities, this carillon brings to life in present-day Albany one of the most characteristic traditions of medieval Dutch towns. So long as Philip Schuyler guards the civic authorities and the daily noon hour carillon concert rings out over automobile horns climbing Capitol Hill and pile drivers constructing the monumental South Mall state office project, the Albany Dutch tradition, like that of the cities in the Netherlands, will be not only the foundation of the city's history but the continuing symbol of its civic identity.

270

CONCLUSION

The Patrician Legacy

The legacy of the Hudson Valley Dutch patricians to the American tradition has been often underestimated because the interpretation of the American way of life dominant in the twentieth century has emphasized aspects of it with which the Dutch tradition appears to be in conflict. A tradition of preeminent loyalty to a local community makes little sense to a people who identify themselves with a nation covering half a continent; a tradition of local and class privilege flies in the face of the belief that all men are created equal; a tradition of heterogeneity finds it difficult to exist in a community which stresses similarities rather than differences. But all these characteristics of the American tradition are themselves now beginning to be recognized as peculiar to a particular era in which the American nation was forced to assert its unity against the centrifugal forces of regional secession prevented only by war; massive immigration representing many different traditions; and blatant social inequalities ingrained even in the law of the land. It was finally necessary to use that unity, perilously forged and perilously maintained, as a weapon of defense in a worldwide conflict for the preservation of the values which it claimed to embody. It was to be expected in such a long-drawn and critical struggle for existence that other values less central to that struggle but equally important in the American tradition should have been given less attention for a time, until those who remembered them for the most part passed from the scene and new generations growing up in the midst of the conflict, having never experienced their reality, came to forget that they had ever existed.

The present generation, having to live in a nation in which local, state, and regional particularisms often interfere with the attainment of national goals, in which individuals and groups of all sorts claim and exert special privileges in both private and public affairs, and in which Americans unhesitatingly and often defiantly assert their deviation from "normal" American standards of values, is learning by daily experience that the values of particularism, privilege, and heterogeneity are not only consistent with the American tradition, but to appreciable numbers of Americans are the most important part of it. In order to assure them of their inalienable rights to life, liberty, and the pursuit of happiness, and at the same time to preserve the equally inalienable rights to life, liberty, and the pursuit of happiness of those who prefer to accept the values of nationality, equality, and homogeneity, it is urgently necessary to come to a better understanding of the part that particularism, privilege, and heterogeneity have played in the formation of the present American tradition. Both as a case study and as a demonstration of a method of attacking the problem, the history of the Hudson Valley Dutch patricians is a good place to start.

To do so, it is necessary first to consider the Dutch tradition as it contributed to the economic, social, and political structure of the American tradition. Perhaps the most conspicuous feature of the Dutch tradition is its concentration upon commerce and trade. Albany was settled by traders whose exercise of free competition carried them to such an extreme of economic anarchy that a state-imposed monopoly appeared to be their only recourse. But this monopoly was unable to enforce its privileges from so great a distance, and Albany was in effect a community of independent traders until the Dongan Charter vested the privilege of monopoly in the community itself. Thus the Dutch tradition of economic leadership by individuals organized into communities, as opposed to the French system of colony-wide monopolies, became a formal part of the Hudson Valley way of doing business. This local monopoly of a single branch of commerce, on which many Dutch cities had made and maintained their fortunes for centuries, was however very soon made obsolete by the increase of population on the American frontier and by the development of the diversified American economy. At first the Dutch merchants of Albany kept pace with these developments, sending their sons to extend their businesses to newer communities and expanding their trade from protected furs to agricultural products and general merchandise which they carried advantageously among both Old and New World markets. When the American Revolution cut off their trade within the British Empire and swept their London-centered system of credit and currency from under their feet, they took leading parts in founding banks and in financing and developing transportation facilities. Only later in the nineteenth century, when these institutions began to be organized on a continental basis, was their influence decisively overshadowed, and in the local banking and finance which are still the indispensable foundations of the nationwide financial structure, such Dutch fortunes as still exist in Albany in the mid-twentieth century are to this day quietly significant.

Dutch social structure also contributed to that of the emerging American tradition. By the early eighteenth century there had developed in Albany a definite stratification reflecting the patrician system normal in Dutch towns, in which the merchants who in their everyday commerce exercised the city's particular privileges and monopolies also controlled the civic organizations by which the responsibilities of maintaining these privileges were apportioned and enforced among the entire community. It was taken for granted that wealth would be accumulated by families rather than by individuals, and would be convertible into both power and prestige which would be shared by all the members of the family. The custom of dividing the family fortune equally among all the children, including daughters (as opposed to the English custom of primogeniture), had the effects of keeping families together, particularly when their inheritance was a going business, of insuring women of status commensurate with the size of their fortunes, and of eliminating the phenomenon of the younger son born and educated to a way of life beyond his prospective means. Dutch patricians' younger sons often took their fortunes into some other line of business or some other place or used them as supplements to professional income, but they were not forced, as were English younger sons, to support themselves by entering the army or the church, becoming followers of some great man who could provide them with preferment, or marrying an heiress.

Particularly through marriage, the English gentry maintained close connections with wealthy mercantile families, but both merchants and gentry regarded life on a country estate as socially superior to continuing in business in town. English trading fortunes therefore went to purchase country estates as a means of social mobility for tradesmen, while Dutch patricians, who considered their civic position quite as respectable and in many cases more profitable and powerful than that of their country cousins, invested in rural development when they thought it might be profitable, but in general kept their fortunes and the center of their existence in the same city over several generations. This tradition the Albany Dutch patricians followed, and those who are still there follow it yet. By encouraging ambitious, wealthy, and powerful plebeians and newcomers to join the patriciate by marriage, the Albany Dutch patricians provided for orderly adjustments to shifts in real power within the community and eventually dispersed much of the Albany Dutch tradition among families of other ethnic backgrounds but similar values.

To Dutch patricians the political process was only one of a variety of means by which they advanced the profit and prestige of their families, for which reason the Albanians quickly became involved in the emerging American political tradition. Seeking the most direct routes to power in the colonial period, they placed primary emphasis on influence with governors and administrative officials with whom they dealt in the normal course of their business, and upon seeking appointment to local offices. As a rule they stood aside from the assembly, whose quest for power was rather in the tradition of the English Glorious Revolution, until it had accomplished that quest and for all practical purposes controlled the governor's use of his administrative and appointive powers. The Dutch patricians then learned to work with the assembly, but they treated it as a small community of powerful individuals who happened to be chosen by election rather than cooptation, instead of as the representatives of the people in the democratic sense. As the American party system developed, Dutch plebeian and patrician leaders learned from their Yankee neighbors how to appeal to voters on issues, but unlike the Yankees they addressed themselves not to the voters' rational judgment but to their emotional conscience. In so doing they sincerely believed themselves to be seeking the ultimate will of the vast majority of the electorate who, having little formal education, in fact judged issues more surely on the basis of their immediate experience than according to rational processes which they did not habitually use. The organization of their various parties, most notably the Albany Regency and the nationwide Jacksonian Democratic Party, resembled the organization of a Dutch community, except that its patricians held their power in terms of votes rather than dollars, and used it to build political machines rather than families.

This description of the relationship between the Dutch patrician tradition and the American tradition as it is usually understood falls far short of the fundamental significance of either. Neither economic, social, nor political explanations, separately or together, explain what was distinctive about the Hudson Valley Dutch tradition, nor do they by any means include all the available information about it. Politics was important to the Dutch, but they had no comprehension of a written constitution, the two-party system, or the concept of popular sovereignty. They were shrewd and effective businessmen, but the corporate organization, union agitation, and government regulation of nineteenth- and twentieth-century American economic development would certainly astonish them. Their social system determined status by birth, intermarriage, and inherited wealth, quite different criteria from occupation, ethnic identity, and religious affiliation. Intellectually they were unconcerned; even their piety expressed itself in their everyday behavior toward their neighbors rather than in theological disputation. It is simply impossible to read their

275

history aright by approaching it like American national history.

It is therefore necessary to go back and look at the Hudson Valley Dutch tradition from the viewpoint of its own beginning. In order to reach this beginning it is necessary to go very far back indeed, for the way of life of the seventeenth-century Netherlands from which the colonists came makes sense only in the context of the cumulative experience of the Netherlanders since they first appeared as a distinct ethnic group in the tenth century. This search requires an acquaintance with medieval history which most readers in all probability do not possess, since for the last generation social studies instruction has stressed the present and considered the past only as it helped to form the present. The result is described by an English-born historian now naturalized in this country:

Like other peoples, we Americans often use history as though it were a shallow mirror, to look in it only for ourselves, our present institutions, and our immediate origins. . . . Our voyage in history is hastily conceived and self-centered. Leaving antique Rome [totally behind, in my generation—APK] we spend our middle ages in England and our modern times in America. Our history is forever colonial, always a record of the province just beginning to be filled up.[1]

Under these educational circumstances, it is quite possible that a coming generation of American historians may find the Middle Ages their most fruitful source of new insights into colonial history—although it may be necessary to revise the textbook interpretation of the Middle Ages before this becomes widely apparent. In the meantime, leading medievalist Lynn White, Jr., has suggested some intriguing starting points.

A blind spot in the study of the history of the United States is failure to recognize our detailed and massive continuity with the European Middle Ages. One reason for this is our angle of vision. . . . Indeed, a good case could be made for the thesis that today the United States is closer to the Middle Ages than is Europe. Many of the . . . early immigrants . . . established loose-jointed late mediaeval communities . . . and at the end of the eighteenth century mediaeval pluralism became the cornerstone of our Constitution. . . . The central issue in American domestic politics at the present time is whether, or the extent to which, our mediaeval legacy of pluralism is still viable. . . . By far the larger part of man's ecology is what is inside his skull: a new external problem rarely begets an authentically novel solution. And what was the mental, emotional and technical equipment in the heads of the men and women who swept the frontier westward? . . . Our frontiersmen . . . were particularly beneficiaries of the Middle Ages. Their essential equipment was very largely the culture of the mediaeval lower classes. . . . they generally followed mediaeval patterns of action because these were the patterns that they knew. . . . What the American frontiersman did was to select, and gradually to elaborate, useful elements in the highly diversified mediaeval tradition which he took for granted.[2]

White's description of this North European cultural tradition, which runs unbroken from the tenth to the eighteenth centuries and crosses the Atlantic and the American continent, is in terms of technological history, a very new, very significant, but as yet highly specialized area in American studies. His point will be clearer to most readers if it is restated in a more familiar form.

The settlement of the American continent was indeed unprecedented in the history of mankind in the expanse of territory covered, the number of people who participated, the speed with which it was accomplished, the extent of publicity it received, and the mass of documentation it left behind. But as a human achievement it was not unprecedented at all. One of the fundamental reasons why American pioneers opened the continent so swiftly, so efficiently, and so effectively was that their ancestors before them had been pioneering in Europe for over a thousand years. England, northern France, and Germany were once covered with dense forests in which barbarian tribes made migration a normal way of life. Little by little they settled down in river valleys and natural clearings, nibbling away at the woodland one tree at a time. Individual peasants carved out homesteads called "assarts." Lords sent settlers whose rents added to their incomes. Kings sent colonists to increase the area of their dominions. Monks built retreats from the world or missionary centers for converting the heathen. They were interrupted and driven away by migrations, invasions, local wars, general wars, famines, and

277

plagues, but they always came back. Little by little they felled the forests of England, France, and Germany, drained the marshes of the Low Countries, scaled the mountains of Scandinavia and Switzerland. Little by little they built up a reservoir of tools and techniques for performing essential tasks; a repository of customs and traditions for ordering everyday living; a repertory of institutions and organizations for governing group relationships. When some of their descendants migrated to America, their response to wilderness conditions reflected—and in many cases continued to reflect for generations—the response of their medieval ancestors to similar conditions. The American pioneer tradition, so distinctively American in its total response to American conditions, was a composite of various contributions, each of which by itself represented some aspect of a transplanted medieval culture.

Such an interpretation of the Westward Movement might appear to refute the "Turner thesis," but as a matter of fact it merely replaces it in its original context. Frederick Jackson Turner wrote for readers who had studied European history almost exclusively; in pointing out that American history had distinctive characteristics worthy of their attention he did not envision the present situation in which it is possible to specialize entirely in American studies. His intention may be seen even more sharply by comparing his thesis to his contemporary Henri Pirenne's thesis concerning the origin of Dutch towns, with which it has surprising similarities. Both Pirenne and Turner started from the conception of a "frontier" as a boundary line between two states, but to both these states were less political than socio-cultural—a "state" of civilization and a "state" of barbarism. *Civilization* to Pirenne was the decadent society of ancient Rome; to Turner it was the equally decadent society of the Old World in general. *Barbarism* carried to Pirenne's classically-educated readers reminders of Tacitus' noble Teutons, particularly the heroic Batavii of the Rhine delta, and may be compared to Turner's idea of the wilderness, which bears considerable resemblance to that of James Fenimore Cooper. Both Pirenne and Turner then extended the conception of the frontier from the line itself to the area through which it ran—in Roman terms the *limes* (or threshold) as well as the *limen* (or boundary line)—and chose as their particular subject the institutions which settlers developed when they moved into these areas. The basic difference between them was that Turner described a society in which these institutions were erected on a rural economy and were constantly reproduced by settlers moving to new lands, while Pirenne described a society with an urban economy which remained stationary for centuries behind substantial city walls. Both delineated the gradual evolution of a way of life which became traditional, but Turner's society evolved in space while Pirenne's evolved in time.

Besides setting readers on a search for the medieval origins of the American way of life, the Hudson Valley Dutch tradition challenges them to find meaning in many sources infrequently used by historians. Most history is based upon written accounts by participants and observers of events, but the Dutch colonists were not nearly so accustomed to writing down their ideas and experiences as were their English counterparts. The Pilgrims produced a major history of their settlement in the first generation, and the Puritans of Massachusetts Bay soon founded a printing press to provide the people with books and the ministers with a means of publication. The Hudson Valley Dutch imported few books, except for schoolbooks and manuals of devotion, supported no presses, and produced no authors—not even of publishable sermons. Nor did they write many letters or diaries in Dutch.

Before deploring the literary poverty of the Hudson Valley Dutch tradition too deeply, it is wise to remember that while English culture was producing Shakespeare, Spenser, and Milton, Dutch culture was producing Rembrandt, Hals, and Vermeer. These great painters represented a vigorous and widespread tradition of artistic creativity and popular appreciation which descended unbroken from the time of the medieval Flemish masters. It would be reasonable to expect, therefore, that Dutch colonists in the Hudson Valley might likewise have expressed in line, color, and mass some of the feelings that English colonists expressed in words. The substantial solidity of Dutch colonial architecture has long been recognized, not only in books but also in the preserva-

279

tion of a number of characteristic Hudson Valley houses as museums. Interesting observations about population movement have been based upon comparison of architectural features from Hudson Valley buildings with those peculiar to particular districts in the Netherlands. Within the last few years it has also been discovered that eighteenth-century Albany was a center of silversmithing, and that the upper Hudson Valley produced a distinctive group of limners, itinerant amateur portrait-painters, a full century before the well-known "Hudson River School." The significance of these artistic discoveries is still being assessed, but it is certain that as we find out more about the Dutch taste in material objects we will learn more about Dutch values and the Dutch way of life.

Other characteristics of the Hudson Valley Dutch tradition are equally important but even less tangible. Unwritten, sometimes unspoken, attitudes, standards, and habits of behavior, handed down by example from parents to children, are very important in understanding any way of life. We often learn about them by comparing observations made by foreign visitors with the casual details disclosed by letters, memoirs, and even fictional representations. In spite of Albany's isolation, a few penetrating and articulate travelers visited the city while the Dutch patricians still ruled it. Albanians wrote few memoirs, but the immense Gansevoort family correspondence serves this purpose equally well. There are also a few novels which convey, either from the author's memory or by imaginative reconstruction based on research, an effective sense of what it meant to be a Hudson Valley Dutchman.

To interpret the insights offered by all of these unusual sources, readers must be prepared to use imagination in a way more often demanded by novels than by historical treatises. In twentieth-century America it is customary to approach from a nonfictional viewpoint many aspects of human experience which in the nineteenth century were discussed in novels, in the eighteenth century in poems, and in the seventeenth century in plays. English critic John Bayley describes this shift in form as it affected Sir

Walter Scott, and further points out the significance of his novels to historians:

Scott was able to make effective use of the Shakespearean tradition. . . . Romantic poetry imitated Shakespeare's style, but neither poetry nor the drama was able to profit from the world of his plays. Fiction did so; the conflict between two worlds, two ideals, which is the basis of so many—and of the histories in particular—is profoundly understood by Scott and adapted to his own purposes, unconsciously perhaps, but with results of the highest importance.[3]

This statement can be placed in a Hudson Valley setting by reading "Cooper" for "Scott" and remembering that Cooper saw the Hudson Valley as the scene of conflicts among Dutch, English, and Yankees as well as between civilization and noble savagery. It can be placed in a context more familiar to historians by reading "Parkman" for "Cooper" and remembering that Parkman saw the Hudson Valley, with its northward extension the Champlain Valley, as the theater of conflict between the English and the French.

Such conflict is one of the main themes of the great novels about families in European literature. Sometimes it is conflict between a leading family and its community, or between two such families in the community. It may also be conflict between a community organized on the basis of kinship and a society organized on the basis of wealth or power. At other times it is conflict among family members caused by the cumulative effect of everyday community tensions. Still another form of it is conflict within families reflecting extraordinary upheavals in the community, the world beyond the community, or both. All of these themes appear in the history of the Gansevoort family and all must be developed to display the Hudson Valley Dutch tradition fully. But for this purpose the usual methods of American history are inappropriate, and those methods familiar to us from American novels are even more inadequate. Bayley, comparing English and American fiction, suggests some reason for this which historians would do well to ponder:

The greatest English literature is not about the Human Condition. . . . the portrayal of "Nature" suggests an almost involuntary fidelity to what is constant in human types and human affairs; to the repetition of birth and death, joy and sorrow; to the humors of men and women and the peculiarities that are at once recognized as universal. . . . The Human Condition, on the other hand, implies a personal sense of where life is significant, of where humanity suffers especially or feels intensively; of unusual violence and unusual modes of feeling; of interesting development or of illuminating decay. The subject matter may even be the same, but those who write about Nature take it for granted, while those who write about the Human Condition take an attitude toward it. . . .

We might begin by observing that there is no Nature in American literature. . . . The processes of living which give their substance to the literary idea of Nature of course existed in America as much as anywhere else, but . . . the complex kinds of traditional authority that Nature implies were specifically disowned by the American idea and left out of the American dream. For America, Nature had to become the Human Condition.

Not at all unjustly, the new civilization distrusted taking anything for granted, particularly the assumptions about hierarchy which are clearly implied in the eighteenth century view of Nature. But in fact Nature was connected not as much with the hierarchy of class (though that comes into it), as with the hierarchy of the feelings and responses. He who portrays Nature must have a sense of proportion and a sense of what is important, for only in a scale of proportions can things be taken for granted. In the scale, public custom and process is more important than personal habit and the world of the individual, the family more important than sex, average tranquillity more important than exceptional violence.[4]

When the Hudson Valley tradition is viewed as a manifestation of human nature rather than the human condition it suddenly begins to make sense—a kind of sense supported by Pirenne, who wrote of Dutch cities:

Everybody knew everybody else in the "great towns" of the Middle Ages, and party strife was intensified by personal rivalries and quarrels. The personal identity of the individual was not in those days lost in a nameless crowd. Each individual man with his passions and interests appeared in the full light of day. There was nothing abstract or theoretical about politics. It was not a fight for a programme: the adversaries met face to face and marched against each other as foes. Political convictions, sharpened by personal antipathies, were easily exasperated to the point of ferocity. . . . Each man became conscious of his own worth. If he were without pity for his adversary in times of strife, he also knew how to do his duty to the utmost when the interests of the town were at stake. If the need arose he was ready to lay down his life for his town.[5]

Thus it becomes evident that Dutch communities were not held together by structures of institutional organization as are those of modern America, but by a complex network of human relationships among individuals and families. Therefore it is by no means inappropriate to describe the binding force of Dutch communities as the centripetal power of human feelings, particularly love of money, love of family members, and love of God.

That the Albany Dutch loved money was one point on which all observers agreed. Traders founded Fort Orange and Beverwyck and chose to stay there because they found it profitable. Most of the lawsuits in their magistrates' court concerned the collection of debts. Members of families participated in trade, invested in ships, and obtained land grants, all for the purpose of accumulating a family fortune. Other important steps were acquisition of political offices, partly as a direct means of increasing the family fortune, but primarily as a means of forwarding its ambition for wealth, power, and prestige. The family fortune was the material indication of the family's status in the community, commonly invested locally and often devoted to civic purposes as well as to the support of the family. When no family members were left to inherit it, it was likely to be distributed for the benefit of the community rather than left to outsiders or to causes of a general or national nature. Conversely, personal quarrels over the division of inheritances were a very important cause of dissension both within families and within the community.

Love of family members was an equally conspicuous characteristic of the Albany Dutch. During their Dutch-speaking period they wrote each other very few letters, mostly business letters, but with the English language they learned a vocabulary of sentiment which prompted many of them to express their feelings toward their relatives with habitual warmth. The excesses of the nineteenth-century rhetoric of the heart—which become often amusingly excessive when used by Dutchmen whose materialistic imaginations obstinately over-freighted the delicate imagery used for far more abstract purposes by English, and still more by Irish and Welsh, popular authors—must not be allowed to obscure the fact that these correspondents sought to convey genuine emotions which they considered important subjects for communication. The repeated burden of these expressions of affection, particularly between husbands and wives, was regret over the necessity of separation and homesickness for the ordinary intrafamily contacts of everyday, which contacts, of course, extended to children and parents living in the same house, and also to aunts, uncles, and cousins who lived nearby. As a feeling binding the community together as well as individual families within it, it is to be distinguished from English "homeliness," which has been elevated to an abstract virtue as well as a fact of everyday life, but which does not extend from the family to the community as a whole. It must also be distinguished sharply from the modern American conception of "love" as the attainment of mutual personal fulfillment between two individuals, which leads in the course of nature to the procreation of other individuals. The contact by which this Dutch family feeling was maintained took place primarily face to face within the community; although distant family members assembled for weddings and funerals, removal from the locality was quite likely to break up a Dutch family unless business connections were also continued.

Love of God was not a subject on which the Albany Dutch wrote extensively, nor, since Americans insist on separating affairs of church and state and historians concern themselves primarily with matters of state, is it an easy subject for an American historian to discuss. Nevertheless, the political and social morality of the eighteenth- and nineteenth-century Hudson Valley Dutchmen who did write about these matters bears obvious relationships to the principal preoccupations of the medieval Dutch religious tradition. The primary similarity is definition of the moral responsibility of the individual as essentially a human, personal responsibility for maintaining certain standards of conduct in everyday situations. The Dutch tradition avoided the often explicitly biological imagery which characterized the relationship between God and man and also the nature of right and wrong in the German tradition, and the equally political imagery for both in the English tradition; examples would be the temptations of Goethe's Mephistopheles and Milton's Lucifer as compared with those depicted in the infernal scenes of Hieronymus Bosch. When faced with instances of secular evil, the Dutch conscience responded neither with physical revulsion nor with metaphysical speculation, but with practical activity suggested by an emotional rather than a rational judgment of the situation. Usually this response was by an individual or at farthest a community to distress of an obvious and immediate nature; the American concept of organizing a nationwide cause to eradicate a long-term evil was outside its frame of reference. For example, the question of whether the institution of slavery as such was right or wrong would probably have been dismissed by Erasmus as one of those futile abstract speculations about the never-to-be-comprehended manner in which angels understand, but the Dutch patricians were noted for their generous and kindly treatment of the slaves they possessed.

The scientific techniques commonly used by modern historians offer little help in understanding the tradition which thus emerges from the available information about the Hudson Valley Dutch patricians. The science of economics has much to say about the processes of acquiring wealth, but little about the forces which motivate individuals—to say nothing of families—to accumulate fortunes over generations and to disperse them in one manner rather than another. The science of psychology says much about the abnormalities of human love, but hardly anything about the emotional forces which hold together happy families. The science of theology says much about doctrine and church government, but very little about the force of faith which compels believers to discharge the religious and moral responsibilities of their creed in the face of opposition and indifference.

Furthermore, when information on these unexplored subjects is collected, it cannot be profitably exploited by the method of scientific analysis. Its meaning only emerges when isolated facts are grouped together on the basis of some observed similarity, and this similarity then contrasted and compared with a similar similarity among some other group of assorted isolated facts. It is thus the associations among facts, rather than the facts themselves, which form the distinctive feature of a tradition. For example, it is not pretended that all of the isolated facts about the Hudson Valley Dutch are necessarily peculiar to them; indeed, many of them are common to several north European traditions. What is uniquely Dutch is the way in which they all fit together, a matter of perspective, of proportion, and of the totality of their cumulative effect.

This catalytic method of research is of course subject to many errors of false and superficial association, particularly because it requires a broader background than many students possess, but with the caution and care necessary in any kind of scholarship, it is an indispensable process for the proper understanding of certain kinds of subjects. The criticism sometimes leveled at it, that it is "intuitive" and therefore not a legitimate process of investigation, is ill-founded. It is quite true that the bases for catalytic association are nonrational, but so long as history takes for its province all events in the human past there are going to be among the subjects of history some effects of nonrational forces, which can never be adequately described and in the meantime can be dangerously misinterpreted in a purely rational, analytic framework. The Hudson Valley Dutch tradition is an obvious test case for the usefulness of the catalytic approach in understanding history precisely because it was so obstinately and outspokenly nonrational in its approach to the problems whose solutions are the foundations of the American tradition.

The necessary background for the use of the catalytic approach is only in part that of the modern research scholar. Of course, anyone trying to write any kind of history does well to be thoroughly familiar with the current conventions of historical communication, including the consensus of established facts, the techniques of social science and statistical research, the areas of historiographical controversy, and the fundamental conflicts of historical philosophy. He also does well to make himself familiar with the obvious fundamentals of literary communication, of which an entire generation, taught on the undergraduate level that the function of literature is more to express the inexpressible than to communicate anything, has by no fault of its own grown up sadly ignorant. But still more important, and overlooked by most graduate schools, are the techniques of organizing and directing wide-ranging reading in subjective as well as objective sources, and of utilizing nonliterary and even nonverbal materials. There are better and worse ways of doing all of these things, and of applying the results, so that the next generation may learn to use their trained imaginations to distinguish as subtly between fact and fantasy as their elders now use their trained intellects to distinguish between truth and falsehood.

At present, this deficiency in the education of American historians unfits them to perceive or approach some subjects in the American past and leads them instead, if they insist upon being interested in them anyway, to study them by inappropriate and misleading methods. It further reflects that deficiency in the tradition of American thought which was noted in the passage by John Bayley. Historians of the American tradition have been particularly suspicious of all forms of hierarchy, sometimes going to the opposite extreme and giving the impression that all facts are created equal and are endowed with an equal inalienable right to be remembered. The idea is that the most memorable facts will automatically call attention to themselves by the magnetic power of their own intrinsic importance, but it breaks down as soon as two individuals approach the same facts from different viewpoints. This presupposition, reinforced by the mechanics of nationwide mass examinations and intensified by the pressure of the information explosion, has produced a generation of readers so overwhelmed by masses of facts all clamoring for equal attention that their most urgent requirement is to have significant facts singled out for specific reasons and presented in some explicitly defined order. Historians have recently been borrowing systems of order and organization from the social sciences, but the historical discipline has resources of its own in this area which American specialists have not yet put to use. One reason for this apparent oversight has been their well-founded recognition that European philosophies of history as such have had little relevance to the facts of American history. Nor would it be appropriate to attempt to devise an American "philosophy of history" in the European sense from the highly unphilosophical American way of life.

But since change is the very essence of the American tradition, it is quite in the mainstream of that tradition to suggest that the failure of Americans to come to terms with these questions in the past is no sufficient reason why they should not do so in the future. Bayley points out that the tradition of American thought does not in fact cover all the facts of American experience. It might be consistent with the idealism of Athens to deny these facts in order to preserve a traditional theory, but American pragmatism has always insisted that theories which do not fit the facts must be altered until they do. It is perhaps not sufficiently recognized that this insistence that theories account for all the facts they profess to explain does not mean in the American tradition what it commonly means in European pragmatism, that "whatever is, is right" and that all standards of value are relative. In most formal European philosophy, moral standards are determined by rational processes, as religious doctrines have in modern times been determined by the fiat of the state church, but in the American pragmatic tradition, standards of value are determined by conscience independently of reason, as religious doctrines are laid down by denominations in total independence of the state. In this respect, as Lynn White, Jr., pointed out, the fundamental basis of the American tradition is to this day obstinately medieval, based on the traditions brought over by lower-class colonists whose counterparts in Europe were not touched by "modern" ideas until the time of the French Revolution.

This close connection between the traditions of the American colonists and the traditions of their ancestors in medieval Europe is particularly clearly demonstrated by the history of the Hudson

288

Valley Dutch patricians, precisely because of their Dutch characteristics of particularism, privilege, and heterogeneity. Their particularism kept them isolated from the other colonists for a century and a half, thus permitting their tradition to develop without interference on its medieval foundation. Their ambition to retain and expand their individual and corporate privileges led them to participate in the British Empire, the Revolution against that Empire, and the formation of the American nation. Their heterogeneity—particularly in retaining the Dutch language— helped them to retain their distinct identity while helping to create the American tradition. As they pursued these advantages for their families and their community, the Hudson Valley Dutch patricians were quite willing to learn from other Americans the importance of nationality, equality, and homogeneity. It was because they accepted these values and incorporated them into their Dutch tradition that it eventually became woven into the American tradition, until in the twentieth century the orange thread, while indistinguishable to the keenest analysis, is nevertheless an indispensable element of the fabric as a whole.

NOTES TO THE CHAPTERS

CHAPTER I

1. Arnold Johan Ferdinand Van Laer, trans., *Minutes of the Court of Fort Orange and Beverwyck*, II, 30 ff.

2. Jonathan Pearson, trans., *Early Records of the City and County of Albany and County of Rensselaerswyck*, III, 41–45.

3. Arnold Johan Ferdinand Van Laer, trans. *Minutes of the Court of Albany, Rensselaerswyck and Schenectady*, II, 367–73.

4. Joel Munsell, *Annals of Albany*, II, 68.

5. Edmund Bailey O'Callaghan, ed., *Documentary History of the State of New York*, II, 109.

6. *Ibid.*, 112.

7. *Ibid.*, 121.

8. *Ibid.*, 122.

9. *Ibid.*, 123.

10. *Ibid.*, 128.

11. *Ibid.*, 130.

12. *Ibid.*, 132.

CHAPTER II

1. Jan Baptist Van Rensselaer to Jeremias Van Rensselaer, Oct. 8, 1659, Jeremias Van Rensselaer, *Correspondence*, trans. A. J. F. Van Laer, 182.

2. Pearson, *Early Records*, III, 320.

3. Victor H. Paltsits, ed., *Albany Minutes*, II, p. 396.

4. Victor S. Clark, *History of Manufactures in the United States* (New York: McGraw-Hill, 1929), I, 166.

5. New York Colonial Documents: Land Papers, 13:108, NYSL (New York State Library).

6. Rutger Bleecker, Daybook, April 17, 1735, Bleecker Papers, NYPL (New York Public Library).

7. Leonard Gansevoort, Jr., "Memoir," GLC (Gansevoort-Lansing Collection).

8. Peter Kalm, *Travels in North America*, trans. Adolph B. Benson, 343.

9. *Ibid.*, 344–45.

10. *Ibid.*, 607–608.

CHAPTER III

1. John Chambers, notes in *Wraxall v. Gansevoort*, NYSL.

2. Judgment Roll, *Wraxall v. Gansevoort*, New York Supreme Court Records, Hall of Records, New York, N.Y.

3. Daniel Horsmanden to Cadwallader Colden, Jan. 24, 1733/4, quoted in Fox, *Land Speculation*, 5.

4. Peter Wraxall, *Abridgement of the Indian Affairs*, ed. Charles McIlwain, 6.

5. *Wraxall v. Gansevoort*, Judgment Roll.

6. Kalm, *Travels*, 346, 614.

7. Deputy Quartermaster General's office to Volkert P. Douw, Jan. 19, 1756, Box 9, Schuyler Papers, NYPL.

8. John Macomb to —— (aide of General Amherst), Aug. 22, 1759, quoted in Edna L. Jacobsen, "Eighteenth Century Merchants in Colonial Albany," Dutch Settlers Society of Albany, *Yearbook*, XX (1944), 5–15.

9. William Corry to Sir William Johnson, Aug. 23, 1759, *Sir William Johnson Papers*, III, 129.

10. Anne Grant, *Memoirs of an American Lady*, 120–21.

11. Witham Marsh to Sir William Johnson, March 28, 1762, *Johnson Papers*, III, 657.

12. John Tabor Kempe to John Bradstreet, Aug. 29, 1763, John Tabor Kempe Papers, NYHS (New-York Historical Society).

13. Witham Marsh to Sir William Johnson, Oct. 2, 1762, *Johnson Papers*, III, 887–88.

14. *Ibid.*

15. *Idem* to *idem*, Oct. 14, 1762, *ibid.*, 902.

16. Sir William Johnson to Witham Marsh, Feb. 4, 1763, *ibid.*, IV, 40.

17. Witham Marsh to Sir William Johnson, Jan. 30, 1763, *ibid.*, 33–34.

18. *Idem* to *idem*, Feb. 28, 1763, *ibid.*, XIII, 284.

19. *Idem* to *idem*, April 21, 1763, *ibid.*, IV, 88.

20. *Idem* to *idem*, Dec. 11, 1763, *ibid.*, XIII, 303.

21. *Idem* to *idem*, May 28, 1764, *ibid.*, 327.

22. *Idem* to *idem*, Sept. 28, 1764, *ibid.*, 331.

23. Leonard Gansevoort to Philip Schuyler, Albany, Dec. 19, 1788, "minor and uncalendared" Schuyler Papers, NYPL.

CHAPTER IV

1. Abraham Yates to Robert Livingston, Jr., Feb. 7, 1761, Yates Papers, NYPL.

2. *Ibid.*

3. *Ibid.*

4. *Ibid.*

5. *Ibid.*

6. Leonard Gansevoort to Peter Gansevoort, Aug. 28, 1775, PGMP (Peter Gansevoort Military Papers), GLC.

7. *Journals of the Provincial Congress, Provincial Convention, Committee of Safety, Council of Safety of New York State, 1775–77* (Albany: T. Weed, 1842), 536, 538.

8. Leonard Gansevoort to Peter Gansevoort, Sept. 2, 1776, PGMP.

9. *Idem* to *idem,* Aug. 21, 1778, *ibid.*

10. Peter Gansevoort to Robert Yates, Dec. 5, 1776, *ibid.*

11. John Adams to Abigail Adams, Aug. 21, 1776, *Adams Family Correspondence,* ed. Lyman H. Butterfield (Cambridge, Mass.: Harvard Univ. Press, 1963), II, 320.

12. Leonard Gansevoort to Peter Gansevoort, July 9, 1777, PGMP.

13. Dr. Jonathan Potts to Peter Gansevoort, July 12, 1777, PGMP.

14. Caty Van Schaick to Peter Gansevoort, July 31, 1777, GFL (Gansevoort Family Letters), GLC.

15. William A. Willett, *Narrative of the Military Actions of Col. Marinus Willett* (New York: C., G., and H. Carvill, 1831), 57–58.

16. Peter Gansevoort to Colonel Barry St. Leger, Aug. 9, 1777, PGMP.

17. John Adams to Abigail Adams, Sept. 2, 1777, *Adams Family Correspondence,* II, 336.

18. Caty Van Schaick to Peter Gansevoort, July 31, 1777, GFL.

CHAPTER V

1. Bernard Mason, *Road to Independence,* 230.

2. *Ibid.,* 231.

3. Henry C. Van Schaack, *Life of Peter Van Schaack* (New York: Appleton, 1842), 110.

4. Peter Gansevoort to William Duer and Gouverneur Morris, Jan. 26, 1778, PGMP.

5. Caty Gansevoort to Peter Gansevoort, July 21, 1778, GFL.

6. *Idem* to *idem,* Aug. 22, 1778, *ibid.*

7. Peter Gansevoort to Caty Gansevoort, July 8, 1780, *ibid.*

8. *Idem* to *idem,* Aug. 14, 1780, *ibid.*

9. ——, diary, March 26, 1783, excerpt transcribed by Catherine Gansevoort Lansing, in "Miscellaneous Historical Collections," GLC.

10. *New York Gazetteer,* Sept. 22, 1783.

11. *Ibid.,* Oct. 21, 1784.

12. *Ibid.,* Nov. 4, 1784.

13. Philip S. Van Rensselaer to Leonard Gansevoort, Aug. 27, 1788, PGTE (collection of Peter G. Ten Eyck, Altamont, N.Y.).

14. Leonard Gansevoort, Jr., to Leonard Gansevoort, Jan. 8, 1788, *ibid.*

15. *Idem* to *idem,* Jan. 10, 1788, *ibid.*

16. *Idem* to *idem,* March 18, 1788, *ibid.*

17. *Albany Journal,* March 17, 1788, NYSL.

18. Leonard Gansevoort, Jr., to Leonard Gansevoort, April 2, 1788, PGTE.

19. Leonard Gansevoort to Stephen Van Rensselaer, April 6, 1788, NYSL.
20. *Albany Gazette,* Aug. 28, 1788, quoted in Munsell, *Annals,* I (2 ed.), 228–35.

CHAPTER VI

1. Leonard Gansevoort to Leonard Gansevoort, Jr., Dec. 16, 1792, NYHS.
2. Jabez D. Hammond, *History of Political Parties in the State of New York* (Albany: Van Benthuysen, 1842), I, 581.
3. Leonard Gansevoort to General Peter Gansevoort, April 18, 1792, GFL.
4. *Idem* to *idem,* March 5, 1788, PGMP.
5. Lieutenant George Armistead to General Peter Gansevoort, July 21, 1806, PGMP.
6. Testimony in *Munro v. Gansevoort,* Dec. 13–28, 1855, Peter Gansevoort Legal Papers, GLC.
7. L. H. Gansevoort to (young) Peter Gansevoort, Dec. 21, 1805, GFL.
8. *Munro v. Gansevoort* testimony.
9. L. H. Gansevoort to (young) Peter Gansevoort, Oct. 4, 1804, GFL.
10. Peter Gansevoort to L. H. Gansevoort, Dec. 11, 1805, *ibid.*
11. L. H. Gansevoort to Peter Gansevoort, Dec. 21, 1805, *ibid.*
12. *Ibid.*
13. Peter Gansevoort to General Peter Gansevoort, March 5, 1811, *ibid.*
14. *Idem* to *idem,* April 16, 1811, *ibid.*
15. *Ibid.*
16. *Idem* to *idem,* Sept. 3, 1811, *ibid.*
17. Martin Van Buren, *Autobiography,* ed. John Fitzgerald (Washington, D.C.: American Historical Ass'n., 1918), 168.
18. Pierre Van Cortlandt to Peter Gansevoort, Nov. 12, 1823, PGC (Peter Gansevoort Correspondence), GLC.
19. Van Buren, *Autobiography,* 13.
20. Assembly of the State of New York, *Journal,* 54th session, 1831, 395.
21. James Stevenson to Peter Gansevoort, Sept. 13, 1831, PGC.
22. Senate of the State of New York, *Journal,* 1836, 616.

CHAPTER VII

1. John C. Olin, *Erasmus and the Age of Reformation* (New York: Harpers, 1965), 95–97.
2. Grant, *Memoirs,* 62–63.
3. *Ibid.,* 56–57.
4. *Ibid.,* 46.
5. *Ibid.,* 58–59.
6. *Ibid.,* 74–75.
7. *Ibid.,* 43.
8. *Ibid.,* 85.
9. *Ibid.,* 45.

10. Leonard Gansevoort, Jr., Memoir, "Miscellaneous Genealogical Collections," GLC.

11. Raesly, *Portrait of New Netherland*, 163.

12. Anna Gansevoort to Leonard Gansevoort, Albany, Sept. 2, 1769, PGTE.

13. Caty Van Schaick to Colonel Gansevoort, Dec. 16, 1777, GFL.

14. Colonel Gansevoort to Caty Gansevoort, June 21, 1778, GFL.

15. Caty Gansevoort to Colonel Gansevoort, June 26, 1778, GFL.

16. Leonard Gansevoort to Leonard Gansevoort, Jr., Dec. 16, 1792, NYHS.

17. Leonard Gansevoort, Will, recorded Dec. 27, 1810, Albany County Surrogate's Office.

18. Peter Gansevoort to Caty Gansevoort, July 21, 1819, GFL.

19. *Idem to idem*, n.d. [1821?], GFL.

20. *Idem to idem*, Sept. 5, 1829, GFL.

21. Peter Gansevoort to Maria Gansevoort, Oct., 1811, GFL.

22. Allan Melville to Maria Melville, July 29, 1818, Melville Family Papers, GLC.

23. Allan Melville to Caty Gansevoort, Boston, Oct. 20, 1814, *ibid.*

24. Peter Gansevoort to Allan Melville, n.d., PGC, GLC.

25. Allan Melville to Robert Melvil at Amsterdam, July –, 1818, *ibid.*

26. Allan Melville to Peter Gansevoort, June 28, 1818, *ibid.*

27. Allan Melville to Maria Melville, July 29, 1818, *ibid.*

28. Maria Melville to Peter Gansevoort, June 26, 1823, PGC, GLC.

29. Mary Sanford to Edward Sanford, Feb. 3, 1832, Mary S. Gansevoort Papers, GLC.

30. Peter Gansevoort to Mary Sanford, "Monday Evening," 1833, *ibid.*

31. Mary Sanford to Edward Sanford, April 10, 1833, *ibid.*

32. *Idem to idem*, June 10, 1833, *ibid.;* James Stevenson to Peter Gansevoort, Sept. 17, 1833, GFL.

33. Peter Gansevoort to Mary B. Sanford, Feb. 24, 1840, PGC, GLC.

34. *Idem to idem*, March 11, 1841, *ibid.*

35. Herman Gansevoort to Peter Gansevoort, Jan. 8, 1842, *ibid.*

36. Susan Gansevoort to Peter Gansevoort, June 29, 1853, *ibid.*

37. Maria Melville to Kate Gansevoort, Jan. 17, 1866, Kate Lansing Correspondence, GLC.

CHAPTER VIII

1. *The Spectator*, ed. G. Gregory Smith (New York: Scribners, 1897), No. 174, Sept. 19, 1711, III:22.

2. Harme Gansevoort to Leonard Gansevoort, April 29, 1788, PGTE. Trans. APK.

3. Leonard Gansevoort to Leonard Gansevoort, Jr., Dec. 16, 1792, NYHS.

4. Maria Melville to Peter Gansevoort, Nov. 21, 1823, PGC, GLC.

5. Leonard Gansevoort, Jr., to Rensselaer Gansevoort, n.d., Hun Papers, Albany Institute of History and Art.

6. Herman Gansevoort to Peter Gansevoort, Jan. 15, 1823, PGC, GLC.

7. Herman Gansevoort, Check Roll and Remembrancer B, Jan. 26, 1823, GLC.

8. Herman Gansevoort to Peter Gansevoort, April 14, 1823, GFL.

9. *Idem* to *idem*, Oct. 23, 1827, PGC.

10. Allan Melville to Maria Melville, journal letter, May, 1818, Melville Family Papers, GLC.

11. Gansevoort Melville to Maria Melville, Nov. 3, 1845, Melville Family Papers, GLC.

12. Munsell, *Annals*, IX, 247.

13. Stanwix Hall, advertisement, Jan. 27, 1836, Stanwix Hall Papers, GLC.

14. Jno. Bloodgood, *et al.*, Citizens of Albany, to Peter Gansevoort and Herman Gansevoort, May 6, 1833, PGC.

15. Stanwix Hall accounts, GLC.

16. L. H. Gansevoort to Caty Gansevoort, May 17, 1812, GFL.

17. Undated account of L. H. Gansevoort, in possession of Mrs. Josephine Sofio, Oxnard, Calif.

18. Mary Ann Gansevoort to Peter Gansevoort, March 4, 1826, PGC.

19. *Idem* to *idem*, Aug. 22, 1832, *ibid.*

20. Maria Melville to Peter Gansevoort, Dec. 8, 1826, *ibid.*

21. Peter L. Gansevoort to Peter Gansevoort, Jan. 4, 1832, *ibid.*

22. Catherine Q. Gansevoort to Peter Gansevoort, March 28, 1847, *ibid.*

CHAPTER IX

1. Raesly, *Portrait of New Netherland*, 128.

2. Olin, *Erasmus*, 98.

3. Herman Melville, *Pierre*, 240.

4. Herman Melville, *Clarel*, 522–23.

5. *Pierre*, 10–11.

6. *Ibid.*, 232–34.

7. *Ibid.*, 28.

8. *Clarel*, 97.

9. *Ibid.*, 98.

10. *Ibid.*, 89.

11. *Ibid.*, 522–23.

12. Peter Gansevoort to Henry Gansevoort, Dec. 4, 1851, PGC.

13. Henry Gansevoort to Susan Gansevoort, Nov. 16, 1853, Susan Gansevoort Correspondence, GLC.

14. C. A. Stockly to Henry Gansevoort, July 9, 1855, HSGC.

15. Kate Gansevoort to Henry Gansevoort, Oct. 21, 1855, *ibid.*

16. Letter to editor, Jan. 4, 1856, HSG Papers.

17. Kate Gansevoort to Henry Gansevoort, June 11, 1858, HSGC.

18. Henry Gansevoort to Peter Gansevoort, May 26, 1858, PGC.

19. *Ibid.*

20. Henry James, *A Small Boy and Others* (New York: Scribners, 1913), 189–90.

21. Henry Gansevoort to Kate Gansevoort, May 30, 1868, CGLC.

22. Henry Gansevoort to Abe Lansing, Aug. 15, 1858, March 27, 1860, ALC.
23. Kate Gansevoort to Henry Gansevoort, May 7, 1861, HSG Memoirs.
24. Henry Gansevoort to Peter Gansevoort, Oct. 9, 1861, *ibid.*
25. Peter Gansevoort to Henry Gansevoort, Oct. 7, 1862, HSGC.
26. Kate Gansevoort to Henry Gansevoort, March 18, 1864, HSGC.
27. Peter Gansevoort to Henry Gansevoort, Feb. 18, 1865, HSGC.

CHAPTER X

1. Mary Ann Gansevoort to Guert Gansevoort, May 11, 1848, Guert Gansevoort Papers, GLC.
2. Herman Gansevoort Ledger, Oct. 19, 1855, GLC. The ladle inscribed in memory of Herman's death is in the Albany Institute of History and Art.
3. Kate Gansevoort to Susan Gansevoort, Aug. 21 and 17, 1867, Susan Gansevoort Correspondence, GLC.
4. Maria Melville to Kate Gansevoort, Oct. 18, 1865, CGLC.
5. Kate Gansevoort to Henry Gansevoort, April 30, 1867, HSGC.
6. *Ibid.*, June 27, 1867.
7. *Ibid.*, Nov. 2, 1869.
8. *Ibid.*, July 31, 1870.
9. Henry Gansevoort to Kate Gansevoort, June 30, 1867, CGLC.
10. *Ibid.*, June 6, 1868.
11. *Clarel,* 483.
12. Henry Gansevoort to Kate Gansevoort, Jan. 21, 1868, CGLC.
13. Henry Gansevoort to George H. Brewster, July 10, 1868, HSGC.
14. Susan Gansevoort to Henry Gansevoort, May 26, 1868, *ibid.*
15. Henry Gansevoort to Kate Gansevoort, March 6, 1867, CGLC.
16. *Ibid.*, April 6, 1869.
17. Henry Gansevoort to Peter Gansevoort, Jan. 21, 1856, PGC.
18. Kate Gansevoort, Diary, Jan. 9, 1862, GLC.
19. *Ibid.*, Feb. 11, 1862.
20. Abe Lansing to Kate Gansevoort, May 30, 1872, CGLC.
21. Kate Gansevoort to Abe Lansing, Aug. 25, 1873, ALC.
22. Kate Gansevoort, Diary, Oct. 3, 1865.
23. Henry Gansevoort to Susan Gansevoort, Jan. 22, 1871, Susan Gansevoort Correspondence, GLC.
24. Robert Sofio and Josephine Sofio to Alice P. Kenney, May 9, 1967.
25. Huybertje Pruyn Hamlin, "Aunt Kitty Lansing," typescript memoir, Albany Institute of History and Art.
26. Kate Lansing to Abe Lansing, July 17, 1877, ALC, GLC.
27. Hamlin, "Aunt Kitty Lansing."
28. National Mary Washington Association circular, n.d., 1893.
29. Catherine Gansevoort Lansing probate records, Albany County Surrogate's Office, Albany, N.Y.
30. *Ibid.*
31. *Albany Evening Journal,* Jan. 23, 1918, Albany Institute.

32. Catherine Gansevoort Lansing, Will, Albany Surrogate's Office.

33. In Catherine Van Rensselaer Bonney, *Legacy of Historical Gleanings* (Albany: J. Munsell, 1875), 2 Volumes, 396.

34. Cuyler Reynolds, *Hudson-Mohawk Genealogical and Family Memoirs* (New York: Lewis Historical Pub. Co., 1911), I, 66.

CONCLUSION

1. John H. Mundy and Peter Riesenberg, *Mediaeval Town* (Princeton, N.J.: Van Nostrand, 1958), 94.

2. Lynn White, Jr., "The Legacy of the Middle Ages in the American Wild West," *Speculum*, April 1965, 191–94.

3. John Bayley, *Romantic Survival* (London: Constable, 1957), 29–30.

4. John Bayley, *Characters of Love* (New York: Basic Books, 1960), 268–71.

5. Henri Pirenne, *Early Democracies in the Low Countries*, 106.

BIBLIOGRAPHY

Standard histories of the Dutch tradition in the Netherlands are Henri Pirenne's *Early Democracies in the Low Countries* (New York: Harper and Row, 1963), Johan Huizinga's *Waning of the Middle Ages* (Garden City, N.Y.: Doubleday-Anchor Books, 1956), and Pieter Geyl's *Revolt of the Netherlands* (New York: Barnes and Noble, 1958). A recent and available work which presents a very similar picture of the Dutch tradition is Charles R. Boxer's *Dutch Seaborne Empire* (New York: Knopf, 1965). The most inclusive book about the Hudson Valley Dutch way of life is Ellis M. Raesly's *Portrait of New Netherland* (New York: Columbia University Press, 1945). Esther M. Singleton, in *Dutch New York* (New York: Dodd, Mead & Co., 1909), gives many useful details about the transplantation of customs. Helen Reynolds, in *Dutch Houses in the Hudson Valley before 1776* (New York: Payson and Clarke, Ltd., 1929), draws together information about architecture. Thomas J. Wertenbaker's *Founding of American Civilization: The Middle Colonies* (New York: Scribners, 1938), demonstrates how historical conclusions may be drawn from architectural facts. Some Hudson Valley houses which have been opened to the public as museums are the Schuyler Mansion and Cherry Hill at Albany, Fort Crailo at Rensselaer, the Bronck House at Coxsackie, and the Van Cortlandt Manor House at Tarrytown.

The most recent and readable history of Albany is Codman Hislop's *Albany: Dutch, English and American* (Albany: Argus, 1936). Arthur J. Weise's *History of Albany, New York* (Albany: E. H. Bender, 1884) offers much detail about the colonial and Revolutionary periods, but less for the nineteenth century. Francis J. Kimball, in *Capital Region of New York State* (New York: Lewis Historical Pub. Co., 1942), 3 volumes, covers the upper Hudson Valley as well as the city of Albany. Also fundamentally important are two remarkable miscellanies of Albaniana by the public-spirited editor, printer, and avid antiquarian, Joel Munsell, *Annals of Albany* (Albany: J. Munsell, 1850–60), 10 volumes, expanded second edition, Volumes 1–4 (1869), and *Collections on the History of Albany* (Albany, 1865–72), 4 volumes. In a very literal sense these works are the monument of the Dutch patrician community, for Munsell knew its last generation intimately and included not only documents from the past but also extensive quotations, particularly obituaries, from newspapers of his own time.

THE GANSEVOORTS OF ALBANY

Among the other documents in these compendiums, Munsell published the Minutes of the Albany Common Council from the city charter in 1686 to 1790. Especially in the earlier years he sometimes omitted items without comment, so the precision of close study requires comparison with the originals (Volumes II–X; I and VIII are wanting) in the New York State Library at Albany. Other colonial local records were translated from the Dutch by Jonathan Pearson, who amassed great quantities of useful information but was capable of making some inexplicably elementary errors. His *Early Records of the City and County of Albany and Colony of Rensselaerswyck* (Albany: University of the State of New York, 1865; 1916–19), like all of his books, must be used with extreme caution and copious reference to as many original documents as are available. Arnold Johan Ferdinand Van Laer's translations of *Minutes of the Court of Fort Orange and Beverwyck* (Albany: University of the State of New York, 1920–23), 2 volumes, and *Minutes of the Court of Albany, Rensselaerswyck and Schenectady* (Albany, 1926–32), 3 volumes, are much more trustworthy. Van Laer was a Dutch historian who settled in Albany late in the nineteenth century and made the translation of Hudson Valley Dutch records a lifetime project. His work is always knowledgeable, reliable, and easily readable. Some records of the Albany Dutch Reformed Church were published by Munsell, more by the Holland Society of New York, in its *Yearbook*, 1904–1908, 1922–27, and others in the *Yearbooks* of the Dutch Settlers Society. In the Church archives are more, untranslated and uncataloged.

The best-known traveler's account of Albany is that of a Swedish scientist who passed through on botanizing expeditions in 1749 and 1750, Peter Kalm, *Travels in North America*, translated by Adolph B. Benson (New York: Dover, 1964). Mrs. Anne McVicar Grant wrote *Memoirs of an American Lady* (London: Longman, 1808) many years after she spent part of her girlhood in Albany, but her insights, though limited, were keen and her memory by and large trustworthy. Imaginative interpretations of the Hudson Valley Dutch include Washington Irving's humorous account of the Dutch tradition, *Diedrich Knickerbocker's History of New York* (Philadelphia: Bradford & Inskeep, 1809), written at a time when the resistance to social change of many Dutchmen was laying them open to ridicule, and his even more famous use of Dutch superstitions and folklore in "Rip Van Winkle" and "The Legend of Sleepy Hollow." James Fenimore Cooper's *Satanstoe* (New York: Stringer & Co., 1845) takes place partly in a Dutch Albany that he probably reconstructed from the reminiscences of Dutch patricians whom he knew during his schooldays there; his scenes are certainly consistent with the available facts. Mary Hun Sears, herself an Albany patrician—incidentally, a descendant of the Gansevoort family —reconstructed the world of her ancestors, predominantly from public records, in *Hudson Crossroads* (New York: Exposition Press, 1953). The most sensitive depiction of Dutch Albany that I have seen is a story for young people, Erick Berry's *Seven Beaver Skins* (New York: John C. Winston Co., 1948), which is both a fine regional novel and an exploration of fundamental human problems of the transit of civilization to the wilderness.

The Gansevoort-Lansing Collection in the New York Public Library is as hard to describe as Munsell's compendiums. Mrs. Lansing (Kate Gansevoort, 1838–1918), who grew up on Munsell's publications, was as fascinated as he by every kind of historical detail, and, like him, never threw anything away. While Munsell's special emphasis was on the community of Albany, however, Kate's was on her own family. Her remote ancestors Harmen Gansevoort (ca. 1635–1710) and Leendert Gansevoort (1683–1763) left to her only a few deeds and their wills. Her great-grandfather, Harme Gansevoort (1712–1801), left his merchant's account books and some business letters. Her grandfather, General Peter Gansevoort (1749–1812), left Revolutionary papers including military records, correspondence with his brother Leonard (1751–1810) in the New York Assembly, and a few letters written from active service to his parents and his sweetheart, later his wife, Caty Van Schaick (1751–1830). Later in life he preserved some other interesting records from his service as U.S. Military Agent (1802–1809) and Brigadier General, U.S. Army (1809–1812).

The portion of the collection centering around General Gansevoort's son, Peter Gansevoort (1789–1876), is much more extensive. After the General's death Peter managed the business affairs of his mother, the widow and six small children of his brother Leonard (1783–1821), and his widowed sister Maria Gansevoort Melville (1791–1872). He also handled the paper work of building Stanwix Hall, in partnership with his eldest brother Herman (1779–1862), who spent his life developing the town of Gansevoort in Saratoga County. Peter also left fifty boxes of papers from his legal practice, irrelevant to this study, but very few written traces, either in the Gansevoort papers or in the public records, of his equally active political career. Finally, he preserved a number of letters from his first wife, Mary Sanford (1814–41), considerable correspondence with some of her relatives, and his own diaries and household accounts.

Peter's only son, Henry Sanford Gansevoort (1835–71), left some sporadic diaries, a fluent though somewhat less than free correspondence with his father, many letters from devoted friends including some attentive ladies, records from his Civil War regiment, and lengthy letters to his sister Kate from his various postwar military stations. Kate kept mammoth and meticulous diaries, wrote at great length to Henry until he died, corresponded frequently with Abraham Lansing (1835–99) during their protracted courtship, and kept up contact with all the cousins, particularly the numerous highly literate Melvilles. She also preserved great quantities of newspaper clippings, extracts from books, and pictures, particularly photographs of her home, her relatives, and vanishing Albany landmarks. Among other oddments she treasured her school composition books, her stepmother's recipe book, drawings of the tombstones of a dozen Gansevoorts mentioned in no other connection and apparently unidentifiable, and even a lock of her father's greying light-brown hair.

CHAPTER I

Hudson Valley physiography is described in John H. Thompson, *Geography of New York State* (Syracuse, N.Y.: Syracuse University Press, 1966). Boxer tells the story of the West India Company. Raesly is indispensable for the transmission of culture to New Netherland. The early history of Fort Orange and Beverwyck is related, with some differing emphases, by Weise, Hislop, and Kimball. Rensselaerswyck, equally important, is exhaustively studied in S. G. Nissenson, *The Patroon's Domain* (New York: Columbia University Press, 1937). Primary sources include *Van Rensselaer-Bowier Manuscripts* (Albany, 1908), Jeremias Van Rensselaer's *Correspondence* (Albany, 1932), and Maria Van Rensselaer's *Correspondence* (Albany, 1936), all published by the University of the State of New York and translated by A. J. F. Van Laer.

The contest between the Van Rensselaers and the Albanians after the English conquest is described in Nissenson's Chapter 8, "The English Period." Alice P. Kenney's "Dutch Patricians in Colonial Albany," *New York History*, July, 1968, shows the relevance of Pirenne's thesis for understanding Albany history. The Schuyler group is depicted in Lawrence H. Leder's *Robert Livingston and the Politics of Colonial New York* (Chapel Hill: University of North Carolina Press, 1961). Jerome R. Reich, in *Leisler's Rebellion* (Chicago: University of Chicago Press, 1953), deals with Albany only briefly and pays little attention to the local aspects of the conflict. The minutes of the Albany Convention are in *Documentary History of the State of New York* (Albany: Weed, Parsons, 1849–51), II, edited by Edmund Bailey O'Callaghan; accounts of the Schenectady massacre are collected in Munsell's *Annals*, IV, 262–74.

CHAPTER II

Dutch patricians of the Golden Age are described by Violet Barbour in *Capitalism in Seventeenth-Century Amsterdam* (Baltimore: Johns Hopkins Press, 1950). The activities of Harmen Gansevoort and his associates in Beverwyck and Albany are from the sources previously described. The picture by James Eights, which shows Harmen Harmense's house, is in the Albany Institute of History and Art, Albany, New York; for general information about Dutch houses and the appearance of Albany at this time see Rev. Charles Maar's "Housing and Homes of New Netherland," Dutch

Settlers Society of Albany, *Yearbook,* III (1927), 5–10, and Benjamin Wadsworth's "Albany in 1694," excerpt from *ibid.,* VI (1930), 9–12.

The basic source for Albany genealogy is Jonathan Pearson, "Contributions for the Genealogies of the First Settlers of the Ancient County of Albany, 1730–1800," in Munsell, *Collections,* IV. (It was also published separately in 1872, but this volume is rare.) Like all of Pearson's work, it needs to be checked against the original sources, primarily the baptism and marriage records of the Albany Dutch Reformed Church, which are conveniently available in Holland Society of New York's *Yearbook,* 1904–1908. Cuyler Reynolds' *Hudson-Mohawk Genealogical and Family Memoirs* (New York: Lewis Historical Pub. Co., 1911), 4 volumes, contains much of the same information and quantities of family tradition, every word of which has to be verified by primary sources. The Albany church records are ideal sources for the new method of "family reconstitution" described by E. A. Wrigley in *Introduction to English Historical Demography* (New York: Basic Books, 1966). It is evident from preliminary work on such a study that its results will be sufficiently significant in their own right to warrant separate publication; therefore no attempt is made to anticipate them here.

Information about Leendert Gansevoort and his relatives is drawn together from widely scattered references in the public records of Albany and of the Province of New York. The process of brewing is described by Stanley Baron in *Brewed in America* (Boston, 1962), 14–74 *passim.* Essential to study of the fur traders is David A. Armour's "Merchants of Albany, N.Y., 1686–1760" (Ph.D dissertation, Northwestern University, 1965). Mohawk Valley land grants and land frauds are described by Edith M. Fox in *Land Speculation in the Mohawk Country* (Ithaca, N.Y.: Cornell University Press, 1949); the complex politics of the 1740's are detailed by Beverly McAnear in "Politics in Provincial New York, 1689–1761" (Ph.D. dissertation, Stanford University, 1935). Some conception of Pieter Gansevoort's medical training may be inferred from Richard Shryock's *Medicine and Society in America 1600–1800* (Ithaca, N.Y.: Cornell University Press, 1960), 9–17.

Leendert Gansevoort's silver tankard and several other pieces of Gansevoort silver are in the Metropolitan Museum of Art, New York City. Other family pieces are depicted in Norman S. Rice, *Albany Silver, 1650–1825* (Albany, 1964), 34–35. The Gansevoort portraits are the property of Mr. and Mrs. Stephen Clark, Cooperstown, New York, and are reproduced in James T. Flexner's *American Painting: First Flowers of our Wilderness* (New York: Houghton-Mifflin, 1947), 185–86. "Pau de Wandelaer," the property of the Albany Institute of History and Art, is reproduced in the Albany Institute's *Hudson Valley Paintings, 1700–1750* (Albany, 1959), 20. Another portrait in the Institute's collection has been tentatively identified as Leendert's daughter Sara. "Magdalena Douw" is at the Henry

Francis DuPont Winterthur Museum, Winterthur, Delaware. Dutch non-literateness is discussed in Raesly, 240–65. James Tanis in *Dutch Calvinistic Pietism in the Middle Colonies* (The Hague: Nijhoff, 1967), explores the Hudson Valley Dutch religious tradition.

CHAPTER III

The meaning of *empire*, both generally and in the eighteenth-century British Empire, is the principal subject of Richard Koebner in *Empire* (Cambridge: Cambridge University Press, 1965). Relations between the Albanians, the French, and the Indians are discussed in detail by Armour and by Allen W. Trelease, *Indian Affairs in Colonial New York: The Seventeenth Century* (Ithaca, N.Y.: Cornell University Press, 1960). The Albanians' part in intercolonial trade rivalries is seen from the viewpoint of Pennsylvania Indians in Francis Jennings' "The Indian Trade of the Susquehanna Valley," *Proceedings of the American Philosophical Society*, Dec., 1966, and "Glory, Death and Transfiguration: The Susquehannock Indians in the Seventeenth Century," *Proceedings of the American Philosophical Society*, Jan., 1968. For Viele's expedition, see John Bartlett Brebner, *Explorers of North America* (Garden City, N.Y.: Doubleday, 1955), 259. McAnear's account of New York politics in the eighteenth century gives more information about the Albanians than any other. Stanley N. Katz, in *Newcastle's New York* (Cambridge, Mass.: Harvard University Press, 1968), discusses English ramifications of New York politics. James Thomas Flexner's *Mohawk Baronet* (New York: Harpers, 1959) will soon be superseded by a life of Johnson by Milton Hamilton, most recent editor of the *Johnson Papers* (Albany: University of the State of New York, 1921–), 13 volumes. Materials on the Wraxall case are widely scattered in court records, general public records, and Peter Wraxall's own *Abridgement of the Indian Affairs*, edited by Charles McIlwain, Harvard Historical Studies, Volume 21 (Cambridge, Mass.: Harvard University Press, 1915), c–cii. A standard narrative history of the French and Indian War is Francis Parkman's *Montcalm and Wolfe* (Boston, 1884). Lawrence W. Gipson's *British Empire Before the American Revolution* (New York, Knopf), 13 volumes to date, is a monumental history of the entire British Empire during this period of conflict and transition; Volume III deals particularly with New York. The Marsh case is almost entirely described in the *Johnson Papers*.

CHAPTER IV

McAnear is the most detailed history of the New York Assembly factions, but it sometimes lacks coherence before the emergence of the Livingston faction. Milton M. Klein, in *"The American Whig,* William

Livingston of New York" (Ph.D. dissertation, Columbia University, 1954), describes Livingston's background and activities. Philip Schuyler's relationship with the Livingston faction is detailed by Don W. Gerlach in *Philip Schuyler and the American Revolution in New York* (Lincoln, Neb.: University of Nebraska Press, 1964). The Livingstons' tactics in New York City received their classic description in Carl L. Becker's *History of Political Parties in the Province of New York* (Madison, Wisc.: University of Wisconsin Press, 1909). Two recent articles on the family in late colonial New York politics which are one-dimensional because they do not make clear the relationship between family and faction are Roger Champagne's "Family Politics versus Constitutional Principles: The New York Assembly Elections of 1768 and 1769," *William and Mary Quarterly*, 3rd Ser. XX (Jan. 1963), 57–79, and Bernard Friedman's "New York Assembly Elections of 1768 and 1769: The Disruption of Family Politics," *New York History* XLVI (Jan. 1965), 3–24. "The Albany Stamp Act Riot" is described by Beverly McAnear in *William and Mary Quarterly*, 3rd Ser. IV (1947), 486–98.

Fundamental for the history of the Revolution in Albany is Albany Committee of Correspondence, *Minutes*, edited by James Sullivan (Albany: University of the State of New York, 1923). Civic organization is described by Bernard Mason in *Road to Independence* (Lexington, Ky.: University of Kentucky Press, 1966) and by Gerlach. The Albany Tory problem is described by Alice P. Kenney in "Dutch Tories in Albany County, N.Y.," *New York History*, Oct. 1961. Essential for an understanding of the Kinderhook situation is Henry C. Van Schaack's *Life of Peter Van Schaack* (New York: Appleton, 1842). Besides Peter Gansevoort's military and family papers in GLC, Robert W. Venables' "Valley of Nettles: The Revolutionary War in the Mohawk Valley, Summer, 1777" (M.A. Thesis, Vanderbilt University, 1965) is indispensable.

CHAPTER V

The most recent study of the political and constitutional revolution in New York, which contains a useful bibliography of this entire subject, is Mason's. Primary sources for the local revolution in Albany are the Albany Committee *Minutes*, the minutes of the Albany Common Council, and Commissioners for Detecting and Defeating Conspiracies, Albany County Sessions, *Minutes*, edited by Victor H. Paltsits (Albany: University of the State of New York, 1909–11), 3 volumes. *Journals of the Military Expedition of Major General John Sullivan Against the Six Nations of Indians* (Auburn, N.Y.: Knapp, Peck & Thomson, 1887) edited by Frederick Cook, includes journals of officers from many units of the expedition—but not from Gansevoort's regiment. A narrative account of the expedition is

Charles P. Whittemore's *A General of the Revolution: John Sullivan of New Hampshire* (New York: Columbia University Press 1961), 135–48, and the correspondence concerning Peter's capture of the Indians is in *Letters and Papers of Major General John Sullivan* (Concord, N.H.: New Hampshire Historical Society Collections, 1930–39), Volumes 13–15, edited by Otis G. Hammond.

The business correspondence of Cuyler and Gansevoort is in the possession of Peter G. Ten Eyck, Altamont, New York, as are a number of political letters about the 1786 and 1788 campaigns. Leonard Gansevoort's account books for his Van Rensselaer partnership include two volumes in NYSL and another in the possession of Robert Ten Eyck, Loudonville, N.Y. Local tradition about the founding of Gansevoort, N.Y., is recorded in Mrs. J. B. Vanderwerker's *Early Days in Gansevoort and Vicinity* (privately printed, n.d.). Much more detail is scattered through Peter Gansevoort's notes on testimony in *George F. Munro v. Gansevoort*, December 13–28, 1855, in Peter Gansevoort Legal Papers, GLC. Letters and accounts from the early days in the mill are in Peter Gansevoort Letters and Accounts, GLC, and a box of miscellaneous Gansevoort accounts in NYHS; a more detailed analysis of this material is Alice P. Kenney's "General Peter Gansevoort's Standard of Living," *New-York Historical Society Quarterly*, July, 1964. The most recent history of the ratification of the Constitution in New York and its antecedent events is Linda G. DePauw's *The Eleventh Pillar* (Ithaca, N.Y.: Cornell University Press, 1966), which contains a full bibliography. Other local campaigns in the upper Hudson Valley are described by Staughton Lynd in *Anti-Federalism in Dutchess County, N.Y.* (Chicago: Loyola University Press, 1962) and by George Dangerfield in *Chancellor Robert R. Livingston of New York* (New York: Harcourt, Brace & Co., 1960). Abraham Yates's "History of the Movement for the United States Constitution," edited by Staughton Lynd, is in *William and Mary Quarterly*, 3rd Ser. XX (1963), 223–45. Interesting corroborative information about Robert Yates is in Forrest McDonald's "The Anti-Federalists, 1781–1789," *Wisconsin Magazine of History*, XLVI:3 (Spring, 1963), 206–14.

CHAPTER VI

The civic tradition of the Dutch patricians is described by Pirenne in Chapter IV; see also Huizinga, particularly for patronage of art and the importance of bells in Flemish towns. A musical composition by Jan Sweelinck, "Orsus, serviteurs du seigneur," conveys very effectively by means of organ and chorus the particular nature of the Flemish carillon tradition. Another musical composition important for understanding the Dutch tradition is *Maastricht Easter Play* (New York: G. Schirmer, 1968), edited by Wilbur W. Hollman.

Several contemporary newspaper accounts of the 1793 fire are reprinted in Munsell's *Collections*, II, 378–82; the deposition of the slave, Bet, November 28, 1793, is in NYSL. "Whitehall" was described by Matilda M. Ten Eyck, Leonard's great-granddaughter, many years after it was destroyed by fire in 1883, in a typescript "Whitehall" in GLC. Many of Leonard's heirlooms are still in the possession of his descendants, including the Peter G. Ten Eycks and the Robert Ten Eycks. His service to his church is mentioned in Ebenezer P. Rogers' *Historical Discourse on the Reformed Protestant Dutch Church of Albany* (New York: Board of Publications R.P.D. Church, 1858).

General Gansevoort's business affairs are from his accounts in GLC and NYHS. For the "Gansworths" among the Senecas I am indebted to Miss Barbara Graymont. The military agency papers, 1802–1809, are in PGMP, as are a few of General Gansevoort's militia papers and some from his brigadier generalship, 1809–1812. One of the discipline cases he had to settle is described in detail by Alice P. Kenney in "The Bathtub Court-Martial," *New-York Historical Society Quarterly* (July, 1966). James Ripley Jacobs in *Beginnings of the U.S. Army, 1783–1812* (Princeton, N.J.: Princeton University Press, 1947) provides necessary background; Jacobs' *Tarnished Warrior* (New York: Macmillan, 1938), 267–75, discusses the Wilkinson trial. The family's memories of the General's funeral were recorded by Herman Melville in *Pierre* (New York: Hendricks, 1949), 26.

Since all three were notoriously remiss as correspondents, the history of Herman, L. H., and Wessel at Snock Kill Falls had to be pieced together from widely scattered references throughout the GLC. Especially important are the testimony in *Munro v. Gansevoort*, Herman Gansevoort's account books, Caty Gansevoort's land papers and accounts, and folders of miscellaneous material relating to L. H. and Wessel. Mr. Clifford L. Rugg, Saratoga County historian, kindly showed me Herman's mansion, which now belongs to the Gansevoort Masonic lodge.

The Yankee invasion is described by Yankees in Gorham A. Worth's *Random Recollections of Albany, 1800–08* (Albany: C. Van Benthuysen, 1849), republished by Munsell in 1866 with lengthy and informative footnotes, and Elkanah Watson's *Men and Times of the Revolution* (New York: Dana & Co., 1856). Peter's career in state government is reconstructed from very scanty documentation scattered through his correspondence, legal papers, accounts, and miscellaneous legislative papers in GLC. Most works on the politics of the period, notably Dixon Ryan Fox's *Decline of Aristocracy in the Politics of New York* (New York: Longmans, 1919), Alvin Kass's *Politics in New York State, 1800–1830* (Syracuse: Syracuse University Press, 1965), and Lee Benson's *The Concept of Jacksonian Democracy: New York as a Test Case* (Princeton N.J.: Princeton University Press, 1961), concentrate on the victory of the Many over the Few and define the Few more in terms of their economic possessions than their inherited and ethnic social status. Robert V. Remini, in *Martin Van Buren and the Making of the Democratic Party* (New York: Columbia University Press, 1959), comes closer to depicting the side of Van Buren which eventually held the loyalty of Peter Gansevoort as well as that which attracted ordinary voters. Van Buren's *Autobiography* (Washington: American Historical Association, 1919) makes this point even more clearly. Ross E. Paulson's *Radicalism and Reform: The Vrooman Family and American Social Thought, 1837–1937* (Lexington: University of Kentucky Press, 1968) depicts the Dutch plebeian tradition as it was handed down to a later generation and transferred to the Middle West.

CHAPTER VII

Information about women in the Dutch patrician tradition is widely scattered and usually superficial. Raesly and Singleton are helpful; Grant and Kalm give the only extended descriptions of women in colonial Albany. Two girls in novels are noteworthy, Anneke Mordaunt in James Fenimore Cooper's *Satanstoe* and Lydia Van den Bosch in William M. Thackeray's *The Virginians*. In their business acumen, their matter-of-fact acceptance of humble origins, their practical efforts to purchase improved social position, and Lydia's eventual achievement of that ambition by marriage—as well as in their open, downright family affection—she and her grandfather are a very fair comic representation of eighteenth-century Albanians. Thackeray visited Albany only a few months before *The Virginians* appeared; it is a tribute to his qualities of observation and imagination that he not only noticed the distinctive characteristics of Albany Dutchmen of his own time but also was so successful in projecting them back into a past of which no literary accounts and but few written records of any kind were available to him. The competitive conspicuous consumption of early nineteenth-century New York is described by Francis J. Grund in *Aristocracy in America* (New York: Harper & Row, 1959) and James Fenimore Cooper in *Home as Found* (Philadelphia: Lea & Blanchard, 1838). The most complete source of biographical and social information about Maria Melville is Leon Howard's *Herman Melville* (Berkeley, Calif.: University of California Press, 1951); William H. Gilman, in *Melville's Early Life and Redburn* (New York: New York University Press, 1951), collects much information about her, the Gansevoorts, and Albany in the 1830's.

CHAPTER VIII

At this point the Albany Dutch tradition diverges decisively from its Dutch roots, and historians have not yet described the areas of the American tradition to which it contributed in the nineteenth century. The vast mass of the Gansevoort papers deals with aspects of American culture which have formed the subjects of few books, those often either highly specialized or overly superficial. Dixon Ryan Fox, in *Decline of Aristocracy*, touches tangentially on the subject of this chapter. The situation and behavior of the Osborns bears considerable resemblance to that of "Aaron Thousand-acres" and his family in James Fenimore Cooper's *The Chainbearer* (New York: Burgess, Streuger & Co., 1845), although the Osborns' principal offense was debt rather than timber-stealing. It is interesting that the "Chainbearer" himself, who spoke for the landowners, was explicitly a Dutchman and that the story took place in Washington County, just across the Hudson from Gansevoort, only twenty years before the Osborn affair. More detail about Allan Melville's mercantile difficulties is available in Gilman and Howard; Robert G. Albion's *Rise of New York Port* (New York: Scribners, 1939) is invaluable for background. Most complete on the *Somers* incident is Harrison Hayford's *Somers Mutiny Affair* (Engle-wood Cliffs, N.J.: Prentice-Hall, 1959).

CHAPTERS IX AND X

The principal works on Herman Melville are Gilman, Howard, Jay Leyda's *Melville Log* (New York: Harcourt, Brace & Co., 1951), 2 volumes, and Eleanor M. Metcalf's *Herman Melville* (Cambridge, Mass.: Harvard University Press, 1953). It is not the purpose of the present chapter to enter into detailed debate with the many literary critics who have studied Melville's works; the introductions to *Pierre* and *Clarel* (New York: Hendricks, 1960) are extensive and effectively summarize the present critical viewpoints concerning these books. Walter Houghton, in *Victorian Frame of Mind* (New Haven, Conn.: Yale University Press, 1957), provides valuable background on mid-nineteenth-century attitudes in both England and America, particularly the sentimental tradition and the problem of religious doubt.

Henry Gansevoort's Correspondence and Papers are in the GLC. The family's trip to Europe is described in greater detail by Alice P. Kenney in "Kate Gansevoort's Grand Tour," *New York History*, Oct. 1966. Henry's military career is summarized in *Memorial of Henry Sanford Gansevoort* (privately printed, 1875), which consists mostly of extracts from his letters. This *Memorial* is the most convenient source for Henry's military career, and gives an expanded account of many incidents which have been summarized or omitted here. But the letters in the *Memorial* were severely edited, sometimes without indication, and it is wise to con-sult the original letters, which are bound into volumes of the *Memorial* in GLC, for the unexpurgated version. The printed *Memorial* of course also excludes almost all family material. The citation HSGMemoirs in the notes therefore refers to the *originals* of letters included in the *Memorial* and not necessarily to passages printed in that work.

INDEX

Abercrombie, Gen. James: 65–67, 106
Adgate, Matthew: 111–12
Albany, N.Y.: xvi, 3, 5–6, 13, 23–25, 189, 299; appearance, 25, 45–46, 262; water supply and fire protection, 29, 134–36, 153; city hall, 45–46, 134, 270; Plan of Union, 46, 64; trade, 52, 119; patricians, 53–54, 64, 68–70, 95, 109; see also Indian trade; Merchants; Patricians; Plebeians
Albany city charter: 14–17, 20, 34–35, 43, 50, 59, 73–74, 113, 272
Albany city council: xxii, 14, 20, 31, 36–37, 43–45, 52, 63, 78, 94; Netherlands, xv, xx, 108; Beverwyck, 8–9, 22; Leisler's Rebellion, 16–20; Gansevoorts on, 28–29, 37, 154, 167; personnel, 34–35, 62, 79; Revolution, 113–14, 118
Albany city courts: 28, 59, 70–77 passim
Albany city defenses: 25, 31, 43–46 passim, 134; garrison, 28, 35, 43–44, 63; wars, 51–52, 65–68, 105–107
Albany city monopoly: 14–15, 32–33, 50–57 passim, 189, 272–73
Albany city officials: 78; mayor, 14, 35–37, 56, 71–79 passim, 86, 113, 124, 126; recorder, 14, 36, 95, 113, 124; clerk, 58–61, 72–78
Albany city politics: 124–29; see also American Revolution; Anti-Leislerians; Cuyler faction; Leisler's Rebellion; Leislerians; Schuyler faction
Albany city records: xxiii, 11, 58, 73–78, 105, 111, 167, 300
Albany Committee of Correspondence: 88, 130; Tories, 94–96, 99, 106; Burgoyne campaign, 101, 106; 1777 constitution, 110–12
Albany Co.: colonial, 6, 39, 40, 52–56

passim, 65–66; Revolution, 99, 106, 111–13; N.Y. state, 123–32
Albany Regency: 156–59, 231, 275
American Revolution: xxii–xxiii, 33, 44, 63, 66, 80, 87–119, 122, 125, 136, 168–70, 174–75, 189, 203, 210, 220, 241, 243, 273, 289; theory, 80–81, 96–97, 108
American tradition: xiii–xiv, xxiv, xxv, 108, 132, 157, 185, 210–13, 223, 271–76, 282, 286–89
Amherst, Gen. Jeffrey: 67, 68, 71, 73
Andros, Gov. Edmund: 13, 16, 58
Anglicans: 63, 83, 165; Albany, 43–45, 67, 113, 134, 135; see also St. Peter's Church
Anne, queen of England: 43, 54
Anti-Federalists: 125–28, 141, 184
Anti-Leislerians: 16–20, 28, 51, 129
Appointments: see Patronage
Aristocrats: xxi, xxiii, 33, 39–40, 71, 82, 155–56, 222–23
Arnold, Gen. Benedict: xxv, 90–91, 104–105; 115–16
Art: 133, 236, 253; Dutch, xx–xxi, 42, 215, 219, 279–80; American, 42, 280; architecture, see Churches; Houses; see also Religious pictures
Artisans: see Craftsmen

Banks: xxii, 120, 141, 175, 189–90, 202, 210–11, 273; Gansevoorts and, 158, 159, 178, 198, 262, 266
Baptisms: 27–30, 43, 192, 269
Bath, N.Y.: 212, 261
Battles: Saratoga, xxv, 104, 106, 114, 119; Lake George, 64, 66; Oriskany, 102, 104, 115; Newtown, 117; Yorktown, 119; Queenston Heights, 192; Antietam, 238; Gettysburg, 239

311

Bellomont, Gov. Robert: 28, 30

Bever, Claes: 10–12, 23, 24, 31

Beverwyck: 7–9, 13–14, 22, 26, 283; see also Albany; Fort Orange

Bible: 162–64, 226–27, 247; pictures, xxi, 165; see also Religious pictures

Boston, Mass.: 42, 54, 87, 91, 174–77, 197–98, 200, 252, 255, 257

Bradstreet, Gen. John: 67, 73–74, 85, 136

British Empire: see Empire, British

Bronck, Pieter: 9–10, 22, 26

Buffalo, N.Y.: 142, 201, 230–31, 252

Burgoyne, Gen. John: 98–107, 114, 170

Burnet, Gov. William: 33, 55, 82

Burr, Aaron: 143–44, 156

Canada: xxiii–xxiv, 17, 45–47, 52, 68, 167, 192, 210; trade competition, 32–33, 50–51; Albany trade with, 37, 46–47, 54–56; invasions, 53, 65–68, 89–92, 94, 98, 101, 104; Tory refuge, 99, 122; see also France; Montreal

Carillons: 133, 270

Carleton, Gen. Guy: 91-93

Catskill, N.Y.: 23, 29, 39

Caughnawagas: see Indians

Charles II, king of England: 13, 23, 81

Cherry Valley, N.Y.: 35–36, 117

Christmas: see New Years

Churches: 133, 152, 236, 266; see also Anglican; Dutch Reformed; Lutheran

Civic activities: banquets and balls, 30, 128, 158, 173; public works, 133–35, 158–59; charities, 133, 158, 162, 266

Civil War: see Wars

Clarke, Lt. Gov. George: 35–36

Claverack, N.Y.: 39, 95, 105, 112, 191

Clinton, Gov. De Witt: 154–57, 159

Clinton, Gov. George (N.Y. colony): 37, 56–61 passim, 82

Clinton, Gov. George (N.Y. state): 113, 114, 123

Clinton, Sir Henry: 105–06

Clinton, Gen. James: 117

Clinton-Sullivan Expedition: 117–18, 142

Clinton Square: 159, 182, 199, 214, 257

Clothing: 41, 46, 70, 164, 167, 173, 177, 247

Colden, Lt. Gov. Cadwallader: 58, 62

Commerce: see Merchants

Communal tradition: Netherlands, xiv, xvi, xxi; Hudson Valley, 25, 78, 109, 156–57, 221–27 passim, 243

Connecticut: 18–19, 63, 151–53; River, 5, 50, 53

Conscience: see Feeling

Constitution: Dutch, xix, 8, 275; British, 109; New York, 1777, 110–13, 154–56; 1821, 150, 154–55; Pennsylvania, 112; U.S., 125–27, 247, 276

Continental Army: 89–91; 3rd N.Y., 98, 100–107 passim, 114–19 passim

Continental Congress: 91–93, 101, 105, 114–15, 125–29 passim, 141

Conyn, Maritje: see Gansevoort, Maritje (Conyn)

Conyn family: 25–27

Cooper, James Fenimore: 150, 178, 278, 281

Co-optation, xv, 8, 78, 275

Cosby, Gov. William: 34–36, 48, 55, 63, 71, 82

Coxsackie, N.Y.: 25, 29, 124

Craftsmen: xv, 34, 108, 128

Crimes: 94, 114, 135–36, 166, 223–24

Currency: 12, 38, 40, 119–21, 189–90, 273

Curtis, Catherine (Gansevoort) (Mrs. George): 206–208, 248, 261

Curtis, George: 206–209, 260

Curtis family: 260–61

Cuyler, Abraham C.: 79, 85, 89, 92, 94, 111, 221

Cuyler, Cornelis: 56, 79, 84–85

Cuyler, Henry: 94

Cuyler, Jacob: 92–93, 125–28; and Gansevoort, 119–21, 123, 190

Cuyler, Johannes: 15–17

Cuyler faction: 32, 57, 71, 88, 97

Cuyler family: 70, 78, 129

Daughters of the American Revolution: 263, 266, 268

De Lancey, James: 57–58, 82

De Lancey, Stephen: 95

De Lancey faction: 57–59, 71, 79, 82–86 *passim*, 95, 109, 111, 129

De Wandelaer, Catarina: *see* Gansevoort, Catarina (de Wandelaer)

De Wandelaer, Johannes: 29, 34, 167

De Wandelaer, John: 119

De Wandelaer, Pau: 41–42, 167

Dellius, Godefridus: 18–20, 43, 52

Democratic Party: xxv, 156–59, 215, 218, 239–41, 245

Depressions: 188–89, 211; *1780's*, 120–21, 189–90; *1815*, 176; *1819*, 196–97; *1837*, 199, 202, 208, 215, 234; *1857*, 231, 234

Dongan, Gov. Thomas: 13–14, 50–51

Dongan Charter: *see* Albany city charter

Douw, Magdalena: *see* Gansevoort, Magdalena (Douw)

Douw, Maritje: *see* Gansevoort, Maritje (Douw)

Douw, Petrus, 39–40, 167, 191

Douw, Volkert Janse: 15, 22, 39

Douw, Volkert P.: 40, 70–72, 77, 79, 84–89 *passim*, 167, 171, 263

Douw family: 39–40, 88

Dutch language: xx–xxiii, 14, 37, 42–46 *passim*, 58, 103, 119, 153, 164, 168, 177, 190, 244, 250, 283, 289

Dutch Reformed Church: xvii–xx, xxiii, 15, 18, 20, 25, 52, 172, 244, 269; buildings, 43–45, 134, 138, 182, 208, 247, 257, 264, 269; controversies, 44–45, 69–70, 73–74; Revolution, 90, 153; Gansevoorts and, 137–38, 175–76, 183, 250, 256–57

Dutch Settlers Society of Albany: 269

Dutch tradition: Hudson Valley, xiii–xiv, xxiv–xxvi, 299; American history, xiii, xxiv, 129, 271–89; Netherlands, xiv–xxi, 108, 299; defense, xviii, 1, 52, 100–107, 168; Albany, xxi–xxii, 65–66, 96–97; hospitality, xxii, 231, 258; decline of in Albany, xxii, 189, 214, 231, 242, 250, 265, 270; and English culture, xxiv, 61–63, 72–78,

83; family, 21–22, 133–34, 157; marriage customs, 26–27, 163, 193; and Yankees, 62–63, 101, 153–54; in American politics, 81, 127–32, 153–59; funeral customs: 136, 246, 256, 263–64, 267, 284; women, 152–53, 160–64, 173, 185, 308; inheritance, 161, 170–71, 178, 191, 273, 283; fortunes, 188, 210–13, 273; in Herman Melville's works, 214–28; *see also* Aristocrats; Fortunes; Patricians; Plebeians

Dutch West India Co.: 1, 4–7, 15, 26

Education: xvi; in Albany, 42–43, 83, 128, 150, 172, 269; Gansevoorts, 150–53, 158, 198–99, 229–30, 252, 261, 266; women, 160, 252; religious, 162, 185; gentlemen, 175; Albany Academy, 198, 229, 261–62; Albany Law School, 230, 253; Albany Institute of History and Art, 266, 269

Elections: 96, 152, 275; Albany city, 14, 34, 36–37, 88–89, 106–10 *passim*, 113, 123–24, 154; N.Y. colony, 35, 37, 82; N.Y. state, 125–27, 129–32, 154–56; *see also* Fraud; Issues

Electorate: 111–12, 126, 155–59 *passim;* voters, 64, 78, 83–86 *passim*, 108, 127, 131, 279

Empire: 49–51, 79; Holy Roman, xv, xvii; British, 49, 55–56, 68, 82, 88, 189, 273, 289; French, 49; Empire State, 109, 129–32; *see also* Canada; Montreal

England: xv, xviii, xix, xxiv, 6, 16, 37, 51–69 *passim*, 114, 143; Parliament, 16, 80–81, 106; Glorious Revolution, 16, 51, 80–81, 274; Board of Trade, 54–60 *passim*; party system, 63, 81; U.S. trade with, 121, 189–90; Gansevoorts to, 199, 216, 235, 237; medieval, 276–78; *see also* London

English conquest: xxi, 13, 15, 22, 50–51, 62

English language: 13, 14, 39, 42, 44, 58, 62, 164, 168, 177, 283

313

Merchants: Netherlands, xiv–xv, xix;
British, xxii–xxiii, 22, 79, 85, 94–95;
Albany, 34, 37–40, 48, 52, 56, 70–
71, 82, 98, 128, 174–76, 272–73,
283; supply armies, 53, 65–66, 70, 89,
102–104, 106, 119, 142; *see also*
Fortunes; Indian trade
Methodists: 204, 208, 257
Middle Ages: xiv–xvii, 276–79, 282–83,
288–89
Milborne, Jacob: 17–19
Militia: Revolution, 89, 96, 102–106,
114–15; N.Y. state, 119, 142, 150,
158; Civil War, 237, 239
Mobs: 87, 108, 128, 130
Mohawks: *see* Iroquois
Mohawk River: 2, 18, 34, 36, 50, 98,
117; valley, 37, 57, 64, 72, 79, 142;
in Revolution, 98–105, 110, 117
Monarchy: xix, 49, 93–94, 109–10, 188–
89
Montcalm, Marquis de: 65, 67
Montgomery, Gen. Richard: 90–92
Montreal: 32, 33, 51, 54, 68, 90–91,
182; *see also* Canada
Mosby, John S.: 240
Munro family: 122, 210; *see also* Gan-
sevoort lawsuits
Museums: xxiii, 65–66, 186, 226, 269,
299
Music: xvi, 170, 173

Negroes: xxii, 38, 135–40 *passim,* 172,
285
Netherlands: xxv, 13, 16, 23, 29, 45,
52, 100, 108, 120–22, 160–63, 188–
89, 237, 269; medieval, xiv–xviii, 162,
276–83 *passim;* Golden Age, xix–xxi,
1, 3–4, 49; *Stadhouder,* xix, 16; States-
General, xix–xx, 4, 133, 188–89; *see
also* William the Silent
Newcastle, Thomas Pelham, Duke of:
55, 58, 81
New England: 26, 42, 53, 63, 143, 257;
Revolution, 94, 101, 106, 114
New Jersey: xxi, 25, 44, 51, 91, 105,
123; New Brunswick, 30, 47

Newspapers: 42, 125–27, 153, 231, 238,
249
New Years customs: 40, 186, 231, 244,
267
New York City: 27, 29, 35, 42, 44, 83,
142, 180, 199, 206, 209, 269; settlement, xiii, 2, 5, 6; politics, 16, 37,
82–83, 115, 127–28, 156; trade, 34,
46–47, 147–48, 176–79, 196–98; Revolution, 87–93 *passim,* 103, 105;
Gansevoorts in, 172, 176–79, 197,
214, 234, 258
New York Colony: 16, 28, 95; assembly,
31–35 *passim,* 40, 55–56, 71–72, 78,
81–87 *passim;* governors, 34, 52, 55ff,
109–10, 274; courts, 34, 75–76, 109–
10; council, 36, 55, 58, 73; politics,
55–57, 63–64, 81, 88, 109–10, 127–
32; *see also* Bellomont; Clinton,
George; Cosby; Elections; Electorate; De Lancey, Johnson, Livingston,
Schuyler factions; Patronage; Prerogative powers
New York State: 143, 270; Revolution,
91–113; Assembly, 110, 113, 123–25,
136, 150, 156–59, 170, 180, 274; politics, 110, 127–32, 154–59; Council
of Appointment, 124, 133, 154–55;
Senate, 124, 158–59, 201, 213, 262;
U.S. Constitution, 125–28; *see also*
Constitution; Clinton, De Witt;
Clinton, George; Patronage; Schuyler,
Van Buren, Yates factions
Nicolls, Gov. Richard: 13, 23
Northumberland, N.Y.: 149, 194, 196,
200, 203; *see also* Gansevoort, N.Y.;
Snock Kill Falls
Novels: 173, 180, 215–25, 252, 280–
82, 300–301, 309

Ohio Valley: 50–51, 63
Orange, House of: xix, 16, 188–89
Osborn, Ephraim: 193–96
Oswego: 33, 38, 57, 65, 98

Palatines: 31, 33
Paris: 174, 183, 192, 235, 237